"This book is a tremendous achievem___  yourself to have a copy on your shelf. '_ is the most comprehensive and unders that subject I've seen to date."

Al Stevens
Contributing Editor, Doctor Dobbs Journal

"Eckel's book is the only one to so clearly explain how to rethink program construction for object orientation. That the book is also an excellent tutorial on the ins and outs of C++ is an added bonus."

Andrew Binstock
Editor, Unix Review

"Bruce continues to amaze me with his insight into C++, and *Thinking in C++* is his best collection of ideas yet. If you want clear answers to difficult questions about C++, buy this outstanding book."

Gary Entsminger
Author, *The Tao of Objects*

"*Thinking in C++* patiently and methodically explores the issues of when and how to use inlines, references, operator overloading, inheritance and dynamic objects, as well as advanced topics such as the proper use of templates, exceptions and multiple inheritance. The entire effort is woven in a fabric that includes Eckel's own philosophy of object and program design. A must for every C++ developer's bookshelf, *Thinking in C++* is the one C++ book you must have if you're doing serious development with C++."

Richard Hale Shaw
Contributing Editor, PC Magazine

in

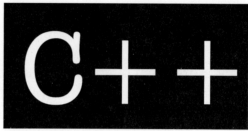

Bruce Eckel

Prentice Hall, Englewood Cliffs, New Jersey 07632

Publisher: Alan Apt
Production Editor: Mona Pompilli
Development Editor: Sondra Chavez
Book Design, Cover Design and Cover Photo:
  Daniel Will-Harris, daniel@will-harris.com
Copy Editor: Shirley Michaels
*Production Coordinator:*Lori Bulwin
Editorial Assistant: Shirley McGuire

The information in this book is distributed on an "as is" basis, without warranty. While every precaution has been taken in the preparation of this book, neither the author nor the publisher shall have any liability to any person or entitle with respect to any liability, loss or damage caused or alleged to be caused directly or indirectly by instructions contained in this book or by the computer software or hardware products described herein.

Printed in the United States of America
10 9 8 7 6 5
ISBN   0-13-917709-4

Prentice-Hall International (UK) Limited, *London*
Prentice-Hall of Australia Pty. Limited, *Sydney*
Prentice-Hall Canada, Inc., *Toronto*
Prentice-Hall Hisapnoamericana, S.A., *Mexico*
Prentice-Hall of India Private Limited, *New Delhi*
Prentice-Hall of Japan, Inc., *Tokyo*
Simon & Schuster Asia Pte. Ltd., *Singapore*
Editora Prentice-Hall do Brasil, Ltda., *Rio de Janeiro*

Thinking

in

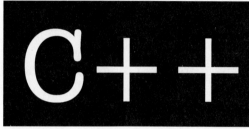

C++

Bruce Eckel

Prentice Hall, Englewood Cliffs, New Jersey 07632

Publisher: Alan Apt
Production Editor: Mona Pompilli
Development Editor: Sondra Chavez
Book Design, Cover Design and Cover Photo:
      Daniel Will-Harris, daniel@will-harris.com
Copy Editor: Shirley Michaels
*Production Coordinator:*Lori Bulwin
Editorial Assistant: Shirley McGuire

© 1995 by Prentice Hall, Inc.
A Paramount Communications Company
Englewood Cliffs, New Jersey 07632

Printed in the United States of America
10 9 8 7 6 5
ISBN   0-13-917709-4

Prentice-Hall International (UK) Limited, *London*
Prentice-Hall of Australia Pty. Limited, *Sydney*
Prentice-Hall Canada, Inc., *Toronto*
Prentice-Hall Hisapnoamericana, S.A., *Mexico*
Prentice-Hall of India Private Limited, *New Delhi*
Prentice-Hall of Japan, Inc., *Tokyo*
Simon & Schuster Asia Pte. Ltd., *Singapore*
Editora Prentice-Hall do Brasil, Ltda., *Rio de Janeiro*

dedication

to the scholar, the healer, and the muse

what's inside...

preface

Like any human language, C++ provides a way to express concepts. If successful, this medium of expression will be significantly easier and more flexible than the alternatives as problems grow larger and more complex.

You can't just look at C++ as a collection of features; some of the features make no sense in isolation. You can only use the sum of the parts if you are thinking about *design*, not simply coding. And to understand C++ in this way, you must understand the problems with C and with programming in general. This book discusses programming problems, why they are problems, and the approach C++ has taken to solve such problems. Thus, the set of features I explain in each chapter will be based on the way I see a particular type of problem being solved with the language. In this way I hope to move you, a little at a time, from understanding C to the point where the C++ mindset becomes your native tongue.

Throughout, I'll be taking the attitude that you want to build a model in your head that allows you to understand the language all the way down to the bare metal; if you encounter a puzzle you'll be able to feed it to your model and deduce the answer. I will try to convey to you the insights which have rearranged my brain to make me start "thinking in C++."

prerequisites

Although I taught C & C++ together in my first C++ book[1] and many people have said they appreciate that, I've since decided that there are many fine tutorials on C and many fine teachers of the C language. I feel it is more useful to assume that someone else has taught you C and that you have at least a reading level of comfort with it. I will focus on simplifying what I found difficult — the C++ language. On the other hand, just as you learn many new words intuitively by seeing them in context in a novel, it's possible to learn a great deal about C from the context in which it is used in this book.

I have also discovered that I don't have the endurance to teach a course that covers both C and C++. I can keep up a nice level of enthusiasm and energy for three days and then I begin to flag. That also seems to be the point at which audience brains become full, so that's how long my training seminars last for small hands-on groups. With larger groups where it's not possible to perform

---

[1] Bruce Eckel, *Using C++*, Osborne/McGraw-Hill, 1989. The second edition was renamed *C++ Inside & Out*, Osborne/McGraw-Hill, 1993. This book was intended for audiences who had programmed in some language other than C.

exercises, I cover most of the material in two to three days, depending on the material presented.

I've endeavored not to use any particular vendor's version of C++ because, for learning the language, I don't feel like the details of a particular implementation are as important as the language itself. Most vendors' documentation concerning their own implementation specifics is adequate.

learning C++

I clawed my way into C++ from exactly the same position as I expect the readers of this book will: as a C programmer with a very no-nonsense, nuts-and-bolts attitude about programming. Worse, my background and experience was in hardware-level embedded programming, where C has often been considered a high-level language and an inefficient overkill for pushing bits around. I discovered later that I wasn't even a very good C programmer, hiding my ignorance of structures, **malloc( )** & **free( )**, **setjmp( )** & **longjmp( )**, and other "sophisticated" concepts, scuttling away in shame when the subjects came up in conversation rather than reaching out for new knowledge.

When I began my struggle to understand C++, the only decent book was Stroustrup's self-professed "expert's guide,[2] " so I was left to simplify the basic concepts on my own. This resulted in my first C++ book,[3] which was essentially a brain dump of my experience. That was designed as a reader's guide, to bring programmers into C

---

[2] Bjarne Stroustrup, *The C++ Programming Language*, Addison-Wesley, 1986 (first edition).

[3] *Using C++*, ibid.

and C++ at the same time. Both editions[4] of the book garnered an enthusiastic response and I still feel it is a valuable resource.

At about the same time that *Using C++* came out, I began teaching the language. Teaching C++ has become my profession; I've seen nodding heads, blank faces, and puzzled expressions in audiences all over the world since 1989. As I began giving in-house training with smaller groups of people, I discovered something during the exercises. Even those people who were smiling and nodding were confused about many issues. I found out, by chairing the C++ track at the Software Development Conference for the last three years, that I and other speakers tended to give the typical audience too many topics, too fast. So eventually, through both variety in the audience level and the way that I presented the material, I would end up losing some portion of the audience. Maybe it's asking too much, but because I am one of those people resistant to traditional lecturing (and for most people, I believe, such resistance results from boredom), I wanted to try to keep everyone up to speed.

For a time, I was creating a number of different presentations in fairly short order. Thus, I ended up learning by experiment and iteration (a technique that also works well in C++ program design). Eventually I developed a course using everything I had learned from my teaching experience, one I would be happy giving for a long time. It tackles the learning problem in discrete, easy-to-digest steps and for a hands-on seminar (the ideal learning situation), there are exercises following each of the short lessons.

This book developed over the course of two years, and the material in this book has been road-tested in many forms in many different seminars. The feedback that I've gotten from each seminar has helped me change and refocus the material until I feel it works well as a teaching medium. But it isn't just a seminar handout — I tried to pack as much information as I could within these pages, and

---

[4] *Using C++* and *C++ Inside & Out*, ibid.

structure it to draw you through, onto the next subject. More than anything, the book is designed to serve the solitary reader, struggling with a new programming language.

goals

My goals in this book are to:

- Present the material a simple step at a time, so the reader can easily digest each concept before moving on.

- Use examples that are as simple and short as possible. This sometimes prevents me from tackling "real-world" problems, but I've found that beginners are usually happier when they can understand every detail of an example rather than being impressed by the scope of the problem it solves. Also, there's a severe limit to the amount of code that can be absorbed in a classroom situation. For this I will no doubt receive criticism for using "toy examples," but I'm willing to accept that in favor of producing something pedagogically useful. Those who want more complex examples can refer to the later chapters of *C++ Inside & Out*.[5]

- Carefully sequence the presentation of features so that you aren't seeing something you haven't been exposed to. Of course, this isn't always possible; in those situations, a brief introductory description will be given.

- Give you what I think is important for you to understand about the language, rather than everything I know. I believe there is an "information importance hierarchy," and there are some facts that 95% of programmers will never need to know, but would just confuse people and add to their perception of the complexity of the language — and C++ is now considered to be more complex than ADA! To take an example from C, if you memorize the operator

---

[5] Ibid.

---

precedence table (I never did) you can write clever code. But if you have to think about it, it will confuse the reader/maintainer of that code. So forget about precedence, and use parentheses when things aren't clear. This same attitude will be taken with some information in the C++ language, which I think is more important for compiler writers than for programmers.

- Keep each section focused enough so the lecture time — and the time between exercise periods — is small. Not only does this keep the audience' minds more active and involved during a hands-on seminar, but it gives the reader a greater sense of accomplishment.

- Provide the reader with a solid foundation so they can understand the issues well enough to move on to more difficult coursework and books.

chapters

C++ is a language where new and different features are built on top of an existing syntax. (Because of this it is referred to as a *hybrid* object-oriented programming language.) As more people have passed through the learning curve, we've begun to get a feel for the way C programmers move through the stages of the C++ language features. Because it appears to be the natural progression of the C-trained mind, I decided to understand and follow this same path, and accelerate the process by posing and answering the questions that came to me as I learned the language and that came from audiences as I taught it.

This course was designed with one thing in mind: the way people learn the C++ language. Audience feedback helped me understand which parts were difficult and needed extra illumination. In the areas where I got ambitious and included too many features all at once, I came to know — through the process of presenting the material — that if you include a lot of new features, you have to explain them all, and the student's confusion is easily compounded. As a result, I've taken a great deal of trouble to introduce the features as few at a time as possible; ideally, only one at a time per chapter.

The goal, then, is for each chapter to teach a single feature, or a small group of associated features, in such a way that no additional features are relied upon. That way you can digest each piece in the context of your current knowledge before moving on. To accomplish this, I leave many C features in place much longer than I would prefer. For example, I would like to be using the C++ iostreams IO library right away, instead of using the **printf( )** family of functions so familiar to C programmers, but that would require introducing the subject prematurely, and so many of the early chapters carry the C library functions with them. This is also true with many other features in the language. The benefit is that you, the C programmer, will not be confused by seeing all the C++ features used before they are explained, so your introduction to the language will be gentle and will mirror the way you will assimilate the features if left to your own devices.

Here is a brief description of the chapters contained in this book.

(0) The evolution of objects. When projects became too big and too complicated to easily maintain, the "software crisis" was born, saying, "We can't get projects done, and if we can they're too expensive!" This precipitated a number of responses, which are discussed in this chapter along with the ideas of object-oriented programming (OOP) and how it attempts to solve the software crisis. You'll also learn about the benefits and concerns of adopting the language and suggestions for moving into the world of C++.

(1) Data abstraction. Most features in C++ revolve around this key concept: the ability to create new data types. Not only does this provide superior code organization, but it lays the ground for more powerful OOP abilities. You'll see how this idea is facilitated by the simple act of putting functions inside structures, the details of how to do it, and what kind of code it creates.

(2) Hiding the implementation. You can decide that some of the data and functions in your structure are unavailable to the user of the new type by making them **private**. This means you can separate the underlying implementation from the interface that the client programmer sees, and thus allow that implementation to be easily changed without affecting client code. The keyword **class** is also introduced as a fancier way to describe a new data type, and the meaning of the word "object" is demystified (it's a variable on steroids).

(3) Initialization & cleanup. One of the most common C errors results from uninitialized variables. The *constructor* in C++ allows you to guarantee that variables of your new data type ("objects of your class") will always be properly initialized. If your objects also require some sort of cleanup, you can guarantee that this cleanup will always happen with the C++ *destructor*.

(4) Function overloading & default arguments. C++ is intended to help you build big, complex projects. While doing this, you may bring in multiple libraries that use the same function name, and you may also choose to use the same name with different meanings within a single library. C++ makes this easy with *function overloading*, which allows you to reuse the same function name as long as the argument lists are different. Default arguments allow you to call the same function in different ways by automatically providing default values for some of your arguments.

(5) Introduction to iostreams. One of the original C++ libraries — the one that provides the essential I/O facility — is called iostreams. Iostreams is intended to replace C's STDIO.H with an I/O library that is easier to use, more flexible, and extensible — you can adapt it to work with your new classes. This chapter teaches you the ins and outs of how to make the best use of the existing iostream library for standard I/O, file I/O, and in-memory formatting.

(6) Constants. This chapter covers the **const** and **volatile** keywords that have additional meaning in C++, especially inside classes. It also shows how the meaning of **const** varies inside and outside classes and how to create compile-time constants in classes.

(7) Inline functions. Preprocessor macros eliminate function call overhead, but the preprocessor also eliminates valuable C++ type checking. The inline function gives you all the benefits of a preprocessor macro plus all the benefits of a real function call.

(8) Name control. Creating names is a fundamental activity in programming, and when a project gets large, the number of names can be overwhelming. C++ allows you a great deal of control over names: creation, visibility, placement of storage, and linkage. This chapter shows how names are controlled using two techniques. First, the **static** keyword is used to control visibility and linkage, and its special meaning with classes is explored. A far more useful technique for controlling names at the global scope is C++'s **namespace** feature, which allows you to break up the global name space into distinct regions.

 (9) References & the copy-constructor. C++ pointers work like C pointers with the additional benefit of stronger C++ type checking. There's a new way to handle addresses; from Algol and Pascal, C++ lifts the *reference* which lets the compiler handle the address manipulation while you use ordinary notation. You'll also meet the copy-constructor, which controls the way objects are passed into and out of functions by value. Finally, the C++ pointer-to-member is illuminated.

(10) Operator overloading. This feature is sometimes called "syntactic sugar." It lets you sweeten the syntax for using your type by allowing operators as well as function calls. In this chapter you'll learn that operator overloading is just a different type of function call and how to write your own, especially the sometimes-confusing uses of arguments, return types, and making an operator a member or friend.

(11) Dynamic object creation. How many planes will an air-traffic system have to handle? How many shapes will a CAD system need?

In the general programming problem, you can't know the quantity, lifetime or type of the objects needed by your running program. In this chapter, you'll learn how C++'s **new** and **delete** elegantly solve this problem by safely creating objects on the heap.

(12) Inheritance & composition. Data abstraction allows you to create new types from scratch; with composition and inheritance, you can create new types from existing types. With composition you assemble a new type using other types as pieces, and with inheritance you create a more specific version of an existing type. In this chapter you'll learn the syntax, how to redefine functions, and the importance of construction and destruction for inheritance & composition.

(13) Polymorphism & virtual functions. On your own, you might take nine months to discover and understand this cornerstone of OOP. Through small, simple examples you'll see how to create a family of types with inheritance and manipulate objects in that family through their common base class. The **virtual** keyword allows you to treat all objects in this family generically, which means the bulk of your code doesn't rely on specific type information. This makes your programs extensible, so building programs and code maintenance is easier and cheaper.

(14) Templates & container classes. Inheritance and composition allow you to reuse object code, but that doesn't solve all your reuse needs. Templates allow you to reuse *source* code by providing the compiler with a way to substitute type names in the body of a class or function. This supports the use of *container class* libraries, which are important tools for the rapid, robust development of object-oriented programs. This extensive chapter gives you a thorough grounding in this essential subject.

(15) Multiple inheritance. This sounds simple at first: A new class is inherited from more than one existing class. However, you can end up with ambiguities and multiple copies of base-class objects. That problem is solved with virtual base classes, but the bigger issue remains: When do you use it? Multiple inheritance is only essential when you need to manipulate an object through more than one common base class. This chapter explains the syntax for multiple inheritance, and shows alternative approaches — in particular, how templates solve one common problem. The use of multiple inheritance to repair a "damaged" class interface is demonstrated as a genuinely valuable use of this feature.

(16) Exception handling. Error handling has always been a problem in programming. Even if you dutifully return error information or set a flag, the function caller may simply ignore it. Exception handling is a primary feature in C++ that solves this problem by allowing you to "throw" an object out of your function when a critical error happens. You throw different types of objects for different errors, and the function caller "catches" these objects in separate error handling routines. If you throw an exception, it cannot be ignored, so you can guarantee that *something* will happen in response to your error.

(17) Run-time type identification. Run-time type identification (RTTI) lets you find the exact type of an object when you only have a pointer or reference to the base type. Normally, you'll want to intentionally ignore the exact type of an object and let the virtual function mechanism implement the correct behavior for that type. But occasionally it is very helpful to know the exact type of an object for which you only have a base pointer; often this information allows you to perform a special-case operation more efficiently. This chapter explains what RTTI is for and how to use it.

Appendix A: Etcetera. At this writing, the C++ Standard is unfinished. Although virtually all the features that will end up in the language have been added to the standard, some haven't appeared in all compilers. This appendix briefly mentions some of the other features you should look for in your compiler (or in future releases of your compiler).

Appendix B: Programming guidelines. This appendix is a series of suggestions for C++ programming. They've been collected over the course of my teaching and programming experience, and also from the insights of other teachers. Many of these tips are summarized from the pages of this book.

Appendix C: Simulating virtual constructors. The constructor cannot have any virtual qualities, and this sometimes produces awkward code. This appendix demonstrates two approaches to "virtual construction."

exercises

I've discovered that simple exercises are exceptionally useful during a seminar to complete a student's understanding, so you'll find a set at the end of each chapter.

These are fairly simple, so they can be finished in a reasonable amount of time in a classroom situation while the instructor observes, making sure all the students are absorbing the material. Some exercises are a bit more challenging to keep advanced students entertained. They're all designed to be solved in a short time and are only there to test and polish your knowledge rather than present major challenges (presumably, you'll find those on your own — or more likely they'll find you).

source code

The source code for this book is copyrighted freeware, distributed as a single package. You should be able to find it on many bulletin board systems (such as CompuServe and AOL), Internet nodes (Such as the SimTel archives; oak.oakland.edu is one node; see SimTel/msdos/cpluspls), and included in product vendor packages. This means you may freely share the package, post it on bulletin boards and the Internet, and include it in shareware packages. However, you cannot distribute the code in pieces (that is, you must distribute the whole package together). The copyright prevents you from republishing the code in print media without permission.

You should search for a file that begins with the letters ECKELT. Two additional characters in the name will be used to represent a version number; for example, ECKELT01.ZIP will represent version 1 in PKZIP form (other compression utilities may be used as appropriate for other systems). In each source-code file you will find the following copyright notice:

You may use the code in your projects and in the classroom as long as the copyright notice that appears in each source file is retained.

If you cannot easily find the code you can get it on a 3 1/2" MSDOS disk by sending a U.S. check in U.S. funds for $25 (add $7 for overseas shipping) to:

EckelBits
5343 Valle Vista
La Mesa, CA 91941-4259

Please request the "Source code for *Thinking in C++*." You may freely distribute the contents of this disk.

coding standards

In the text of this book, identifiers (function, variable, and class names) will be set in **bold**. Most keywords will also be set in bold, except for those keywords which are used so much that the bolding can become tedious, like class and virtual.

I use a particular coding style for the examples in this book. It was developed over a number of years, and was inspired by Bjarne Stroustrup's style in his original *The C++ Programming Language*.[6] The subject of formatting style is good for hours of hot debate, so I'll just say I'm not trying to dictate correct style via my examples; I have my own motivation for using the style that I do. Because C++ is a free-form programming language, you can continue to use whatever style you're comfortable with.

The programs in this book are files that are automatically included by the word processor in the text, directly from compiled files. (I use a special format on the first line of each file to facilitate this inclusion; the line begins with //: and the file name.) Thus, the code files printed in the book should all work without compiler errors. The errors that *should* cause compile-time error messages are

---

[6] Ibid.

---

commented out with the comment //! so they can be easily discovered and tested using automatic means. Errors discovered and reported to the author will appear first in the distributed source code and later in updates of the book.

One of the standards in this book is that all programs will compile and link without errors (although they will sometimes cause warnings). To this end, some of the programs, which only demonstrate a coding example and don't represent stand-alone programs, will have empty **main( )** functions, like this

```
main() {}
```

This allows the linker to complete without an error.

The standard for **main( )** is to return an **int**, but Standard C++ states that if there is no **return** statement inside **main( )**, the compiler will automatically generate code to **return 0**. This option will be used in this book (although some compilers may still generate warnings for this).

language standards

Throughout this book, when referring to conformance to the ANSI/ISO C standard, I will use the term *Standard C*.

Although at this writing the ANSI/ISO C++ committee was still working on the language, the process seemed assured: all the features accepted by the committee eventually make their way into the implementations, and all the "major" features had been added. Thus, I will use the term *Standard C++* when referring to features in what, at this writing, was the ANSI/ISO C++ draft document. Keep in mind, however, that this information was based on the draft that was current as I was writing the book, and there's some chance that a feature described in this book could be changed before the standard is finalized.

language support

Your compiler may not support all the features discussed in this book, especially if you don't have the newest version of your compiler. Implementing a language like C++ is a Herculean task, and you can expect that the features will appear in pieces rather than all at once. But if you attempt one of the examples in the book and get a lot of errors from the compiler, it's not necessarily a bug in the code or the compiler — it may simply not be implemented in your particular compiler yet.

seminars & mentoring

My company provides three-day, hands-on, in-house training seminars based on the material in this book. Selected material from each chapter represents a lesson, which is followed by a monitored exercise period so each student receives personal attention. For more information, contact

Bruce Eckel C++ Training
20 Sunnyside Avenue, Suite A129
Mill Valley, CA 94941
eckel@aol.com

Two-day public seminars (in larger groups, without exercises) and three-day public training courses are also held; contact the above address for information. If you want to organize a public seminar or training session in your city, send a message requesting more information.

I also provide mentoring services to help guide your project through its development cycle, especially your company's first C++ project. This involves regular visits including training time (in the early parts of the project) and coaching in design and coding.

errors

No matter how many tricks a writer uses to detect errors, some always creep in and these often leap off the page for a fresh reader. If you discover anything you believe to be an error, please send the original source file (which you can find on the internet and other sources, as mentioned on page 26) with a loudly commented error and suggested correction via electronic mail to **eckel@aol.com** so it may be fixed in the next printing of the book. Also, suggestions for additional exercises or requests to cover specific topics in the next edition are welcome. Your help is appreciated.

acknowledgements

The ideas and understanding in this book have come from many sources: friends like Dan Saks, Scott Meyers, Charles Petzold, and Michael Wilk; pioneers of the language like Bjarne Stroustrup, Andrew Koenig, and Rob Murray; members of the C++ Standards Committee like Tom Plum, Reg Charney, Tom Penello, Chuck Allison, Sam Druker, Nathan Myers, and Uwe Stienmueller; people who have spoken in my C++ track at the Software Development Conference; and very often students in my seminars, who ask the questions I need to hear in order to make the material clearer.

I have been presenting this material on tours produced by Miller Freeman Inc. with my friend Richard Hale Shaw. Richard's insights and support have been very helpful (and Kim's, too). Thanks also to KoAnn Vikoren, Lisa Monson, Julie Shaw, Nicole Freeman, Cindy Blair, Barbara Hanscome, Yvonne Labat, Regina Ridley, Alex Dunne, Judy DeMocker, and the rest of the cast and crew at MFI.

A form of this material was first published in Embedded Systems Programming magazine, edited by Tyler Sperry.

The book design, cover design, and cover photo were created by my friend Daniel Will-Harris, noted author and designer, who used to play with rub-on letters in junior high school while he awaited the invention of computers and desktop publishing. However, I produced the camera-ready pages myself, so the typesetting errors are mine. Microsoft® Word for Windows 6 was used to write the book and to create camera-ready pages. The body typeface is ITC Cheltenham and the headlines are in ITC American Typewriter.

The people at Prentice Hall were wonderful; this is the best book-publishing experience I've had. Thanks to Alan Apt, Sondra Chavez, Mona Pompili, Shirley McGuire, and everyone else there who made life easy for me.

Thanks very much to Eric Lang and Steve Ross at Microsoft, and to Eric Nagler — they all gave wonderful specific feedback and suggested changes, an author's dream. Thanks also for feedback from Robin Rowe, Rowe Technology; Leigh Sneddon; John H. Carson, Management Science Department, The George Washington University; and Mark T. Ellis, Reuters.

Alex Matthews was my intern for part of this book's development cycle and was responsible for research on parts of Chapter 0, as well as the integration of error reports from technical readers. My great friend Mark Bennett Western helped me out at the last minute integrating copy edits. Diane Anderson also helped with edits, and Toni Will-Harris gave opinions and general useful feedback.

Thanks to the vendors who supplied me with compilers: Borland, Microsoft & MetaWare. General thank-you to: Rich Friedman at SIGS, Greg Cross, Walter Bright, P.J. Plauger, Hank Shiffman, Steve Ross, Tim Gooch, Jan Gray, Steven Sheetz, and Jim Meador at the Exploratorium.

A special thanks to all my teachers, and all my students (who are my teachers as well).

Personal thanks to my friends Gen Kiyooka and Kraig Brockschmidt, who've shown me that computers can too be part of a path to enlightenment. The supporting cast of friends includes, but is not limited to: Zack Urlocker, Andrew Binstock, Neil

Rubenking, Steve Sinofsky, JD Hildebrandt (& Bobbi), Tom Keffer, Brian McElhinney, Brinkley Barr, Larry O'Brien, Bill Gates at Midnight Engineering Magazine, Larry Constantine & Lucy Lockwood, Tom Keffer, Greg Perry, Dan Putterman, Christi Westphal, Gene Wang, Dave Mayer, David Intersimone, Andrea Rosenfield, Claire Sawyers, Claire Jones, The Italians (Andrea Provaglio, Laura Fallai, Marco Cantu, Corrado, Ilsa and Christina Giustozzi), Chris & Laura Strand, The Almquists, Brad Jerbic, Marilyn Cvitanic, The Mabrys, The Haflingers, The Pollocks, Peter Vinci, The Robbins Families, The Moelter Families (& the McMillans), The Wilks, Dave Stoner, Laurie Adams, The Penneys, The Cranstons, Larry Fogg, Mike & Karen Sequeira, Gary Entsminger & Allison Brody, Chester Andersen, Joe Lordi, Dave & Brenda Bartlett, Robert Herald, The Rentschlers, The Sudeks, Dick, Patty, and Lee Eckel, Lynn & Todd, and their families. And of course, Mom & Dad.

the evolution
of objects

The genesis of the computer revolution was in a machine. The genesis of our programming languages thus tends to look like that machine.

But the computer is not so much a machine as it is a mind amplification tool and a different kind of expressive medium. As a result, the tools are beginning to look less like machines and more like parts of our minds, and more like other expressive mediums like writing, painting, sculpture, animation or filmmaking. Object-oriented programming is part of this movement toward the computer as an expressive medium.

This chapter will introduce you to the basic concepts of object-oriented programming (OOP), followed by a discussion of OOP development methods. Finally, strategies for moving yourself, your projects, and your company to object-oriented programming are presented.

This chapter is background and supplementary material. If you're eager to get to the specifics of the language, feel free to jump ahead to Chapter 1. You can always come back here and fill in your knowledge later.

key concepts

Although C++ encompasses much more than the basics of object-oriented programming, the language revolves around certain key concepts you need to understand before looking at design and development issues.

objects: characteristics + behaviors[1]

The first object-oriented programming language was Simula-67, developed in the sixties to solve, as the name implies, simulation problems. A classic simulation is the bank teller problem, which involves a bunch of tellers, customers, transactions, units of money — a lot of "objects." Objects that are identical except for their state during a program's execution are grouped together into "classes of objects" and that's where the word *class* came from.

A class describes a set of objects that have identical characteristics (data elements) and behaviors (functionality). So a class is really a data type because a floating point number (for example) also has a set of characteristics and behaviors. The difference is that a programmer defines a class to fit a problem rather than being

---

[1] Parts of this description were adapted from my introduction to *The Tao of Objects* by Gary Entsminger, M&T/Holt, 1995.

forced to use an existing data type that was designed to represent a unit of storage in a machine. You extend the programming language by adding new data types specific to your needs. The programming system welcomes the new classes and gives them all the care and type-checking that it gives to built-in types.

This approach was not limited to building simulations. Whether or not you agree that any program is a simulation of a system you design, the use of OOP techniques can easily reduce a large set of problems to a simple solution. This discovery spawned a number of OOP languages, most notably Smalltalk — the most successful OOP language until C++.

Abstract data typing is a fundamental concept in object-oriented programming. Abstract data types work almost exactly like built-in types: You can create variables of a type (called *objects* or *instances* in object-oriented parlance) and manipulate those variables (called *sending messages* or *requests*; you send a message and the object figures out what to do with it).

inheritance: type relationships

A type does more than describe the constraints on a set of objects; it also has a relationship with other types. Two types can have characteristics and behaviors in common, but one type may contain more characteristics than another and may also handle more messages (or handle them differently). *Inheritance* expresses this similarity between types with the concept of base types and derived types. A base type contains all the characteristics and behaviors that are shared among the types derived from it. You create a base type to represent the core of your ideas about some objects in your system. From the base type, you derive other types to express the different ways that core can be realized.

For example, a garbage-recycling machine sorts pieces of garbage. The base type is "garbage," and each piece of garbage has a weight, a value, and so on and can be shredded, melted, or decomposed. From this, more specific types of garbage are derived that may have additional characteristics (a bottle has a color) or behaviors (an aluminum can may be crushed, a steel can is magnetic). In addition, some behaviors may be different (the value of paper depends on its type and condition). Using inheritance, you can build a type hierarchy that expresses the problem you're trying to solve in terms of its types.

A second example is the classic shape problem, perhaps used in a computer-aided design system or game simulation. The base type is "shape," and each shape has a size, a color, a position, and so on. Each shape can be drawn, erased, moved, colored, and so on. From this, specific types of shapes are derived (inherited): circle, square, triangle, and so on, each of which may have additional characteristics and behaviors. Certain shapes can be flipped, for example. Some behaviors may be different (calculating the area of a shape). The type hierarchy embodies both the similarities and differences between the shapes.

Casting the solution in the same terms as the problem is tremendously beneficial because you don't need a lot of intermediate models (used with procedural languages for large problems) to get from a description of the problem to a description of the solution; in pre-object-oriented languages the solution was inevitably described in terms of computers. With objects, the type hierarchy is the primary model, so you go directly from the description of the system in the real world to the description of the system in code. Indeed, one of the difficulties people have with object-oriented design is that it's too simple to get from the beginning to the end. A mind trained to look for complex solutions is often stumped by this simplicity at first.

polymorphism

When dealing with type hierarchies, you often want to treat an object not as the specific type that it is but as a member of its base type. This allows you to write code that doesn't depend on specific types. In the shape example, functions manipulate generic shapes without respect to whether they're circles, squares, triangles, and so on. All shapes can be drawn, erased, and moved, so these functions simply send a message to a shape object; they don't worry about how the object copes with the message.

Such code is unaffected by the addition of new types, which is the most common way to extend an object-oriented program to handle new situations. For example, you can derive a new subtype of shape called pentagon without modifying the functions that deal only with generic shapes. The ability to extend a program easily by deriving new subtypes is important because it greatly reduces the cost of software maintenance. (The so-called "software crisis" was caused by the observation that software was costing more than people thought it ought to.)

There's a problem, however, with attempting to treat derived-type objects as their generic base types (circles as shapes, bicycles as vehicles, cormorants as birds). If a function is going to tell a generic shape to draw itself, or a generic vehicle to steer, or a generic bird to fly, the compiler cannot know at compile-time precisely what piece of code will be executed. That's the point — when the message is sent, the programmer doesn't w*ant* to know what piece of code will be executed; the draw function can be applied equally to a circle, square, or triangle, and the object will execute the proper code depending on its specific type. If you add a new subtype, the code it executes can be different without changes to the function call. The compiler cannot know precisely what piece of code is executed, so what does it do?

The answer is the primary twist in object-oriented programming: The compiler cannot make a function call in the traditional sense. The function call generated by a non-OOP compiler causes what is called *early binding*, a term you may not have heard before because you've never thought about it any other way. It means the compiler generates a call to a specific function name, and the linker resolves that call to the absolute address of the code to be executed. In OOP, the program cannot determine the address of the code until run-time, so some other scheme is necessary when a message is sent to a generic object.

To solve the problem, object-oriented languages use the concept of *late binding*. When you send a message to an object, the code being called isn't determined until run-time. The compiler does ensure that the function exists and performs type checking on the arguments and return value (a language where this isn't true is called *weakly typed*), but it doesn't know the exact code to execute.

To perform late binding, the compiler inserts a special bit of code in lieu of the absolute call. This code calculates the address of the function body to execute at run-time using information stored in the object itself (this subject is covered in great detail in Chapter 13). Thus, each object can behave differently according to the contents of that pointer. When you send a message to an object, the object actually does figure out what to do with that message.

You state that you want a function to have the flexibility of late-binding properties using the keyword *virtual*. You don't need to understand the mechanics of *virtual* to use it, but without it you can't do object-oriented programming in C++. Virtual functions allow you to express the differences in behavior of classes in the same family. Those differences are what cause polymorphic behavior.

manipulating concepts: what an OOP program looks like

You know what a procedural program in C looks like: data definitions and function calls. To find the meaning of such a program you have to work a little, looking through the function calls and low-level concepts to create a model in your mind. This is the reason we need intermediate representations for procedural programs — they tend to be confusing because the terms of expression are oriented more toward the computer than the problem you're solving.

Because C++ adds many new concepts to the C language, your natural assumption may be that, of course, the **main( )** in a C++

program will be far more complicated than the equivalent C program. Here, you'll be pleasantly surprised: A well-written C++ program is generally far simpler and much easier to understand than the equivalent C program. What you'll see are the definitions of the objects that represent concepts in your problem space (rather than the issues of the computer representation) and messages sent to those objects to represent the activities in that space. One of the delights of object-oriented programming is that it's generally very easy to understand the code by reading it. Usually there's a lot less code, as well, because many of your problems will be solved by reusing existing library code.

why C++ succeeds

Part of the reason C++ has been so successful is that the goal was not just to turn C into an OOP language (although it started that way), but to solve many other problems facing developers today, especially those who have large investments in C. Traditionally, OOP languages have suffered from the attitude that you should dump everything you know and start from scratch with a new set of concepts and a new syntax, arguing that it's better in the long run to lose all the old baggage that comes with procedural languages. This may be true, in the long run. But in the short run, a lot of that baggage was valuable. The most valuable elements may not be the existing code base (which, given adequate tools, could be translated), but instead the existing *mind base*. If you're a functioning C programmer and must drop everything you know about C in order to adopt a new language, you immediately become nonproductive for many months, until your mind fits around the new paradigm. Whereas if you can leverage off of your existing C knowledge and expand upon it, you can continue to be productive with what you already know while moving into the world of object-oriented programming. As everyone has his/her own mental model of programming, this move is messy enough as it is without the added expense of starting with a new language model from square one. So the reason for the success of C++, in a nutshell, is economic: It still costs to move to OOP, but C++ costs a lot less.

The goal of C++ is improved productivity. This productivity comes in many ways, but the language is designed to aid you as much as possible, while hindering you as little as possible with arbitrary rules or any requirement that you use a particular set of features. The reason C++ is successful is that it is designed with practicality in mind: Decisions are based on providing the maximum benefits to the programmer.

a better C

You get an instant win even if you continue to write C code because C++ has closed the holes in the C language and provides better type checking and compile-time analysis. You're forced to declare functions so the compiler can check their use. The preprocessor has virtually been eliminated for value substitution and macros, which removes a set of difficult-to-find bugs. C++ has a feature called *references* that allows more convenient handling of addresses for function arguments and return values. The handling of names is improved through function overloading, which allows you to use the same name for different functions. Namespaces also improve the control of names. There are numerous other small features that improve the safety of C.

you're already on the learning curve

The problem with learning a new language is productivity: No company can afford to suddenly lose a productive software engineer because she's learning a new language. C++ is an extension to C, not a complete new syntax and programming model. It allows you to continue creating useful code, applying the features gradually as you learn and understand them. This may be one of the most important reasons for the success of C++.

In addition, all your existing C code is still viable in C++, but because the C++ compiler is pickier, you'll often find hidden errors when recompiling the code.

efficiency

Sometimes it is appropriate to trade execution speed for programmer productivity. A financial model, for example, may be useful for only a short period of time, so it's more important to create the model rapidly than to execute it rapidly. However, most applications require some degree of efficiency, so C++ always errs on the side of greater efficiency. Because C programmers tend to be very efficiency-conscious, this is also a way to ensure they won't be able to argue that the language is too fat and slow. A number of features in C++ are intended to allow you to tune for performance when the generated code isn't efficient enough.

Not only do you have the same low-level control as in C (and the ability to directly write assembly language within a C++ program), but anecdotal evidence suggests that the program speed for an object-oriented C++ program tends to be within ±10% of a program written in C, and often much closer. The design produced for an OOP program may actually be more efficient than the C counterpart.

systems are easier to express and understand

Classes designed to fit the problem tend to express it better. This means that when you write the code, you're describing your solution in the terms of the problem space ("put the grommet in the bin") rather than the terms of the computer, which is the solution space ("set the bit in the chip that means that the relay will close"). You deal with higher-level concepts and can do much more with a single line of code.

The other benefit of this ease of expression is maintenance, which (if reports can be believed) takes a huge portion of the cost over a program's lifetime. If a program is easier to understand, then it's easier to maintain. This can also reduce the cost of creating and maintaining the documentation.

maximal leverage with libraries

The fastest way to create a program is to use code that's already written: a library. A major goal in C++ is to make library use easier. This is accomplished by casting libraries into new data types (classes), so bringing in a library is adding a new data type to the language. Because the compiler takes care of how the library is used — guaranteeing proper initialization and cleanup, ensuring functions are called properly — you can focus on what you want the library to do, not how you have to do it.

Because names can be sequestered to portions of your program, you can use as many libraries as you want without the kinds of name clashes you'd run into with C.

source-code reuse with templates

There is a significant class of types that require source-code modification in order to reuse them effectively. The template performs the source code modification automatically, making it an especially powerful tool for reusing library code. A type you design using templates will work effortlessly with many other types. Templates are especially nice because they hide the complexity of this type of code reuse from the client programmer.

error handling

Error handling in C is a notorious problem, and one that is often ignored — finger-crossing is usually involved. If you're building a large, complex program, there's nothing worse than having an error buried somewhere with no vector telling you where it came from. C++ *exception handling* (the subject of Chapter 16) is a way to guarantee that an error is noticed and that something happens as a result.

programming in the large

Many traditional languages have built-in limitations to program size and complexity. BASIC, for example, can be great for pulling together quick solutions for certain classes of problems, but if the program gets more than a few pages long or ventures out of the normal problem domain of that language, it's like trying to run through an ever-more viscous solution. C, too, has these limitations. For example, when a program gets beyond perhaps 50,000 lines of code, name collisions start to become a problem. In short, you run out of function and variable names. Another particularly bad problem is the little holes in the C language — errors can get buried in a large program that are extremely difficult to find.

There's no clear line that tells when your language is failing you, and even if there were, you'd ignore it. You don't say, "My BASIC program just got too big; I'll have to rewrite it in C!" Instead, you try to shoehorn a few more lines in to add that one extra feature. So the extra costs come creeping up on you.

C++ is designed to aid *programming in the large*, that is, to erase those creeping-complexity boundaries between a small program and a large one. You certainly don't need to use OOP, templates, namespaces, and exception handling when you're writing a hello-world-class utility program, but those features are there when you need them. And the compiler is aggressive about ferreting out bug-producing errors for small and large programs alike.

introduction to methods

A *method* is a set of processes and heuristics used to break down the complexity of a programming problem. Especially in OOP, methodology is a field of many experiments, so it is important to understand the problem the method is trying to solve before you consider adopting one. This is particularly true with C++, where the programming language itself is intended to reduce the complexity involved in expressing a program. This may in fact

---

alleviate the need for ever-more-complex methodologies. Instead, simpler ones may suffice in C++ for a much larger class of problems than you could handle with simple methods for procedural languages.

Its also important to realize that the term "methodology" is often too grand and promises too much. Whatever you do now when you design and write a program is a method. It may be your own method, and you may not be conscious of doing it, but it is a process you go through as you create. If it is an effective process, it may need only a small tune-up to work with C++. If you are not satisfied with your productivity and the way your programs turn out, you may want to consider adopting a formal method.

complexity

To analyze this situation, I shall start with a premise:

> *Computer programming is about managing complexity by imposing discipline.*

This *discipline* appears two ways, each of which can be examined separately:

1. *Internal discipline* is seen in the structure of the program itself, through the expressiveness of the programming language and the cleverness and insight of the programmers.

2. *External discipline* is seen in the meta-information about the program, loosely described as "design documentation" (not to be confused with product documentation).

I maintain these two forms of discipline are at odds with each other: one is the *essence* of a program, driven by the need to make the program work the first time, and the other is the *analysis* of a program, driven by the need to understand and maintain the program in the future. Both creation and maintenance are fundamental properties of a program's lifetime, and a useful

Thinking in C++   *Bruce Eckel*

programming method will integrate both in the most expedient fashion, without going overboard in one direction or another.

internal discipline

The evolution of computer programming (in which C++ is just a step on the path) began by imposing internal discipline on the programming model, allowing the programmer to alias names to machine locations and machine instructions. This was such a jump from numerical machine programming that it spawned other developments over the years, generally involving further abstractions away from the low-level machine and toward a model more suited to solving the problem at hand. Not all these developments caught on; often the ideas originated in the academic world and spread into the computing world at large depending on the set of problems they were well suited for.

The creation of named subroutines as well as linking techniques to support libraries of these subroutines was a huge leap forward in the 50's and spawned two languages that would be heavy-hitters for decades: FORTRAN ("FORmula-TRANslation") for the scientific crowd and COBOL ("COmmon Business-Oriented Language") for the business folks. The successful language in "pure" computer science was Lisp ("List-Processing"), while the more mathematically oriented could use APL ("A Programming Language").

All of these languages had in common their use of procedures. Lisp and APL were created with language elegance in mind — the "mission statement" of the language is embodied in an engine that handles all cases of that mission. FORTRAN and COBOL were created to solve specific types of problems, and then evolved when those problems got more complex or new ones appeared. Even in their twilight years they continue to evolve: Versions of both FORTRAN and COBOL are appearing with object-oriented extensions. (A fundamental tenet of post-modern philosophy is that any organization takes on an independent life of its own; its primary goal becomes to perpetuate that life.)

The named subroutine was recognized as a major leverage point in programming, and languages were designed around the concept, Algol and Pascal, in particular. Other languages also appeared, successfully solved a subset of the programming problem, and took their place in the order of things. Two of the most interesting of these were Prolog, built around an *inference engine* (something you see popping up in other languages, often as a library) and FORTH, which is an extensible language. FORTH allows the programmer to re-form the language itself until it fits the problem, a concept akin to object-oriented programming. However, FORTH also allows you to change the base language itself. Because of this, it becomes a maintenance nightmare and is thus probably the purest expression of the concept of internal discipline, where the emphasis is on the one-time solution of the problem rather than the maintenance of that solution.

Numerous other languages have been invented to solve a portion of the programming problem. Usually, these languages begin with a particular objective in mind. BASIC ("Beginners All-purpose Symbolic Instruction Code"), for example, was designed in the 60's to make programming simpler for the beginner. APL was designed for mathematical manipulations. Both languages can solve other problems, but the question becomes whether they are the most ideal solutions for the entire problem set. The joke is, "To a three-year-old with a hammer, everything looks like a nail," but it displays an underlying economic truth: If your only language is BASIC or APL, then that's probably the best solution for your problem, especially if the deadline is short term and the solution has a limited lifetime.

However, two factors eventually creep in: the management of complexity, and maintenance (discussed in the next section). Of course, complexity is what the language was created to manage in the first place, and the programmer, loath to give up the years of time invested in fluency with the language, will go to greater and greater lengths to bend the language to the problem at hand. In fact, the boundary of chaos is fuzzy rather than clear: who's to say when your language begins to fail you? It doesn't, not all at once.

The solution to a problem begins to take longer and becomes more of a challenge to the programmer. More cleverness is required to get around the limitations of the language, and this cleverness becomes standard lore, things you "just have to do to make the language work." This seems to be the way humans operate; rather than grumbling every time we encounter a flaw, we stop calling it a flaw.

But eventually the programming problems became too difficult to solve *and* to maintain — that is, the solutions were too expensive. It was finally clear that the complexity was more than we could handle. Although a large class of programming problems involves doing most of the work during development and creating a solution that requires minimal maintenance (or might simply be thrown away or replaced with a different solution), this is only a subset of the general problem. In the general problem, you view the software as providing a service to people. As the needs of the users evolve, that service must evolve with it. Thus a project is not finished when version one ships; it is a living entity that continues to evolve, and the evolution of a program becomes part of the general programming problem.

external discipline

The need to evolve a program requires new ways of thinking about the problem. It's not just "How do we make it work?" but "How do we make it work *and* make it easy to change?" And there's a new problem: When you're just trying to make a program work, you can assume that the team is stable (you can hope, anyway), but if you're thinking in terms of a program's lifetime, you must assume that team members will change. This means that a new team member must somehow learn the essentials about a program that previous team members communicated to each other (probably using spoken words). Thus the program needs some form of design documentation.

Because documentation is not essential to making a program work, there are no rules for its creation as there are rules imposed by a programming language on a program. Thus, if you require your documentation to satisfy a particular need, you must impose an external discipline. Whether documentation "works" or not is much more difficult to determine (and requires a program's lifetime to verify), so the "best" form of external discipline can be more hotly debated than the "best" programming language.

The important question to keep in mind when making decisions about external discipline is, *"What problem am I trying to solve?"* The essence of the problem was stated above: "How do we make it work *and* make it easy to change?" However, this question has often gone through so many interpretations that it becomes "How can I conform to the FoobleBlah documentation specifications so the government will pay me for this project?" That is, the goal of the external discipline becomes the creation of a *document* rather than a good, maintainable program design; the document may become more important than the program itself.

When asking questions about the directions of the future in general, and computing in particular, I start by applying an economic Occam's Razor: Which solution costs less? Assuming the solution satisfies the needs, is the price difference enough to motivate you out of your current, comfortable way of doing things? If your method involves saving every document ever created during the analysis and design of the project *and maintaining* all those documents as the project evolves, then you will have a system that maximizes the overhead of evolving a project in favor of complete understanding by new team members (assuming there's not so much documentation that it becomes daunting to read). Taken to an extreme, such a method can conceivably cost as much for program creation and maintenance as the approaches it is intended to replace.

At the other end of the external-structure spectrum are the minimalist methods. Perform enough of an analysis to be able to come up with a design, then throw the analysis away so you don't spend time and money maintaining it. Do enough of a design to begin coding, then throw the design away, again, so you don't spend time and money to maintain the document. (The following may or may not be ironic, depending on your situation.) Then the code is so elegant and clear that it needs minimal comments. The code and comments together are enough for the new team member to get up to speed on the project. Because less time is spent with all that tedious documentation (which no one really understands anyway), new members integrate faster.

Throwing *everything* away, however, is probably not the best idea, although if you don't maintain your documents, that's effectively what you do. Some form of document is usually necessary. (See the description of *scripting*, described later in this chapter.)

communication

Expecting your code to suffice as documentation for a larger project is not particularly reasonable, even though it happens more often than not in practice. But it contains the essence of what we really want an external discipline to produce: communication. You'd like to communicate *just enough* to a new team member that she can help evolve the program. But you'd also like to keep the amount of money you spend on external discipline to a minimum because ultimately people are paying for the service the program provides, not the design documentation behind it. And to be truly useful, the external discipline should do more than just generate documentation — it should be a way for team members to communicate about the design as they're creating it. The goal of the ideal external discipline is to facilitate communication about the analysis and design of a program. This helps the people working on the program now and those who will work on the program in the future. The focus is not just to enable communication, but to create good designs.

Because people (and programmers, in particular) are drawn to computers because the machine does work for you — again, an economic motivation — external disciplines that require the developer to do a lot of work *for* the machine seem doomed from the beginning. A successful method (that is, one that gets used) has two important features:

1. It helps you analyze and design. That is, it's much easier to think about and communicate the analysis and design with the method than without it. The difference between your current productivity and the productivity you'll have using the method must be significant; otherwise you might as well stay where you are. Also, it must be simple enough to use that you don't need to carry a handbook. When you're solving *your* problem, that's what you want to think about, not whether you're using symbols or techniques properly.

2. It doesn't impose overhead without short-term payback. Without some short-term reward in the form of visible progress toward your goal, you aren't going to feel very productive with a method, and you're going to find ways to avoid it. This progress cannot be in the guise of the transformation of one intermediate form to another. You've got to see your classes appear, along with the messages they send each other. To someone creating a method this may seem like an arbitrary constraint, but it's simple psychology: People want to feel like they're doing real creative work, and if your method keeps them from a goal rather than helping them gallop toward it, they'll find a way to get around your method.

magnitude

One of the arguments against my view on the subject of methodologies is, "Well, *yes*, you can get away with anything as long as you're working with *small* projects," with "small" apparently meaning anything the listener is capable of imagining. Although this attitude is often used to intimidate the unconverted, there is a kernel of truth inside: What you need may depend on the scale of the problem you're attempting to solve. Tiny projects need no external discipline at all other than the patterns of problem solving learned in the lifetime of the individual programmer. Big projects with many people have little communication among those people and so must have a formal way for that communication to occur effectively and accurately.

The gray area is the projects in between. Their needs may vary depending on the complexity of the project and the experience of the developers. Certainly *all* medium-sized projects don't require adherence to a full-blown method, generating many reports, lots of paper, and lots of work. Some probably do, but many can get away with "methodology lite" (more code, less documentation). The complexity of all the methodologies we are faced with may fall under an 80% – 20% (or less) rule: We are being deluged with details of methodologies that may be needed for less than 20% of the programming problems being solved. If your designs are adequate and maintenance is not a nightmare, maybe you don't need it, or not all of it anyway.

structured OOP?

An even more significant question arises. Suppose a methodology is needed to facilitate communication. This meta-communication about the program is necessary because the programming language is inadequate — it is too oriented toward the machine paradigm and is not very helpful for talking about the problem. The procedural-programming model of the world, for example, requires you to talk about a program in terms of data and functions that transform the data. Because this is not the way we discuss the real problem that's being solved, you must translate back and forth between the problem description and the solution description. Once you get a solution description and implement it, proper etiquette requires that you make changes to the problem description anytime you change the solution. This means you must translate from the machine paradigm *backward* into the problem space. To get a truly maintainable program that can be adapted to changes in the problem space, this is necessary. The overhead and organization required seem to demand an external discipline of some sort. The most important methodology for procedural programming is the *structured techniques*.

Now consider this: What if the language in the solution space were uprooted from the machine paradigm? What if you could force the solution space to use the same terminology as the problem space?

For example, an air conditioner in your climate-controlled building becomes an air conditioner in your climate-control program, a thermostat becomes a thermostat, and so on. (This is what you do, not coincidentally, with OOP.) Suddenly, translating from the problem space to the solution space becomes a minor issue. Conceivably, each phase in the analysis, design, and implementation of a program could use the same terminology, the same representation. So the question becomes, "Do we still need a document about the document, if the essential document (the program) can adequately describe itself?" If OOP does what it claims, then the shape of the programming problem may have changed to the point that all the difficulties solved by the structured techniques might not exist in this new world.

This is not just a fanciful argument, as a thought experiment will reveal. Suppose you need to write a little utility, for example, one that performs an operation on a text file like those you'll find in the latter pages of Chapter 5. Some of those took a few minutes to write; the most difficult took a few hours. Now suppose you're back in the 50's and the project must be done in machine language or assembly, with minimal libraries. It goes from a few minutes for one person to weeks or months and many people. In the 50's you'd need a lot of external discipline and management; now you need none. Clearly, the development of tools has greatly increased the complexity of the problems we're able to solve without external discipline (and just as clearly, we go find problems that are more complicated).

This is not to suggest that no external discipline is necessary, simply that a useful external discipline for OOP will solve different problems than those solved by a useful external discipline for procedural programming. In particular, the goal of an OOP method must be first and foremost to generate a good design. Not only do good designs of any kind promote reuse, but the need for a good design is directly in line with the needs of developers at all levels of a project. Thus, they will be more likely to adopt such a system.

With these points in mind, let's consider some of the issues of an OOP design method.

five stages of object design

The design life of an object is not limited to the period of time when you're writing the program. Instead, the design of an object appears to happen over a sequence of stages. It's helpful to have this perspective because you stop expecting perfection right away; instead, you realize that the understanding of what an object does and what it should look like happens over time. This view also applies to the design of various types of programs; the pattern for a particular type of program emerges through struggling again and again with that problem.[2] Objects, too, have their patterns that emerge through understanding, use, and reuse.

The following is a description, not a method. It is simply an observation of when you can expect design of an object to occur.

1. object discovery

This phase occurs during the initial analysis of a program. Objects may be discovered by looking for external factors and boundaries, duplication of elements in the system, and the smallest conceptual units. Some objects are obvious if you already have a set of class libraries. Commonality between classes suggesting base classes and inheritance may appear right away, or later in the design process.

2. object assembly

As you're building an object you'll discover the need for new members that didn't appear during discovery. The internal needs of the object may require new classes to support it.

---

[2] See *Design Patterns: Elements of Reusable Object-Oriented Software* by Erich Gamma et al., Addison-Wesley, 1995.

3. system construction

Once again, more requirements for an object may appear at this later stage. As you learn, you evolve your objects. The need for communication and interconnection with other objects in the system may change the needs of your classes or require new classes.

4. system extension

As you add new features to a system you may discover that your previous design doesn't support easy system extension. With this new information, you can restructure parts of the system, very possibly adding new classes.

5. object reuse

This is the real stress test for a class. If someone tries to reuse it in an entirely new situation, they'll probably discover some shortcomings. As you change a class to adapt to more new programs, the general principles of the class will become clearer, until you have a truly reusable object.

guidelines for object development

These stages suggest some guidelines when thinking about developing your classes:

1. Let a specific problem generate a class, then let the class grow and mature during the solution of other problems.

2. Remember, discovering the classes you need is the majority of the system design. If you already had those classes, this would be a trivial project.

3. Don't force yourself to know everything at the beginning; learn as you go. That's the way it will happen anyway.

4. Start programming; get something working so you can prove or disprove your design. Don't fear procedural-style spaghetti code — classes partition the problem and help control anarchy and entropy. Bad classes do not break good classes.

5. Always keep it simple. Little clean objects with obvious utility are better than big complicated interfaces. You can always start small and simple and expand the class interface when you understand it better. It can be impossible to reduce the interface of an existing class.

what a method promises

For various reasons methods have often promised a lot more than they can deliver. This is unfortunate because programmers are already a suspicious lot when it comes to strategies and unrealistic expectations; the bad reputation of some methods can cause others to be discarded out of hand. Because of this, valuable techniques can be ignored at significant financial and productivity costs.

a manager's silver bullet

The worst promise is to say, "This method will solve all your problems." Such a promise will more likely come couched in the idea that a method will solve problems that don't really have a solution, or at least not in the domain of program design: An impoverished corporate culture; exhausted, alienated, or adversarial team members; insufficient schedule and resources; or attempting to solve a problem that may in fact be insoluble (insufficient research). The best methodology, regardless of what it promises, will solve none of these problems or any problems in the same class. For that matter, OOP and C++ won't help either. Unfortunately, a manager in such a situation is precisely the person that's most vulnerable to the siren song of the silver bullet.[3]

a tool for productivity

This is what a method *should* be. Increased productivity should come not only in the form of easy and inexpensive maintenance

---

[3] A reference to vampires made in *The Mythical Man-Month*, by Fred Brooks, Addison-Wesley, 1975.

but especially in the creation of a good *design* in the first place. Because the motivating factor for the creation of methodologies was improved maintenance, some methods ignore the beauty and integrity of the program design in favor of maintenance issues. Instead, a good design should be the foremost goal; a good OOP design will have easy maintenance as a side-effect.

what a method should deliver

Regardless of what claims are made for a particular method, it should provide a number of essential features, covered in this section: A contract to allow you to communicate about what the project will accomplish and how it will do it; a system to support the structuring of that project; and a set of tools to represent the project in some abstract form so you can easily view and manipulate it. A more subtle issue, covered last, is the "attitude" of the method concerning that most precious of all resources, The enthusiasm of the team members.

a communication contract

For very small teams, you can keep in such close contact that communication happens naturally. This is the ideal situation. One of the great benefits of C++ is that it allows projects to be built with fewer team members, so this intimate style of communication can be maintained, which means communication overhead is lower and projects can be built more quickly.

The situation is not always so ideal. There can come a point where there are too many team members or the project is too complex, and some form of communication discipline is necessary. A method provides a way to form a "contract" between the members of a team. You can view the concept of such a contract in two ways:

1. **Adversarial**. The contract is an expression of suspicion between the parties involved, to make sure that no one gets out of line and everyone does what they're supposed to. The contract spells out the bad things that happen if they don't. If you are looking at any contract this way, you've already lost the game because you already

think the other party is not trustworthy. If you can't trust someone, a contract won't ensure good behavior.

2. **Informational**. The contract is an attempt to make sure everyone knows what we've agreed upon. It is an aid to communication so everyone can look at it and say, "Yes, that's what I think we're going to do." It's an expression of an agreement *after* the agreement has been made, just to clean up misunderstandings. This sort of contract can be minimalist and easy to read.

A useful method will not foment an adversarial contract; the emphasis will be on communication.

a structuring system

The structure is the heart of your system. If a method accomplishes nothing else it must be able to tell programmers:

1. What classes you need.

2. How you hook them together to build a working system.

A method generates these answers through a process that begins with an analysis of the problem and ends with some sort of representation of the classes, the system, and the messages passed between the classes in the system.

tools for representation

The model should not be more complex than the system it represents. A good model presents an abstraction.

You are certainly not constrained to using the representation tools that come with a particular method. You can make up your own to suit your needs. (For example, later in this chapter there's a suggested notation for use with a commercial word processor.) Following are guidelines for a useful notation:

1. Include no more detail than necessary. Remember the "seven plus or minus two" rule of complexity. (You can only hold that many

items in your mind at one moment.) Extra detail becomes baggage that must be maintained and costs money.

2. You should be able to get as much information as you need by probing deeper into the representation levels. That is, levels can be created if necessary, hidden at higher levels of abstraction and made visible on demand.

3. The notation should be as minimal as possible. "Too much magic causes software rot."

4. System design and class design are separate issues. Classes are reusable tools, while systems are solutions to specific problems (although a system design, too, may be reusable). The notation should focus first on system design.

5. Is a class design notation necessary? The expression of classes provided by the C++ language seems to be adequate for most situations. If a notation doesn't give you a significant boost over describing classes in their native language, then it's a hindrance.

6. The notation should hide the implementation internals of the objects. Those are generally not important during design.

7. Keep it simple. The analysis *is* the design. Basically, all you want to do in your method is discover your objects and how they connect with each other to form a system. If a method and notation require more from you, then you should question whether that method is spending your time wisely.

don't deplete
the most important resource

My friend Michael Wilk, after allowing that he came from academia and perhaps wasn't qualified to make a judgment (the type of preamble you hear from someone with a fresh perspective), observed that the most important resource that a project, team, or company has is *enthusiasm*. It seems that no matter how thorny the problem, how badly you've failed in the past, the primitiveness of your tools or what the odds are, enthusiasm can overcome the obstacle.

Unfortunately, various management techniques often do not consider enthusiasm at all, or, because it cannot easily be measured, consider it an "unimportant" factor, thinking that if enough management structure is in place, the project can be forced through. This sort of thinking has the effect of damping the enthusiasm of the team, because they can feel like no more than a means to a company's profit motive, a cog. Once this happens a team member becomes an "employee," watching the clock and seeking interesting distractions.

A method and management technique built upon motivation and enthusiasm as the most precious resources would be an interesting experiment indeed. At least, you should consider the effect that an OOP design method will have on the morale of your team members.

"required" reading

Before you choose any method, it's helpful to gain perspective from those who are not trying to sell one. It's easy to adopt a method without really understanding what you want out of it or what it will do for you. Others are using it, which seems a compelling reason. However, humans have a strange little psychological quirk: If they want to believe something will solve their problems, they'll try it. (This is experimentation, which is good.) But if it doesn't solve their problems, they may redouble their efforts and begin to announce loudly what a great thing they've discovered. (This is denial, which is not good.) The assumption here may be that if you can get other people in the same boat, you won't be lonely, even if it's going nowhere.

This is not to suggest that all methodologies go nowhere, but that you should be armed to the teeth with mental tools that help you stay in experimentation mode ("It's not working; let's try something else") and out of denial mode ("No, that's not really a problem.

Everything's wonderful, we don't need to change"). I think the following books, read *before* you choose a method, will provide you with these tools.

Software Creativity, by Robert Glass (Prentice-Hall, 1995). This is the best book I've seen that discusses *perspective* on the whole methodology issue. It's a collection of short essays and papers that Glass has written and sometimes acquired (P.J. Plauger is one contributor), reflecting his many years of thinking and study on the subject. They're entertaining and only long enough to say what's necessary; he doesn't ramble and lose your interest. He's not just blowing smoke, either; there are hundreds of references to other papers and studies. All programmers and managers should read this book before wading into the methodology mire.[4]

Peopleware, by Tom Demarco and Timothy Lister (Dorset House, 1987). Although they have backgrounds in software development, this book is about projects and teams in general. But the focus is on the *people* and their needs rather than the technology and its needs. They talk about creating an environment where people will be happy and productive, rather than deciding what rules those people should follow to be adequate components of a machine. This latter attitude, I think, is the biggest contributor to programmers smiling and nodding when XYZ method is adopted and then quietly doing whatever they've always done.

Complexity, by M. Mitchell Waldrop (Simon & Schuster, 1992). This chronicles the coming together of a group of scientists from different disciplines in Santa Fe, New Mexico, to discuss real problems that the individual disciplines couldn't solve (the stock market in economics, the initial formation of life in biology, why people do what they do in sociology, etc.). By crossing physics, economics, chemistry, math, computer science, sociology, and

---

[4] Another good "perspective" book is *Object Lessons* by Tom Love, SIGS Books, 1993.

others, a multidisciplinary approach to these problems is developing. But more importantly, a different way of *thinking* about these ultra-complex problems is emerging: Away from mathematical determinism and the illusion that you can write an equation that predicts all behavior and toward first *observing* and looking for a pattern and trying to emulate that pattern by any means possible. (The book chronicles, for example, the emergence of genetic algorithms.) This kind of thinking, I believe, is useful as we observe ways to manage more and more complex software projects.

scripting: a minimal method

I'll start by saying this is not tried or tested anywhere. I make no promises — it's a starting point, a seed for other ideas, and a thought experiment, albeit after a great deal of thought and a fair amount of reading and observation of myself and others in the process of development. It was inspired by a writing class I took called "Story Structure," taught by Robert McKee,[5] primarily to aspiring and practicing screenwriters, but also for novelists and playwrights. It later occurred to me that programmers have a lot in common with that group: Our concepts ultimately end up expressed in some sort of textual form, and the structure of that expression is what determines whether the product is successful or not. There are a few amazingly well-told stories, many stories that are uninspired but competent and get the job done, and a lot of badly told stories, some of which don't get published. Of course, stories seem to *want* to be told while programs *demand* to be written.

---

[5] Through Two Arts, Inc., 12021 Wilshire Blvd. Suite 868, Los Angeles, CA 90025.

Writers have an additional constraint that does not always appear in programming: They generally work alone or possibly in groups of two. Thus they must be very economical with their time, and any method that does not bear significant fruit is discarded. Two of McKee's goals were to reduce the typical amount of time spent on a screenplay from one year to six months and to significantly increase the quality of the screenplays in the process. Similar goals are shared by software developers.

Getting everyone to agree on anything is an especially tough part of the startup process of a project. The minimal nature of this system should win over even the most independent of programmers.

premises

I'm basing the method described here on two significant premises, which you must carefully consider before you adopt the rest of the ideas:

1. C++, unlike typical procedural languages (and most existing languages, for that matter) has many guards in the language and language features so you can build in your own guards. These guards are intended to prevent the program you create from losing its structure, both during the process of creating it and over time, as the program is maintained.

2. No matter how much analysis you do, there are some things about a system that won't reveal themselves until design time, and more things that won't reveal themselves until a program is up and running. Because of this, it's critical to move fairly quickly through analysis and design to implement a test of the proposed system. Because of Point 1, this is far safer than when using procedural languages, because the guards in C++ are instrumental in preventing the creation of "spaghetti code."

This second point is worth emphasizing. Because of the history we've had with procedural languages, it is commendable that a team will want to proceed carefully and understand every minute detail before moving to design and implementation. Certainly, when creating a DBMS, it pays to understand a customer's needs thoroughly. But a DBMS is in a class of problems that is very well-posed and well-understood. The class of programming problem discussed in this chapter is of the "wild-card" variety, where it isn't simply re-forming a well-known solution, but instead involves one or more wild-card factors — elements where there is no well-understood previous solution, and research is necessary.[6] Attempting to thoroughly analyze a wild-card problem before moving into design and implementation results in *analysis paralysis* because you don't have enough information to solve this kind of problem during the analysis phase. Solving such a problem requires iteration through the whole cycle, and that requires risk-taking behavior (which makes sense, because you're trying to do something new and the potential rewards are higher). It may seem like the risk is compounded by "rushing" into a preliminary implementation, but it can instead reduce the risk in a wild-card project because you're finding out early whether a particular design is viable.

The goal of this method is to attack wild-card projects by producing the most rapid development of a proposed solution, so the design can be proved or disproved as early as possible. Your efforts will not be lost. It's often proposed that you "build one to throw away." With OOP, you may still throw *part* of it away, but because code is encapsulated into classes, you will inevitably produce some useful class designs and develop some worthwhile ideas about the system design during the first iteration that do not need to be thrown away. Thus, the first rapid pass at a problem not only produces critical information for the next analysis, design, and implementation iteration, it also creates a code foundation for that iteration.

---

[6] My rule of thumb for estimating such projects: If there's more than one wild card, don't even try to plan how long it's going to take or how much it will cost. There are too many degrees of freedom.

Another important feature of this method is support for brainstorming at the early part of a project. By keeping the initial document small and concise, it can be created in a few sessions of group brainstorming with a leader who dynamically creates the description. This not only solicits input from everyone, it also fosters initial buy-in and agreement by everyone on the team. Perhaps most importantly, it can kick off a project with a lot of enthusiasm (as noted previously, the most essential resource).

representation

The writer's most valuable computer tool is the word processor, because it easily supports the structure of a document. With programming projects, the structure of the program is usually supported and described by some form of separate documentation. As the projects become more complex, the documentation is essential. This raises a classic problem, stated by Brooks:[7]

> *A basic principle of data processing teaches the folly of trying to maintain independent files in synchronism .... Yet our practice in programming documentation violates our own teaching. We typically attempt to maintain a machine-readable form of a program and an independent set of human-readable documentation ...."*

A good tool will connect the code and its documentation.

I consider it very important to use familiar tools and modes of thinking; the change to OOP is challenging enough by itself. Early OOP methodologies have suffered by using elaborate graphical notation schemes. You inevitably change your design a lot, so expressing it with a notation that's difficult to modify is a liability because you'll resist changing it to avoid the effort involved. Only recently have tools been appearing that manipulate these graphical notations. Tools for easy use of a design notation must already be in

[7] *The Mythical Man-Month*, ibid.

place *before* you can expect people to use a method. Combining this with the fact that documents are usually expected during the software design process, the most logical tool is a full-featured word processor.[8] Virtually every company already has these in place (so there's no cost to trying this method), most programmers are familiar with them, and as programmers they are comfortable creating tools using the underlying macro language. This follows the spirit of C++, where you build on your existing knowledge and tool base rather than throwing it away.

The mode of thinking used by this method also follows that spirit. Although a graphical notation is useful[9] to express a design in a report, it is not fast enough to support brainstorming. However, everyone understands outlining, and most word processors have some sort of outlining mode that allows you to grab pieces of the outline and quickly move them around. This is perfect for rapid design evolution in an interactive brainstorming session. In addition, you can expand and collapse outlines to see various levels of granularity in the system. And (as described later), as you create the design, you create the design document, so a report on the state of the project can be produced with a process not unlike running a compiler.

1. high concept

Any system you build, no matter how complicated, has a fundamental purpose, the business that it's in, the basic need that it satisfies. If you can look past the user interface, the hardware- or

---

[8] My observations here are based on what I am most familiar with: the extensive capabilities of Microsoft Word, which was used to produce the camera-ready pages of this book.

[9] I encourage the choice of one that uses simple boxes, lines, and symbols that are available in the drawing package of the word processor, rather than amorphous shapes that are difficult to produce.

system-specific details, the coding algorithms and the efficiency problems, you will eventually find the core of its being, simple and straightforward. Like the so-called *high concept* from a Hollywood movie, you can describe it in one or two sentences. This pure description is the starting point.

The high concept is quite important because it sets the tone for your project; it's a mission statement. You won't necessarily get it right the first time (you may be developing the treatment or building the design before it becomes completely clear), but keep trying until it feels right. For example, in an air-traffic control system you may start out with a high concept focused on the system that you're building: "The tower program keeps track of the aircraft." But consider what happens when you shrink the system to a very small airfield; perhaps there's only a human controller or none at all. A more useful model won't concern the solution you're creating as much as it describes the problem: "Aircraft arrive, unload, service and reload, and depart."

2. treatment

A *treatment* of a script is a summary of the story in one or two pages, a fleshing out of the high concept. The best way to develop the high concept and treatment for a computer system may be in a group situation with a facilitator who has writing ability. Ideas can be suggested in a brainstorming environment, while the facilitator tries to express the ideas on a computer that's networked with the group or projected on screen. The facilitator takes the role of a ghostwriter and doesn't judge the ideas but instead simply tries to make them clear and keep them flowing.

The treatment becomes the jumping-off point for the initial object discovery and first rough cut at design, which can also be performed in a group setting with a facilitator.

3. structuring

Structure is the key to the system. Without structure you have a random collection of meaningless events. With structure you have a story. The structure of a story is expressed through characters, which correspond to objects, and plot, which corresponds to system design.

organizing the system

As mentioned earlier, the primary representation tool for this method is a sophisticated word processor with outlining facility.

You start with level-1 sections for **high concept**, **treatment**, **objects**, and **design**. As the objects are discovered, they are placed as level-2 subsections under **objects**. Object interfaces are added as level-3 subsections under the specific type of object. If essential descriptive text comes up, it is placed as normal text under the appropriate subsection.

Because this technique involves typing and outlining, with no drawing, the brainstorming process is not hindered by the speed of creating the representation.

characters: initial object discovery

The treatment contains nouns and verbs. As you find these, the nouns will suggest classes, and the verbs will become either methods for those classes or processes in the system design. Although you may not be comfortable that you've found everything after this first pass, remember that it's an iterative process. You can add additional classes and methods at further stages and later design passes, as you understand the problem better. The point of this structuring is that you *don't* currently understand the problem, so don't expect the design to be revealed to you all at once.

Start by simply moving through the treatment and creating a level-2 subsection in **objects** for each unique noun that you find. Take verbs that are clearly acting upon an object and place them as level-3 method subsections beneath the appropriate noun. Add the argument list (even if it's initially empty) and return type for each method. This will give you a rough cut and something to talk about and push around.

If a class is inherited from another class, its level-2 subsection should be placed as close as possible after the base class, and its subsection name should indicate the inheritance relationship just as you would when writing the code: **derived : public base**. This allows the code to be properly generated.

Although you can set your system up to express methods that are hidden from the public interface, the intent here is to create only the classes and their public interfaces; other elements are considered part of the underlying implementation and not the high-level design. If expressed, they should appear as text-level notes beneath the appropriate class.

When decision points come up, use a modified Occam's Razor approach: Consider the choices and select the one that is simplest, because simple classes are almost always best. It's easy to add more elements to a class, but as time goes on, it's difficult to take them away.

If you need to seed the process, look at the problem from a lazy programmer's standpoint: What objects would you like to magically appear to solve your problem? It's also helpful to have references on hand for the classes that are available and the various system design patterns, to clarify proposed classes or designs.

You won't stay in the objects section the entire time; instead, you'll move back and forth between objects and system design as you analyze the treatment. Also, at any time you may want to write some normal text beneath any of the subsections as ideas or notes about a particular class or method.

plot: initial system design

From the high concept and treatment, a number of "subplots" should be apparent. Often they may be as simple as "input, process, output," or "user interface, actions." Each subplot has its own level-2 subsection under **design**. Most stories follow one of a set of common plots; in OOP the analogy is being called a "pattern." Refer to resources on OOP design patterns to aid in searching for plots.

At this point, you're just trying to create a rough sketch of the system. During the brainstorming session, people in the group make suggestions about activities they think occur in the system, and each activity is recorded individually, without necessarily working to connect it to the whole. It's especially important to have the whole team, including mechanical design (if necessary), marketing, and managers, included in this session, not only so everyone is comfortable that the issues have been considered, but because everyone's input is valuable at this point.

A subplot will have a set of stages or states that it moves through, conditions for moving between stages, and the actions involved in each transition. Each stage is given its own level-3 subsection under that particular subplot. The conditions and transitions can be described as text under the stage subhead. Ideally, you'll eventually (as the design iteration proceeds) be able to write the essentials of each subplot as the creation of objects and sending messages to them. This becomes the initial code body for that subplot.

The design discovery and object discovery processes will stimulate each other, so you'll be adding subentries to both sections during the session.

4. development

This is the initial conversion from the rough design to a compiling body of code that can be tested, and especially that will prove or disprove your design. This is not a one-pass process, but rather the beginning of a series of writes and rewrites, so the emphasis is on converting from the document into a body of code in such a way that the document can be regenerated using any changes to the structure or associated prose in the code. This way, generating design documentation after coding begins (and the inevitable changes occur) becomes reasonably effortless, and the design document can become a tool for reporting on the progress of the project.

initial translation

By using the standard section names **objects** and **design** at level-1 section headings, you can key your tools to lift out those sections and generate your header files from them. You perform different activities depending on what major section you're in and the level of subsection you're working on. The easiest approach may be to have your tool or macro break the document into pieces and work on each one appropriately.

Each level-2 section in **objects** should have enough information in the section name (the name of the class and its base class, if any) to generate the class declaration automatically, and each level-3 subsection beneath the class name should have enough information in the section name (member function name, argument list, and return type) to generate the member function declaration. Your tool will simply move through these and create the class declarations.

For simplicity, a single class declaration will appear in each header file. The best approach to naming the header files is probably to include the file name as tagged information in the level-2 section name for that class.

Plotting can be more subtle. Each subplot may produce an independent function, called from inside **main( )**, or simply a section in **main( )**. Start with something that gets the job done; a more refined pattern may emerge in future iterations.

code generation

Using automatic tools (most word-processor scripting tools are adequate for this),

1. Generate a header file for each class described in your **objects** section, creating a class declaration for each one, with all the public

---

Thinking in C++   *Bruce Eckel*

interface functions and their associated description blocks, surrounding each with special tags that can be easily parsed later.

2. Generate a header file for each subplot and copy its description as a commented block at the beginning of the file, followed by function declarations.

3. Mark each subplot, class, and method with its outline heading level as a tagged, commented identifier: //#[1], //#[2], etc.). All generated files have document comments in specially identified blocks with tags. Class names and function declarations also retain comment markers. This way, a reversing tool can go through, extract all the information and regenerate the source document, preferably, in a document-description language like Rich Text Format (RTF).

4. The interfaces and plots should be compilable at this point (but not linkable), so syntax checking can occur. This will ensure the high-level integrity of the design. The document can be regenerated from the correctly compiling files.

5. At this point, two things can happen. If the design is still very early, it's probably easiest to work on the document (rather than the code) in brainstorming sessions, or on subparts of the document in groups responsible for them. However, if the design is complete enough, you can begin coding. If interface elements are added during coding, they must be tagged by the programmer along with tagged comments, so the regeneration program can use the new information to produce the document.

   If you had the front end to a compiler, you could certainly do this for classes and functions automatically, but that's a big job and the language is evolving. Using explicit tags is fairly fail-safe, and commercial browsing tools can be used to verify that all public functions have made it into the document (that is, they were tagged).

5. rewriting

This is the analogy of rewriting a screenplay to refine it and make it shine. In programming, it's the process of iteration. It's where your program goes from good to great, and where those issues that you didn't really understand in the first pass become clear. It's also where your classes can evolve from single-project usage to reusable resources.

From a tool standpoint, reversing the process is a bit more complicated. You want to be able to decompose the header files so they can be reintegrated into the design document, including all the changes that have been made during coding. Then, if any changes are made to the design in the design document, the header files must be completely rebuilt, without losing any of the work that was done to get the header file to compile in the first iteration. Thus, your tool must not only look for your tagged information to turn into section levels and text, it must also find, tag, and store the other information such as the **#include**s at the beginning of each file. If you keep in mind that the header file expresses the class design and that you must be able to regenerate the header from your design document, you'll be OK.

Also notice that the text level notes and discussions, which were turned into tagged comments on the initial generation, have more than likely been modified by the programmer as the design evolved. It's essential that these are captured and put into their respective places, so the design document reflects the new information. This allows you to change that information, and it's carried back to the generated header files.

For the system design (**main( )** and any supporting functions) you may want to capture the whole file, add section identifiers like A, B, C, and so on, as tagged comments (do *not* use line numbers, because these may change), and attach your section descriptions (which will then be carried back and forth into the **main( )** file as tagged, commented text).

You have to know when to stop when iterating the design. Ideally, you achieve target functionality and are in the process of refinement and addition of new features when the deadline comes along and forces you to stop and ship that version. (Remember, software is a subscription business.)

logistics

Periodically, you'll want to get an idea of where the project is by reintegrating the document. This process can be painless if it's done over a network using automatic tools. Regularly integrating and maintaining the master design document is the responsibility of the project leader or manager, while teams or individuals are responsible for subparts of the document (that is, their code and comments).

Supplemental features, such as class diagrams, can be generated using third-party tools and automatically included in the document.

A current report can be generated at any time by simply "refreshing" the document. The state of all parts of the program can then be viewed; this also provides immediate updates for support groups, especially end-user documentation. The document is also critically valuable for rapid start-up of new team members.

A single document is more reasonable than all the documents produced by some analysis, design, and implementation methods. Although one smaller document is less impressive, it's "alive," whereas an analysis document, for example, is only valuable for a particular phase of the project and then rapidly becomes obsolete. It's hard to put a lot of effort into a document that you know will be thrown away.

other methods

There is currently a large number (more than 20) of formal methods available for you to choose from.[10] Some are not entirely independent because they share fundamental ideas, but at some higher level they are all unique. Because at the lowest levels most of the methods are constrained by the default behavior of the language, each method would probably suffice for a simple project. The true benefit is claimed to be at the higher levels; one method may excel at the design of real-time hardware controllers, but that method may not as easily fit the design of an archival database.

Each approach has its cheerleading squad, but before you worry too much about a large-scale method, you should understand the language basics a little better, to get a feel for how a method fits your particular style, or whether you even need a method at all. The following descriptions of three of the most popular methods are mainly for flavor, not comparison shopping. If you want to learn more about methods, there are many books and courses available.

Booch

The Booch[11] method is one of the original, most basic, and most widely referenced. Because it was developed early, it was meant to be applied to a variety of programming problems. It focuses on the unique features of OOP: classes, methods, and inheritance. The steps are as follows:

---

[10] These are summarized in *Object Analysis and Design: Description of Methods*, edited by Andrew T.F. Hutt of the Object Management Group (OMG), John Wiley & Sons, 1994.

[11] See *Object-Oriented Design with Applications* by Grady Booch, Benjamin/Cummings, 1991. A more recent edition focuses on C++.

Thinking in C++ *Bruce Eckel*

1. **Identify classes and objects at a certain level of abstraction**. This is predictably a small step. You state the problem and solution in natural language and identify key features such as nouns that will form the basis for classes. If you're in the fireworks business, you may want to identify Workers, Firecrackers, and Customers; more specifically you'll need Chemists, Assemblers, and Handlers; AmateurFirecrackers and ProfessionalFirecrackers; Buyers and Spectators. Even more specifically, you could identify YoungSpectators, OldSpectators, TeenageSpectators, and ParentSpectators.

2. **Identify their semantics**. Define classes at an appropriate level of abstraction. If you plan to create a class, you should identify that class's audience properly. For example, if you create a class Firecracker, who is going to observe it, a Chemist or a Spectator? The former will want to know what chemicals go into the construction, and the latter will respond to the colors and shapes released when it explodes. If your Chemist requests a firecracker's primary color-producing chemicals, it had better not get the reply, "Some really cool greens and reds." Similarly, a Spectator would be puzzled at a Firecracker that spouted only chemical equations when it was lit. Perhaps your program is for a vertical market, and both Chemists and Spectators will use it; in that case, your Firecracker will have both objective and subjective attributes, and will be able to appear in the appropriate guise for the observer.

3. **Identify relationships between them (CRC cards)**. Define how the classes interact with other classes. A common method for tabulating the information about each class uses the Class, Responsibility, Collaboration (CRC) card. This is a small card (usually an index card) on which you write the state variables for the class, the responsibilities it has (i.e., the messages it gives and receives), and references to the other classes with which it interacts. Why an index card? The reasoning is that if you can't fit all you need to know about a class on a small card, the class is too complex. The ideal class should be understood at a glance; index cards are not only readily available, they also happen to hold what

most people consider a reasonable amount of information. A solution that doesn't involve a major technical innovation is one that's available to everyone (like the document structuring in the scripting method described earlier in this chapter).

4. **Implement the classes**. Now that you know what to do, jump in and code it. In most projects the coding will affect the design.

5. **Iterate the design**. The design process up to this point has the feeling of the classic waterfall method of program development. Now it diverges. After a preliminary pass to see whether the key abstractions allow the classes to be separated cleanly, iterations of the first three steps may be necessary. Booch writes of a "round-trip gestalt design process." Having a gestalt view of the program should not be impossible if the classes truly reflect the natural language of the solution. Perhaps the most important thing to remember is that by default — by definition, really — if you modify a class its super- and subclasses will still function. You need not fear modification; it cannot break the program, and any change in the outcome will be limited to subclasses and/or specific collaborators of the class you change. A glance at your CRC card for the class will probably be the only clue you need to verify the new version.

Responsibility-Driven Design (RDD)

This method[12] also uses CRC cards. Here, as the name implies, the cards focus on delegation of responsibilities rather than appearance. To illustrate, the Booch method might produce an Employee-BankEmployee-BankManager hierarchy; in RDD this might come out Manager-FinanceManager-BankManager. The bank manager's primary responsibilities are managerial, so the hierarchy reflects that.

More formally, RDD involves the following:

---

[12] See *Designing Object-Oriented Software* by Rebecca Wirfs-Brock et al., Prentice Hall, 1990.

1. **Data or state**. A description of the data or state variables for each class.

2. **Sinks and sources**. Identification of data sinks and sources, classes that process or generate data.

3. **Observer or view**. View or observer classes that separate hardware dependencies.

4. **Facilitator or helper**. Facilitator or helper classes, such as a linked list, that contain little or no state information and simply help other classes to function.

Object Modeling Technique (OMT)

Object Modeling Technique[13] (OMT) adds one more level of complexity to the process. Booch's method emphasizes the fundamental appearance of classes and defines them simply as outgrowths of the natural language solution. RDD takes that one step further by emphasizing the class responsibility more than its appearance. OMT describes not only the classes but various states of the system using detailed diagramming, as follows:

1. **Object model, "what," object diagram**. The object model is similar to that produced by Booch's method and RDD. Object classes are connected by responsibilities.

2. **Dynamic model, "when," state diagram**. The dynamic model describes time-dependent states of the system. Different states are connected by transitions. An example that contains time-dependent states is a real-time sensor that collects data from the outside world.

3. **Functional model, "how," data flow diagram**. The functional model traces the flow of data. The theory is that because the real work at the lowest level of the program is accomplished using

---

[13] See *Object-Oriented Modeling and Design* by James Rumbaugh et al., Prentice Hall, 1991.

procedures, the low-level behavior of the program is best understood by diagramming the data flow rather than by diagramming its objects.

strategies for translation

If you buy into OOP, you next question is probably, "How can I get my manager/colleagues/department/peers to start using objects?" Think about how you — one independent programmer — would go about learning to use a new language and a new programming paradigm. You've done it before. First comes education and examples; then comes a trial project to give you a feel for the basics without doing anything too confusing; then you try to do a "real world" project that actually does something useful. Throughout your first projects you continue your education by reading, asking questions of gurus, and trading hints with friends. In essence, this is the approach many authors suggest for the switch from C to C++. Switching an entire company will of course introduce certain group dynamics, but it will help at each step to remember how one person would do it.

stepping up to OOP

Here are some guidelines to consider when making the transition to OOP and C++:

1. training

The first step is some form of education. Remember the company's investment in plain C code, and try not to throw it all into disarray for 6 to 9 months while everyone puzzles over how multiple inheritance works. Pick a small group for indoctrination, preferably one composed of people who are curious, work well together, and can function as their own support network while they're learning C++.

An alternative approach that is sometimes suggested is the education of all company levels at once, including overview courses for strategic managers as well as design and programming courses for project builders. This is especially good for smaller companies making fundamental shifts in the way they do things, or at the division level of larger companies. Because the cost is higher, however, some may choose to start with project-level training, do a pilot project (possibly with an outside mentor), and let the project team become the teachers for the rest of the company.

2. low-risk project

Try a low-risk project first and allow for mistakes. Once you've gained some experience, you can either seed other projects from members of this first team or use the team members as an OOP technical support staff. This first project may not work right the first time, so it should be not very important in the grand scheme of things. It should be simple, self-contained, and instructive; this means that it should involve creating classes that will be meaningful to the other programmers in the company when they get their turn to learn C++.

3. model from success

Seek out examples of good object-oriented design before starting from scratch. There's a good probability that someone has solved your problem already, and if they haven't solved it exactly you can probably apply what you've learned about abstraction to modify an existing design to fit your needs. This is the general concept of *design patterns*.[14]

4. use existing class libraries

The primary economic motivation for switching to C++ is the easy use of existing code in the form of class libraries; the shortest application development cycle will result when you don't have to write anything but **main( )** yourself. However, some new programmers don't understand this, are unaware of existing class libraries, or through fascination with the language desire to write

---

[14] See Gamma et al., ibid.

classes that may already exist. Your success with OOP and C++ will be optimized if you make an effort to seek out and reuse other people's code early in the transition process.

5. don't rewrite existing code in C++

Although *compiling* your C code in C++ usually produces (sometimes great) benefits by finding problems in the old code, it is not usually the best use of your time to take existing, functional code and rewrite it in C++. There are incremental benefits, especially if the code is slated for reuse. But chances are you aren't going to see the dramatic increases in productivity that you hope for in your first few projects unless that project is a new one. C++ and OOP shine best when taking a project from concept to reality.

management obstacles

If you're a manager, your job is to acquire resources for your team, to overcome barriers to your team's success and in general to try to provide the most productive and enjoyable environment so your team is most likely to perform those miracles that are always being asked of you. Moving to C++ falls in all three of these categories, and it would be wonderful if it didn't cost you anything as well. Although it is arguably cheaper than the OOP alternatives for team of C programmers (and probably for programmers in other procedural languages), it isn't free, and there are obstacles you should be aware of before trying to sell the move to C++ within your company and embarking on the move itself.

startup costs

The cost is more than just the acquisition of a C++ compiler. Your medium- and long-term costs will be minimized if you invest in training (and possibly mentoring for your first project) and also if you identify and purchase class libraries that solve your problem rather than trying to build those libraries yourself. These are hard-money costs that must be factored into a realistic proposal. In addition, there are the hidden costs in loss of productivity while learning a new language and possibly a new programming environment. Training and mentoring can certainly minimize these but team members must overcome their own struggles to understand the issues. During this process they will make more mistakes (this is a feature, because acknowledged mistakes are the fastest path to learning) and be less productive. Even then, with some types of programming problems, the right classes, and the right development environment, it's possible to be more productive while you're learning C++ (even considering that you're making more mistakes and writing fewer lines of code per day) than if you'd stayed with C.

performance issues

A common question is, "Doesn't OOP automatically make my programs a lot bigger and slower?" The answer is, "It depends." Most traditional OOP languages were designed with experimentation and rapid prototyping in mind rather than lean-and-mean operation. Thus, they virtually guaranteed a significant increase in size and decrease in speed. C++, however, is designed with production programming in mind. When your focus is on rapid prototyping, you can throw together components as fast as possible while ignoring efficiency issues. If you're using any third-party libraries, these are usually already optimized by their vendors; in any case it's not an issue while you're in rapid-development mode. When you have a system you like, if it's small and fast enough, then you're done. If not, you begin tuning with a profiling tool, looking first for speedups that can be done with simple applications of built-in C++ features. If that doesn't help, you look for modifications that can be made in the underlying implementation so no code that uses a particular class needs to be changed. Only if nothing else solves the problem do you need to change the design. The fact that performance in that portion of the design is so critical is an indicator that it must be part of the primary design criteria. You have the benefit of finding this out early through rapid prototyping.

As mentioned earlier in this chapter, the number that is most often given for the difference in size and speed between C and C++ is ±10%, and often much closer to par. You may actually get a

---

significant improvement in size and speed for C++ over C because the design you make for C++ could be quite different from the one you'd make for C.

The evidence for size and speed comparisons between C and C++ is so far all anecdotal and is likely to remain so. Regardless of the number of people who suggest that a company try the same project using C and C++, no company is likely to waste money that way, unless it's very big and interested in such research projects. Even then it seems like the money could be better spent. Almost universally, programmers who have moved from C (or some other procedural language) to C++ have had the personal experience of a great acceleration in their programming productivity, and that's the most compelling argument you can find.

common design errors

When starting your team into OOP and C++, programmers will typically go through a series of common design errors. This often happens because of too little feedback from experts during the design and implementation of early projects, because no experts have been developed within the company. It's easy to feel that you understand OOP too early in the cycle and go off on a bad tangent; something that's obvious to someone experienced with the language may be a subject of great internal debate for a novice. Much of this trauma can be skipped by using an outside expert for training and mentoring.

summary

This chapter attempts to give you a feel for the broad issues of object-oriented programming and C++, including why OOP is different, and why C++ in particular is different; concepts of OOP methods and why you should (or should not) use one; a suggestion for a minimal method that I've developed to allow you to get started on an OOP project with minimal overhead; discussions of other methods; and finally the kinds of issues you will encounter when moving your own company to OOP and C++.

OOP and C++ may not be for everyone. It's important to evaluate your own needs and decide whether C++ will optimally satisfy those needs, or if you might be better off with another programming system. If you know that your needs will be very specialized for the foreseeable future and if you have specific constraints that may not be satisfied by C++, then you owe it to yourself to investigate the alternatives. Even if you eventually choose C++ as your language, you'll at least understand what the options were and have a clear vision of why you took that direction.

data abstraction

C++ is a productivity enhancement tool. Why else would you make the effort (and it is an effort, regardless of how easy we attempt to make the transition) to

switch from some language that you already know and are productive in (C, in this case) to a new language where you're going to be *less* productive for a while, until you get the hang of it? It's because you've become convinced that you're going to get big gains by using this new tool.

Productivity, in computer programming terms, means that fewer people can make much more complex and impressive programs in less time. There are certainly other issues when it comes to choosing a language, like efficiency (does the nature of the language cause code bloat?), safety (does the language help you ensure that your program will always do what you plan, and handle errors gracefully?), and maintenance (does the language help you create code that is easy to understand, modify and extend?). These are certainly important factors that will be examined in this book.

But raw productivity means a program that might take three of you a week takes one of you a day or two. This touches several levels of economics. You're happy because you get the rush of power that comes from building something, your client (or boss) is happy because products are produced faster and with fewer people, and the customers are happy because they get products more cheaply. The only way to get massive increases in productivity is to leverage off other people's code, that is, to use libraries.

A library is simply a bunch of code that someone else has written, packaged together somehow. Often, the most minimal package is a file with an extension like .LIB and one or more header files to declare what's in the library to your compiler. The linker knows how to search through the LIB file and extract the appropriate compiled code. But that's only one way to deliver a library. On platforms that span many architectures, like Unix, often the only sensible way to deliver a library is with source code, so it can be recompiled on the new target. And on Microsoft Windows, the *dynamic-link library* (DLL) is a much more sensible approach — for one thing, you can often update your program by sending out a new DLL, which *your* library vendor may have sent you.

So libraries are probably the most important way to improve productivity, and one of the primary design goals of C++ is to make library use easier. This implies that there's something hard about using libraries in C. Understanding this factor will give you a first insight into the design of C++, and thus insight into how to use it.

declarations vs. definitions

First, it's important to understand the difference between declarations and definitions because the terms will be used precisely throughout the book. A *declaration* introduces a name to the compiler. It says, "Here's what this name means." A *definition*, on the other hand, allocates storage for the name. This meaning works whether you're talking about a variable or a function; in either case, at the point of definition the compiler allocates storage. For a variable, it determines how big that variable is and generates space in memory to hold information. For a function, the compiler generates code, which ends up allocating storage in memory. The storage for a function has an address that can be produced using the function name with no argument list, or with the address-of operator.

A definition can also be a declaration. If the compiler hasn't seen the name **A** before and you define **int A**, the compiler sees the name for the first time and allocates storage for it all at once.

Declarations are often made using the **extern** keyword. **extern** is required if you're declaring a variable but not defining it. With a function declaration, **extern** is optional because a function name, argument list, or a return value without a function body is automatically a declaration.

A *function prototype* contains all the information about argument types and return values. **int f(float, char);** is a function prototype because it not only introduces **f** as the name of the function, it tells the compiler what the arguments and return value are so they can be handled properly. C++ requires function prototyping because it adds a significant level of safety.

Here are some examples of declarations:

```
/*: DECLARE.C -- Declaration/definition examples */
extern int i; /* Declaration without definition */
extern float f(float); /* Function declaration */

float b;  /* Declaration & definition */
float f(float a) {  /* Definition */
  return a + 1.0;
}

int i; /* Definition */
int h(int x) { /* Declaration & definition */
  return x + 1;
}

main() {
  b = 1.0;
  i = 2;
  f(b);
  h(i);
}
```

In the function declarations, the argument names are optional. In the definitions, they are required. This is true only in C, not C++.

Throughout this book you'll notice that the first line of a file will be a comment that starts with the open-comment syntax followed by a colon. This is a technique I use to allow easy extraction of information from code files using a text-manipulation tool like "grep" or "awk." The first line also has the name of the file, so it can be referred to in text and in other files, and so you can easily locate it on the source-code disk for the book.

a tiny C library

A small library usually starts out as a collection of functions, but those of you who have used third-party C libraries know that there's usually more to it than that because there's more to life than behavior, actions and functions. There are also characteristics (blue, pounds, texture, luminance), which are represented by data. And when you start to deal with a set of characteristics in C, it is very convenient to clump them together into a **struct**, especially if you want to represent more than one similar thing in your problem space. Then you can make a variable of this **struct** for each thing.

Thus, most C libraries have a set of **struct**s and a set of functions that act on those **struct**s. As an example of what such a system looks like, consider a programming tool that acts like an array, but whose size can be established at run-time, when it is created. I'll call it a **stash**:

```
/*: LIB.H -- Header file: example C library */
/* Array-like entity created at run-time */

typedef struct STASHtag {
  int size;  /* Size of each space */
  int quantity; /* Number of storage spaces */
  int next; /* Next empty space */
  /* Dynamically allocated array of bytes: */
  unsigned char* storage;
} Stash;

void initialize(Stash* S, int Size);
void cleanup(Stash* S);
int add(Stash* S, void* element);
void* fetch(Stash* S, int index);
int count(Stash* S);
void inflate(Stash* S, int increase);
```

The tag name for the **struct** is generally used in case you need to reference the **struct** inside itself. For example, when creating a linked list, you need a pointer to the next **struct**. But almost universally in a C library you'll see the **typedef** as shown above, on every **struct** in the library. This is done so you can treat the **struct** as if it were a new type and define variables of that **struct** like this:

```
stash A, B, C;
```

Note that the function declarations use the Standard C style of function prototyping, which is much safer and clearer than the "old" C style. You aren't just introducing a function name; you're also telling the compiler what the argument list and return value look like.

The **storage** pointer is an **unsigned char***. This is the smallest piece of storage a C compiler supports, although on some machines it can be the same size as the largest. It's implementation dependent. You might think that because the **stash** is designed to hold any type of variable, a **void*** would be more appropriate here. However, the purpose is not to treat this storage as a block of some unknown type, but rather as a block of contiguous bytes.

The source code for the implementation file (which you may not get if you buy a library commercially — you might get only a compiled OBJ or LIB or DLL, etc.) looks like this:

```
/*: LIB.C -- Implementation of
    example C library */
/* Declare structure and functions: */
#include "..\1\lib.h"
/* Error testing macros: */
#include <assert.h>
/* Dynamic memory allocation functions: */
#include <stdlib.h>
#include <string.h> /* memcpy() */
#include <stdio.h>
```

```
void initialize(Stash* S, int Size) {
  S->size = Size;
  S->quantity = 0;
  S->storage = 0;
  S->next = 0;
}

void cleanup(Stash* S) {
  if(S->storage) {
      puts("freeing storage");
      free(S->storage);
  }
}

int add(Stash* S, void* element) {
  /* enough space left? */
  if(S->next >= S->quantity)
    inflate(S, 100);
  /* Copy element into storage,
  starting at next empty space: */
  memcpy(&(S->storage[S->next * S->size]),
      element, S->size);
  S->next++;
  return(S->next - 1); /* Index number */
}

void* fetch(Stash* S, int index) {
  if(index >= S->next || index < 0)
    return 0;  /* Not out of bounds? */
  /* Produce pointer to desired element: */
  return &(S->storage[index * S->size]);
}

int count(Stash* S) {
  /* Number of elements in stash */
  return S->next;
}
```

```
void inflate(Stash* S, int increase) {
  void* v =
    realloc(S->storage,
            (S->quantity + increase)
            * S->size);
  /* Was it successful? */
  assert(v);
  S->storage = v;
  S->quantity += increase;
}
```

Notice the style for local **#includes**: Even though the header file exists in a local directory, its path is given relative to the root directory of this book. By doing this, you can easily create another directory off the book's root and copy code to it for experimentation without worrying about changing **#include** paths.

initialize( ) performs the necessary setup for **struct stash** by setting the internal variables to appropriate values. Initially, the **storage** pointer is set to zero, and the **size** indicator is also zero — no initial storage is allocated.

The **add( )** function inserts an element into the **stash** at the next available location. First, it checks to see if there is any available space left. If not, it expands the storage using the **inflate( )** function, described later.

Because the compiler doesn't know the specific type of the variable being stored (all the function gets is a **void***), you can't just do an assignment, which would certainly be the convenient thing. Instead, you must use the Standard C library function **memcpy( )** to copy the variable byte-by-byte. The first argument is the destination address where **memcpy( )** is to start copying bytes. It is produced by the expression:

```
&(S->storage[S->next * S->size])
```

This indexes from the beginning of the block of storage to the **next** available piece. This number, which is simply a count of the number of pieces used plus one, must be multiplied by the number of bytes occupied by each piece to produce the offset in bytes. This doesn't produce the address, but instead the byte at the address. To produce the address, you must use the address-of operator **&**.

The second and third arguments to **memcpy( )** are the starting address of the variable to be copied and the number of bytes to copy, respectively. The **next** counter is incremented, and the index of the value stored is returned, so the programmer can use it later in a call to **fetch( )** to select that element.

fetch( ) checks to see that the index isn't out of bounds and then returns the address of the desired variable, calculated the same way as it was in **add( )**.

count( ) may look a bit strange at first to a seasoned C programmer. It seems like a lot of trouble to go through to do something that would probably be a lot easier to do by hand. If you have a **struct stash** called **intStash**, for example, it would seem much more straightforward to find out how many elements it has by saying **intStash.next** instead of making a function call (which has overhead) like **count(&intStash)**. However, if you wanted to change the internal representation of **stash** and thus the way the count was calculated, the function call interface allows the necessary flexibility. But alas, most programmers won't bother to find out about your "better" design for the library. They'll look at the **struct** and grab the **next** value directly, and possibly even change **next** without your permission. If only there were some way for the library designer to have better control over things like this! (Yes, that's foreshadowing.)

dynamic storage allocation

You never know the maximum amount of storage you might need for a **stash**, so the memory pointed to by **storage** is allocated from the *heap*. The heap is a big block of memory used for allocating smaller pieces at run-time. You use the heap when you don't know the size of the memory you'll need while you're writing a program. That is, only at run-time will you find out that you need space to hold 200 **airplane** variables instead of 20. Dynamic-memory allocation functions are part of the Standard C library and include **malloc( )**, **calloc( )**, **realloc( )**, and **free( )**.

The **inflate( )** function uses **realloc( )** to get a bigger chunk of space for the **stash**. **realloc( )** takes as its first argument the address of the storage that's already been allocated and that you want to resize. (If this argument is zero — which is the case just after **initialize( )** has been called — it allocates a new chunk of memory.) The second argument is the new size that you want the chunk to be. If the size is smaller, there's no chance the block will need to be copied, so the heap manager is simply told that the extra space is free. If the size is larger, as in **inflate( )**,there may not be enough contiguous space, so a new chunk might be allocated and the memory copied. The **assert( )** checks to make sure that the operation was successful. (**malloc( )**, **calloc( )** and **realloc( )** all return zero if the heap is exhausted.)

Note that the C heap manager is fairly primitive. It gives you chunks of memory and takes them back when you **free( )** them. There's no facility for *heap compaction*, which compresses the heap to provide bigger free chunks. If a program allocates and frees heap storage for a while, you can end up with a heap that has lots of memory free, just not anything big enough to allocate the size of chunk you're looking for at the moment. However, a heap compactor moves memory chunks around, so your pointers won't retain their proper values. Some operating environments, such as Microsoft Windows, have heap compaction built in, but they require you to use special memory *handles* (which can be temporarily converted to pointers, after locking the memory so the heap compactor can't move it) instead of pointers.

assert( ) is a preprocessor macro in ASSERT.H. **assert( )** takes a single argument, which can be any expression that evaluates to true or false. The macro says, "I assert this to be true, and if it's not, the program will exit after printing an error message." When you are no longer debugging, you can define a flag so asserts are ignored. In the meantime, it is a very clear and portable way to test for errors. Unfortunately, it's a bit abrupt in its handling of error situations: "Sorry, mission control. Our C program failed an assertion and bailed out. We'll have to land the shuttle on manual." In Chapter 16, you'll see how C++ provides a better solution to critical errors with *exception handling*.

When you create a variable on the stack at compile-time, the storage for that variable is automatically created and freed by the compiler. It knows exactly how much storage it needs, and it knows the lifetime of the variables because of scoping. With dynamic memory allocation, however, the compiler doesn't know how much storage you're going to need, *and* it doesn't know the lifetime of that storage. It doesn't get cleaned up automatically. Therefore, you're responsible for releasing the storage using **free( )**, which tells the heap manager that storage can be used by the next call to **malloc( )**, **calloc( )** or **realloc( )**. The logical place for this to happen in the library is in the **cleanup( )** function because that is where all the closing-up housekeeping is done.

To test the library, two **stash**es are created. The first holds **int**s and the second holds arrays of 80 **char**s. (You could almost think of this as a new data type. But that happens later.)

```
/*: LIBTESTC.C -- Test demonstration library */
#include "..\1\lib.h"
#include <stdio.h>
#include <assert.h>
#define BUFSIZE 80

main() {
  Stash intStash, stringStash;
  int i;
  FILE* file;
  char buf[BUFSIZE];
  char* cp;
```

```
/* .... */
initialize(&intStash, sizeof(int));
for(i = 0; i < 100; i++)
   add(&intStash, &i);
/* Holds 80-character strings: */
initialize(&stringStash,
          sizeof(char) * BUFSIZE);
file = fopen("LIBTESTC.C", "r");
assert(file);
while(fgets(buf, BUFSIZE, file))
   add(&stringStash, buf);
fclose(file);

for(i = 0; i < count(&intStash); i++)
   printf("fetch(&intStash, %d) = %d\n", i,
         *(int*)fetch(&intStash, i));

i = 0;
while((cp = fetch(&stringStash, i++)) != 0)
   printf("fetch(&stringStash, %d) = %s",
         i - 1, cp);
putchar('\n');
cleanup(&intStash);
cleanup(&stringStash);
}
```

At the beginning of **main( )**, the variables are defined, including the two **stash** structures. Of course, you must remember to initialize these later in the block. One of the problems with libraries is that you must carefully convey to the user the importance of the initialization and cleanup functions. If these functions aren't called, there will be a lot of trouble. Unfortunately, the user doesn't always wonder if initialization and cleanup are mandatory. They know what *they* want to accomplish, and they're not as concerned about you jumping up and down saying, "Hey, wait, you have to do *this* first!" Some users have even been known to initialize the elements of the structure themselves. There's certainly no mechanism to prevent it (more foreshadowing).

The **intStash** is filled up with integers, and the **stringStash** is filled with strings. These strings are produced by opening the source code file, LIBTEST.C, and reading the lines from it into the **stringStash**. Notice something interesting here: The Standard C library functions for opening and reading files use the same techniques as in the **stash** library! **fopen( )** returns a pointer to a **FILE struct**, which it creates on the heap, and this pointer is passed to any function that refers to that file (**fgets( )**, in this case). One of the things **fclose( )** does is release the **FILE struct** back to the heap. Once you start noticing this pattern of a C library consisting of **struct**s and associated functions, you see it everywhere!

After the two stashes are loaded, you can print them out. The **intStash** is printed using a **for** loop, which uses **count( )** to establish its limit. The **stringStash** is printed with a **while**, which breaks out when **fetch( )** returns zero to indicate it is out of bounds.

There are a number of other things you should understand before we look at the problems in creating a C library. (You may already know these because you're a C programmer.) First, although header files are used here because it's good practice, they aren't essential. It's possible in C to call a function that you haven't declared. A good compiler will warn you that you probably ought to declare a function first, but it isn't enforced. This is a dangerous practice, because the compiler can assume that a function that you call with an **int** argument has an argument list containing **int**, and it will treat it accordingly — a very difficult bug to find.

Note that the LIB.H header file *must* be included in any file that refers to **stash** because the compiler can't even guess at what that structure looks like. It can guess at functions, even though it probably shouldn't, but that's part of the history of C.

Each separate C file is a *translation unit*. That is, the compiler is run separately on each translation unit, and when it is running it is aware of only that unit. Thus, any information you provide by including header files is quite important because it provides the compiler's understanding of the rest of your program. Declarations in header files are particularly important, because everywhere the header is included, the compiler will know exactly what to do. If, for example, you have a declaration in a header file that says **void foo(float);**, the compiler knows that if you call it with an integer argument, it should promote the **int** to a **float**. Without the declaration, the compiler would simply assume that a function **foo(int)** existed, and it wouldn't do the promotion.

For each translation unit, the compiler creates an object file, with an extension of **.o** or **.obj** or something similar. These object files, along with the necessary start-up code, must be collected by the linker into the executable program. During linking, all the external references must be resolved. For example, in LIBTEST.C, functions like **initialize( )** and **fetch( )** are declared (that is, the compiler is told what they look like) and used, but not defined. They are defined elsewhere, in LIB.C. Thus, the calls in LIBTEST.C are external references. The linker must, when it puts all the object files together, take the unresolved external references and find the addresses they actually refer to. Those addresses are put in to replace the external references.

It's important to realize that in C, the references are simply function names, generally with an underscore in front of them. So all the linker has to do is match up the function name where it is called and the function body in the object file, and it's done. If you accidentally made a call that the compiler interpreted as **foo(int)** and there's a function body for **foo(float)** in some other object file, the linker will see **_foo** in one place and **_foo** in another, and it will think everything's OK. The **foo( )** at the calling location will push an **int** onto the stack, and the **foo( )** function body will expect a **float** to be on the stack. If the function only reads the value and doesn't write to it, it won't blow up the stack. In fact, the **float** value it reads off the stack might even make some kind of sense. That's worse because it's harder to find the bug.

Thinking in C++   *Bruce Eckel*

bringing it all together: project-building tools

When using *separate compilation* (breaking code into a number of translation units), you need some way to compile them all and to tell the linker to put them with the appropriate libraries and startup code into an executable file. Most compilers allow you to do this with a single command-line statement. For a compiler named **cpp**, for example, you might say

```
cpp libtest.c lib.c
```

The problem with this approach is that the compiler will first compile each individual translation unit, regardless of whether it *needs* to be rebuilt or not. With many files in a project, it can get very tedious to recompile everything if you've only changed a single file.

The first solution to this problem, developed on Unix (which is where C was created), was a program called **make**. **make** compares the date on the source-code file to the date on the object file, and if the object-file date is earlier than the source-code file, **make** invokes the compiler on the source. You can learn more about **make** from your compiler's documentation.[1]

make is powerful, but it's a bit tedious to learn and configure a **makefile**, which is a text file describing the relationships between all the files in a project. Because of this, compiler vendors came up with their own project building tools. These tools ask you which translation units are in your project, and determine all the relationships themselves. They have something similar to a

---

[1] See also *C++ Inside & Out* by the author (Osborne/McGraw-Hill, 1993)

---

makefile, generally called a *project file*, but the programming environment maintains this file so you don't have to worry about it. The configuration and use of project files vary from system to system, so it will be assumed here that you are using the project-building tool of your choice to create these programs, and that you will find the appropriate documentation on how to use them (although project file tools provided by compiler vendors are usually so simple to use that you can learn them quite effortlessly).

file names

One other issue you should be aware of is file naming. In C, it has been traditional to name header files (containing declarations) with an extension of **.h** and implementation files (that cause storage to be allocated and code to be generated) with an extension of **.c**. C++ went through an evolution. It was first developed on Unix, where the operating system was aware of upper and lower case in file names. The original file names were simply capitalized versions of the C extensions: **.H** and **.C**. This of course didn't work for operating systems that didn't distinguish upper and lower case, like MS-DOS. DOS C++ vendors used extensions of **.hxx** and **.cxx** for header files and implementation files, respectively, or **.hpp** and **.cpp**. Later, someone figured out that the only reason you needed a different extension for a file was so the compiler could determine whether to compile it as a C or C++ file. Because the compiler never compiled header files directly, only the implementation file extension needed to be changed. The custom, virtually across all systems, has now become to use **.cpp** for implementation files and **.h** for header files.

what's wrong?

We are remarkably adaptable, even with things where perhaps we *shouldn't* adapt. The style of the **stash** library has been a staple for C programmers, but if you look at it for a while, you might notice that it's rather . . . awkward. When you use it, you have to pass the address of the structure to every single function in the library. When reading the code, the mechanism of the library gets mixed with the meaning of the function calls, which is confusing when you're trying to understand what's going on.

One of the biggest obstacles, however, to using libraries in C is the problem of *name clashes*. C has a single name space for functions; that is, when the linker looks for a function name, it looks in a single master list. In addition, when the compiler is working on a translation unit, it can only work with a single function with a given name.

Now suppose you decide to buy two libraries from two different vendors, and each library has a structure that must be initialized and cleaned up. Both vendors decided that **initialize( )** and **cleanup( )** are good names. If you include both their header files in a single translation unit, what does the C compiler do? Fortunately, Standard C gives you an error, telling you there's a type mismatch in the two different argument lists of the declared functions. But even if you don't include them in the same translation unit, the linker will still have problems. A good linker will detect that there's a name clash, but some linkers take the first function name they find, by searching through the list of object files in the order you give them in the link list. (Indeed, this can be thought of as a feature because it allows you to replace a library function with your own version.)

In either event, you can't use two C libraries that contain a function with the identical name. To solve this problem, C library vendors will often prepend a string of unique characters to the beginning of all their function names. So **initialize( )** and **cleanup( )** might become **stash_initialize( )** and **stash_cleanup( )**. This is a logical thing to do because it "mangles" the name of the **struct** the function works on with the name of the function.

Now it's time to take the very first step into C++. Variable names inside a **struct** do not clash with global variable names. So why not take advantage of this for function names, when those functions operate on a particular **struct**? That is, why not make functions members of structs?

the basic object

Step one in C++ is exactly that. Functions can now be placed inside structs as "member functions." Here's what it looks like with the **stash**:

```
//: LIBCPP.H -- C library converted to C++

struct stash {
  int size;  // Size of each space
  int quantity; // Number of storage spaces
  int next; // Next empty space
   // Dynamically allocated array of bytes:
  unsigned char* storage;
  // Functions!
  void initialize(int Size);
  void cleanup();
  int add(void* element);
  void* fetch(int index);
  int count();
  void inflate(int increase);
};
```

The first thing you'll notice is the new comment syntax, //. This is in addition to C-style comments, which still work fine. The C++ comments only go to the end of the line, which is often very convenient. In addition, in this book we put a colon after the // on the first line of the file, followed by the name of the file and a brief description. This allows an exact inclusion of the file from the source code. In addition, you can easily identify the file in the electronic source code from its name in the book listing.

Next, notice there is no **typedef**. Instead of requiring you to create a **typedef**, the C++ compiler turns the name of the structure into a new type name for the program (just like **int**, **char**, **float** and **double** are type names). The *use* of **stash** is still the same.

All the data members are exactly the same as before, but now the functions are inside the body of the **struct**. In addition, notice that the first argument from the C version of the library has been removed. In C++, instead of forcing you to pass the address of the structure as the first argument to all the functions that operate on that structure, the compiler secretly does this for you. Now the only arguments for the functions are concerned with what the function *does*, not the mechanism of the function's operation.

It's important to realize that the function code is effectively the same as it was with the C library. The number of arguments are the same (even though you don't see the structure address being passed in, it's still there); and there's only one function body for each function. That is, just because you say

```
stash A, B, C;
```

doesn't mean you get a different **add( )** function for each variable.

So the code that's generated is almost the same as you would have written for the C library. Interestingly enough, this includes the "name mangling" you probably would have done to produce **stash_initialize( )**, **stash_cleanup( )**, and so on. When the function name is inside the **struct**, the compiler effectively does the same thing. Therefore, **initialize( )** inside the structure **stash** will not collide with **initialize( )** inside any other structure. Most of the time you don't have to worry about the function name mangling — you use the unmangled name. But sometimes you do need to be able to specify that this **initialize( )** belongs to the **struct stash**, and not to any other **struct**. In particular, when you're defining the function you need to fully specify which one it is. To accomplish this full specification, C++ has a new operator, **::** the *scope resolution operator* (named so because names can now be in different scopes: at global scope, or within the scope of a **struct**). For example, if you want to specify **initialize( ),** which belongs to **stash**, you say **stash::initialize(int Size, int Quantity);**. You can see how the scope resolution operator is used in the function definitions for the C++ version of **stash**:

```
//: LIBCPP.CPP -- C library converted to C++
// Declare structure and functions:
#include "..\1\libcpp.h"
#include <assert.h> // Error testing macros
#include <stdlib.h> // Dynamic memory
#include <string.h> // memcpy()
#include <stdio.h>

void stash::initialize(int Size) {
  size = Size;
  quantity = 0;
  storage = 0;
  next = 0;
}

void stash::cleanup() {
  if(storage) {
    puts("freeing storage");
    free(storage);
  }
}

int stash::add(void* element) {
  if(next >= quantity) // Enough space left?
    inflate(100);
  // Copy element into storage,
  // starting at next empty space:
  memcpy(&(storage[next * size]),
         element, size);
  next++;
  return(next - 1); // Index number
```

```
}

void* stash::fetch(int index) {
  if(index >= next || index < 0)
    return 0;   // Not out of bounds?
  // Produce pointer to desired element:
  return &(storage[index * size]);
}

int stash::count() {
  return next; // Number of elements in stash
}

void stash::inflate(int increase) {
  void* v =
    realloc(storage, (quantity+increase)*size);
  assert(v);   // Was it successful?
  storage = (unsigned char*)v;
  quantity += increase;
}
```

There are several other things that are different about this file. First, the declarations in the header files are *required* by the compiler. In C++ you *cannot* call a function without declaring it first. The compiler will issue an error message otherwise. This is an important way to ensure that function calls are consistent between the point where they are called and the point where they are defined. By forcing you to declare the function before you call it, the C++ compiler virtually ensures you will perform this declaration by including the header file. If you also include the same header file in the place where the functions are defined, then the compiler checks to make sure the declaration in the header and the definition match up. This means that the header file becomes a validated repository for function declarations and ensures that functions are used consistently throughout all translation units in the project.

Of course, global functions can still be declared by hand every place where they are defined and used. (This is so tedious that it becomes very unlikely.) However, structures must always be declared before they are defined or used, and the most convenient place to put a structure definition is in a header file, except for those you intentionally hide in a file).

You can see that all the member functions are virtually the same, except for the scope resolution and the fact that the first argument from the C version of the library is no longer explicit. It's still there, of course, because the function has to be able to work on a particular **struct** variable. But notice that inside the member function the member selection is also gone! Thus, instead of saying **S->size = Size;** you say **size = Size;** and eliminate the tedious **S->**, which didn't really add anything to the meaning of what you were doing anyway. Of course, the C++ compiler must still be doing this for you. Indeed, it is taking the "secret" first argument and applying the member selector whenever you refer to one of the data members of a class. This means that whenever you are inside the member function of another class, you can refer to any member (including another member function) by simply giving its name. The compiler will search through the local structure's names before looking for a global version of that name. You'll find that this feature means that not only is your code easier to write, it's a lot easier to read.

But what if, for some reason, you *want* to be able to get your hands on the address of the structure? In the C version of the library it was easy because each function's first argument was a **stash*** called **S**. In C++, things are even more consistent. There's a special keyword, called **this**, which produces the address of the **struct**. It's the equivalent of **S** in the C version of the library. So we can revert to the C style of things by saying

```
this->size = Size;
```

The code generated by the compiler is exactly the same. Usually, you don't use **this** very often, but when you need it, it's there.

There's one last change in the definitions. In **inflate( )** in the C library, you could assign a **void*** to any other pointer like this:

```
S->storage = v;
```

and there was no complaint from the compiler. But in C++, this statement is not allowed. Why? Because in C, you can assign a **void*** (which is what **malloc( )**, **calloc( )**, and **realloc( )** return) to any other pointer without a cast. C is not so particular about type information, so it allows this kind of thing. Not so with C++. Type is critical in C++, and the compiler stamps its foot when there are any violations of type information. This has always been important, but it is especially important in C++ because you have member functions in **struct**s. If you could pass pointers to **struct**s around with impunity in C++, then you could end up calling a member function for a **struct** that doesn't even logically exist for that **struct**! A real recipe for disaster. Therefore, while C++ allows the assignment of any type of pointer to a **void*** (this was the original intent of **void***, which is required to be large enough to hold a pointer to any type), it will *not* allow you to assign a **void** pointer to any other type of pointer. A cast is always required, to tell the reader and the compiler that you know the type that it is going to. Thus you will see the return values of **calloc( )** and **realloc( )** are explicitly cast to **(unsigned char*)**.

This brings up an interesting issue. One of the important goals for C++ is to compile as much existing C code as possible to allow for an easy transition to the new language. Notice in the above example how Standard C library functions are used. In addition, all C operators and expressions are available in C++. However, this doesn't mean any code that C allows will automatically be allowed in C++. There are a number of things the C compiler lets you get away with that are dangerous and error-prone. (We'll look at them as the book progresses.) The C++ compiler generates warnings and errors for these situations. This is often much more of an advantage than a hindrance. In fact, there are many situations where you are trying to run down an error in C and just can't find it, but as soon as you recompile the program in C++, the compiler points out the problem! In C, you'll often find that you can get the program to compile, but then you have to get it to work. In C++, often when the program compiles correctly, it works, too! This is because the language is a lot stricter about type.

You can see a number of new things in the way the C++ version of **stash** is used, in the following test program:

```
//: LIBTEST.CPP -- Test of C++ library
#include "..\1\libcpp.h"
#include <stdio.h>
#include <assert.h>
#define BUFSIZE 80

main() {
  stash intStash, stringStash;
  int i;
  FILE* file;
  char buf[BUFSIZE];
  char* cp;
  // ....
  intStash.initialize(sizeof(int));
  for(i = 0; i < 100; i++)
    intStash.add(&i);
  // Holds 80-character strings:
  stringStash.initialize(sizeof(char)*BUFSIZE);
  file = fopen("LIBTEST.CPP", "r");
  assert(file);
  while(fgets(buf, BUFSIZE, file))
    stringStash.add(buf);
  fclose(file);

  for(i = 0; i < intStash.count(); i++)
    printf("intStash.fetch(%d) = %d\n", i,
           *(int*)intStash.fetch(i));

  i = 0;
```

```
  while(
    (cp = (char*)stringStash.fetch(i++))!=0)
      printf("stringStash.fetch(%d) = %s",
             i - 1, cp);
  putchar('\n');
  intStash.cleanup();
  stringStash.cleanup();
}
```

The code is quite similar, but when a member function is called, the call occurs using the member selection operator '.' preceded by the name of the variable. This is a convenient syntax because it mimics the selection of a data member of the structure. The difference is that this is a function member, so it has an argument list.

Of course, the call that the compiler *actually* generates looks much more like the original C library function. Thus, considering name mangling and the passing of **this**, the C++ function call **intStash.initialize(sizeof(int), 100)** becomes something like **stash_initialize(&intStash, sizeof(int), 100)**. If you ever wonder what's going on underneath the covers, remember that the original C++ compiler **cfront** from AT&T produced C code as its output, which was then compiled by the underlying C compiler. This approach meant that **cfront** could be quickly ported to any machine that had a C compiler, and it helped to rapidly disseminate C++ compiler technology.

You'll also notice an additional cast in

```
while(cp = (char*)stringStash.fetch(i++))
```

This is due again to the stricter type checking in C++.

what's an object?

Now that you've seen an initial example, it's time to step back and take a look at some terminology. The act of bringing functions inside structures is the root of the changes in C++, and it introduces a new way of thinking about structures as concepts. In C, a structure is an agglomeration of data, a way to package data so you can treat it in a clump. But it's hard to think about it as anything but a programming convenience. The functions that operate on those structures are elsewhere. However, with functions in the package, the structure becomes a new creature, capable of describing both characteristics (like a C **struct** could) *and* behaviors. The concept of an object, a free-standing, bounded entity that can remember *and* act, suggests itself.

The terms "object" and "object-oriented programming" (OOP) are not new. The first OOP language was Simula-67, created in Scandinavia in 1967 to aid in solving modeling problems. These problems always seemed to involve a bunch of identical entities (like people, bacteria, and cars) running around interacting with each other. Simula allowed you to create a general description for an entity that described its characteristics and behaviors and then make a whole bunch of them. In Simula, the "general description" is called a **class** (a term you'll see in a later chapter), and the mass-produced item that you stamp out from a class is called an *object*. In C++, an object is just a variable, and the purest definition is "a region of storage." It's a place where you can store data, and it's implied that there are also operations that can be performed on this data.

Unfortunately there's not complete consistency across languages when it comes to these terms, although they are fairly well-accepted. You will also sometimes encounter disagreement about what an object-oriented language is, although that seems to be fairly well sorted out by now. There are languages that are *object-based*, which means they have objects like the C++ structures-

---

with-functions that you've seen so far. This, however, is only part of the picture when it comes to an object-oriented language, and languages that stop at packaging functions inside data structures are object-based, not object-oriented.

abstract data typing

The ability to package data with functions allows you to create a new data type. This is often called *encapsulation*[2]. An existing data type, like a **float**, has several pieces of data packaged together: an exponent, a mantissa, and a sign bit. You can tell it to do things: add to another **float** or to an **int**, and so on. It has characteristics and behavior.

The **stash** is also a new data type. You can **add( )** and **fetch( )** and **inflate( )**. You create one by saying **stash S**, as you create a **float** by saying **float f**. A **stash** also has characteristics and behavior. Even though it acts like a real, built-in data type, we refer to it as an *abstract data type*, perhaps because it allows us to abstract a concept from the problem space into the solution space. In addition, the C++ compiler treats it like a new data type, and if you say a function expects a **stash**, the compiler makes sure you pass a **stash** to that function. The same level of type checking happens with abstract data types (sometimes called *user-defined types*) as with built-in types.

You can immediately see a difference, however, in the way you perform operations on objects. You say **object.member_function(arglist)**. This is "calling a member function for an object." But in object-oriented parlance, this is also referred to as "sending a message to an object." So for a **stash S,**

---

[2] You should be aware that this term seems to be the subject of ongoing debate. Some people use it as defined here; others use it to describe *implementation hiding*, discussed in Chapter 2.

the statement **S.add(&i)** "sends a message to **S**" saying "**add( )** this to yourself." In fact, object-oriented programming can be summed up in a single sentence as "sending messages to objects." Really, that's all you do — create a bunch of objects and send messages to them. The trick, of course, is figuring out what your objects and messages *are*, but once you accomplish that the implementation in C++ is surprisingly straightforward.

object details

At this point you're probably wondering the same thing that most C programmers do because C is a language that is very low-level and efficiency-oriented. A question that comes up a lot in seminars is "How big is an object, and what does it look like?" The answer is "Pretty much the same as you expect from a C **struct**." In fact, a C **struct**.(with no C++ adornments) will usually look *exactly* the same in the code that the C and C++ compilers produce, which is reassuring to those C programmers who depend on the details of size and layout in their code, and for some reason directly access structure bytes instead of using identifiers, although depending on a particular size and layout of a structure is a nonportable activity.

The size of a **struct** is the combined size of all its members. Sometimes when a **struct** is laid out by the compiler, extra bytes are added to make the boundaries come out neatly — this may increase execution efficiency. In Chapters 13 and 15, you'll see how in some cases "secret" pointers are added to the structure, but you don't need to worry about that right now.

You can determine the size of a **struct** using the **sizeof** operator. Here's a small example:

```
//: SIZEOF.CPP -- Sizes of structs
#include <stdio.h>
#include "..\1\lib.h"
#include "..\1\libcpp.h"
```

```
struct A {
  int I[100];
};

struct B {
  void f();
};

void B::f() {}

main() {
  printf("sizeof struct A = %d bytes\n",
         sizeof(A));
  printf("sizeof struct B = %d bytes\n",
         sizeof(B));
  printf("sizeof Stash in C = %d bytes\n",
         sizeof(Stash));
  printf("sizeof stash in C++ = %d bytes\n",
         sizeof(stash));
}
```

The first print statement produces 200 because each **int** occupies two bytes. **struct B** is something of an anomaly because it is a **struct** with no data members. In C, this is illegal, but in C++ we need the option of creating a **struct** whose sole task is to scope function names, so it is allowed. Still, the result produced by the second **printf( )** statement is a somewhat surprising nonzero value. In early versions of the language, the size was zero, but an awkward situation arises when you create such objects: They have the same address as the object created directly after them, and so are not distinct. Thus, structures with no data members will always have some minimum nonzero size.

The last two **sizeof** statements show you that the size of the structure in C++ is the same as the size of the equivalent version in C. C++ endeavors not to add any overhead.

header file etiquette

When I first learned to program in C, the header file was a mystery to me. Many C books don't seem to emphasize it, and the compiler didn't enforce function declarations, so it seemed optional most of the time, except when structures were declared. In C++ the use of header files becomes crystal clear. They are practically mandatory for easy program development, and you put very specific information in them: declarations. The header file tells the compiler what is available in your library. Because you can use the library without the source code for the CPP file (you only need the object file or library file), the header file is where the interface specification is stored.

The header is a contract between you and the user of your library. It says, "Here's what my library does." It doesn't say how because that's stored in the CPP file, and you won't necessarily deliver the sources for "how" to the user.

The contract describes your data structures, and states the arguments and return values for the function calls. The user needs all this information to develop the application and the compiler needs it to generate proper code.

The compiler enforces the contract by requiring you to declare all structures and functions before they are used *and*, in the case of member functions, before they are defined. Thus, you're forced to put the declarations in the header and to include the header in the file where the member functions are defined and the file(s) where they are used. Because a single header file describing your library is included throughout the system, the compiler can ensure consistency and prevent errors.

There are certain issues that you must be aware of in order to organize your code properly and write effective header files. The first issue concerns what you can put into header files. The basic rule is "only declarations," that is, only information to the compiler

---

but nothing that allocates storage by generating code or creating variables. This is because the header file will probably be included in several translation units in a project, and if storage is allocated in more than one place, the linker will come up with a multiple definition error.

This rule isn't completely hard and fast. If you define a piece of data that is "file static" (has visibility only within a file) inside a header file, there will be multiple instances of that data across the project, but the linker won't have a collision. Basically, you don't want to do anything in the header file that will cause an ambiguity at link time.

The second critical issue concerning header files is redeclaration. Both C and C++ allow you to redeclare a function, as long as the two declarations match, but neither will allow the redeclaration of a structure. In C++ this rule is especially important because if the compiler allowed you to redeclare a structure and the two declarations differed, which one would it use?

The problem of redeclaration comes up quite a bit in C++ because each data type (structure with functions) generally has its own header file, and you have to include one header in another if you want to create another data type that uses the first one. In the whole project, it's very likely that you'll include several files that include the same header file. During a single compilation, the compiler can see the same header file several times. Unless you do something about it, the compiler will see the redeclaration of your structure.

The typical preventative measure is to "insulate" the header file by using the preprocessor. If you have a header file named FOO.H, it's common to do your own "name mangling" to produce a preprocessor name that is used to prevent multiple inclusion of the header file. The inside of FOO.H might look like this:

```
#ifndef FOO_H_
#define FOO_H_
// Rest of header here...
```

```
#endif // FOO_H_
```

Notice a leading underscore was *not* used because Standard C reserves identifiers with leading underscores.

using headers in projects

When building a project in C++, you'll usually create it by bringing together a lot of different types (data structures with associated functions). You'll usually put the declaration for each type or group of associated types in a separate header file, then define the functions for that type in a translation unit. When you use that type, you must include the header file to perform the declarations properly.

Sometimes that pattern will be followed in this book, but more often the examples will be very small, so everything — the structure declarations, function definitions, and the **main( )** function — may appear in a single file. However, keep in mind that you'll want to use separate files and header files in practice.

nested structures

The convenience of taking data and function names out of the global name space extends to structures. You can nest a structure within another structure, and therefore keep associated elements together. The declaration syntax is what you would expect, as you can see in the following structure, which implements a push-down stack as a very simple linked list so it "never" runs out of memory:

```
//: NESTED.H -- Nested struct in linked list
#ifndef NESTED_H_
#define NESTED_H_

struct stack {
  struct link {
    void* data;
```

```
    link* next;
    void initialize(void* Data, link* Next);
  } * head;
  void initialize();
  void push(void* Data);
  void* peek();
  void* pop();
  void cleanup();
};
#endif // NESTED_H_
```

The nested **struct** is called **link**, and it contains a pointer to the next **link** in the list and a pointer to the data stored in the **link**. If the **next** pointer is zero, it means you're at the end of the list.

Notice that the **head** pointer is defined right after the declaration for **struct link**, instead of a separate definition **link* head**. This is a syntax that came from C, but it emphasizes the importance of the semicolon after the structure declaration — the semicolon indicates the end of the list of definitions of that structure type. (Usually the list is empty.)

The nested structure has its own **initialize( )** function, like all the structures presented so far, to ensure proper initialization. **stack** has both an **initialize( )** and **cleanup( )** function, as well as **push( )**, which takes a pointer to the data you wish to store (assumed to have been allocated on the heap), and **pop( )**, which returns the **data** pointer from the top of the stack and removes the top element. (Notice that *you* are responsible for destroying the destination of the **data** pointer.) The **peek( )** function also returns the **data** pointer from the top element, but it leaves the top element on the stack.

cleanup goes through the stack and removes each element *and* frees the **data** pointer (so it *must* be on the heap).

Here are the definitions for the member functions:

```
//: NESTED.CPP -- Linked list with nesting
#include <stdlib.h>
#include <assert.h>
#include "nested.h"

void stack::link::initialize(
    void* Data, link* Next) {
  data = Data;
  next = Next;
}

void stack::initialize() { head = 0; }

void stack::push(void* Data) {
  link* newlink = (link*)malloc(sizeof(link));
  assert(newlink);
  newlink->initialize(Data, head);
  head = newlink;
}

void* stack::peek() { return head->data; }

void* stack::pop() {
  if(head == 0) return 0;
  void* result = head->data;
  link* oldHead = head;
  head = head->next;
  free(oldHead);
  return result;
}

void stack::cleanup() {
  link* cursor = head;
  while(head) {
    cursor = cursor->next;
    free(head->data); // Assumes a malloc!
    free(head);
```

```
        head = cursor;
   }
}
```

The first definition is particularly interesting because it shows you how to define a member of a nested structure. You simply use the scope resolution operator a second time, to specify the name of the enclosing **struct**. The **stack::link::initialize( )** function takes the arguments and assigns them to its members. Although you can certainly do these things by hand quite easily, you'll see a different form of this function in the future, so it will make much more sense.

The **stack::initialize( )** function sets **head** to zero, so the object knows it has an empty list.

stack::push( ) takes the argument, a pointer to the piece of data you want to keep track of using the **stack**, and pushes it on the stack. First, it uses **malloc( )** to allocate storage for the **link** it will insert at the top. Then it calls the **initialize( )** function to assign the appropriate values to the members of the **link**. Notice that the **next** pointer is assigned to the current **head**; then **head** is assigned to the new **link** pointer. This effectively pushes the **link** in at the top of the list.

stack::pop( ) stores the **data** pointer at the current top of the stack; then it moves the **head** pointer down and deletes the old top of the stack. **stack::cleanup( )** creates a **cursor** to move through the stack and **free( )** both the **data** in each link and the link itself.

Here's an example to test the **stack**:

```
//: NESTEST.CPP -- Test of nested linked list
#include "..\1\nested.h"
#include <stdio.h>
#include <stdlib.h>
#include <string.h>
#include <assert.h>
```

```
main(int argc, char** argv) {
  stack textlines;
  FILE* file;
  char* s;
  #define BUFSIZE 100
  char buf[BUFSIZE];
  assert(argc == 2); // File name is argument
  textlines.initialize();
  file = fopen(argv[1], "r");
  assert(file);
  // Read file and store lines in the stack:
  while(fgets(buf, BUFSIZE, file)) {
    char* string = (char*)malloc(strlen(buf)+1);
    assert(string);
    strcpy(string, buf);
    textlines.push(string);
  }
  // Pop the lines from the stack and print them:
  while((s = (char*)textlines.pop()) != 0) {
    printf("%s", s); free(s); }
  textlines.cleanup();
}
```

This is very similar to the earlier example, but it pushes the lines on the stack and then pops them off, which results in the file being printed out in reverse order. In addition, the file name is taken from the command line.

global scope resolution

The scope resolution operator gets you out of situations where the name the compiler chooses by default (the "nearest" name) isn't what you want. For example, suppose you have a structure with a local identifier **A**, and you want to select a global identifier **A** inside a member function. The compiler would default to choosing the local one, so you must tell it to do otherwise. When you want to specify a global name using scope resolution, you use the operator with nothing in front of it. Here's an example that shows global scope resolution for both a variable and a function:

```
//: SCOPERES.CPP -- Global scope resolution
int A;
void f() {}

struct S {
  int A;
  void f();
};

void S::f() {
  ::f();  // Would be recursive otherwise!
  ::A++;  // Select the global A
  A--;    // The A at struct scope
}

main() {}
```

Without scope resolution in **S::f( )**, the compiler would default to selecting the member versions of **f( )** and **A**.

summary

In this chapter, you've learned the fundamental "twist" of C++: that you can place functions inside of structures. This new type of structure is called an *abstract data type*, and variables you create using this structure are called *objects*, or *instances*, of that type. Calling a member function for an object is called *sending a message* to that object. The primary action in object-oriented programming is sending messages to objects.

Although packaging data and functions together is a significant benefit for code organization and makes library use easier because it prevents name clashes by hiding the names, there's a lot more you can do to make programming safer in C++. In the next chapter, you'll learn how to protect some members of a **struct** so that only you can manipulate them. This establishes a clear boundary between what the user of the structure can change and what only the programmer may change.

exercises

1. Create a **struct** declaration with a single member function; then create a definition for that member function. Create an object of your new data type, and call the member function.

2. Write and compile a piece of code that performs data member selection and a function call using the keyword that refers to the address of the current object.

3. Show an example of a structure declared within another structure (a *nested structure*). Also show how members of that structure are defined.

4. How big is a structure? Write a piece of code that prints the size of various structures. Create structures that have data members only and ones that have data members and function members. Then create a structure that has no members at all. Print out the sizes of all these. Explain the reason for the result of the structure with no data members at all.

5. C++ automatically creates the equivalent of a **typedef** for enumerations and unions as well as **struct**s, as you've seen in this chapter. Write a small program that demonstrates this.

hiding the implementation

A typical C library contains a struct and some associated functions to act on that struct. So far, you've seen how C++ takes functions that are conceptually associated and makes them literally associated, by

putting the function declarations inside the scope of the **struct**, changing the way functions are called for the **struct**, eliminating the passing of the structure address as the first argument, and adding a new type name to the program (so you don't have to create a **typedef** for the **struct** tag).

These are all convenient — they help you organize your code and make it easier to write and read. However, there are other important issues when making libraries easier in C++, especially the issues of safety and control. This chapter looks at the subject of boundaries in structures.

setting limits

In any relationship it's important to have boundaries that are respected by all parties involved. When you create a library, you establish a relationship with the user (also called the *client programmer*) of that library, who is another programmer, but one putting together an application or using your library to build a bigger library.

In a C **struct**, as with most things in C, there are no rules. Users can do anything they want with that **struct**, and there's no way to force any particular behaviors. For example, even though you saw in the last chapter the importance of the functions named **initialize( )** and **cleanup( )**, the user could choose whether to call those functions or not. (We'll look at a better approach in the next chapter.) And even though you would really prefer that the user not directly manipulate some of the members of your **struct**, in C there's no way to prevent it. Everything's naked to the world.

There are two reasons for controlling access to members. The first is to keep users' hands off tools they shouldn't touch, tools that are necessary for the internal machinations of the data type, but not part of the interface that users need to solve their particular problems. This is actually a service to users because they can easily see what's important to them and what they can ignore.

The second reason for access control is to allow the library designer to change the internal workings of the structure without worrying about how it will affect the client programmer. In the **stack** example in the last chapter, you might want to allocate the storage in big chunks, for speed, rather than calling **malloc( )** each time an element is added. If the interface and implementation are clearly separated and protected, you can accomplish this and require only a relink by the user.

C++ access control

C++ introduces three new keywords to set the boundaries in a structure: **public**, **private**, and **protected**. Their use and meaning are remarkably straightforward. These *access specifiers* are used only in a structure declaration, and they change the boundary for all the declarations that follow them. Whenever you use an access specifier, it must be followed by a colon.

public means all member declarations that follow are available to everyone. **public** members are like **struct** members. For example, the following **struct** declarations are identical:

```
//: PUBLIC.CPP -- Public is just like C struct

struct A {
   int i;
   char j;
   float f;
   void foo();
};

void A::foo() {}

struct B {
public:
   int i;
   char j;
   float f;
   void foo();
};

void B::foo() {}
```

```
main() {}
```

The **private** keyword, on the other hand, means no one can access
that member except you, the creator of the type, inside function
members of that type. **private** is a brick wall between you and the
user; if someone tries to access a private member, they'll get a
compile-time error. In **struct B** in the above example, you may
want to make portions of the representation (that is, the data
members) hidden, accessible only to you:

```
//: PRIVATE.CPP -- Setting the boundary

struct B {
private:
  char j;
  float f;
public:
  int i;
  void foo();
};

void B::foo() {
  i = 0;
  j = '0';
  f = 0.0;
};

main() {
  B b;
  b.i = 1;     // OK, public
//!  b.j = '1';  // Illegal, private
//!  b.f = 1.0;  // Illegal, private
}
```

Although **foo( )** can access any member of **B**, an ordinary global
function like **main( )** cannot. Of course, neither can member

functions of other structures. Only the functions that are clearly stated in the structure declaration (the "contract") can have access to **private** members.

There is no required order for access specifiers, and they may appear more than once. They affect all the members declared after them and before the next access specifier.

protected

The last access specifier is **protected**. **protected** acts just like **private**, with one exception that we can't really talk about right now: Inherited structures have access to **protected** members, but not **private** members. But inheritance won't be introduced until Chapter 12, so this doesn't have any meaning to you. For the current purposes, consider **protected** to be just like **private**; it will be clarified when inheritance is introduced.

friends

What if you want to explicitly grant access to a function that isn't a member of the current structure? This is accomplished by declaring that function a **friend** *inside* the structure declaration. It's important that the **friend** declaration occurs inside the structure declaration because you (and the compiler) must be able to read the structure declaration and see every rule about the size and behavior of that data type. And a very important rule in any relationship is "who can access my private implementation?"

The class controls which code has access to its members. There's no magic way to "break in"; you can't declare a new class and say "hi, I'm a friend of **Bob**!" and expect to see the **private** and **protected** members of **Bob**.

You can declare a global function as a **friend**, and you can also declare a member function of another structure, or even an entire structure, as a **friend**. Here's an example :

```
//: FRIEND.CPP -- Friend allows special access

struct X; // Declaration (incomplete type spec)

struct Y {
  void f(X*);
};

struct X { // Definition
private:
  int i;
public:
  void initialize();
  friend void g(X*, int); // Global friend
  friend void Y::f(X*);   // Struct member friend
  friend struct Z; // Entire struct is a friend
  friend void h();
};

void X::initialize() { i = 0; }

void g(X* x, int i) { x->i = i; }

void Y::f(X* x) { x->i = 47; }

struct Z {
private:
  int j;
public:
  void initialize();
  void g(X* x);
};

void Z::initialize() { j = 99; }

void Z::g(X* x) { x->i += j; }
```

```
void h() {
  X x;
  x.i = 100; // Direct data manipulation
}

main() {
  X x;
  Z z;
  z.g(&x);
}
```

struct Y has a member function **f( )** that will modify an object of type **X**. This is a bit of a conundrum because the C++ compiler requires you to declare everything before you can refer to it, so **struct Y** must be declared before its member **Y::f(X*)** can be declared as a friend in **struct X**. But for **Y::f(X*)** to be declared, **struct X** must be declared first!

Here's the solution. Notice that **Y::f(X*)** takes the *address* of an **X** object. This is critical because the compiler always knows how to pass an address, which is of a fixed size regardless of the object being passed, even if it doesn't have full information about the size of the type. If you try to pass the whole object, however, the compiler must see the entire structure definition of **X**, to know the size and how to pass it, before it allows you to declare a function such as **Y::g(X)**.

By passing the address of an **X**, the compiler allows you to make an *incomplete type specification* of **X** prior to declaring **Y::f(X*)**. This is accomplished in the declaration **struct X;**. This simply tells the compiler there's a **struct** by that name, so if it is referred to, it's OK, as long as you don't require any more knowledge than the name.

Now, in **struct X**, the function **Y::f(X*)** can be declared as a **friend** with no problem. If you tried to declare it before the compiler had seen the full specification for **Y**, it would have given you an error. This is a safety feature to ensure consistency and eliminate bugs.

Notice the two other **friend** functions. The first declares an ordinary global function **g( )** as a **friend**. But **g( )** has not been previously declared at the global scope! It turns out that **friend** can be used this way to simultaneously declare the function *and* give it **friend** status. This extends to entire structures: **friend struct Z** is an incomplete type specification for **Z**, and it gives the entire structure **friend** status.

nested friends

Making a structure nested doesn't automatically give it access to **private** members. To accomplish this you must follow a particular form: first define the nested structure, then declare it as a **friend** using full scoping. The structure definition must be separate from the **friend** declaration, otherwise it would be seen by the compiler as a nonmember. Here's an example:

```
//: NESTFRND.CPP -- Nested friends
#include <stdio.h>
#include <string.h> // memset()
#define SZ 20

struct holder {
private:
  int a[SZ];
public:
  void initialize();
  struct pointer {
  private:
    holder* h;
    int* p;
  public:
    void initialize(holder* H);
    // Move around in the array:
    void next();
    void previous();
    void top();
```

```cpp
      void end();
      // Access values:
      int read();
      void set(int i);
    };
    friend holder::pointer;
};

void holder::initialize() {
 memset(a, 0, SZ * sizeof(int));
}

void holder::pointer::initialize(holder* H) {
  h = H;
  p = h->a;
}

void holder::pointer::next() {
  if(p < &(h->a[SZ - 1])) p++;
}

void holder::pointer::previous() {
  if(p > &(h->a[0])) p--;
}

void holder::pointer::top() {
  p = &(h->a[0]);
}

void holder::pointer::end() {
  p = &(h->a[SZ - 1]);
}

int holder::pointer::read() {
  return *p;
}
```

```
void holder::pointer::set(int i) {
  *p = i;
}

main() {
  holder h;
  holder::pointer hp, hp2;
  int i;

  h.initialize();
  hp.initialize(&h);
  hp2.initialize(&h);
  for(i = 0; i < SZ; i++) {
    hp.set(i);
    hp.next();
  }
  hp.top();
  hp2.end();
  for(i = 0; i < SZ; i++) {
    printf("hp = %d, hp2 = %d\n",
           hp.read(), hp2.read());
    hp.next();
    hp2.previous();
  }
}
```

The **struct holder** contains an array of **ints** and the **pointer** allows you to access them. Because **pointer** is strongly associated with **holder**, it's sensible to make it a member of that class. Once **pointer** is defined, it is granted access to the private members of **holder** by saying:

```
friend holder::pointer;
```

Notice that the **struct** keyword is not necessary because the compiler already knows what **pointer** is.

Because **pointer** is a separate class from **holder**, you can make more than one of them in **main( )** and use them to select different parts of the array. Because **pointer** is a class instead of a raw C pointer, you can guarantee that it will always safely point inside the **holder**.

is it pure?

The class definition gives you an audit trail, so you can see from looking at the class which functions have permission to modify the private parts of the class. If a function is a **friend**, it means that it isn't a member, but you want to give permission to modify private data anyway, and it must be listed in the class definition so all can see that it's one of the privileged functions.

C++ is a hybrid object-oriented language, not a pure one, and **friend** was added to get around practical problems that crop up. It's fine to point out that this makes the language less "pure," because C++ *is* designed to be pragmatic, not to aspire to an abstract ideal.

object layout

Chapter 1 stated that a **struct** written for a C compiler and later compiled with C++ would be unchanged. This referred primarily to the object layout of the **struct**, that is, where the storage for the individual variables is positioned in the memory allocated for the object. If the C++ compiler changed the layout of C **struct**s, then any C code you wrote that inadvisably took advantage of knowledge of the positions of variables in the **struct** would break.

When you start using access specifiers, however, you've moved completely into the C++ realm, and things change a bit. Within a particular "access block" (a group of declarations delimited by access specifiers), the variables are guaranteed to be laid out contiguously, as in C. However, the access blocks themselves may not appear in the object in the order that you declare them.

Although the compiler will usually lay the blocks out exactly as you see them, there is no rule about it, because a particular machine architecture and/or operating environment may have explicit support for **private** and **protected** that might require those blocks to be placed in special memory locations. The language specification doesn't want to restrict this kind of advantage.

Access specifiers are part of the structure and don't affect the objects created from the structure. All of the access specification information disappears before the program is run; generally this happens during compilation. In a running program, objects become "regions of storage" and nothing more. Thus, if you really want to you can break all the rules and access memory directly, as you can in C. C++ is not designed to prevent you from doing unwise things. It just provides you with a much easier, highly desirable alternative.

In general, it's not a good idea to depend on anything that's implementation-specific when you're writing a program. When you must, those specifics should be encapsulated inside a structure, so any porting changes are focused in one place.

the class

Access control is often referred to as *implementation hiding*. Including functions within structures (encapsulation) produces a data type with characteristics and behaviors, but access control puts boundaries within that data type, for two important reasons. The first is to establish what users can and can't use. You can build your internal mechanisms into the structure without worrying that users will think it's part of the interface they should be using.

This feeds directly into the second reason, which is to separate the interface from the implementation. If the structure is used in a set of programs, but users can't do anything but send messages to the **public** interface, then you can change anything that's **private** without requiring modifications to their code.

Encapsulation and implementation hiding together invent something more than a C **struct**. We're now in the world of object-oriented programming, where a structure is describing a class of objects, as you would describe a class of fishes or a class of birds: Any object belonging to this class will share these characteristics and behaviors. That's what the structure declaration has become, a description of the way all objects of this type will look and act.

In the original OOP language, Simula-67, the keyword **class** was used to describe a new data type. This apparently inspired Stroustrup to choose the same keyword for C++, to emphasize that this was the focal point of the whole language, the creation of new data types that are more than C **struct**s with functions. This certainly seems like adequate justification for a new keyword.

However, the use of **class** in C++ comes close to being an unnecessary keyword. It's identical to the **struct** keyword in absolutely every way except one: **class** defaults to **private**, whereas **struct** defaults to public. Here are two structures that produce the same result:

```
//: CLASS.CPP -- Similarity of struct and class

struct A {
private:
  int i, j, k;
public:
  int f();
  void g();
};

int A::f() { return i + j + k; }

void A::g() { i = j = k = 0; }

// Identical results are produced with:

class B {
```

```
    int i, j, k;
public:
  int f();
  void g();
};

int B::f() { return i + j + k; }

void B::g() { i = j = k = 0; }

main() {}
```

The **class** is the fundamental OOP concept in C++. It is one of the keywords that will *not* be set in bold in this book — it becomes annoying with a word repeated as often as "class." The shift to classes is so important that I suspect Stroustrup's preference would have been to throw **struct** out altogether, but the need for backwards compatibility of course wouldn't allow it.

Many people prefer a style of creating classes that is more **struct**-like than class-like, because you override the "default-to-private" behavior of the class by starting out with **public** elements:

```
class X {
public:
  void interface_function();
private:
  void private_function();
  int internal_representation;
};
```

The logic behind this is that it makes more sense for the reader to see the members they are concerned with first, then they can ignore anything that says **private**. Indeed, the only reasons all the other members must be declared in the class at all are so the compiler knows how big the objects are and can allocate them properly, and so it can guarantee consistency.

The examples in this book, however, will put the **private** members first, like this:

```
class X {
  void private_function();
  int internal_representation;
public:
  void interface_function();
};
```

Some people even go to the trouble of mangling their own private names:

```
class Y {
public:
  void f();
private:
  int mX;   // "self-mangled" name
};
```

Because **mX** is already hidden in the scope of **Y**, the **m** is unnecessary. However, in projects with many global variables (something you should strive to avoid, but is sometimes inevitable in existing projects) it is helpful to be able to distinguish, inside a member function definition, which data is global and which is a member.

modifying stash to use access control

It makes sense to take the examples from Chapter 1 and modify them to use classes and access control. Notice how the user portion of the interface is now clearly distinguished, so there's no possibility of users accidentally manipulating a part of the class that they shouldn't.

```
//: STASH.H -- Converted to use access control
#ifndef STASH_H_
#define STASH_H_
```

```
class stash {
  int size;  // Size of each space
  int quantity; // Number of storage spaces
  int next; // Next empty space
  // Dynamically allocated array of bytes:
  unsigned char* storage;
  void inflate(int increase);
public:
  void initialize(int Size);
  void cleanup();
  int add(void* element);
  void* fetch(int index);
  int count();
};
#endif // STASH_H_
```

The **inflate( )** function has been made **private** because it is used only by the **add( )** function and is thus part of the underlying implementation, not the interface. This means that, sometime later, you can change the underlying implementation to use a different system for memory management.

Other than the name of the include file, the above header is the only thing that's been changed for this example. The implementation file and test file are the same.

modifying stack to use access control

As a second example, here's the **stack** turned into a class. Now the nested data structure is **private**, which is nice because it ensures that the user will neither have to look at it nor be able to depend on the internal representation of the **stack**:

```
//: STACK.H -- Nested structs via linked list
#ifndef STACK_H_
```

```
#define STACK_H_

class stack {
  struct link {
    void* data;
    link* next;
    void initialize(void* Data, link* Next);
  } * head;
public:
  void initialize();
  void push(void* Data);
  void* peek();
  void* pop();
  void cleanup();
};
#endif // STACK_H_
```

As before, the implementation doesn't change and so is not repeated here. The test, too, is identical. The only thing that's been changed is the robustness of the class interface. The real value of access control is during development, to prevent you from crossing boundaries. In fact, the compiler is the only one that knows about the protection level of class members. There is no information mangled into the member name that carries through to the linker. All the protection checking is done by the compiler; it's vanished by run time.

Notice that the interface presented to the user is now truly that of a push-down stack. It happens to be implemented as a linked list, but you can change that without affecting what the user interacts with, or (more importantly) a single line of client code.

handle classes

Access control in C++ allows you to separate interface from implementation, but the implementation hiding is only partial. The compiler must still see the declarations for all parts of an object in order to create and manipulate it properly. You could imagine a programming language that requires only the public interface of an object and allows the private implementation to be hidden, but C++ performs type checking statically (at compile time) as much as possible. This means that you'll learn as early as possible if there's an error. It also means your program is more efficient. However, including the private implementation has two effects: The implementation is visible even if you can't easily access it, and it can cause needless recompilation.

visible implementation

Some projects cannot afford to have their implementation visible to the end user. It may show strategic information in a library header file that the company doesn't want available to competitors. You may be working on a system where security is an issue — an encryption algorithm, for example — and you don't want to expose any clues in a header file that might enable people to crack the code. Or you may be putting your library in a "hostile" environment, where the programmers will directly access the private components anyway, using pointers and casting. In all these situations, it's valuable to have the actual structure compiled inside an implementation file rather than exposed in a header file.

reducing recompilation

The project manager in your programming environment will cause a recompilation of a file if that file is touched *or* if another file it's dependent upon — that is, an included header file — is touched. This means that any time you make a change to a class, whether it's to the public interface or the private implementation, you'll force a recompilation of anything that includes that header file. For a large project in its early stages this can be very unwieldy because the underlying implementation may change often; if the project is very big, the time for compiles can prohibit rapid turnaround.

The technique to solve this is sometimes called *handle classes* or the "Cheshire Cat"[1] — everything about the implementation disappears except for a single pointer, the "smile." The pointer refers to a structure whose definition is in the implementation file along with all the member function definitions. Thus, as long as the interface is unchanged, the header file is untouched. The implementation can change at will, and only the implementation file needs to be recompiled and relinked with the project.

Here's a simple example demonstrating the technique. The header file contains only the public interface and a single pointer of an incompletely specified class:

```
//: HANDLE.H -- Handle classes
#ifndef HANDLE_H_
#define HANDLE_H_

class handle {
  struct cheshire; // Class declaration only
  cheshire* smile;
public:
  void initialize();
  void cleanup();
  int read();
  void change(int);
};
#endif // HANDLE_H_
```

This is all the client programmer is able to see. The line

```
struct cheshire;
```

is an *incomplete type specification* or a *class declaration* (A *class definition* includes the body of the class.) It tells the compiler that

---

[1] This name is attributed to John Carolan, one of the early pioneers in C++, and of course, Lewis Carroll.

cheshire is a structure name, but nothing about the **struct**. This is only enough information to create a pointer to the **struct**; you can't create an object until the structure body has been provided. In this technique, that body contains the underlying implementation and is hidden away in the implementation file:

```
//: HANDLE.CPP -- Handle implementation
#include "..\2\handle.h"
#include <stdlib.h>
#include <assert.h>

// Define handle's implementation:
struct handle::cheshire {
  int i;
};

void handle::initialize() {
  smile = (cheshire*)malloc(sizeof(cheshire));
  assert(smile);
  smile->i = 0;
}

void handle::cleanup() {
  free(smile);
}

int handle::read() {
  return smile->i;
}

void handle::change(int x) {
  smile->i = x;
}
```

cheshire is a nested structure, so it must be defined with scope resolution:

```
struct handle::cheshire {
```

In the **handle::initialize( )**, storage is allocated for a **cheshire** structure,[2] and in **handle::cleanup( )** this storage is released. This storage is used in lieu of all the data elements you'd normally put into the **private** section of the class. When you compile HANDLE.CPP, this structure definition is hidden away in the object file where no one can see it. If you change the elements of **cheshire**, the only file that must be recompiled is HANDLE.CPP because the header file is untouched.

The use of **handle** is like the use of any class: Include the header, create objects, and send messages.

```
//: USEHANDL.CPP -- Use the handle class
#include "..\2\handle.h"

main() {
  handle u;
  u.initialize();
  u.read();
  u.change(1);
  u.cleanup();
}
```

The only thing the client programmer can access is the public interface, so as long as the implementation is the only thing that changes, this file never needs recompilation. Thus, although this isn't perfect implementation hiding, it's a big improvement.

---

[2] Chapter 11 demonstrates a much better way to create an object on the heap with **new**.

summary

Access control in C++ is not an object-oriented feature, but it gives valuable control to the creator of a class. The users of the class can clearly see exactly what they can use and what to ignore. More important, though, is the ability to ensure that no user becomes dependent on any of the underlying implementation of a class. If you know this, you can change the underlying implementation with the knowledge that no one will be affected by the changes because they can't access that part of the class.

When you have the freedom to change the underlying implementation, you can not only improve your design at some later time, but you also have the freedom to make mistakes. No matter how carefully you plan and design, you'll make mistakes. Knowing that it's relatively safe to make these mistakes means you'll be more experimental, you'll learn faster, and you'll finish your project sooner.

The public interface to a class is what the user *does* see, so that is the most important part of the class to get "right" during analysis and design. But even that allows you some leeway for change. If you don't get the interface right the first time, you can *add* more functions, as long as you don't remove any that people have used in their code.

exercises

1. Create a class with **public**, **private**, and **protected** data members and function members. Create an object of this class and see what kind of compiler messages you get when you try to access all the class members.

2. Create a class and a global **friend** function that manipulates the **private** data in the class.

3. Modify **cheshire** in HANDLE.CPP, and verify that your project manager recompiles and relinks only this file, but doesn't recompile USEHANDL.CPP.

initialization
& cleanup

Chapter 1 made a significant improvement in library use by taking all the scattered components of a typical C library and encapsulating them into a structure (an abstract data type, called a class from now on).

This not only provides a single unified point of entry into a library component, but it also hides the names of the functions within the class name. In Chapter 2, access control (implementation hiding) was introduced. This gives the class designer a way to establish clear boundaries for determining what the user is allowed to manipulate and what is off limits. It means the internal mechanisms of a data type's operation are under the control and discretion of the class designer, and it's clear to users what members they can and should pay attention to.

Together, encapsulation and implementation hiding make a significant step in improving the ease of library use. The concept of "new data type" they provide is better in some ways than the existing built-in data types inherited from C. The C++ compiler can now provide type-checking guarantees for that data type and thus ensure a level of safety when that data type is being used.

When it comes to safety, however, there's a lot more the compiler can do for us than C provides. In this and future chapters, you'll see additional features engineered into C++ that make the bugs in your program almost leap out and grab you, sometimes before you even compile the program, but usually in the form of compiler warnings and errors. For this reason, you will soon get used to the unlikely sounding scenario that a C++ program that compiles usually runs right the first time.

Two of these safety issues are initialization and cleanup. A large segment of C bugs occur when the programmer forgets to initialize or clean up a variable. This is especially true with libraries, when users don't know how to initialize a **struct**, or even that they must. (Libraries often do not include an initialization function, so the user is forced to initialize the **struct** by hand.) Cleanup is a special problem because C programmers are used to forgetting about variables once they are finished, so any cleaning up that may be necessary for a library's **struct** is often missed.

In C++ the concept of initialization and cleanup is essential to making library use easy and to eliminating the many subtle bugs that occur when the user forgets to perform these activities. This chapter examines the features in C++ that help guarantee proper initialization and cleanup.

guaranteed initialization with the constructor

Both the **stash** and **stack** classes have had functions called
initialize( ), which hint that it should be called before using the
object in any other way. Unfortunately, this means the user must
ensure proper initialization. Users are prone to miss details like
initialization in their headlong rush to make your amazing library
solve their problem. In C++ initialization is too important to leave
to the user. The class designer can guarantee initialization of every
object by providing a special function called the *constructor*. If a
class has a constructor, the compiler automatically calls that
constructor at the point an object is created, before users can even
get their hands on the object. The constructor call isn't even an
option for the user; it is performed by the compiler at the point the
object is defined.

The next challenge is what to name this function. There are two
issues. The first is that any name you use is something that can
potentially clash with a name you might like to use as a member in
the class. The second is that because the compiler is responsible
for calling the constructor, it must always know which function to
call. The solution Stroustrup chose seems the easiest and most
logical: The name of the constructor is the same as the name of the
class. It makes sense that such a function will be called
automatically on initialization.

Here's a simple class with a constructor:

```
class X {
  int i;
public:
  X();  // constructor
};
```

Now, when an object is defined,

```
void f() {
  X a;
  // ...
}
```

the same thing happens as if **a** were an **int**: Storage is allocated for the object. But when the program reaches the *sequence point* (point of execution) where **a** is defined, the constructor is called automatically. That is, the compiler quietly inserts the call to **X::X( )** for the object **a** at its point of definition. Like any member function, the first (secret) argument to the constructor is the address of the object for which it is being called.

Like any function, the constructor can have arguments to allow you to specify *how* an object is created, give it initialization values, and so on. Constructor arguments provide you with a way to guarantee that all parts of your object are initialized to appropriate values. For example, if the class **tree** has a constructor that takes a single integer argument denoting the height of the tree, you must then create a tree object like this:

```
tree t(12);   // 12-foot tree
```

If **tree(int)** is your only constructor, then the compiler won't let you create an object any other way. (We'll look at multiple constructors and different ways to call constructors in the next chapter.)

That's really all there is to a constructor: It's a specially named function that is called automatically by the compiler for every object. However, it eliminates a large class of problems and makes the code easier to read. In the preceding code fragment, for example, you don't see an explicit function call to some **initialize( )** function that is conceptually separate from definition. In C++, definition and initialization are unified concepts — you can't have one without the other.

Both the constructor and destructor are very unusual types of functions: They have no return value. This is distinctly different from a **void** return value, where the function returns nothing but you still have the option to make it something else. Constructors and destructors return nothing and you don't have an option. The acts of bringing an object into and out of the program are special, like birth and death, and the compiler always makes the function calls itself, to make sure they happen. If there were a return value, and if you could select your own, the compiler would somehow have to know what to do with the return value, or the user would have to explicitly call constructors and destructors, which would eliminate their safety.

guaranteed cleanup with the destructor

As a C programmer, you often think about the importance of initialization, but it's rarer to think about cleanup. After all, what do you need to do to clean up an **int**? Just forget about it. However, with libraries, just "letting go" of an object once you're done with it is not so safe. What if it modifies some piece of hardware, or puts something on the screen, or allocates storage on the heap? If you just forget about it, your object never achieves closure upon its exit from this world. In C++, cleanup is as important as initialization and is therefore guaranteed with the destructor.

The syntax for the destructor is similar to that for the constructor: The class name is used for the name of the function. However, the destructor is distinguished from the constructor by a leading tilde (~). In addition, the destructor never has any arguments because destruction never needs any options. Here's the declaration for a destructor:

```
class Y {
public:
```

```
   ~Y();
};
```

The destructor is called automatically by the compiler when the object goes out of scope. You can see where the constructor gets called by the point of definition of the object, but the only evidence for a destructor call is the closing brace of the scope that surrounds the object. Yet the destructor is called, even when you use **goto** to jump out of a scope. (**goto** still exists in C++, for backward compatibility with C and for the times when it comes in handy.) You should note that a nonlocal **goto**, implemented by the Standard C library functions **setjmp( )** and **longjmp( )**, doesn't cause destructors to be called. (This is the specification, even if your compiler doesn't implement it that way. Relying on a feature that isn't in the specification means your code is nonportable.)

Here's an example demonstrating the features of constructors and destructors you've seen so far:

```
//: CONSTR1.CPP -- Constructors & destructors
#include <stdio.h>

class tree {
  int height;
public:
  tree(int initialHeight);   // Constructor
  ~tree();   // Destructor
  void grow(int years);
  void printsize();
};

tree::tree(int initialHeight) {
  height = initialHeight;
}

tree::~tree() {
  puts("inside tree destructor");
```

```
    printsize();
}

void tree::grow(int years) {
  height += years;
}

void tree::printsize() {
  printf("tree height is %d\n", height);
}

main() {
  puts("before opening brace");
  {
    tree t(12);
    puts("after tree creation");
    t.printsize();
    t.grow(4);
    puts("before closing brace");
  }
  puts("after closing brace");
}
```

Here's the output of the above program:

```
before opening brace
after tree creation
tree height is 12
before closing brace
inside tree destructor
tree height is 16
after closing brace
```

You can see that the destructor is automatically called at the closing brace of the scope that encloses it.

elimination of the definition block

In C, you must always define all the variables at the beginning of a block, after the opening brace. This is not an uncommon requirement in programming languages (Pascal is another example), and the reason given has always been that it's "good programming style." On this point, I have my suspicions. It has always seemed inconvenient to me, as a programmer, to pop back to the beginning of a block every time I need a new variable. I also find code more readable when the variable definition is close to its point of use.

Perhaps these arguments are stylistic. In C++, however, there's a significant problem in being forced to define all objects at the beginning of a scope. If a constructor exists, it must be called when the object is created. However, if the constructor takes one or more initialization arguments, how do you know you will have that initialization information at the beginning of a scope? In the general programming situation, you won't. Because C has no concept of **private**, this separation of definition and initialization is no problem. However, C++ guarantees that when an object is created, it is simultaneously initialized. This ensures you will have no uninitialized objects running around in your system. C doesn't care; in fact, C *encourages* this practice by requiring you to define variables at the beginning of a block before you necessarily have the initialization information.

Generally C++ will not allow you to create an object before you have the initialization information for the constructor, so you don't have to define variables at the beginning of a scope. In fact, the style of the language would seem to encourage the definition of an object as close to its point of use as possible. In C++, any rule that applies to an "object" automatically refers to an object of a built-in type, as well. This means that any class object or variable of a built-in type can also be defined at any point in a scope. It also means that you can wait until you have the information for a variable before defining it, so you can always define and initialize at the same time:

```
//: DEFINIT.CPP -- Defining variables anywhere
#include <stdio.h>
#include <assert.h>
#include <stdlib.h>

class G {
  int i;
public:
  G(int I);
};

G::G(int I) { i = I; }

main() {
  #define SZ 100
  char buf[SZ];
  printf("initialization value? ");
  int retval = (int)gets(buf);
  assert(retval);
  int x = atoi(buf);
  int y = x + 3;
  G g(y);
}
```

You can see that **buf** is defined, then some code is executed, then **x** is defined and initialized using a function call, then **y** and **g** are defined. C, of course, would never allow a variable to be defined anywhere except at the beginning of the scope.

Generally, you should define variables as close to their point of use as possible, and always initialize them when they are defined. (This is a stylistic suggestion for built-in types, where initialization is optional.) This is a safety issue. By reducing the duration of the variable's availability within the scope, you are reducing the chance it will be misused in some other part of the scope. In addition, readability is improved because the reader doesn't have to jump back and forth to the beginning of the scope to know the type of a variable.

for loops

In C++, you will often see a **for** loop counter defined right inside the **for** expression:

```
for(int j = 0; j < 100; j++) {
    printf("j = %d\n", j);
}
for(int i = 0; i < 100; i++)
    printf("i = %d\n", i);
```

The above statements are important special cases, which cause confusion to new C++ programmers.

The variables **i** and **j** are defined directly inside the **for** expression (which you cannot do in C). They are then available for use in the **for** loop. It's a very convenient syntax because the context removes all question about the purpose of **i** and **j**, so you don't need to use such ungainly names as **i_loop_counter** for clarity.

The problem is the lifetime of the variables, which was formerly determined *by the enclosing scope*. This is a situation where a design decision was made from a compiler-writer's view of what is logical because as a programmer you obviously intend **i** to be used only inside the statement(s) of the **for** loop. Unfortunately, however, if you previously took this approach and said

```
for(int i = 0; i < 100; i++)
    printf("i = %d\n", i);
// ....
```

```
for(int i = 0; i < 100; i++){
    printf("i = %d\n", i);
}
```

(with or without curly braces) within the same scope, compilers written for the old specification gave you a multiple-definition error for **i**. The new Standard C++ specification says that the lifetime of a loop counter defined within the control expression of a **for** loop lasts until the end of the controlled expression, so the above statements will work. (However, not all compilers may support this yet, and you may encounter code based on the old style.) If the transition causes errors, the compiler will point them out to you; the solution requires only a small edit. Watch out, though, for local variables that hide variables in the enclosing scope.

I find small scopes an indicator of good design. If you have several pages for a single function, perhaps you're trying to do too much with that function. More granular functions are not only more useful, but it's also easier to find bugs.

storage allocation

A variable can now be defined at any point in a scope, so it might seem initially that the storage for a variable may not be defined until its point of definition. It's more likely that the compiler will follow the practice in C of allocating all the storage for a block at the opening brace of that block. It doesn't matter because, as a programmer, you can't get the storage (a.k.a. the object) until it has been defined. Although the storage is allocated at the beginning of the block, the constructor call doesn't happen until the sequence point where the object is defined because the identifier isn't available until then. The compiler even checks to make sure you don't put the object definition (and thus the constructor call) where the sequence point only conditionally passes through it, such as in a **switch** statement or somewhere a **goto** can jump past it. Uncommenting the statements in the following code will generate a warning or an error:

```
//: NOJUMP.CPP -- Can't jump past constructors

class X {
public:
  X() {}
};

void f(int i) {
  if(i < 10) {
  //! goto jump1; // Error: goto bypasses init
  }
  X x1;  // Constructor called here
 jump1:
  switch(i) {
    case 1 :
      X x2;  // Constructor called here
      break;
  //! case 2 : // Error: case bypasses init
      X x3;  // Constructor called here
      break;
  }
}

main() {}
```

In the above code, both the **goto** and the **switch** can potentially jump past the sequence point where a constructor is called. That object will then be in scope even if the constructor hasn't been called, so the compiler gives an error message. This once again guarantees that an object cannot be created unless it is also initialized.

All the storage allocation discussed here happens, of course, on the stack. The storage is allocated by the compiler by moving the stack pointer "down" (a relative term, which may indicate an increase or decrease of the actual stack pointer value, depending on your machine). Objects can also be allocated on the heap, but that's the subject of Chapter 11.

stash with constructors and destructors

The examples from previous chapters have obvious functions that map to constructors and destructors: **initialize( )** and **cleanup( )**. Here's the **stash** header using constructors and destructors:

```
//: STASH3.H -- With constructors & destructors
#ifndef STASH3_H_
#define STASH3_H_

class stash {
  int size;  // Size of each space
  int quantity; // Number of storage spaces
  int next; // Next empty space
  // Dynamically allocated array of bytes:
  unsigned char* storage;
  void inflate(int increase);
public:
  stash(int Size);
  ~stash();
  int add(void* element);
  void* fetch(int index);
  int count();
};
#endif // STASH3_H_
```

The only member function definitions that are changed are **initialize( )** and **cleanup( )**, which have been replaced with a constructor and destructor:

```
//: STASH3.CPP -- Constructors & destructors
```

```
#include "..\3\stash3.h"
#include <assert.h>
#include <stdlib.h>
#include <string.h>
#include <stdio.h>

stash::stash(int Size) {
  size = Size;
  quantity = 0;
  storage = 0;
  next = 0;
}

stash::~stash() {
  if(storage) {
    puts("freeing storage");
    free(storage);
  }
}

int stash::add(void* element) {
  if(next >= quantity) // Enough space left?
    inflate(100);
  // Copy element into storage,
  // starting at next empty space:
  memcpy(&(storage[next * size]),
         element, size);
  next++;
  return(next - 1); // Index number
}

void* stash::fetch(int index) {
  if(index >= next || index < 0)
    return 0;  // Not out of bounds?
  // Produce pointer to desired element:
  return &(storage[index * size]);
}
```

```
int stash::count() {
  return next; // Number of elements in stash
}

void stash::inflate(int increase) {
  void* v =
    realloc(storage, (quantity+increase)*size);
  assert(v);  // Was it successful?
  storage = (unsigned char*)v;
  quantity += increase;
}
```

Notice, in the following test program, how the definitions for **stash** objects appear right before they are needed, and how the initialization appears as part of the definition, in the constructor argument list:

```
//: STSHTST3.CPP -- Constructors & destructors
#include "..\3\stash3.h"
#include <stdio.h>
#include <assert.h>
#define BUFSIZE 80

main() {
  stash intStash(sizeof(int));
  for(int j = 0; j < 100; j++)
    intStash.add(&j);

  FILE* file = fopen("STASHTST.CPP", "r");
  assert(file);
  // Holds 80-character strings:
  stash stringStash(sizeof(char) * BUFSIZE);
  char buf[BUFSIZE];
  while(fgets(buf, BUFSIZE, file))
    stringStash.add(buf);
  fclose(file);
```

```
  for(int k = 0; k < intStash.count(); k++)
    printf("intStash.fetch(%d) = %d\n", k,
           *(int*)intStash.fetch(k));

  for(int i = 0; i < stringStash.count(); i++)
    printf("stringStash.fetch(%d) = %s",
           i, (char*)stringStash.fetch(i++));
  putchar('\n');
}
```

Also notice how the **cleanup( )** calls have been eliminated, but the destructors are still automatically called when **intStash** and **stringStash** go out of scope.

stack with constructors & destructors

Reimplementing the linked list (inside **stack**) with constructors and destructors shows up a significant problem. Here's the modified header file:

```
//: STACK3.H -- With constructors/destructors
#ifndef STACK3_H_
#define STACK3_H_

class stack {
  struct link {
    void* data;
    link* next;
    void initialize(void* Data, link* Next);
  } * head;
public:
  stack();
```

```
    ~stack();
    void push(void* Data);
    void* peek();
    void* pop();
};
#endif // STACK3_H_
```

Notice that although **stack** has a constructor and destructor, the nested class **link** does not. This has nothing to do with the fact that it's nested. The problem arises when it is used:

```
//: STACK3.CPP -- Constructors/destructors
#include <stdlib.h>
#include <assert.h>
#include "..\3\stack3.h"

void stack::link::initialize(
  void* Data, link* Next) {
  data = Data;
  next = Next;
}

stack::stack() { head = 0; }

void stack::push(void* Data) {
  // Can't use a constructor with malloc!
  link* newlink = (link*)malloc(sizeof(link));
  assert(newlink);
  newlink->initialize(Data, head);
  head = newlink;
}

void* stack::peek() { return head->data; }

void* stack::pop() {
  if(head == 0) return 0;
  void* result = head->data;
```

```
    link* oldHead = head;
    head = head->next;
    free(oldHead);
    return result;
}

stack::~stack() {
  link* cursor = head;
  while(head) {
    cursor = cursor->next;
    free(head->data); // Assumes malloc!
    free(head);
    head = cursor;
  }
}
```

link is created inside **stack::push**, but it's created on the heap and there's the rub. How do you create an object on the heap if it has a constructor? So far we've been saying, "OK, here's a piece of memory on the heap and I want you to pretend that it's actually a real object." But the constructor doesn't allow us to hand it a memory address upon which it will build an object.[1] The creation of an object is critical, and the C++ constructor wants to be in control of the whole process to keep things safe. There is an easy solution to this problem, the operator **new**, that we'll look at in Chapter 11, but for now the C approach to dynamic allocation will have to suffice. Because the allocation and cleanup are hidden within **stack** — it's part of the underlying implementation — you don't see the effect in the test program:

```
//: STKTST3.CPP -- Constructors/destructors
#include "..\3\stack3.h"
```

------

[1]Actually, there's a syntax that *does* allow you to do this. But it's for special cases and doesn't solve the general problem described here.

```
#include <stdio.h>
#include <stdlib.h>
#include <string.h>
#include <assert.h>

main(int argc, char** argv) {
  assert(argc == 2); // File name is argument
  FILE* file = fopen(argv[1], "r");
  assert(file);
  #define BUFSIZE 100
  char buf[BUFSIZE];
  stack textlines;  // Constructor called here
  // Read file and store lines in the stack:
  while(fgets(buf, BUFSIZE, file)) {
    char* string =
      (char*)malloc(strlen(buf) + 1);
    assert(string);
    strcpy(string, buf);
    textlines.push(string);
  }
  // Pop lines from the stack and print them:
  char* s;
  while((s = (char*)textlines.pop()) != 0) {
    printf("%s", s); free(s); }
}  // Destructor called here
```

The constructor and destructor for **textlines** are called automatically, so the user of the class can focus on what to do with the object and not worry about whether or not it will be properly initialized and cleaned up.

aggregate initialization

An *aggregate* is just what it sounds like: a bunch of things clumped together. This definition includes aggregates of mixed types, like **struct**s and **class**es. An array is an aggregate of a single type.

Initializing aggregates can be error-prone and tedious. C++ *aggregate initialization* makes it much safer. When you create an object that's an aggregate, all you must do is make an assignment, and the initialization will be taken care of by the compiler. This assignment comes in several flavors, depending on the type of aggregate you're dealing with, but in all cases the elements in the assignment must be surrounded by curly braces. For an array of built-in types this is quite simple:

```
int a[5] = { 1, 2, 3, 4, 5 };
```

If you try to give more initializers than there are array elements, the compiler gives an error message. But what happens if you give *fewer* initializers, such as

```
int b[6] = {0};
```

Here, the compiler will use the first initializer for the first array element, and then use zero for all the elements without initializers. Notice this initialization behavior doesn't occur if you define an array without a list of initializers. So the above expression is a very succinct way to initialize an array to zero, without using a **for** loop, and without any possibility of an off-by-one error (Depending on the compiler, it may also be more efficient than the **for** loop.)

A second shorthand for arrays is *automatic counting*, where you let the compiler determine the size of the array based on the number of initializers:

```
int c[] = { 1, 2, 3, 4 };
```

Now if you decide to add another element to the array, you simply add another initializer. If you can set your code up so it needs to be changed in only one spot, you reduce the chance of errors during modification. But how do you determine the size of the array? The expression **sizeof c** / **sizeof *c** (size of the entire array divided by the size of the first element) does the trick in a way that doesn't need to be changed if the array size changes:

```
for(int i = 0; i < sizeof c / sizeof *c; i++)
  c[i]++;
```

Because structures are also aggregates, they can be initialized in a similar fashion. Because a C-style **struct** has all its members **public**, they can be assigned directly:

```
struct X {
  int i;
  float f;
  char c;
};
```

```
X x1 = { 1, 2.2, 'c' };
```

If you have an array of such objects, you can initialize them by using a nested set of curly braces for each object:

```
X x2[3] = { {1, 1.1, 'a'}, {2, 2.2, 'b'} };
```

Here, the third object is initialized to zero.

If any of the data members are **private**, or even if everything's public but there's a constructor, things are different. In the above examples, the initializers are assigned directly to the elements of the aggregate, but constructors are a way of forcing initialization to occur through a formal interface. Here, the constructors must be called to perform the initialization. So if you have a **struct** that looks like this,

```
struct Y {
  float f;
  int i;
  Y(int A); // presumably assigned to i
};
```

You must indicate constructor calls. The best approach is the explicit one as follows:

```
Y y2[] = { Y(1), Y(2), Y(3) };
```

You get three objects and three constructor calls. Any time you have a constructor, whether it's a **struct** with all members **public** or a **class** with **private** data members, all the initialization must go through the constructor, even if you're using aggregate initialization.

Here's a second example showing multiple constructor arguments:

```
//: MULTIARG.CPP -- Multiple constructor arguments
// with aggregate initialization

class X {
  int i, j;
public:
  X(int I, int J) {
    i = I;
    j = J;
  }
};

main() {
  X xx[] = { X(1,2), X(3,4), X(5,6), X(7,8) };
}
```

Notice that it looks like an explicit but unnamed constructor is called for each object in the array.

default constructors

A *default constructor* is one that can be called with no arguments. A default constructor is used to create a "vanilla object," but it's also very important when the compiler is told to create an object but isn't given any details. For example, if you take **Y** and use it in a definition like this,

```
Y y4[2] = { Y(1) };
```

the compiler will complain that it cannot find a default constructor. The second object in the array wants to be created with no arguments, and that's where the compiler looks for a default constructor. In fact, if you simply define an array of **Y** objects,

```
Y y5[7];
```

or an individual object,

```
Y y;
```

the compiler will complain because it must have a default constructor to initialize every object in the array. (Remember, if you have a constructor the compiler ensures it is *always* called, regardless of the situation.)

The default constructor is so important that *if* (and only if) there are no constructors for a structure (**struct** or **class**), the compiler will automatically create one for you. So this works:

```
class Z {
  int i;  // private
}; // no constructor

Z z, z2[10];
```

If any constructors are defined, however, and there's no default constructor, the above object definitions will generate compile-time errors.

You might think that the default constructor should do some intelligent initialization, like setting all the memory for the object to zero. But it doesn't — that would add extra overhead but be out of the programmer's control. This would mean, for example, that if you compiled C code under C++, the effect would be different. If you want the memory to be initialized to zero, you must do it yourself.

The automatic creation of default constructors was not simply a feature to make life easier for new C++ programmers. It's virtually

---

required to aid backward compatibility with existing C code, which is a critical issue in C++. In C, it's not uncommon to create an array of **struct**s. Without the default constructor, this would cause a compile-time error in C++.

If you had to modify your C code to recompile it under C++ just because of stylistic issues, you might not bother. When you move C code to C++, you will almost always have new compile-time error messages, but those errors are because of genuine bad C code that the C++ compiler can detect because of its stronger rules. In fact, a good way to find obscure errors in a C program is to run it through a C++ compiler.

summary

The seemingly elaborate mechanisms provided by C++ should give you a strong hint about the critical importance placed on initialization and cleanup in the language. As Stroustrup was designing C++, one of the first observations he made about productivity in C was that a very significant portion of programming problems are caused by improper initialization of variables. These kinds of bugs are very hard to find, and similar issues apply to improper cleanup. Because constructors and destructors allow you to *guarantee* proper initialization and cleanup (the compiler will not allow an object to be created and destroyed without the proper constructor and destructor calls), you get complete control and safety.

Aggregate initialization is included in a similar vein — it prevents you from making typical initialization mistakes with aggregates of built-in types and makes your code more succinct.

Safety during coding is a big issue in C++. Initialization and cleanup are an important part of this, but you'll also see other safety issues as the book progresses.

exercises

1. Modify the HANDLE.H, HANDLE.CPP, and USEHANDL.CPP files at the end of Chapter 2 to use constructors and destructors.

2. Create a class with a nondefault constructor and destructor, each of which print something to announce their presence. Write code that demonstrates when the constructor and destructor are called.

3. Demonstrate automatic counting and aggregate initialization with an array of objects of the class you created in Exercise 2. Add a member function to that class that prints a message. Calculate the size of the array and move through it, calling your new member function.

4. Create a class without any constructors, and show you can create objects with the default constructor. Now create a nondefault constructor (one with an argument) for the class, and try compiling again. Explain what happened.

function overloading & default arguments

One of the important features in any programming language is the convenient use of names.

When you create an object (a variable), you give a name to a region of storage. A function is a name for an action. By using names that you make up to describe the system at hand, you create a program that is easier for people to understand and change. It's a lot like writing prose — the goal is to communicate with your readers.

A problem arises when mapping the concept of nuance in human language onto a programming language. Often, the same word expresses a number of different meanings, depending on context. That is, a single word has multiple meanings — it's *overloaded*. This is very useful, especially when it comes to trivial differences. You say "wash the shirt, wash the car." It would be silly to be forced to say, "shirt_wash the shirt, car_wash the car" just so the hearer doesn't have to make any distinction about the action performed. Most human languages are redundant, so even if you miss a few words, you can still determine the meaning. We don't need unique identifiers — we can deduce meaning from context.

Most programming languages, however, require that you have a unique identifier for each function. If you have three different types of data you want to print, **int**, **char**, and **float**, you generally have to create three different function names, for example, **print_int( )**, **print_char( )**, and **print_float( )**. This loads extra work on you as you write the program, and on readers as they try to understand it.

In C++, another factor forces the overloading of function names: the constructor. Because the constructor's name is predetermined by the name of the class, there can be only one constructor name. But what if you want to create an object in more than one way? For example, suppose you build a class that can initialize itself in a standard way and also by reading information from a file. You need two constructors, one that takes no arguments (the *default* constructor) and one that takes a character string as an argument, which is the name of the file to initialize the object. Both are constructors, so they must have the same name — the name of the class. Thus function overloading is essential to allow the same function name, the constructor in this case, to be used with different argument types.

Although function overloading is a must for constructors, it's a general convenience and can be used with any function, not just class member functions. In addition, function overloading means that if you have two libraries that contain functions of the same name, the chances are they won't conflict as long as the argument lists are different. We'll look at all these factors in detail throughout this chapter.

The theme of this chapter is convenient use of function names. Function overloading allows you to use the same name for different functions, but there's a second way to make calling a function more convenient. What if you'd like to call the same function in different ways? When functions have long argument lists, it can become tedious to write and confusing to read the function calls when most of the arguments are the same for all the calls. A very commonly used feature in C++ is called *default arguments*. A default argument is one the compiler inserts if the person calling a function doesn't specify it. Thus the calls **f("hello")**, **f("hi", 1)** and **f("howdy", 2, 'c')** can all be calls to the same function. They could also be calls to three overloaded functions, but when the argument lists are this similar, you'll usually want similar behavior that calls for a single function.

Function overloading and default arguments really aren't very complicated. By the time you reach the end of this chapter, you'll understand when to use them and the underlying mechanisms used during compiling and linking to implement them.

more mangling

In Chapter 1 the concept of *name mangling* was introduced. (Sometimes the more gentle term *decoration* is used.) In the code

```
void f();
class X { void f(); };
```

the function **f( )** inside the scope of **class X** does not clash with the global version of **f( )**. The compiler performs this scoping by manufacturing different internal names for the global version of **f( )** and **X::f( )**. In Chapter 1 it was suggested that the names are simply the class name "mangled" together with the function name, so the internal names the compiler uses might be **_f** and **_X_f**. It turns out that function name mangling involves more than the class name.

Here's why. Suppose you want to overload two function names

```
void print(char);
void print(float);
```

It doesn't matter whether they are both inside a class or at the global scope. The compiler can't generate unique internal identifiers if it uses only the scope of the function names. You'd end up with **_print** in both cases. The idea of an overloaded function is that you use the same function name, but different argument lists. Thus, for overloading to work the compiler must mangle the names of the argument types with the function name. The above functions, defined at global scope, produce internal names that might look something like **_print_char** and **_print_float**. It's worth noting there is no standard for the way names must be mangled by the compiler, so you will see very different results from one compiler to another. (You can see what it looks like by telling the compiler to generate assembly-language output.) This, of course, causes problems if you want to buy compiled libraries for a particular compiler and linker, but those problems can also exist because of the way different compilers generate code.

That's really all there is to function overloading: You can use the same function name for different functions, as long as the argument lists are different. The compiler mangles the name, the scope, and the argument lists to produce internal names for it and the linker to use.

overloading on return values

It's common to wonder "why just scopes and argument lists? Why not return values?" It seems at first that it would make sense to also mangle the return value with the internal function name. Then you could overload on return values, as well:

```
void f();
```

```
int f();
```

This works fine when the compiler can unequivocally determine the meaning from the context, as in **int x = f( );**. However, in C you've always been able to call a function and ignore the return value. How can the compiler distinguish which call is meant in this case? Possibly worse is the difficulty the reader has in knowing which function call is meant. Overloading solely on return value is a bit too subtle, and thus isn't allowed in C++.

type-safe linkage

There is an added benefit to all this name mangling. A particularly sticky problem in C occurs when the user misdeclares a function, or, worse, a function is called without declaring it first, and the compiler infers the function declaration from the way it is called. Sometimes this function declaration is correct, but when it isn't, it can be a very difficult bug to find.

Because all functions *must* be declared before they are used in C++, the opportunity for this problem to pop up is greatly diminished. The compiler refuses to declare a function automatically for you, so it's likely you will include the appropriate header file. However, if for some reason you still manage to misdeclare a function, either by declaring it yourself by hand or by including the wrong header file (perhaps one that is out of date), the name-mangling provides a safety net that is often referred to as *type-safe linkage*.

Consider the following scenario. In one file is the definition for a function:

```
//: DEF.CPP -- Function definition
void f(int) {}
```

In the second file, the function is misdeclared and then called:

```
//: USE.CPP -- Function misdeclaration
void f(char);
```

```
main() {
//!  f(1); // Causes a linker error
}
```

Even though you can see that the function is actually **f(int)**, the compiler doesn't know this because it was told — through an explicit declaration — that the function is **f(char)**. Thus, the compilation is successful. In C, the linker would also be successful, but *not* in C++. Because the compiler mangles the names, the definition becomes something like **f_int**, whereas the use of the function is **f_char**. When the linker tries to resolve the reference to **f_char**, it can find only **f_int**, and it gives you an error message. This is type-safe linkage. Although the problem doesn't occur all that often, when it does it can be incredibly difficult to find, especially in a large project. This is one of the cases where you can find a difficult error in a C program simply by running it through the C++ compiler.

overloading example

Consider the examples we've been looking at so far in this series, modified to use function overloading. As stated earlier, an immediately useful place for overloading is in constructors. You can see this in the following version of the **stash** class:

```
//: STASH4.H -- Function overloading
#ifndef STASH4_H_
#define STASH4_H_

class stash {
  int size;  // Size of each space
  int quantity; // Number of storage spaces
  int next; // Next empty space
  // Dynamically allocated array of bytes:
  unsigned char* storage;
```

```
    void inflate(int increase);
public:
    stash(int Size); // Zero quantity
    stash(int Size, int InitQuant);
    ~stash();
    int add(void* element);
    void* fetch(int index);
    int count();
};
#endif // STASH4_H_
```

The first **stash( )** constructor is the same as before, but the second one has a **Quantity** argument to indicate the initial quantity of storage places to be allocated. In the definition, you can see that the internal value of **quantity** is set to zero, along with the **storage** pointer:

```
//: STASH4.CPP -- Function overloading
#include "..\4\stash4.h"
#include <assert.h>
#include <stdlib.h>
#include <string.h>
#include <stdio.h>

stash::stash(int Size) {
    size = Size;
    quantity = 0;
    next = 0;
    storage = 0;
}

stash::stash(int Size, int InitQuant) {
    size = Size;
    quantity = 0;
    next = 0;
    storage = 0;
    inflate(InitQuant);
```

```
}

stash::~stash() {
  if(storage) {
    puts("freeing storage");
    free(storage);
  }
}

int stash::add(void* element) {
  if(next >= quantity) // Enough space left?
    inflate(100); // Add space for 100 elements
  // Copy element into storage,
  // starting at next empty space:
  memcpy(&(storage[next * size]),
         element, size);
  next++;
  return(next - 1); // Index number
}

void* stash::fetch(int index) {
  if(index >= next || index < 0)
    return 0;   // Not out of bounds?
  // Produce pointer to desired element:
  return &(storage[index * size]);
}

int stash::count() {
  return next; // Number of elements in stash
}

void stash::inflate(int increase) {
  void* v =
    realloc(storage, (quantity+increase)*size);
  assert(v);   // Was it successful?
  storage = (unsigned char*)v;
  quantity += increase;
```

```
}
```

When you use the first constructor no memory is allocated for **storage**. The allocation happens the first time you try to **add( )** an object and any time the current block of memory is exceeded inside **add( )**.

This is demonstrated in the test program, which exercises the first constructor:

```
//: STSHTST4.CPP -- Function overloading
#include "..\4\stash4.h"
#include <stdio.h>
#include <assert.h>
#define BUFSIZE 80

main() {
  int i;
  FILE* file;
  char buf[BUFSIZE];
  char* cp;
  // ....
  stash intStash(sizeof(int));
  for(i = 0; i < 100; i++)
    intStash.add(&i);
  file = fopen("STSHTST4.CPP", "r");
  assert(file);
  // Holds 80-character strings:
  stash stringStash(sizeof(char) * BUFSIZE);
  while(fgets(buf, BUFSIZE, file))
    stringStash.add(buf);
  fclose(file);

  for(i = 0; i < intStash.count(); i++)
    printf("intStash.fetch(%d) = %d\n", i,
           *(int*)intStash.fetch(i));
```

```
  i = 0;
  while(
    (cp = (char*)stringStash.fetch(i++)) != 0)
    printf("stringStash.fetch(%d) = %s",
           i - 1, cp);
  putchar('\n');
}
```

You can modify this code to use the second constructor just by adding another argument; presumably you'd know something about the problem that allows you to choose an initial size for the **stash**.

default arguments

Examine the two constructors for **stash( )**. They don't seem all that different, do they? In fact, the first constructor seems to be the special case of the second one with the initial **size** set to zero. In this situation it seems a bit of a waste of effort to create and maintain two different versions of a similar function.

C++ provides a remedy with *default arguments*. A default argument is a value given in the declaration that the compiler automatically inserts if you don't provide a value in the function call. In the **stash** example, we can replace the two functions:

```
stash(int Size); // zero quantity
stash(int Size, int Quantity);
```

with the single declaration

```
stash(int Size, int Quantity = 0);
```

The **stash(int)** definition is simply removed — all that is necessary is the single **stash(int, int)** definition.

Now, the two object definitions

```
stash A(100), B(100, 0);
```

will produce exactly the same results. The identical constructor is called in both cases, but for **A**, the second argument is automatically substituted by the compiler when it sees the first argument is an **int** and there is no second argument. The compiler has seen the default argument, so it knows it can still make the function call if it substitutes this second argument, which is what you've told it to do by making it a default.

Default arguments are a convenience, as function overloading is a convenience. Both features allow you to use a single name in different situations. The difference is that the compiler is substituting arguments when you don't want to put them in yourself. The preceding example is a good place to use default arguments instead of function overloading; otherwise you end up with two or more functions that have similar signatures and similar behaviors. Obviously, if the functions have very different behaviors, it usually doesn't make sense to use default arguments.

There are two rules you must be aware of when using default arguments. First, only trailing arguments may be defaulted. That is, you can't have a default argument followed by a nondefault argument. Second, once you start using default arguments, all the remaining arguments must be defaulted. (This follows from the first rule.)

Default arguments are only placed in the declaration of a function, which is placed in a header file. The compiler must see the default value before it can use it. Sometimes people will place the commented values of the default arguments in the function definition, for documentation purposes

```
void fn(int x /* = 0 */) { // ...
```

Default arguments can make arguments declared without identifiers look a bit funny. You can end up with

```
void f(int x, int = 0, float = 1.1);
```

In C++ you don't need identifiers in the function definition, either:

```
void f(int x, int, float f) { /* ... */ }
```

In the function body, **x** and **f** can be referenced, but not the middle argument, because it has no name. The calls must still use a placeholder, though: **f(1)** or **f(1,2,3.0)**. This syntax allows you to put the argument in as a placeholder without using it. The idea is that you might want to change the function definition to use it later, without changing all the function calls. Of course, you can accomplish the same thing by using a named argument, but if you define the argument for the function body without using it, most compilers will give you a warning message, assuming you've made a logical error. By intentionally leaving the argument name out, you suppress this warning.

More important, if you start out using a function argument and later decide that you don't need it, you can effectively remove it without generating warnings, and yet not disturb any client code that was calling the previous version of the function.

a bit vector class

As a further example of operator overloading and default arguments, consider the problem of efficiently storing a set of true-false flags. If you have a number of pieces of data that can be expressed as "on" or "off," it may be convenient to store them in an object called a *bit vector*. Sometimes a bit vector is not a tool to be used by the application developer, but a part of other classes.

Of course, the easiest way to code a group of flags is with a byte of data for each flag, as shown in this example:

```
//: FLAGS.CPP -- List of true/false flags
#include <stdio.h>
#include <string.h>
#include <assert.h>
#define FSIZE 100
#define TRUE 1
```

```
#define FALSE 0

class flags {
  unsigned char f[FSIZE];
public:
  flags();
  void set(int i);
  void clear(int i);
  int read(int i);
  int size();
};

flags::flags() {
  memset(f, FALSE, FSIZE);
}

void flags::set(int i) {
  assert(i >= 0 && i < FSIZE);
  f[i] = TRUE;
}

void flags::clear(int i) {
  assert(i >= 0 && i < FSIZE);
  f[i] = FALSE;
}

int flags::read(int i) {
  assert(i >= 0 && i < FSIZE);
  return f[i];
}

int flags::size() { return FSIZE; }

main() {
  flags fl;
  for(int i = 0; i < fl.size(); i++)
    if(i % 3 == 0) fl.set(i);
```

```
  for(int j = 0; j < fl.size(); j++)
    printf("fl.read(%d)= %d\n", j, fl.read(j));
}
```

However, this is wasteful, because you're using eight bits for a flag that could be expressed as a single bit. Sometimes this storage is important, especially if you want to build other classes using this class. So consider instead the following **BitVector**, which uses a bit for each flag. The function overloading occurs in the constructor and the **bits( )** function:

```
//: BITVECT.H -- Bit Vector
#ifndef BITVECT_H_
#define BITVECT_H_

class BitVector {
  unsigned char* bytes;
  int Bits, numBytes;
public:
  BitVector(); // Default: 0 size
  // init points to an array of bytes
  // size is measured in bytes
  BitVector(unsigned char* init,
            int size = 8);
  // binary is a string of 1s and 0s
  BitVector(char* binary);
  ~BitVector();
  void set(int bit);
  void clear(int bit);
  int read(int bit);
  int bits(); // Number of bits in the vector
  void bits(int sz); // Set number of bits
  void print(const char* msg = "");
};
#endif // BITVECT_H_
```

The first (default) constructor creates a **BitVector** of size zero. You can't set any bits in this vector because there are none. First you have to increase the size of the vector with the overloaded **bits( )** function. The version with no arguments returns the current size of the vector in bits, and **bits(int)** changes the size to what is specified in the argument. Thus you both set and read the size using the same function name. Note that there's no restriction on the new size — you can make it smaller as well as larger.

The second constructor takes a pointer to an array of **unsigned chars**, that is, an array of raw bytes. The second argument tells the constructor how many bytes are in the array. If the first argument is zero rather than a valid pointer, the array is initialized to zero. If you don't give a second argument, the default size is eight bytes.

You might think you can create a **BitVector** of size eight bytes and set it to zero by saying **BitVector b(0);**. This would work if not for the third constructor, which takes a **char*** as its only argument. The argument **0** could be used in either the second constructor (with the second argument defaulted) or the third constructor. The compiler has no way of knowing which one it should choose, so you'll get an ambiguity error. To successfully create a **BitVector** this way, you must cast zero to a pointer of the proper type: **BitVector b((unsigned char*)0)**. This is awkward, so you may instead want to create an empty vector with **BitVector b** and then expand it to the desired size with **b.bits(64)** to allocate eight bytes.

It's important that the compiler distinguish **char*** and **unsigned char*** as two distinct data types. If it did not (a problem in the past) then **BitVector(unsigned char*, int)** (with the second argument defaulted) and **BitVector(char*)** would look the same when the compiler tried to match the function call.

Note that the **print( )** function has a default argument for its **char*** argument. This may look a bit puzzling if you know how the compiler handles string constants. Does the compiler create a new default character string every time you call the function? The answer is no; it creates a single string in a special area reserved for static and global data, and passes the *address* of that string every time it needs to use it as a default.

a string of bits

The third constructor for the **BitVector** takes a pointer to a character string that represents a string of bits. This is a convenient syntax for the user because it allows the vector initialization values to be expressed in the natural form **0110010**. The object is created to match the length of the string, and each bit is set or cleared according to the string.

The other functions are the all-important **set( )**, **clear( )**, and **read( )**, each of which takes the bit number of interest as an argument. The **print( )** function prints a message, which has a default argument of an empty string, and then the bit pattern of the **BitVector**, again using ones and zeros.

Two issues are immediately apparent when implementing the **BitVector** class. One is that if the number of bits you need doesn't fall on an 8-bit boundary (or whatever word size your machine uses), you must round up to the nearest boundary. The second is the care necessary in selecting the bits of interest. For example, when creating a **BitVector** using an array of bytes, each byte in the array must be read in from left to right so it will appear the way you expect it in the **print( )** function.

Here are the member function definitions:

```
//: BITVECT.CPP -- BitVector Implementation
#include <stdio.h>
#include <assert.h>
#include <stdlib.h>
#include <string.h>
#include "..\4\bitvect.h"
#include <limits.h> //CHAR_BIT = # bits in char
// A byte with the high bit set:
const unsigned char highbit =
  1 << (CHAR_BIT - 1);
```

```
BitVector::BitVector() {
  numBytes = 0;
  Bits = 0;
  bytes = 0;
}
// Notice default args are not duplicated:
BitVector::BitVector(unsigned char* init,
                     int size) {
  numBytes = size;
  Bits = numBytes * CHAR_BIT;
  bytes = (unsigned char*)calloc(numBytes, 1);
  assert(bytes);
  if(init == 0) return; // Default to all 0
  // Translate from bytes into bit sequence:
  for(int index = 0; index<numBytes; index++)
    for(int offset = 0;
        offset < CHAR_BIT; offset++)
      if(init[index] & (highbit >> offset))
        set(index * CHAR_BIT + offset);
}

BitVector::BitVector(char* binary) {
  Bits = strlen(binary);
  numBytes =  Bits / CHAR_BIT;
  // If there's a remainder, add 1 byte:
  if(Bits % CHAR_BIT) numBytes++;
  bytes = (unsigned char*)calloc(numBytes, 1);
  assert(bytes);
  for(int i = 0; i < Bits; i++)
    if(binary[i] == '1') set(i);
}

BitVector::~BitVector() {
  free(bytes);
}
```

```
void BitVector::set(int bit) {
  assert(bit >= 0 && bit < Bits);
  int index = bit / CHAR_BIT;
  int offset = bit % CHAR_BIT;
  unsigned char mask = (1 << offset);
  bytes[index] |= mask;
}

int BitVector::read(int bit) {
  assert(bit >= 0 && bit < Bits);
  int index = bit / CHAR_BIT;
  int offset = bit % CHAR_BIT;
  unsigned char mask = (1 << offset);
  return bytes[index] & mask;
}

void BitVector::clear(int bit) {
  assert(bit >= 0 && bit < Bits);
  int index = bit / CHAR_BIT;
  int offset = bit % CHAR_BIT;
  unsigned char mask = ~(1 << offset);
  bytes[index] &= mask;
}

int BitVector::bits() { return Bits; }

void BitVector::bits(int size) {
  int oldsize = Bits;
  Bits = size;
  numBytes = Bits / CHAR_BIT;
  // If there's a remainder, add 1 byte:
  if(Bits % CHAR_BIT) numBytes++;
  void* v = realloc(bytes, numBytes);
  assert(v);
  bytes = (unsigned char*)v;
  for(int i = oldsize; i < Bits; i++)
    clear(i); // Erase additional bits
```

```
}

void BitVector::print(const char* msg) {
  puts(msg);
  for(int i = 0; i < Bits; i++){
    if(read(i)) putchar('1');
      else putchar('0');
    // Format into byte blocks:
    if((i + 1) % CHAR_BIT == 0) putchar(' ');
  }
  putchar('\n');
}
```

The first constructor is trivial because it just sets everything to zero. The second constructor allocates storage and initializes the number of bits, and then it gets a little tricky. The outer **for** loop indexes through the array of bytes, and the inner **for** loop indexes through each byte a bit at a time. However, the bit is selected from the byte from left to right using the expression **init[index] & (0x80 >> offset)**. Notice this is a bitwise AND, and the hex **0x80** (a 1-bit in the highest location) is shifted to the right by **offset** to create a mask. If the result is nonzero, there is a one in that particular bit position, and the **set( )** function is used to set the bit inside the **BitVector**. It was important to scan the source bytes from left to right so the **print( )** function makes sense to the viewer.

The third constructor converts from a character string representing a binary sequence of ones and zeroes into a **BitVector**. The number of bits is taken at face value — the length of the character string. But because the character string may produce a number of bits that isn't a multiple of eight, the number of bytes **numBytes** is calculated by first doing an integer division and then checking to see if there's a remainder by using the modulus operator. In this case, unlike the second constructor, the bits are scanned in from left to right from the source string.

The **set( )**, **clear( )**, and **read( )** functions follow a nearly identical format. The first three lines are identical in each case: **assert( )** that the argument is in range, and create an **index** into the array of bytes and an **offset** into the selected byte. Both **set( )** and **read( )** create their **mask** the same way: by shifting a bit left into the desired position. But **set( )** forces the bit in the array to be set by ORing the appropriate byte with the **mask**, and **read( )** checks the value by ANDing the **mask** with the byte and seeing if the result is nonzero. **clear( )** creates its **mask** by shifting the one into the desired position, then flipping all the bits with the binary NOT operator (the tilde: **~**), then ANDing the mask onto the byte so only the desired bit is forced to zero.

Note that **set( )**, **read( )**, and **clear( )** could be written much more succinctly. For example, **clear( )** could be reduced to

```
bytes[bit/CHAR_BIT] &= ~(1 << (bit % CHAR_BIT));
```

While this is more efficient, it certainly isn't as readable.

The two overloaded **bits( )** functions are quite different in their behavior. The first is simply an *access function* (a function that produces a value based on **private** data without allowing access to that data) that tells how many bits are in the array. The second uses its argument to calculate the new number of bytes required, **realloc( )**s the memory (which allocates fresh memory if **bytes** is zero) and zeroes the additional bits. Note that if you ask for the same number of bits you've already got, this may actually reallocate the memory (depending on the implementation of **realloc( )**) but it won't hurt anything.

The **print( )** function puts out the **msg** string. The Standard C library function **puts( )** always adds a new line, so this will result in a new line for the default argument. Then it uses **read( )** on each successive bit to print the appropriate character. For easier visual scanning, after each eight bits it prints out a space. Because of the way the second **BitVector** constructor reads in its array of bytes, the **print( )** function will produce results in a familiar form.

The following program tests the **BitVector** class by exercising all the functions:

```
//: BVTEST.CPP -- Testing the BitVector class
#include "..\4\bitvect.h"

main() {
  unsigned char b[] = {
    0x0f, 0xff, 0xf0,
    0xAA, 0x78, 0x11
  };
  BitVector bv1(b, sizeof b / sizeof *b),
    bv2("1001010011110010101000101001010010010101");
  bv1.print("bv1 before modification");
  for(int i = 36; i < bv1.bits(); i++)
    bv1.clear(i);
  bv1.print("bv1 after modification");
  bv2.print("bv2 before modification");
  for(int j=bv2.bits()-10; j<bv2.bits(); j++)
    bv2.clear(j);
  bv2.set(30);
  bv2.print("bv2 after modification");
  bv2.bits(bv2.bits() / 2);
  bv2.print("bv2 cut in half");
  bv2.bits(bv2.bits() + 10);
  bv2.print("bv2 grown by 10");
  BitVector bv3((unsigned char*)0);
}
```

The objects **bv1**, **bv2**, and **bv3** show three different types of **BitVector**s and their constructors. The **set( )** and **clear( )** functions are demonstrated. (**read( )** is exercised inside **print( )**.) Toward the end of this example, **bv2** is cut in half and then grown to demonstrate a way to zero the end of the **BitVector**.

You should be aware that the Standard C++ library contains **bits** and **bitstring** classes which are much more complete (and standard) implementations of bit vectors.

summary

Both function overloading and default arguments provide a convenience for calling function names. It can seem confusing at times to know which technique to use. For example, in the **BitVector** class it seems like the two **bits( )** functions could be combined into a single version:

```
int bits(int sz = -1);
```

If you called it without an argument, the function would check for the -1 default and interpret that as meaning that you wanted it to tell you the current number of bits. The use appears to be the same as the previous scheme. However, there are a number of significant differences that jump out, or at least should make you feel uncomfortable.

Inside **bits( )** you'll have to do a conditional based on the value of the argument. If you have to *look* for the default rather than treating it as an ordinary value, that should be a clue that you will end up with two different functions inside one: one version for the normal case, and one for the default. You might as well split it up into two distinct function bodies and let the compiler do the selection. This results in a slight increase in efficiency, because the extra argument isn't passed and the extra code for the conditional isn't executed. The slight efficiency increase for two functions could make a difference if you call the function many times.

You do lose something when you use a default argument in this case. First, the default has to be something you wouldn't ordinarily use, -1 in this case. Now you can't tell if a negative number is an accident or a default substitution. Second, there's only one return value with a single function, so the compiler loses the information that was available for the overloaded functions. Now, if you say

```
int i = bv1.set(10);
```

the compiler will accept it and no longer sees something that you, as the class designer, might want, to be an error.

And consider the plight of the user, always. Which design will make more sense to users of your class as they peruse the header file? What does a default argument of -1 suggest? Not much. The two separate functions are much clearer because one takes a value and doesn't return anything and the other doesn't take a value but returns something. Even without documentation, it's far easier to guess what the two different functions do.

As a guideline, you shouldn't use a default argument as a flag upon which to conditionally execute code. You should instead break the function into two or more overloaded functions if you can. A default argument should be a value you would ordinarily put in that position. It's a value that is more likely to occur than all the rest, so users can generally ignore it or use it only if they want to change it from the default value.

The default argument is included to make function calls easier, especially when those functions have many arguments with typical values. Not only is it much easier to write the calls, it's easier to read them, especially if the class creator can order the arguments so the least-modified defaults appear latest in the list.

An especially important use of default arguments is when you start out with a function with a set of arguments, and after it's been used for a while you discover you need to add arguments. By defaulting all the new arguments, you ensure that all client code using the previous interface is not disturbed.

exercises

1. Create a **message** class with a constructor that takes a single **char***
   with a default value. Create a private member **char***, and assume
   the constructor will be passed a static quoted string; simply assign
   the argument pointer to your internal pointer. Create two
   overloaded member functions called **print( )**: one that takes no
   arguments and simply prints the message stored in the object, and
   one that takes a **char*** argument, which it prints in addition to the
   internal message. Does it make sense to use this approach rather
   than the one used for the constructor?

2. Determine how to generate assembly output with your compiler,
   and run experiments to deduce the name-mangling scheme.

3. Modify STASH4.H and STASH4.CPP to use default arguments in the
   constructor. Test the constructor by making two different versions
   of a **stash** object.

4. Compare the execution speed of the **flags** class versus the
   BitVector class. To ensure there's no confusion about efficiency,
   first remove the **index**, **offset**, and **mask** clarification definitions in
   set( ), **clear( )** and **read( )** by combining them into a single
   statement that performs the appropriate action. (Test the new code
   to make sure you haven't broken anything.)

5. Change FLAGS.CPP so it dynamically allocates the storage for the
   flags. Give the constructor an argument that is the size of the
   storage, and put a default of 100 on that argument. Make sure you
   properly clean up the storage in the destructor.

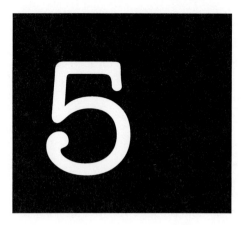

introduction to iostreams

So far in this book we've used the old reliable C standard I/O library, a perfect example of a library that begs to be turned into a class.

In fact, there's much more you can do with the general I/O problem than just take standard I/O and turn it into a class. Wouldn't it be nice if you could make all the usual "receptacles" — standard I/O, files and even blocks of memory — look the same, so you need to remember only one interface? That's the idea behind iostreams. They're much easier, safer, and often more efficient than the assorted functions from the Standard C stdio library.

Iostream is usually the first class library that new C++ programmers learn to use. This chapter explores the *use* of iostreams, so they can replace the C I/O functions through the rest of the book. In future chapters, you'll see how to set up your own classes so they're compatible with iostreams.

why iostreams?

You may wonder what's wrong with the good old C library. And why not "wrap" the C library in a class and be done with it? Indeed, there are situations when this is the perfect thing to do, when you want to make a C library a bit safer and easier to use. For example, suppose you want to make sure a stdio file is always safely opened and properly closed, without relying on the user to remember to call the **close( )** function:

```
//: FILECLAS.H -- Stdio files wrapped
#ifndef FILECLAS_H_
#define FILECLAS_H_
#include <stdio.h>

class file {
  FILE* f;
public:
  file(const char* fname, const char* mode="r");
  ~file();
  FILE* fp();
};
#endif // FILECLAS_H_
```

In C when you perform file I/O, you work with a naked pointer to a FILE **struct**, but this class wraps around the pointer and guarantees it is properly initialized and cleaned up using the constructor and destructor. The second constructor argument is the file mode, which defaults to "r" for "read."

To fetch the value of the pointer to use in the file I/O functions, you use the **fp( )** access function. Here are the member function definitions:

```
//: FILECLAS.CPP -- Stdio files wrapped
#include <stdlib.h>
#include "..\5\fileclas.h"

file::file(const char* fname, const char* mode) {
  f = fopen(fname, mode);
  if(f == NULL) {
    printf("%s: file not found\n", fname);
    exit(1);
  }
}

file::~file() {
  fclose(f);
}

FILE* file::fp() {
  return f;
}
```

The constructor calls **fopen( )**, as you would normally do, but it also checks to ensure the result isn't zero, which indicates a failure upon opening the file. If there's a failure, the name of the file is printed and **exit( )** is called.

The destructor closes the file, and the access function **fp( )** returns **f**. Here's a simple example using **class file**:

```
//: FCTEST.CPP -- Testing class file
#include <assert.h>
#include "..\5\fileclas.h"

main(int argc, char* argv[]) {
  assert(argc == 2);
```

```
    file f(argv[1]); // Opens and tests
    #define BSIZE 100
    char buf[BSIZE];
    while(fgets(buf, BSIZE, f.fp()))
      puts(buf);
  } // File automatically closed by destructor
```

You create the **file** object and use it in normal C file I/O function
calls by calling **fp( )**. When you're done with it, just forget about it,
and the file is closed by the destructor at the end of the scope.

true wrapping

Even though the FILE pointer is private, it isn't particularly safe
because **fp( )** retrieves it. The only effect seems to be guaranteed
initialization and cleanup, so why not make it public, or use a **struct**
instead? Notice that while you can get a copy of **f** using **fp( )**, you
cannot assign to **f** — that's completely under the control of the
class. Of course, once the user has the pointer returned by **fp( )**, he
can still assign to the structure elements, so the safety is in
guaranteeing a valid FILE pointer rather than proper contents of the
structure.

If you want complete safety, you have to prevent the user from
direct access to the FILE pointer. This means some version of all the
normal file I/O functions will have to show up as class members, so
everything you can do with the C approach is available in the C++
class:

```
//: FULLWRAP.H -- Completely hidden file IO
#ifndef FULLWRAP_H_
#define FULLWRAP_H_
#include <stdio.h>

class File {
  FILE* f;
  FILE* F(); // Produces checked pointer to f
public:
```

```
    File(); // Create object but don't open file
    File(const char* path,
        const char* mode = "r");
    ~File();
    int open(const char* path,
            const char* mode = "r");
    int reopen(const char* path,
              const char* mode);
    int Getc();
    int Ungetc(int c);
    int Putc(int c);
    int puts(const char* s);
    char* gets(char* s, int n);
    int printf(const char* format, ...);
    size_t read(void* ptr, size_t size,
                size_t n);
    size_t write(const void* ptr,
                 size_t size, size_t n);
    int eof();
    int close();
    int flush();
    int seek(long offset, int whence);
    int getpos(fpos_t* pos);
    int setpos(const fpos_t* pos);
    long tell();
    void rewind();
    void setbuf(char* buf);
    int setvbuf(char* buf, int type, size_t sz);
    int error();
    void Clearerr();
};
#endif // FULLWRAP_H_
```

This class contains almost all the file I/O functions from STDIO.H.
vfprintf( ), is missing; it is used to implement the **printf( )** member
function.

File has the same constructor as in the previous example, and it also has a default constructor. The default constructor is important if you want to create an array of **File** objects or use a **File** object as a member of another class where the initialization doesn't happen in the constructor (but sometime after the enclosing object is created).

The default constructor sets the private **FILE** pointer **f** to zero. But now, before any reference to **f**, its value must be checked to ensure it isn't zero. This is accomplished with the last member function in the class, **F( )**, which is **private** because it is intended to be used only by other member functions. (We don't want to give the user direct access to the **FILE** structure in this class.)[1]

This is not a terrible solution by any means. It's quite functional, and you could imagine making similar classes for standard (console) I/O and for in-core formatting (reading/writing a piece of memory rather than a file or the console).

The big stumbling block is the run-time interpreter used for the variable-argument list functions. This is the code that parses through your format string at run time and grabs and interprets arguments from the variable argument list. It's a problem for four reasons.

1. Even if you use only a fraction of the functionality of the interpreter, the whole thing gets loaded. So if you say:

```
printf("%c", 'x');
```

you'll get the whole package, including the parts that print out floating-point numbers and strings. There's no option for reducing the amount of space used by the program.

---

[1] The implementation and test files for FULLWRAP are available in the freely distributed source code for this book. See preface for details.

2. Because the interpretation happens at run-time there's a performance overhead you can't get rid of. It's frustrating because all the information is *there* in the format string at compile time, but it's not evaluated until run time. However, if you could parse the arguments in the format string at compile time you could make hard function calls that have the potential to be much faster than a run-time interpreter (although the **printf( )** family of functions is usually quite well optimized).

3. A worse problem occurs because the evaluation of the format string doesn't happen until run-time: there can be no compile-time error checking. You're probably very familiar with this problem if you've tried to find bugs that came from using the wrong number or type of arguments in a **printf( )** statement. C++ makes a big deal out of compile-time error checking to find errors early and make your life easier. It seems a shame to throw it away for an I/O library, especially because I/O is used a lot.

4. For C++, the most important problem is that the **printf( )** family of functions is not particularly extensible. They're really designed to handle the four basic data types in C (**char, int, float, double** and their variations). You might think that every time you add a new class, you could add an overloaded **printf( )** and **scanf( )** function (and their variants for files and strings) but remember, overloaded functions must have different types in their argument lists and the **printf( )** family hides its type information in the format string and in the variable argument list. For a language like C++, whose goal is to be able to easily add new data types, this is an ungainly restriction.

iostreams to the rescue

All these issues make it clear that one of the first standard class libraries for C++ should handle I/O. Because "hello, world" is the first program just about everyone writes in a new language, and because I/O is part of virtually every program, the I/O library in C++

must be particularly easy to use. It also has the much greater challenge that it can never know all the classes it must accommodate, but it must nevertheless be adaptable to use any new class. Thus its constraints required that this first class be a truly inspired design.

This chapter won't look at the details of the design and how to add iostream functionality to your own classes (you'll learn that in a later chapter). First, you need to learn to use iostreams. In addition to gaining a great deal of leverage and clarity in your dealings with I/O and formatting, you'll also see how a really powerful C++ library can work.

sneak preview of operator overloading

Before you can use the iostreams library, you must understand one new feature of the language that won't be covered in detail until a later chapter. To use iostreams, you need to know that in C++ all the operators can take on different meanings. In this chapter, we're particularly interested in **<<** and **>>**. The statement "operators can take on different meanings" deserves some extra insight.

In Chapter 4, you learned how function overloading allows you to use the same function name with different argument lists. Now imagine that when the compiler sees an expression consisting of an argument followed by an operator followed by an argument, it simply calls a function. That is, an operator is simply a function call with a different syntax.

Of course, this is C++, which is very particular about data types. So there must be a previously declared function to match that operator and those particular argument types, or the compiler will not accept the expression.

What most people find immediately disturbing about operator overloading is the thought that maybe everything they know about operators in C is suddenly wrong. This is absolutely false. Here are two of the sacred design goals of C++:

Thinking in C++ *Bruce Eckel*

1. A program that compiles in C will compile in C++. The only compilation errors and warnings from the C++ compiler will result from the "holes" in the C language, and fixing these will require only local editing. (Indeed, the complaints by the C++ compiler usually lead you directly to undiscovered bugs in the C program.)

2. The C++ compiler will not secretly change the behavior of a C program by recompiling it under C++.

   Keeping these goals in mind will help answer a lot of questions; knowing there are no capricious changes to C when moving to C++ helps make the transition easy. In particular, operators for built-in types won't suddenly start working differently — you cannot change their meaning. Overloaded operators can be created only where new data types are involved. So you can create a new overloaded operator for a new class, but the expression

```
1 << 4;
```

   won't suddenly change its meaning, and the illegal code

```
1.414 << 1;
```

   won't suddenly start working.

inserters and extractors

In the iostreams library, two operators have been overloaded to make the use of iostreams easy. The operator **<<** is often referred to as an *inserter* for iostreams, and the operator **>>** is often referred to as an *extractor*.

A *stream* is an object that formats and holds bytes. You can have an input stream (*istream*) or an output stream (*ostream*). There are different types of istreams and ostreams: *ifstreams* and *ofstreams* for files, *istrstreams* , and *ostrstreams* for **char*** memory (in-core formatting), and *istringstreams* & *ostringstreams* for interfacing with the Standard C++ **string** class. All these stream objects have the same interface, regardless of whether you're working with a file, standard I/O, a piece of memory or a **string** object. The single interface you learn also works for extensions added to support new classes.

If a stream is capable of producing bytes (an istream), you can get information from the stream using an extractor. The extractor produces and formats the type of information that's expected by the destination object. To see an example of this, you can use the **cin** object, which is the iostream equivalent of **stdin** in C, that is, redirectable standard input. This object is pre-defined whenever you include the IOSTREAM.H header file. (Thus, the iostream library is automatically linked with most compilers.)

```
int i;
cin >> i;

float f;
cin >> f;

char c;
cin >> c;

char buf[100];
cin >> buf;
```

There's an overloaded operator **>>** for every data type you can use as the right-hand argument of **>>** in an iostream statement. (You can also overload your own, which you'll see in a later chapter.)

To find out what you have in the various variables, you can use the **cout** object (corresponding to standard output; there's also a **cerr** object corresponding to standard error) with the inserter **<<**:

```
cout << "i = ";
cout << i;
cout << "\n";
cout << "f = ";
cout << f;
cout << "\n";
```

Thinking in C++ *Bruce Eckel*

```
cout << "c = ";
cout << c;
cout << "\n";
cout << "buf = ";
cout << buf;
cout << "\n";
```

This is notably tedious, and doesn't seem like much of an improvement over **printf( )**, type checking or no. Fortunately, the overloaded inserters and extractors in iostreams are designed to be chained together into a complex expression that is much easier to write:

```
cout << "i = " << i << endl;
cout << "f = " << f << endl;
cout << "c = " << c << endl;
cout << "buf = " << buf << endl;
```

You'll understand how this can happen in a later chapter, but for now it's sufficient to take the attitude of a class user and just know it works that way.

manipulators

One new element has been added here: a *manipulator* called **endl**. A manipulator acts on the stream itself; in this case it inserts a newline and *flushes* the stream (puts out all pending characters that have been stored in the internal stream buffer but not yet output). You can also just flush the stream:

```
cout << flush;
```

There are additional basic manipulators that will change the number base to **oct** (octal), **dec** (decimal) or **hex** (hexadecimal):

```
cout << hex << "0x" << i << endl;
```

There's a manipulator for extraction that "eats" white space:

```
cin >> ws;
```

---

and a manipulator called **ends**, which is like **endl**, only for strstreams (covered in a while). These are all the manipulators in IOSTREAM.H, but there are more in IOMANIP.H you'll see later in the chapter.

common usage

Although **cin** and the extractor **>>** provide a nice balance to **cout** and the inserter **<<**, in practice using formatted input routines, especially with standard input, has the same problems you run into with **scanf( )**. If the input produces an unexpected value, the process is skewed, and it's very difficult to recover. In addition, formatted input defaults to whitespace delimiters. So if you collect the above code fragments into a program

```
//: IOSEXAMP.CPP -- Iostream examples
#include <iostream.h>

main() {
   int i;
   cin >> i;

   float f;
   cin >> f;

   char c;
   cin >> c;

   char buf[100];
   cin >> buf;

   cout << "i = " << i << endl;
   cout << "f = " << f << endl;
   cout << "c = " << c << endl;
   cout << "buf = " << buf << endl;

   cout << flush;
```

```
    cout << hex << "0x" << i << endl;
}
```

and give it the following input,

```
12 1.4 c this is a test
```

you'll get the same output as if you give it

```
12
1.4
c
this is a test
```

and the output is, somewhat unexpectedly,

```
i = 12
f = 1.4
c = c
buf = this
0xc
```

Notice that **buf** got only the first word because the input routine looked for a space to delimit the input, which it saw after "this." In addition, if the continuous input string is longer than the storage allocated for **buf**, you'll overrun the buffer.

It seems **cin** and the extractor are provided only for completeness, and this is probably a good way to look at it. In practice, you'll usually want to get your input a line at a time as a sequence of characters and then scan them and perform conversions once they're safely in a buffer. This way you don't have to worry about the input routine choking on unexpected data.

Another thing to consider is the whole concept of a command-line interface. This has made sense in the past when the console was little more than a glass typewriter, but the world is rapidly changing to one where the graphical user interface (GUI) dominates. What is the meaning of console I/O in such a world? It makes much more sense to ignore **cin** altogether other than for very simple examples or tests, and take the following approaches:

1. If your program requires input, read that input from a file — you'll soon see it's remarkably easy to use files with iostreams. Iostreams for files still works fine with a GUI.

2. Read the input without attempting to convert it. Once you've got it someplace where it can't foul things up during conversion, then you can safely scan it.

3. Output is different. If you're using a GUI, **cout** doesn't work and you must send it to a file (which is identical to sending it to **cout**) or use the GUI facilities for data display. Otherwise it often makes sense to send it to **cout**. In both cases, the output formatting functions of iostreams are highly useful.

line-oriented input

To grab input a line at a time, you have two choices: the member functions **get( )** and **getline( )**. Both functions take three arguments: a pointer to a character buffer in which to store the result, the size of that buffer (so they don't overrun it), and the terminating character, to know when to stop reading input. The terminating character has a default value of '**\n**', which is what you'll usually use. Both functions store a zero in the result buffer when they encounter the terminating character in the input.

So what's the difference? Subtle, but important: **get( )** stops when it *sees* the delimiter in the input stream, but it doesn't extract it from the input stream. Thus, if you did another **get( )** using the same delimiter it would immediately return with no fetched input. (Presumably, you either use a different delimiter in the next **get( )** statement or a different input function.) **getline( )**, on the other hand, extracts the delimiter from the input stream, but still doesn't store it in the result buffer.

Generally, when you're processing a text file that you read a line at a time, you'll want to use **getline( )**.

Thinking in C++   *Bruce Eckel*

overloaded versions of get( )

get( ) also comes in three other overloaded versions: one with no arguments that returns the next character, using an **int** return value; one that stuffs a character into its **char** argument, using a *reference* (You'll have to jump forward to Chapter 9 if you want to understand it right this minute . . . .); and one that stores directly into the underlying buffer structure of another iostream object. That is explored later in the chapter.

reading raw bytes

If you know exactly what you're dealing with and want to move the bytes directly into a variable, array, or structure in memory, you can use **read( )**. The first argument is a pointer to the destination memory, and the second is the number of bytes to read. This is especially useful if you've previously stored the information to a file, for example, in binary form using the complementary **write( )** member function for an output stream. You'll see examples of all these functions later.

error handling

All the versions of **get( )** and **getline( )** return the input stream from which the characters came *except* for **get( )** with no arguments, which returns the next character or EOF. If you get the input stream object back, you can ask it if it's still OK. In fact, you can ask *any* iostream object if it's OK using the member functions **good( )**, **eof( )**, **fail( )**, and **bad( )**. These return state information based on the **eofbit** (indicates the buffer is at the end of sequence), the **failbit** (indicates some operation has failed because of formatting issues or some other problem that does not affect the buffer) and the **badbit** (indicates something has gone wrong with the buffer).

However, as mentioned earlier, the state of an input stream generally gets corrupted in weird ways only when you're trying to do input to specific types and the type read from the input is inconsistent with what is expected. Then of course you have the problem of what to do with the input stream to correct the problem. If you follow my advice and read input a line at a time or as a big glob of characters (with **read( )**) and don't attempt to use the input formatting functions except in simple cases, then all you're concerned with is whether you're at the end of the input (EOF). Fortunately, testing for this turns out to be simple and can be done inside of conditionals, such as **while(cin)** or **if(cin)**. For now you'll have to accept that when you use an input stream object in this context, the right value is safely, correctly and magically produced to indicate whether the object has reached the end of the input. You can also use the Boolean NOT operator **!**, as in **if(!cin)**, to indicate the stream is *not* OK; that is, you've probably reached the end of input and should quit trying to read the stream.

There are times when the stream becomes not-OK, but you understand this condition and want to go on using it. For example, if you reach the end of an input file, the **eofbit** and **failbit** are set, so a conditional on that stream object will indicate the stream is no longer good. However, you may want to continue using the file, by seeking to an earlier position and reading more data. To correct the condition, simply call the **clear( )** member function.[2]

file iostreams

Manipulating files with iostreams is much easier and safer than using STDIO.H in C. All you do to open a file is create an object; the constructor does the work. You don't have to explicitly close a file (although you can, using the **close( )** member function) because the destructor will close it when the object goes out of scope.

To create a file that defaults to input, make an **ifstream** object. To create one that defaults to output, make an **ofstream** object.

---

[2] Newer implementations of iostreams will still support this style of handling errors, but in some cases will also throw exceptions.

Here's an example that shows many of the features discussed so far. Note the inclusion of FSTREAM.H to declare the file I/O classes; this also includes IOSTREAM.H.

```cpp
//: STRFILE.CPP -- Stream I/O with files
// The difference between get() & getline()
#include <fstream.h>  // Includes iostream.h
#include <assert.h>
#define SZ 100  // Buffer size

main() {
  char buf[SZ];
  {
    ifstream in("strfile.cpp"); // Read
    assert(in); // Ensure successful open
    ofstream out("strfile.out"); // Write
    assert(out);
    int i = 1; // Line counter

    // A less-convenient approach for line input:
    while(in.get(buf, SZ)) { // Leaves \n in input
      in.get(); // Throw away next character (\n)
      cout << buf << endl; // Must add \n
      // File output just like standard I/O:
      out << i++ << ": " << buf << endl;
    }
  } // Destructors close in & out

  ifstream in("strfile.out");
  assert(in);
  // More convenient line input:
  while(in.getline(buf, SZ)) { // Removes \n
    char* cp = buf;
    while(*cp != ':')
      cp++;
    cp += 2; // Past ": "
    cout << cp << endl; // Must still add \n
```

```
        }
    }
```

The creation of both the **ifstream** and **ofstream** are followed by an **assert( )** to guarantee the file has been successfully opened. Here again the object, used in a situation where the compiler expects an integral result, produces a value that indicates success or failure. (To do this, an automatic type conversion member function is called. These are discussed in Chapter 10.)

The first **while** loop demonstrates the use of two forms of the **get( )** function. The first gets characters into a buffer and puts a zero terminator in the buffer when either **SZ – 1** characters have been read or the third argument (defaulted to '\n') is encountered. **get( )** leaves the terminator character in the input stream, so this terminator must be thrown away via **in.get( )** using the form of **get( )** with no argument, which fetches a single byte and returns it as an **int**. You can also use the **ignore( )** member function, which has two defaulted arguments. The first is the number of characters to throw away, and defaults to one. The second is the character at which the **ignore( )** function quits (after extracting it) and defaults to EOF.

Next you see two output statements that look very similar: one to **cout** and one to the file **out**. Notice the convenience here; you don't need to worry about what kind of object you're dealing with because the formatting statements work the same with all **ostream** objects. The first one echoes the line to standard output, and the second writes the line out to the new file and includes a line number.

To demonstrate **getline( )**, it's interesting to open the file we just created and strip off the line numbers. To ensure the file is properly closed before opening it to read, you have two choices. You can surround the first part of the program in braces to force the **out** object out of scope, thus calling the destructor and closing the file, which is done here. You can also call **close( )** for both files; if you want, you can even reuse the **in** object by calling the **open( )**

member function (you can also create and destroy the object dynamically on the heap as is in Chapter 11).

The second **while** loop shows how **getline( )** removes the terminator character (its third argument, which defaults to '\n') from the input stream when it's encountered. Although **getline( )**, like **get( )**, puts a zero in the buffer, it still doesn't insert the terminating character.

open modes

You can control the way a file is opened by changing a default argument. The following table shows the flags that control the mode of the file:

Flag	Function
ios::in	Opens an input file. Use this as an open mode for an **ofstream** to prevent truncating an existing file.
ios::out	Opens an output file. When used for an **ofstream** without **ios::app**, **ios::ate** or **ios::in**, **ios::trunc** is implied.
ios::app	Opens an output file for appending.
ios::ate	Opens an existing file (either input or output) and seeks the end.
ios::nocreate	Opens a file only if it already exists. (Otherwise it fails.)
ios::noreplace	Opens a file only if it does not exist. (Otherwise it fails.)
ios::trunc	Opens a file and deletes the old file, if it already exists.

Flag	Function
ios::binary	Opens a file in binary mode. Default is text mode.

These flags can be combined using a bitwise OR.

iostream buffering

Whenever you create a new class, you should endeavor to hide the details of the underlying implementation as possible from the user of the class. Try to show them only what they need to know and make the rest **private** to avoid confusion. Normally when using iostreams you don't know or care where the bytes are being produced or consumed; indeed, this is different depending on whether you're dealing with standard I/O, files, memory, or some newly created class or device.

There comes a time, however, when it becomes important to be able to send messages to the part of the iostream that produces and consumes bytes. To provide this part with a common interface and still hide its underlying implementation, it is abstracted into its own class, called **streambuf**. Each iostream object contains a pointer to some kind of **streambuf**. (The kind depends on whether it deals with standard I/O, files, memory, etc.) You can access the **streambuf** directly; for example, you can move raw bytes into and out of the **streambuf**, without formatting them through the enclosing iostream. This is accomplished, of course, by calling member functions for the **streambuf** object.

Currently, the most important thing for you to know is that every iostream object contains a pointer to a **streambuf** object, and the **streambuf** has some member functions you can call if you need to.

To allow you to access the **streambuf**, every iostream object has a member function called **rdbuf( )** that returns the pointer to the object's **streambuf**. This way you can call any member function for the underlying **streambuf**. However, one of the most interesting things you can do with the **streambuf** pointer is to connect it to another iostream object using the **<<** operator. This drains all the bytes from your object into the one on the left-hand side of the **<<**. This means if you want to move all the bytes from one iostream to another, you don't have to go through the tedium (and potential coding errors) of reading them one byte or one line at a time. It's a much more elegant approach.

For example, here's a very simple program that opens a file and sends the contents out to standard output (similar to the previous example):

```
//: STYPE.CPP -- Type a file to standard output
#include <fstream.h>
#include <assert.h>

main(int argc, char* argv[]) {
  assert(argc == 2); // Must have a command line
  ifstream in(argv[1]);
  assert(in); // Exits if it doesn't exist
  cout << in.rdbuf(); // Outputs entire file
}
```

After making sure there is an argument on the command line, an **ifstream** is created using this argument. The open will fail if the file doesn't exist, and this failure is caught by the **assert(in)**.

All the work really happens in the statement

```
cout << in.rdbuf();
```

which causes the entire contents of the file to be sent to **cout**. This is not only more succinct to code, it is often more efficient than moving the bytes one at a time.

using get( ) with a streambuf

There is a form of **get( )** that allows you to write directly into the **streambuf** of another object. The first argument is the destination **streambuf** (whose address is mysteriously taken using a *reference*, discussed in Chapter 9), and the second is the terminating character, which stops the **get( )** function. So yet another way to print a file to standard output is

```
//: SBUFGET.CPP -- Get directly into a streambuf
#include <fstream.h>

main() {
  ifstream in("sbufget.cpp");
  while(in.get(*cout.rdbuf()))
    in.ignore();
}
```

rdbuf( ) returns a pointer, so it must be dereferenced to satisfy the function's need to see an object. The **get( )** function, remember, doesn't pull the terminating character from the input stream, so it must be removed using **ignore( )** so **get( )** doesn't just bonk up against the newline forever (which it will, otherwise).

You probably won't need to use a technique like this very often, but it may be useful to know it exists.

seeking in iostreams

Each type of iostream has a concept of where its "next" character will come from (if it's an **istream**) or go (if it's an **ostream**). In some situations you may want to move this stream position. You can do it using two models: One uses an absolute location in the stream called the **streampos**; the second works like the Standard C library functions **fseek( )** for a file and moves a given number of bytes from the beginning, end, or current position in the file.

The **streampos** approach requires that you first call a "tell" function: **tellp( )** for an **ostream** or **tellg( )** for an **istream**. (The "p" refers to the "put pointer" and the "g" refers to the "get pointer.") This function returns a **streampos** you can later use in the single-argument version of **seekp( )** for an **ostream** or **seekg( )** for an **istream**, when you want to return to that position in the stream.

The second approach is a relative seek and uses overloaded versions of **seekp( )** and **seekg( )**. The first argument is the number of bytes to move: it may be positive or negative. The second argument is the seek direction:

ios::beg	From beginning of stream
ios::cur	Current position in stream
ios::end	From end of stream

Here's an example that shows the movement through a file, but remember, you're not limited to seeking within files, as you are with C and STDIO.H. With C++, you can seek in any type of iostream (although the behavior of **cin** & **cout** when seeking is undefined):

```
//: SEEKING.CPP -- Seeking in iostreams
#include <fstream.h>
#include <assert.h>

main(int argc, char* argv[]) {
  assert(argc == 2);
  ifstream in(argv[1]);
  assert(in); // File must already exist
  in.seekg(0, ios::end); // End of file
  streampos sp = in.tellg(); // Size of file
  cout << "file size = " << sp << endl;
  in.seekg(-sp/10, ios::end);
  streampos sp2 = in.tellg();
  in.seekg(0, ios::beg); // Start of file
  cout << in.rdbuf(); // Print whole file
```

```
  in.seekg(sp2); // Move to streampos
  // Prints the last 1/10th of the file:
  cout << endl << endl << in.rdbuf() << endl;
}
```

This program picks a file name off the command line and opens it as an **ifstream**. **assert( )** detects an open failure. Because this is a type of **istream**, **seekg( )** is used to position the "get pointer." The first call seeks zero bytes off the end of the file, that is, to the end. Because a **streampos** is a **typedef** for a **long**, calling **tellg( )** at that point also returns the size of the file, which is printed out. Then a seek is performed moving the get pointer 1/10 the size of the file — notice it's a negative seek from the end of the file, so it backs up from the end. If you try to seek positively from the end of the file, the get pointer will just stay at the end. The **streampos** at that point is captured into **sp2**, then a **seekg( )** is performed back to the beginning of the file so the whole thing can be printed out using the **streambuf** pointer produced with **rdbuf( )**. Finally, the overloaded version of **seekg( )** is used with the **streampos sp2** to move to the previous position, and the last portion of the file is printed out.

creating read/write files

Now that you know about the **streambuf** and how to seek, you can understand how to create a stream object that will both read and write a file. The following code first creates an **ifstream** with flags that say it's both an input and an output file. The compiler won't let you write to an **ifstream**, however, so you need to create an **ostream** with the underlying stream buffer:

```
ifstream in("filename", ios::in|ios::out);
ostream out(in.rdbuf());
```

You may wonder what happens when you write to one of these objects. Here's an example:

```
//: IOFILE.CPP -- Reading & writing one file
#include <fstream.h>
```

```
main() {
  ifstream in("iofile.cpp");
  ofstream out("iofile.out");
  out << in.rdbuf(); // Copy file
  in.close();
  out.close();
  // Open for reading and writing:
  ifstream in2("iofile.out",ios::in|ios::out);
  ostream out2(in2.rdbuf());
  cout << in2.rdbuf();   // Print whole file
  out2 << "Where does this end up?";
  out2.seekp(0, ios::beg);
  out2 << "And what about this?";
  in2.seekg(0, ios::beg);
  cout << in2.rdbuf();
}
```

The first five lines copy the source code for this program into a file
called **iofile.out**, and then close the files. This gives us a safe text
file to play around with. Then the aforementioned technique is used
to create two objects that read and write to the same file. In **cout
<< in2.rdbuf( )**, you can see the "get" pointer is initialized to the
beginning of the file. The "put" pointer, however, is set to the end of
the file because "Where does this end up?" appears appended to
the file. However, if the put pointer is moved to the beginning with a
seekp( ), all the inserted text *overwrites* the existing text. Both
writes are seen when the get pointer is moved back to the
beginning with a **seekg( )**, and the file is printed out. Of course, the
file is automatically saved and closed when **out2** goes out of scope
and its destructor is called.

strstreams

The third standard type of iostream works directly with memory
instead of a file or standard output. It allows you to use the same

---

reading and formatting functions to manipulate bytes in memory. On old computers the memory was referred to as *core* so this type of functionality is often called *in-core formatting*.

The class names for strstreams echo those for file streams. If you want to create a strstream to extract characters from, you create an **istrstream**. If you want to put characters into a strstream, you create an **ostrstream**.

String streams work with memory, so you must deal with the issue of where the memory comes from and where it goes. This isn't terribly complicated, but you must understand it and pay attention. The benefits of strstreams far outweigh this minor inconvenience.

user-allocated storage

The easiest approach to understand is when the user is responsible for allocating the storage. With **istrstream**s this is the only allowed approach. There are two constructors:

```
istrstream::istrstream(char* buf);
istrstream::istrstream(char* buf, int size);
```

The first constructor takes a pointer to a zero-terminated character array; you can extract bytes until the zero. The second constructor additionally requires the size of the array, which doesn't have to be zero-terminated. You can extract bytes all the way to **buf[size]**, whether or not you encounter a zero along the way.

When you hand an **istrstream** constructor the address of an array, that array must already be filled with the characters you want to extract and presumably format into some other data type. Here's a simple example:[3]

---

[3] Note the name has been truncated to handle the DOS limitation on file names. You may need to adjust the header file name if your system supports longer file names (or simply copy the header file).

```
//: ISTRING.CPP -- Input strstreams
#include <strstrea.h>

main() {
  istrstream s("1.414 47 This is a test");
  int i;
  float f;
  s >> i >> f; // Whitespace-delimited input
  char buf2[100];
  s >> buf2;
  cout << "i = " << i << ", f = " << f;
  cout << " buf2 = " << buf2 << endl;
  cout << s.rdbuf(); // Get the rest...
}
```

You can see that this is a more flexible and general approach to transforming character strings to typed values than the Standard C Library functions like **atof( )**, **atoi( )**, and so on.

The compiler handles the static storage allocation of the string in

```
istrstream s("1.414 47 This is a test");
```

You can also hand it a pointer to a zero-terminated string allocated on the stack or the heap.

In **s >> i >> f**, the first number is extracted into **i** and the second into **f**. This isn't "the first whitespace-delimited set of characters" because it depends on the data type it's being extracted into. For example, if the string were instead, "**1.414 47 This is a test**," then **i** would get the value one because the input routine would stop at the decimal point. Then **f** would get **0.414**. This could be useful if you want to break a floating-point number into a whole number and a fraction part. Otherwise it would seem to be an error.

As you may already have guessed, **buf2** doesn't get the rest of the string, just the next whitespace-delimited word. In general, it seems the best place to use the extractor in iostreams is when you know the exact sequence of data in the input stream and you're converting to some type other than a character string. However, if you want to extract the rest of the string all at once and send it to another iostream, you can use **rdbuf( )** as shown.

output strstreams

Output strstreams also allow you to provide your own storage; in this case it's the place in memory the bytes are formatted *into*. The appropriate constructor is

```
ostrstream::ostrstream(char*, int, int = ios::out);
```

The first argument is the preallocated buffer where the characters will end up, the second is the size of the buffer, and the third is the mode. If the mode is left as the default, characters are formatted into the starting address of the buffer. If the mode is either **ios::ate** or **ios::app** (same effect), the character buffer is assumed to already contain a zero-terminated string, and any new characters are added starting at the zero terminator.

The second constructor argument is the size of the array and is used by the object to ensure it doesn't overwrite the end of the array. If you fill the array up and try to add more bytes, they won't go in.

An important thing to remember about **ostrstream**s is that the zero terminator you normally need at the end of a character array *is not* inserted for you. When you're ready to zero-terminate the string, use the special manipulator **ends**.

Once you've created an **ostrstream** you can insert anything you want, and it will magically end up formatted in the memory buffer. Here's an example:

```
//: OSTRING.CPP -- Output strstreams
#include <strstrea.h>
#define SZ 100

main() {
```

```
    cout << "type an int, a float and a string:";
    int i;
    float f;
    cin >> i >> f;
    cin >> ws; // Throw away white space
    char buf[SZ];
    cin.getline(buf, SZ); // Get rest of the line
    // (cin.rdbuf() would be awkward)
    ostrstream os(buf, SZ, ios::app);
    os << endl;
    os << "integer = " << i << endl;
    os << "float = " << f << endl;
    os << ends;
    cout << buf;
    cout << os.rdbuf(); // Same effect
    cout << os.rdbuf(); // NOT the same effect
}
```

This is similar to the previous example in fetching the **int** and **float**. You might think the logical way to get the rest of the line is to use **rdbuf( )**; this works, but it's awkward because all the input including carriage returns is collected until the user presses control-Z (control-D on Unix) to indicate the end of the input. The approach shown, using **getline( )**, gets the input until the user presses the carriage return. This input is fetched into **buf**, which is subsequently used to construct the **ostrstream os**. If the third argument **ios::app** weren't supplied, the constructor would default to writing at the beginning of **buf**, overwriting the line that was just collected. However, the "append" flag causes it to put the rest of the formatted information at the end of the string.

You can see that, like the other output streams, you can use the ordinary formatting tools for sending bytes to the **ostrstream**. The only difference is that you're responsible for inserting the zero at the end with **ends**. Note that **endl** inserts a newline in the strstream, but no zero.

Now the information is formatted in **buf**, and you can send it out directly with **cout << buf**. However, it's also possible to send the information out with **os.rdbuf( )**. When you do this, the get pointer inside the **streambuf** is moved forward as the characters are output. For this reason, if you say **cout << os.rdbuf( )** a second time, nothing happens — the get pointer is already at the end.

automatic storage allocation

Output strstreams (but *not* **istrstream**s) give you a second option for memory allocation: they can do it themselves. All you do is create an **ostrstream** with no constructor arguments:

```
ostrstream A;
```

Now **A** takes care of all its own storage allocation on the heap. You can put as many bytes into **A** as you want, and if it runs out of storage, it will allocate more, moving the block of memory, if necessary.

This is a very nice solution if you don't know how much space you'll need, because it's completely flexible. And if you simply format data into the strstream and then hand its **streambuf** off to another iostream, things work perfectly:

```
A << "hello, world. i = " << i << endl << ends;
cout << A.rdbuf();
```

This is the best of all possible solutions. But what happens if you want the physical address of the memory that **A**'s characters have been formatted into? It's readily available — you simply call the **str( )** member function:

```
char* cp = A.str();
```

There's a problem now. What if you want to put more characters into **A**? It would be OK if you knew **A** had already allocated enough storage for all the characters you want to give it, but that's not true. Generally, **A** will run out of storage when you give it more characters, and ordinarily it would try to allocate more storage on the heap. This would usually require moving the block of memory. But the stream objects has just handed you the address of its memory block, so it can't very well move that block, because you're expecting it to be at a particular location.

The way an **ostrstream** handles this problem is by "freezing" itself. As long as you don't use **str( )** to ask for the internal **char***, you can add as many characters as you want to the **ostrstream**. It will allocate all the necessary storage from the heap, and when the object goes out of scope, that heap storage is automatically released.

However, if you call **str( )**, the **ostrstream** becomes "frozen." You can't add any more characters to it. Rather, you aren't *supposed* to — implementations are not required to detect the error. Adding characters to a frozen **ostrstream** results in undefined behavior. In addition, the **ostrstream** is no longer responsible for cleaning up the storage. You took over that responsibility when you asked for the **char*** with **str( )**.

To prevent a memory leak, the storage must be cleaned up somehow. There are two approaches. The more common one is to directly release the memory when you're done. To understand this, you need a sneak preview of two new keywords in C++: **new** and **delete**. As you'll see in Chapter 11, these do quite a bit, but for now you can think of them as replacements for **malloc( )** and **free( )** in C. The operator **new** returns a chunk of memory, and **delete** frees it. It's important to know about them here because virtually all memory allocation in C++ is performed with **new**, and this is also true with **ostrstream**. If it's allocated with **new**, it must be released with **delete**, so if you have an **ostrstream A** and you get the **char*** using **str( )**, the typical way to clean up the storage is

```
delete A.str();
```

This satisfies most needs, but there's a second, much less common way to release the storage: You can unfreeze the **ostrstream**. You do this by calling **freeze( )**, which is a member function of the

ostrstream's **streambuf. freeze( )** has a default argument of one, which freezes the stream, but an argument of zero will unfreeze it:

```
A.rdbuf()->freeze(0);
```

Now the storage is deallocated when **A** goes out of scope and its destructor is called. In addition, you can add more bytes to **A**. However, this may cause the storage to move, so you better not use any pointer you previously got by calling **str( )** — it won't be reliable after adding more characters.

The following example tests the ability to add more characters after a stream has been unfrozen:

```
//: WALRUS.CPP -- Freezing a strstream
#include <strstrea.h>

main() {
  ostrstream s;
  s << "'The time has come', the walrus said,";
  s << ends;
  cout << s.str() << endl; // String is frozen
  // S is frozen; destructor won't delete
  // the streambuf storage on the heap
  s.seekp(-1, ios::cur); // Back up before NULL
  s.rdbuf()->freeze(0); // Unfreeze it
  // Now destructor releases memory, and
  // you can add more characters (but you
  // better not use the previous str() value)
  s << " 'To speak of many things'" << ends;
  cout << s.rdbuf();
}
```

After putting the first string into **s**, an **ends** is added so the string can be printed using the **char*** produced by **str( )**. At that point, **s** is frozen. We want to add more characters to **s**, but for it to have any effect, the put pointer must be backed up one so the next character is placed on top of the zero inserted by **ends**. (Otherwise the string would be printed only up to the original zero.) This is accomplished with **seekp( )**. Then **s** is unfrozen by fetching the underlying **streambuf** pointer using **rdbuf( )** and calling **freeze(0)**. At this point **s** is like it was before calling **str( )**: We can add more characters, and cleanup will occur automatically, with the destructor.

It is *possible* to unfreeze an **ostrstream** and continue adding characters, but it is not common practice. Normally, if you want to add more characters once you've gotten the **char*** of a **ostrstream**, you create a new one, pour the old stream into the new one using **rdbuf( )** and continue adding new characters to the new **ostrstream**.

proving movement

If you're still not convinced you should be responsible for the storage of a **ostrstream** if you call **str( )**, here's an example that demonstrates the storage location is moved, therefore the old pointer returned by **str( )** is invalid:

```
//: STRMOVE.CPP -- Ostrstream memory movement
#include <strstrea.h>

main() {
  ostrstream s;
  s << "hi";
  char* old = s.str(); // Freezes s
  s.rdbuf()->freeze(0); // Unfreeze
  for(int i = 0; i < 100; i++)
    s << "howdy"; // Should force reallocation
  cout << "old = " << (void*)old << endl;
  cout << "new = " << (void*)s.str(); // Freezes
  delete s.str(); // Release storage
}
```

After inserting a string to **s** and capturing the **char*** with **str( )**, the string is unfrozen and enough new bytes are inserted to virtually assure the memory is reallocated and most likely moved. After

---

printing out the old and new **char*** values, the storage is explicitly released with **delete** because the second call to **str( )** froze the string again.

To print out addresses instead of the strings they point to, you must cast the **char*** to a **void***. The operator **<<** for **char*** prints out the string it is pointing to, while the operator **<<** for **void*** prints out the hex representation of the pointer.

It's interesting to note that if you don't insert a string to **s** before calling **str( )**, the result is zero. This means no storage is allocated until the first time you try to insert bytes to the **ostrstream**.

a better way

The Standard C++ **string** class and the associated **stringstream** class that works with it is a much-improved approach to the problem. When you use these two classes instead of **char*** and **strstream**, you don't need to worry about responsibility for storage — everything's automatically cleaned up for you.[4]

output stream formatting

The whole goal of this effort, and all these different types of iostreams, is to allow you to easily move and translate bytes from one place to another. It certainly wouldn't be very useful if you couldn't do all the formatting with the **printf( )** family of functions. In this section, you'll learn all the output formatting functions that are available for iostreams, so you can get your bytes the way you want them.

---

[4] At this writing, these classes were specified in the draft standard but not implemented for any available compiler.

The formatting functions in iostreams can be somewhat confusing at first because there's often more than one way to control the formatting: through both member functions and manipulators. To further confuse things, there is a generic member function to set state flags to control formatting, such as left- or right-justification, whether to use uppercase letters for hex notation, whether to always use a decimal point for floating-point values, and so on. On the other hand, there are specific member functions to set and read values for the fill character, the field width, and the precision.

In an attempt to clarify all this, the internal formatting data of an iostream is examined first, along with the member functions that can modify that data. (Everything can be controlled through the member functions.) The manipulators are covered separately.

internal formatting data

The class **ios** (which you can see in the header file IOSTREAM.H) contains data members to store all the formatting data pertaining to that stream. Some of this data has a range of values and is stored in variables: the floating-point precision, the output field width, and the character used to pad the output (normally a space). The rest of the formatting is determined by flags, which are usually combined to save space and are referred to collectively as the *format flags*. You can find out the value of the format flags with the **ios::flags( )** member function, which takes no arguments and returns a **long** (**typedef**ed to **fmtflags**) that contains the current format flags. All the rest of the functions make changes to the format flags and return the previous value of the format flags.

```
fmtflags ios::flags(fmtflags newflags);
fmtflags ios::setf(fmtflags ored_flag);
fmtflags ios::unsetf(fmtflags clear_flag);
fmtflags ios::setf(fmtflags bits, fmtflags field);
```

The first function forces *all* the flags to change, which you do sometimes. More often, you change one flag at a time using the remaining three functions.

The use of **setf( )** can seem more confusing: To know which overloaded version to use, you must know what type of flag you're changing. There are two types of flags: ones that are simply on or off, and ones that work in a group with other flags. The on/off flags are the simplest to understand because you turn them on with **setf(fmtflags)** and off with **unsetf(fmtflags)**. These flags are

on/off flag	effect
ios::skipws	Skip white space. (For input; this is the default.)
ios::showbase	Indicate the numeric base (dec, oct, or hex) when printing an integral value. The format used can be read by the C++ compiler.
ios::showpoint	Show decimal point and trailing zeros for floating-point values.
ios::uppercase	Display uppercase A-F for hexadecimal values and E for scientific values.
ios::showpos	Show plus sign (+) for positive values.
ios::unitbuf	"Unit buffering." The stream is flushed after each insertion.
ios::stdio	Synchronizes the stream with the C standard I/O system.

For example, to show the plus sign for **cout**, you say **cout.setf(ios::showpos)**. To stop showing the plus sign, you say **cout.unsetf(ios::showpos)**.

The last two flags deserve some explanation. You turn on unit buffering when you want to make sure each character is output as soon as it is inserted into an output stream. You could also use unbuffered output, but unit buffering provides better performance.

The **ios::stdio** flag is used when you have a program that uses both iostreams and the C standard I/O library (not unlikely if you're using C libraries). If you discover your iostream output and **printf( )** output are occurring in the wrong order, try setting this flag.

format fields

The second type of formatting flags work in a group. You can have only one of these flags on at a time, like the buttons on old car radios — you push one in, the rest pop out. Unfortunately this doesn't happen automatically, and you have to pay attention to what flags you're setting so you don't accidentally call the wrong **setf( )** function. For example, there's a flag for each of the number bases: hexadecimal, decimal, and octal. Collectively, these flags are referred to as the **ios::basefield**. If the **ios::dec** flag is set and you call **setf(ios::hex)**, you'll set the **ios::hex** flag, but you *won't* clear the **ios::dec** bit, resulting in undefined behavior. The proper thing to do is call the second form of **setf( )** like this: **setf(ios::hex, ios::basefield)**. This function first clears all the bits in the **ios::basefield**, *then* sets **ios::hex**. Thus, this form of **setf( )** ensures that the other flags in the group "pop out" whenever you set one. Of course, the **hex( )** manipulator does all this for you, automatically, so you don't have to concern yourself with the internal details of the implementation of this class or to even *care* that it's a set of binary flags. Later you'll see there are manipulators to provide equivalent functionality in all the places you would use **setf( )**.

Here are the flag groups and their effects:

ios::basefield	effect
ios::dec	Format integral values in base 10 (decimal) (default radix).

ios::basefield	effect
ios::hex	Format integral values in base 16 (hexadecimal).
ios::oct	Format integral values in base 8 (octal).

ios::floatfield	effect
ios::scientific	Display floating-point numbers in scientific format. Precision field indicates number of digits after the decimal point.
ios::fixed	Display floating-point numbers in fixed format. Precision field indicates number of digits after the decimal point.
"automatic" (Neither bit is set.)	Precision field indicates the total number of significant digits.

ios::adjustfield	effect
ios::left	Left-align values; pad on the right with the fill character.
ios::right	Right-align values. Pad on the left with the fill character. This is the default alignment.
ios::internal	Add fill characters after any leading sign or base indicator, but before the value.

width, fill and precision

The internal variables that control the width of the output field, the fill character used when the data doesn't fill the output field, and the precision for printing floating-point numbers are read and written by member functions of the same name.

function	effect
int ios::width( )	Reads the current width. (Default is 0.) Used for both insertion and extraction.
int ios::width(int n)	Sets the width, returns the previous width.
int ios::fill( )	Reads the current fill character. (Default is space.)
int ios::fill(int n)	Sets the fill character, returns the previous fill character.
int ios::precision( )	Reads current floating-point precision. (Default is 6.)
int ios::precision(int n)	Sets floating-point precision, returns previous precision. See **ios::floatfield** table for the meaning of "precision."

The fill and precision values are fairly straightforward, but width requires some explanation. When the width is zero, inserting a value will produce the minimum number of characters necessary to represent that value. A positive width means that inserting a value will produce at least as many characters as the width; if the value has less than width characters, the fill character is used to pad the field. However, the value will never be truncated, so if you try to print 123 with a width of two, you'll still get 123. The field width specifies a *minimum* number of characters; there's no way to specify a maximum number.

The width is also distinctly different because it's reset to zero by each inserter or extractor that could be influenced by its value. It's really not a state variable, but an implicit argument to the inserters and extractors. If you want to have a constant width, you have to call **width( )** after each insertion or extraction.

an exhaustive example

To make sure you know how to call all the functions previously discussed, here's an example that calls them all:

```
//: FORMAT.CPP -- Formatting functions
#include <fstream.h>
#define D(a) T << #a << endl; a
ofstream T("format.out");

main() {
  D(int i = 47;)
  D(float f = 2300114.414159;)
  char* s = "Is there any more?";

  D(T.setf(ios::unitbuf);)
  D(T.setf(ios::stdio);)

  D(T.setf(ios::showbase);)
  D(T.setf(ios::uppercase);)
  D(T.setf(ios::showpos);)
  D(T << i << endl;) // Default to dec
  D(T.setf(ios::hex, ios::basefield);)
  D(T << i << endl;)
  D(T.unsetf(ios::uppercase);)
  D(T.setf(ios::oct, ios::basefield);)
  D(T << i << endl;)
  D(T.unsetf(ios::showbase);)
  D(T.setf(ios::dec, ios::basefield);)
```

```
D(T.setf(ios::left, ios::adjustfield);)
D(T.fill('0');)
D(T << "fill char: " << T.fill() << endl;)
D(T.width(10);)
T << i << endl;
D(T.setf(ios::right, ios::adjustfield);)
D(T.width(10);)
T << i << endl;
D(T.setf(ios::internal, ios::adjustfield);)
D(T.width(10);)
T << i << endl;
D(T << i << endl;) // Without width(10)

D(T.unsetf(ios::showpos);)
D(T.setf(ios::showpoint);)
D(T << "prec = " << T.precision() << endl;)
D(T.setf(ios::scientific, ios::floatfield);)
D(T << endl << f << endl;)
D(T.setf(ios::fixed, ios::floatfield);)
D(T << f << endl;)
D(T.setf(0, ios::floatfield);) // Automatic
D(T << f << endl;)
D(T.precision(20);)
D(T << "prec = " << T.precision() << endl;)
D(T << endl << f << endl;)
D(T.setf(ios::scientific, ios::floatfield);)
D(T << endl << f << endl;)
D(T.setf(ios::fixed, ios::floatfield);)
D(T << f << endl;)
D(T.setf(0, ios::floatfield);) // Automatic
D(T << f << endl;)

D(T.width(10);)
T << s << endl;
D(T.width(40);)
T << s << endl;
D(T.setf(ios::left, ios::adjustfield);)
```

```
  D(T.width(40);)
  T << s << endl;

  D(T.unsetf(ios::showpoint);)
  D(T.unsetf(ios::unitbuf);)
  D(T.unsetf(ios::stdio);)
}
```

This example uses a trick to create a trace file so you can monitor what's happening. The macro **D(a)** uses the preprocessor "stringizing" to turn **a** into a string to print out. Then it reiterates **a** so the statement takes effect. The macro sends all the information out to a file called **T**, which is the trace file. The output is

```
int i = 47;
float f = 2300114.414159;
T.setf(ios::unitbuf);
T.setf(ios::stdio);
T.setf(ios::showbase);
T.setf(ios::uppercase);
T.setf(ios::showpos);
T << i << endl;
+47
T.setf(ios::hex, ios::basefield);
T << i << endl;
+0X2F
T.unsetf(ios::uppercase);
T.setf(ios::oct, ios::basefield);
T << i << endl;
+057
T.unsetf(ios::showbase);
T.setf(ios::dec, ios::basefield);
T.setf(ios::left, ios::adjustfield);
T.fill('0');
T << "fill char: " << T.fill() << endl;
fill char: 0
T.width(10);
```

```
+470000000
T.setf(ios::right, ios::adjustfield);
T.width(10);
0000000+47
T.setf(ios::internal, ios::adjustfield);
T.width(10);
+000000047
T << i << endl;
+47
T.unsetf(ios::showpos);
T.setf(ios::showpoint);
T << "prec = " << T.precision() << endl;
prec = 6
T.setf(ios::scientific, ios::floatfield);
T << endl << f << endl;

2.300115e+06
T.setf(ios::fixed, ios::floatfield);
T << f << endl;
2300114.500000
T.setf(0, ios::floatfield);
T << f << endl;
2.300115e+06
T.precision(20);
T << "prec = " << T.precision() << endl;
prec = 20
T << endl << f << endl;

2300114.5000000020000000000
T.setf(ios::scientific, ios::floatfield);
T << endl << f << endl;

2.30011450000000020000e+06
T.setf(ios::fixed, ios::floatfield);
T << f << endl;
2300114.5000000020000000000
T.setf(0, ios::floatfield);
```

```
T << f << endl;
2300114.5000000002000000000
T.width(10);
Is there any more?
T.width(40);
000000000000000000000000Is there any more?
T.setf(ios::left, ios::adjustfield);
T.width(40);
Is there any more?00000000000000000000000
T.unsetf(ios::showpoint);
T.unsetf(ios::unitbuf);
T.unsetf(ios::stdio);
```

Studying this output should clarify your understanding of the iostream formatting member functions.

formatting manipulators

As you can see from the previous example, calling the member functions can get a bit tedious. To make things easier to read and write, a set of manipulators is supplied to duplicate the actions provided by the member functions.

Manipulators with no arguments are provided in IOSTREAM.H. These include **dec**, **oct**, and **hex** , which perform the same action as, respectively, **setf(ios::dec, ios::basefield)**, **setf(ios::oct, ios::basefield)**, and **setf(ios::hex, ios::basefield)**, albeit more succinctly. IOSTREAM.H[5] also includes **ws**, **endl**, **ends**, and **flush** and the additional set shown here:

----

[5] These only appear in the revised library; you won't find them in older implementations of iostreams.

manipulator	effect
showbase noshowbase	Indicate the numeric base (dec, oct, or hex) when printing an integral value. The format used can be read by the C++ compiler.
showpos noshowpos	Show plus sign (+) for positive values
uppercase nouppercase	Display uppercase A-F for hexadecimal values, and E for scientific values
showpoint noshowpoint	Show decimal point and trailing zeros for floating-point values.
skipws noskipws	Skip white space on input.
left right internal	Left-align, pad on right. Right-align, pad on left. Fill between leading sign or base indicator and value.
scientific fixed	Use scientific notation **setprecision( )** or **ios::precision( )** sets number of places after the decimal point.

manipulators with arguments

If you are using manipulators with arguments, you must also include the header file IOMANIP.H. This contains code to solve the general problem of creating manipulators with arguments. In addition, it has six predefined manipulators:

manipulator	effect
setiosflags (fmtflags n)	Sets only the format flags specified by n. Setting remains in effect until the next change, like **ios::setf( )**.
resetiosflags(fmtflags n)	Clears only the format flags specified by n. Setting remains in effect until the next change, like **ios::unsetf( )**.
setbase(base n)	Changes base to n, where n is 10, 8, or 16. (Anything else results in 0.) If n is zero, output is base 10, but input uses the C conventions: 10 is 10, 010 is 8, and 0xf is 15. You might as well use **dec**, **oct**, and **hex** for output.
setfill(char n)	Changes the fill character to n, like **ios::fill( )**.
setprecision(int n)	Changes the precision to n, like **ios::precision( )**.
setw(int n)	Changes the field width to n, like **ios::width( )**.

If you're using a lot of inserters, you can see how this can clean things up. As an example, here's the previous program rewritten to use the manipulators. (The macro has been removed to make it easier to read.)

```
//: MANIPS.CPP -- FORMAT.CPP using manipulators
#include <fstream.h>
#include <iomanip.h>

main() {
  ofstream T("trace.out");
  int i = 47;
  float f = 2300114.414159;
  char* s = "Is there any more?";

  T << setiosflags(
        ios::unitbuf | ios::stdio
        | ios::showbase | ios::uppercase
        | ios::showpos
      );
  T << i << endl; // Default to dec
  T << hex << i << endl;
  T << resetiosflags(ios::uppercase)
    << oct << i << endl;
  T.setf(ios::left, ios::adjustfield);
  T << resetiosflags(ios::showbase)
    << dec << setfill('0');
  T << "fill char: " << T.fill() << endl;
  T << setw(10) << i << endl;
  T.setf(ios::right, ios::adjustfield);
  T << setw(10) << i << endl;
  T.setf(ios::internal, ios::adjustfield);
  T << setw(10) << i << endl;
  T << i << endl; // Without setw(10)

  T << resetiosflags(ios::showpos)
    << setiosflags(ios::showpoint)
    << "prec = " << T.precision() << endl;
  T.setf(ios::scientific, ios::floatfield);
  T << f << endl;
  T.setf(ios::fixed, ios::floatfield);
  T << f << endl;
```

```
T.setf(0, ios::floatfield); // Automatic
T << f << endl;
T << setprecision(20);
T << "prec = " << T.precision() << endl;
T << f << endl;
T.setf(ios::scientific, ios::floatfield);
T << f << endl;
T.setf(ios::fixed, ios::floatfield);
T << f << endl;
T.setf(0, ios::floatfield); // Automatic
T << f << endl;

T << setw(10) << s << endl;
T << setw(40) << s << endl;
T.setf(ios::left, ios::adjustfield);
T << setw(40) << s << endl;

T << resetiosflags(
      ios::showpoint | ios::unitbuf
      | ios::stdio
   );
}
```

You can see that a lot of the multiple statements have been condensed into a single chained insertion. Note the calls to **setiosflags( )** and **resetiosflags( )**, where the flags have been bitwise-ORed together. This could also have been done with **setf( )** and **unsetf( )** in the previous example.

creating manipulators

(Note: This section contains some material that will not be introduced until later chapters.) Sometimes you'd like to create your own manipulators, and it turns out to be remarkably simple. A zero-argument manipulator like **endl** is simply a function that takes as its argument an **ostream** reference (references are a different way to pass arguments, discussed in Chapter 9). The declaration for **endl** is

```
ostream& endl(ostream&);
```

Now, when you say:

```
cout << "howdy" << endl;
```

the **endl** produces the *address* of that function. So the compiler says "is there a function I can call that takes the address of a function as its argument?" There is a pre-defined function in IOSTREAM.H to do this; it's called an *applicator*. The applicator calls the function, passing it the **ostream** object as an argument.

You don't need to know how the applicator works to create your own manipulator; you only need to know the applicator exists. Here's an example that creates a manipulator called **nl** that emits a newline *without* flushing the stream:

```
//: NL.CPP -- Creating a manipulator
#include <iostream.h>

ostream& nl(ostream& os) {
  return os << '\n';
}

main() {
  cout << "newlines" << nl << "between" << nl
       << "each" << nl << "word" << nl;
}
```

The expression

```
os << '\n';
```

calls a function that returns **os**, which is what is returned from **nl**.[6]

People often argue that the **nl** approach shown above is preferable to using **endl** because the latter always flushes the output stream, which may incur a performance penalty.

effectors

As you've seen, zero-argument manipulators are quite easy to create. But what if you want to create a manipulator that takes arguments? The iostream library has a rather convoluted and confusing way to do this, but Jerry Schwarz, the creator of the iostream library, suggests[7] a scheme he calls *effectors*. An effector is a simple class whose constructor performs the desired operation, along with an overloaded **operator<<** that works with the class. Here's an example with two effectors. The first outputs a truncated character string, and the second prints a number in binary (the process of defining an overloaded **operator<<** will not be discussed until Chapter 10):

```
//: EFFECTOR.CPP -- Jerry Schwarz's "effectors"
#include<iostream.h>
#include <stdlib.h>
#include <string.h>
#include <assert.h>
#include <limits.h> // ULONG_MAX

// Put out a portion of a string:
class fixw {
  char* s;
public:
  fixw(const char* S, int width);
```

---

[6] Before putting **nl** into a header file, you should make it an **inline** function (see Chapter 7).

[7] In a private conversation.

```
    ~fixw();
    friend ostream& operator<<(ostream&, fixw&);
};

fixw::fixw(const char* S, int width) {
  s = (char*)malloc(width + 1);
  assert(s);
  strncpy(s, S, width);
  s[width] = 0; // Null-terminate
}

fixw::~fixw() { free(s); }

ostream& operator<<(ostream& os, fixw& fw) {
  return os << fw.s;
}

// Print a number in binary:
typedef unsigned long ulong;

class bin {
  ulong n;
public:
  bin(ulong N);
  friend ostream& operator<<(ostream&, bin&);
};

bin::bin(ulong N) { n = N; }

ostream& operator<<(ostream& os, bin& b) {
  ulong bit = ~(ULONG_MAX >> 1); // Top bit set
  while(bit) {
    os << (b.n & bit ? '1' : '0');
    bit >>= 1;
  }
  return os;
}
```

```
main() {
  char* string =
    "Things that make us happy, make us wise";
  for(int i = 1; i <= strlen(string); i++)
    cout << fixw(string, i) << endl;
  ulong x = 0xFEDCBA98UL;
  ulong y = 0x76543210UL;
  cout << "x in binary: " << bin(x) << endl;
  cout << "y in binary: " << bin(y) << endl;
}
```

The constructor for **fixw** creates a shortened copy of its **char***
argument, and the destructor releases the memory created for this
copy. The overloaded **operator<<** takes the contents of its second
argument, the **fixw** object, and inserts it into the first argument, the
ostream, then returns the **ostream** so it can be used in a chained
expression. When you use **fixw** in an expression like this:

```
cout << fixw(string, i) << endl;
```

a *temporary object* is created by the call to the **fixw** constructor,
and that temporary is passed to **operator<<**. The effect is that of a
manipulator with arguments.

The **bin** effector relies on the fact that shifting an unsigned number
to the right shifts zeros into the high bits. ULONG_MAX (the largest
unsigned long value, from the standard include file LIMITS.H) is
used to produce a value with the high bit set, and this value is
moved across the number in question (by shifting it), masking each
bit.

Initially the problem with this technique was that once you created
a class called **fixw** for **char*** or **bin** for **unsigned long**, no one else
could create a different **fixw** or **bin** class for their type. However,
with *namespaces* (covered in Chapter 8), this problem is
eliminated.

Thinking in C++ *Bruce Eckel*

iostream examples

In this section you'll see some examples of what you can do with all the information you've learned in this chapter. Although many tools exist to manipulate bytes (stream editors like **sed** and **awk** from Unix are perhaps the most well known, but a text editor also fits this category), they generally have some limitations. **sed** and **awk** can be slow and can only handle lines in a forward sequence, and text editors usually require human interaction, or at least learning a proprietary macro language. The programs you write with iostreams have none of these limitations: They're fast, portable, and flexible. It's a very useful tool to have in your kit.

code generation

The first examples concern the generation of programs that, coincidentally, fit the format used in this book. This provides a little extra speed and consistency when developing code. The first program creates a file to hold **main( )** (assuming it takes no command-line arguments and uses the iostream library):

```
//: MAKEMAIN.CPP -- Create a shell main() file
#include <fstream.h>
#include <strstrea.h>
#include <assert.h>
#include <string.h>
#include <ctype.h>

main(int argc, char* argv[]) {
  assert(argc == 2);
  // Don't replace it if it exists:
  ofstream mainfile(argv[1], ios::noreplace);
  assert(mainfile);
  istrstream name(argv[1]);
  ostrstream CAPname;
  char c;
```

```
  while(name.get(c))
    CAPname << char(toupper(c));
  CAPname << ends;
  mainfile << "//:" << ' ' << CAPname.rdbuf()
    << " -- " << endl
    << "#include <iostream.h>" << endl
    << endl
    << "main() {" << endl << endl
    << "}" << endl;
}
```

The file is opened using **ios::noreplace** to make sure you don't accidentally overwrite an existing file. Then the argument on the command line is used to create an **istrstream**, so the characters can be extracted one at a time and converted to upper case with the Standard C library macro **toupper( )**. This returns an **int** so it must be explicitly cast to a **char**. This name is used in the headline, followed by the remainder of the generated file.

maintaining class library source

The second example performs a more complex and useful task. Generally, when you create a class you think in library terms, and make a header file NAME.H for the class declaration and a file where the member functions are implemented, called NAME.CPP. These files have certain requirements: a particular coding standard (the program shown here will use the coding format for this book), and in the header file the declarations are generally surrounded by some preprocessor statements to prevent multiple declarations of classes. (Multiple declarations confuse the compiler — it doesn't know which one you want to use. They could be different, so it throws up its hands and gives an error message.)

This example allows you to create a new header-implementation pair of files, or to modify an existing pair. If the files already exist, it checks and potentially modifies the files, but if they don't exist, it creates them using the proper format.

```
//: CPPCHECK.CPP -- Configures .H & .CPP files
```

```
// To conform to style standard.
// Tests existing files for conformance
#include <fstream.h>
#include <strstrea.h>
#include <string.h>
#include <ctype.h>
#include <assert.h>
#define SZ 40   // Buffer sizes
#define BSZ 100

main(int argc, char* argv[]) {
  assert(argc == 2); // File set name
  enum bufs { base, header, implement,
    Hline1, guard1, guard2, guard3,
    CPPline1, include, bufnum };
  char b[bufnum][SZ];
  ostrstream osarray[] = {
    ostrstream(b[base], SZ),
    ostrstream(b[header], SZ),
    ostrstream(b[implement], SZ),
    ostrstream(b[Hline1], SZ),
    ostrstream(b[guard1], SZ),
    ostrstream(b[guard2], SZ),
    ostrstream(b[guard3], SZ),
    ostrstream(b[CPPline1], SZ),
    ostrstream(b[include], SZ),
  };
  osarray[base] << argv[1] << ends;
  // Find any '.' in the string using the
  // Standard C library function strchr():
  char* period = strchr(b[base], '.');
  if(period) *period = 0; // Strip extension
  // Force to upper case:
  for(int i = 0; b[base][i]; i++)
    b[base][i] = toupper(b[base][i]);
  // Create file names and internal lines:
  osarray[header] << b[base] << ".H" << ends;
```

```
osarray[implement] << b[base] << ".CPP" << ends;
osarray[Hline1] << "//:" << ' ' << b[header]
  << " -- " << ends;
osarray[guard1] << "#ifndef " << b[base]
                << "_H_" << ends;
osarray[guard2] << "#define " << b[base]
                << "_H_" << ends;
osarray[guard3] << "#endif // " << b[base]
                << "_H_" << ends;
osarray[CPPline1] << "//:" << ' '
                  << b[implement]
                  << " -- " << ends;
osarray[include] << "#include \""
                 << b[header] << "\"" <<ends;
// First, try to open existing files:
ifstream existh(b[header]),
         existcpp(b[implement]);
if(!existh) { // Doesn't exist; create it
  ofstream newheader(b[header]);
  newheader << b[Hline1] << endl
    << b[guard1] << endl
    << b[guard2] << endl << endl
    << b[guard3] << endl;
}
if(!existcpp) { // Create cpp file
  ofstream newcpp(implement);
  newcpp << b[CPPline1] << endl
    << b[include] << endl;
}
if(existh) { // Already exists; verify it
  strstream hfile; // Write & read
  ostrstream newheader; // Write
  hfile << existh.rdbuf() << ends;
  // Check that first line conforms:
  char buf[BSZ];
  if(hfile.getline(buf, BSZ)) {
    if(!strstr(buf, "//:") ||
```

```
              !strstr(buf, b[header]))
          newheader << b[Hline1] << endl;
    }
    // Ensure guard lines are in header:
    if(!strstr(hfile.str(), b[guard1]) ||
       !strstr(hfile.str(), b[guard2]) ||
       !strstr(hfile.str(), b[guard3])) {
        newheader << b[guard1] << endl
            << b[guard2] << endl
            << buf
            << hfile.rdbuf() << endl
            << b[guard3] << endl << ends;
    } else
      newheader << buf
        << hfile.rdbuf() << ends;
    // If there were changes, overwrite file:
    if(strcmp(hfile.str(),newheader.str())!=0){
      existh.close();
      ofstream newH(b[header]);
      newH << "//@//" << endl // change marker
        << newheader.rdbuf();
    }
    delete hfile.str();
    delete newheader.str();
  }
  if(existcpp) { // Already exists; verify it
    strstream cppfile;
    ostrstream newcpp;
    cppfile << existcpp.rdbuf() << ends;
    char buf[BSZ];
    // Check that first line conforms:
    if(cppfile.getline(buf, BSZ))
      if(!strstr(buf, "//:") ||
         !strstr(buf, b[implement]))
        newcpp << b[CPPline1] << endl;
    // Ensure header is included:
    if(!strstr(cppfile.str(), b[include]))
```

```
        newcpp << b[include] << endl;
      // Put in the rest of the file:
      newcpp << buf << endl; // First line read
      newcpp << cppfile.rdbuf() << ends;
      // If there were changes, overwrite file:
      if(strcmp(cppfile.str(),newcpp.str())!=0){
        existcpp.close();
        ofstream newCPP(b[implement]);
        newCPP << "//@//" << endl // change marker
          << newcpp.rdbuf();
      }
      delete cppfile.str();
      delete newcpp.str();
    }
}
```

This example requires a lot of string formatting in many different buffers. Rather than creating a lot of individually named buffers and **ostrstream** objects, a single set of names is created in the **enum bufs**. Then two arrays are created: an array of character buffers and an array of **ostrstream** objects built from those character buffers. Note that in the definition for the two-dimensional array of **char** buffers **b**, the number of **char** arrays is determined by **bufnum**, the last enumerator in **bufs**. When you create an enumeration, the compiler assigns integral values to all the **enum** labels starting at zero, so the sole purpose of **bufnum** is to be a counter for the number of enumerators in **buf**. The length of each string in **b** is **SZ**.

The names in the enumeration are **base**, the capitalized base file name without extension; **header**, the header file name; **implement**, the implementation file (CPP) name; **Hline1**, the skeleton first line of the header file; **guard1**, **guard2**, and **guard3**, the "guard" lines in the header file (to prevent multiple inclusion); **CPPline1**, the skeleton first line of the CPP file; and **include**, the line in the CPP file that includes the header file.

osarray is an array of **ostrstream** objects created using aggregate initialization and automatic counting. Of course, this is the form of the **ostrstream** constructor that takes two arguments (the buffer address and buffer size), so the constructor calls must be formed accordingly inside the aggregate initializer list. Using the **bufs** enumerators, the appropriate array element of **b** is tied to the corresponding **osarray** object. Once the array is created, the objects in the array can be selected using the enumerators, and the effect is to fill the corresponding **b** element. You can see how each string is built in the lines following the **ostrstream** array definition.

Once the strings have been created, the program attempts to open existing versions of both the header and CPP file as **ifstream**s. If you test the object using the operator '!' and the file doesn't exist, the test will fail. If the header or implementation file doesn't exist, it is created using the appropriate lines of text built earlier.

If the files *do* exist, then they are verified to ensure the proper format is followed. In both cases, a **strstream** is created and the whole file is read in; then the first line is read and checked to make sure it follows the format by seeing if it contains both a "//:" and the name of the file. This is accomplished with the Standard C library function **strstr( )**. If the first line doesn't conform, the one created earlier is inserted into an **ostrstream** that has been created to hold the edited file.

In the header file, the whole file is searched (again using **strstr( )**) to ensure it contains the three "guard" lines; if not, they are inserted. The implementation file is checked for the existence of the line that includes the header file (although the compiler effectively guarantees its existence).

In both cases, the original file (in its **strstream**) and the edited file (in the **ostrstream**) are compared to see if there are any changes. If there are, the existing file is closed, and a new **ofstream** object is created to overwrite it. The **ostrstream** is output to the file after a special change marker is added at the beginning, so you can use a

---

text search program to rapidly find any files that need reviewing to make additional changes.

detecting compiler errors

All the code in this book is designed to compile as shown without errors. Any line of code that should generate a compile-time error is commented out with the special comment sequence "//!". The following program will remove these special comments and append a numbered comment to the line, so that when you run your compiler it should generate error messages and you should see all the numbers appear when you compile all the files. It also appends the modified line to a special file so you can easily locate any lines that don't generate errors:

```
//: SHOWERR.CPP -- Un-comment error generators
#include <fstream.h>
#include <strstrea.h>
#include <stdio.h>
#include <string.h>
#include <ctype.h>
#include <assert.h>
char* marker = "//!";

char* usage =
"usage: showerr filename chapnum\n"
"where filename is a C++ source file\n"
"and chapnum is the chapter name it's in.\n"
"Finds lines commented with //! and removes\n"
"comment, appending //(#) where # is unique\n"
"across all files, so you can determine\n"
"if your compiler finds the error.\n"
"showerr /r\n"
"resets the unique counter.";

// File containing error number counter:
char* errnum = "..\\errnum.txt";
// File containing error lines:
```

```
char* errfile = "..\\errlines.txt";
ofstream errlines(errfile,ios::app);

main(int argc, char* argv[]) {
  if(argc < 2) {
    cerr << usage << endl;
    return 1;
  }
  if(argv[1][0] == '/' || argv[1][0] == '-') {
    // Allow for other switches:
    switch(argv[1][1]) {
      case 'r': case 'R':
        cout << "reset counter" << endl;
        remove(errnum); // Delete files
        remove(errfile);
        return 0;
      default:
        cerr << usage << endl;
        return 1;
    }
  }
  char* chapter = argv[2];
  strstream edited; // Edited file
  int counter = 0;
  {
    ifstream infile(argv[1]);
    assert(infile);
    ifstream count(errnum);
    if(count) count >> counter;
    int linecount = 0;
    #define sz 255
    char buf[sz];
    while(infile.getline(buf, sz)) {
      linecount++;
      // Eat white space:
      int i = 0;
      while(isspace(buf[i]))
```

```
        i++;
      // Find marker at start of line:
      if(strstr(&buf[i], marker) == &buf[i]) {
        // Erase marker:
        memset(&buf[i], ' ', strlen(marker));
        // Append counter & error info:
        ostrstream out(buf, sz, ios::ate);
        out << "//(" << ++counter << ") "
            << "Chapter " << chapter
            << " File: " << argv[1]
            << " Line " << linecount << endl
            << ends;
          edited << buf;
        errlines << buf; // Append error file
      } else
        edited << buf << "\n"; // Just copy
    }
  } // Closes files
  ofstream outfile(argv[1]); // Overwrites
  outfile << edited.rdbuf();
  ofstream count(errnum); // Overwrites
  count << counter; // Save new counter
}
```

The marker can be replaced with one of your choice.

Each file is read a line at a time, and each line is searched for the marker appearing at the head of the line; the line is modified and put into the error line list and into the **strstream edited**. When the whole file is processed, it is closed (by reaching the end of a scope), reopened as an output file and **edited** is poured into the file. Also notice the counter is saved in an external file, so the next time this program is invoked it continues to sequence the counter.

a simple datalogger

This example shows an approach you might take to log data to disk and later retrieve it for processing. The example is meant to produce a temperature-depth profile of the ocean at various points. To hold the data, a class is used:

```
//: DATALOG.H -- Datalogger record layout
#ifndef DATALOG_H_
#define DATALOG_H_
#include <time.h>
#include <iostream.h>
#define BSZ 10

class datapoint {
  tm Tm; // Time & day
  // Ascii degrees (*) minutes (') seconds ("):
  char Latitude[BSZ], Longitude[BSZ];
  double Depth, Temperature;
public:
  tm Time(); // read the time
  void Time(tm T); // set the time
  const char* latitude(); // read
  void latitude(const char* l); // set
  const char* longitude(); // read
  void longitude(const char* l); // set
  double depth(); // read
  void depth(double d); // set
  double temperature(); // read
  void temperature(double t); // set
  void print(ostream& os);
};
#endif // DATALOG_H_
```

The access functions provide controlled reading and writing to each of the data members. The **print( )** function formats the **datapoint** in a readable form onto an **ostream** object (the argument to **print( )**). Here's the definition file:

```
//: DATALOG.CPP -- Datapoint member functions
#include "..\5\datalog.h"
#include <iomanip.h>
#include <string.h>

tm datapoint::Time() { return Tm; }

void datapoint::Time(tm T) { Tm = T; }

const char* datapoint::latitude() {
  return Latitude;
}

void datapoint::latitude(const char* l) {
  Latitude[BSZ - 1] = 0;
  strncpy(Latitude, l, BSZ - 1);
}

const char* datapoint::longitude() {
  return Longitude;
}

void datapoint::longitude(const char* l) {
  Longitude[BSZ - 1] = 0;
  strncpy(Longitude, l, BSZ - 1);
}

double datapoint::depth() { return Depth; }

void datapoint::depth(double d) { Depth = d; }

double datapoint::temperature() {
  return Temperature;
}

void datapoint::temperature(double t) {
  Temperature = t;
```

```
      }

      void datapoint::print(ostream& os) {
        os.setf(ios::fixed, ios::floatfield);
        os.precision(4);
        os.fill('0'); // Pad on left with '0'
        os << setw(2) << Time().tm_mon << '\\'
           << setw(2) << Time().tm_mday << '\\'
           << setw(2) << Time().tm_year << ' '
           << setw(2) << Time().tm_hour << ':'
           << setw(2) << Time().tm_min << ':'
           << setw(2) << Time().tm_sec;
        os.fill(' '); // Pad on left with ' '
        os << " Lat:" << setw(9) << latitude()
           << ", Long:" << setw(9) << longitude()
           << ", depth:" << setw(9) << depth()
           << ", temp:" << setw(9) << temperature()
           << endl;
      }
```

In **print( )**, the call to **setf( )** causes the floating-point output to be fixed-precision, and **precision( )** sets the number of decimal places to four.

The default is to right-justify the data within the field. The time information consists of two digits each for the hours, minutes and seconds, so the width is set to two with **setw( )** in each case. (Remember that any changes to the field width affect only the next output operation, so **setw( )** must be given for each output.) But first, to put a zero in the left position if the value is less than 10, the fill character is set to '0'. Afterwards, it is set back to a space.

The latitude and longitude are zero-terminated character fields, which hold the information as degrees (here, '*' denotes degrees), minutes ('), and seconds("). You can certainly devise a more efficient storage layout for latitude and longitude if you desire.

generating test data

Here's a program that creates a file of test data in binary form (using **write( )**) and a second file in ASCII form using **datapoint::print( )**. You can also print it out to the screen but it's easier to inspect in file form.

```
//: DATAGEN.CPP -- Test data generator
#include <fstream.h>
#include <stdlib.h>
#include <string.h>
#include "..\5\datalog.h"

main() {
  ofstream data("data.txt");
  ofstream bindata("data.bin", ios::binary);
  time_t timer = time(NULL);  // Get time
  // Seed random generator:
  srand((unsigned)timer);
  for(int i = 0; i < 100; i++) {
    datapoint d;
    // Convert date/time to a structure:
    d.Time(*localtime(&timer));
    timer += 55; // Reading each 55 seconds
    d.latitude("45*20'31\"");
    d.longitude("22*34'18\"");
    // Zero to 199 meters:
    double newdepth  = rand() % 200;
    double fraction = rand() % 100 + 1;
    newdepth += double(1) / fraction;
    d.depth(newdepth);
    double newtemp = 150 + rand()%200; //Kelvin
    fraction = rand() % 100 + 1;
    newtemp += (double)1 / fraction;
    d.temperature(newtemp);
    d.print(data);
    bindata.write((unsigned char*)&d,
                sizeof(d));
```

```
        }
    }
```

The file DATA.TXT is created in the ordinary way as an ASCII file, but DATA.BIN has the flag **ios::binary** to tell the constructor to set it up as a binary file.

The Standard C library function **time( )**, when called with a zero argument, returns the current time as a **time_t** value, which is the number of seconds elapsed since 00:00:00 GMT, January 1 1970 (the dawning of the age of Aquarius?). The current time is the most convenient way to seed the random number generator with the Standard C library function **srand( )**, as is done here.

Sometimes a more convenient way to store the time is as a **tm** structure, which has all the elements of the time and date broken up into their constituent parts as follows:

```
struct tm {
    int tm_sec; // 0-59 seconds
    int tm_min; // 0-59 minutes
    int tm_hour; // 0-23 hours
    int tm_mday; // day of month
    int tm_mon; // 1-12 months
    int tm_year; // calendar year
    int tm_wday; // Sunday == 0, etc.
    int tm_yday; // 0-365 day of year
    int tm_isdst; // daylight savings?
};
```

To convert from the time in seconds to the local time in the **tm** format, you use the Standard C library **localtime( )** function, which takes the number of seconds and returns a pointer to the resulting **tm**. This **tm**, however, is a **static** structure inside the **localtime( )** function, which is rewritten every time **localtime( )** is called. To copy the contents into the **tm struct** inside **datapoint**, you might think you must copy each element individually. However, all you must do is a structure assignment, and the compiler will take care of the rest. This means the right-hand side must be a structure, not a pointer, so the result of **localtime( )** is dereferenced. The desired result is achieved with

```
d.Time = *localtime(&timer);
```

After this, the **timer** is incremented by 55 seconds to give an interesting interval between readings.

The latitude and longitude used are fixed values to indicate a set of readings at a single location. Both the depth and the temperature are generated with the Standard C library **rand( )** function, which returns a pseudorandom number between zero and the constant RAND_MAX. To put this in a desired range, use the modulus operator **%** and the upper end of the range. These numbers are integral; to add a fractional part, a second call to **rand( )** is made, and the value is inverted after adding one (to prevent divide-by-zero errors).

In effect, the DATA.BIN file is being used as a container for the data in the program, even though the container exists on disk and not in RAM. To send the data out to the disk in binary form, **write( )** is used. The first argument is the starting address of the source block — notice it must be cast to an **unsigned char*** because that's what the function expects. The second argument is the number of bytes to write, which is the size of the **datapoint** object. Because no pointers are contained in **datapoint**, there is no problem in writing the object to disk. If the object is more sophisticated, you must implement a scheme for *serialization* . (Most vendor class libraries have some sort of serialization structure built into them.)

verifying & viewing the data

To check the validity of the data stored in binary format, it is read from the disk and put in text form in DATA2.TXT, so that file can be compared to DATA.TXT for verification. In the following program, you can see how simple this data recovery is. After the test file is created, the records are read at the command of the user.

```
//: DATASCAN.CPP -- Verify and view logged data
```

```
#include <fstream.h>
#include <strstrea.h>
#include <iomanip.h>
#include <assert.h>
#include "..\5\datalog.h"

main() {
  ifstream bindata("data.bin", ios::binary);
  assert(bindata); // Make sure it exists
  // Create comparison file to verify data.txt:
  ofstream verify("data2.txt");
  datapoint d;
  while(bindata.read((unsigned char*)&d,
                       sizeof d))
    d.print(verify);
  bindata.clear(); // Reset state to "good"
  // Display user-selected records:
  int recnum = 0;
  // Left-align everything:
  cout.setf(ios::left, ios::adjustfield);
  // Fixed precision of 4 decimal places:
  cout.setf(ios::fixed, ios::floatfield);
  cout.precision(4);
  for(;;) {
    bindata.seekg(recnum* sizeof d, ios::beg);
    cout << "record " << recnum << endl;
    if(bindata.read((unsigned char*)&d,
                       sizeof d)) {
      cout << asctime(&(d.Time()));
      cout << setw(11) << "Latitude"
           << setw(11) << "Longitude"
           << setw(10) << "Depth"
           << setw(12) << "Temperature"
           << endl;
      // Put a line after the description:
      cout << setfill('-') << setw(43) << '-'
           << setfill(' ') << endl;
```

```
      cout << setw(11) << d.latitude()
            << setw(11) << d.longitude()
            << setw(10) << d.depth()
            << setw(12) << d.temperature()
            << endl;
    } else {
      cout << "invalid record number" << endl;
      bindata.clear(); // Reset state to "good"
    }
    cout << endl
          << "enter record number, x to quit:";
    char buf[10];
    cin.getline(buf, 10);
    if(buf[0] == 'x') break;
    istrstream input(buf, 10);
    input >> recnum;
  }
}
```

The **ifstream bindata** is created from DATA.BIN as a binary file, with the **ios::nocreate** flag on to cause the **assert( )** to fail if the file doesn't exist. The **read( )** statement reads a single record and places it directly into the **datapoint d**. (Again, if **datapoint** contained pointers this would result in meaningless pointer values.) This **read( )** action will set **bindata's failbit** when the end of the file is reached, which will cause the **while** statement to fail. At this point, however, you can't move the get pointer back and read more records because the state of the stream won't allow further reads. So the **clear( )** function is called to reset the **failbit**.

Once the record is read in from disk, you can do anything you want with it, such as perform calculations or make graphs. Here, it is displayed to further exercise your knowledge of iostream formatting.

The rest of the program displays a record number (represented by **recnum**) selected by the user. As before, the precision is fixed at four decimal places, but this time everything is left justified.

The formatting of this output looks different from before:

```
record 0
Tue Nov 16 18:15:49 1993
Latitude    Longitude  Depth      Temperature
--------------------------------------------
45*20'31"  22*34'18"  186.0172   269.0167
```

To make sure the labels and the data columns line up, the labels are put in the same width fields as the columns, using **setw( )**. The line in between is generated by setting the fill character to '-', the width to the desired line width, and outputting a single '-'.

If the **read( )** fails, you'll end up in the **else** part, which tells the user the record number was invalid. Then, because the **failbit** was set, it must be reset with a call to **clear( )** so the next **read( )** is successful (assuming it's in the right range).

Of course, you can also open the binary data file for writing as well as reading. This way you can retrieve the records, modify them, and write them back to the same location, thus creating a flat-file database management system. In my very first programming job, I also had to create a flat-file DBMS — but using BASIC on an Apple II. It took months, while this took minutes. Of course, it might make more sense to use a packaged DBMS now, but with C++ and iostreams you can still do all the low-level operations that are necessary in a lab.

summary

This chapter has given you a fairly thorough introduction to the iostream class library. In all likelihood, it is all you need to create programs using iostreams. (In later chapters you'll see simple examples of adding iostream functionality to your own classes.) However, you should be aware that there are some additional features in iostreams that are not used often, but which you can discover by looking at the iostream header files and by reading your compiler's documentation on iostreams.

exercises

1. Open a file by creating an **ifstream** object called **in**. Make an **ostrstream** object called **os**, and read the entire contents into the **ostrstream** using the **rdbuf( )** member function. Get the address of **os**'s **char*** with the **str( )** function, and capitalize every character in the file using the Standard C **toupper( )** macro. Write the result out to a new file, and **delete** the memory allocated by **os**.

2. Create a program that opens a file (the first argument on the command line) and searches it for any one of a set of words (the remaining arguments on the command line). Read the input a line at a time, and print out the lines (with line numbers) that match.

3. Write a program that adds a copyright notice to the beginning of all source-code files. This is a small modification to exercise 1.

4. Use your favorite text-searching program (**grep**, for example) to output the names (only) of all the files that contain a particular pattern. Redirect the output into a file. Write a program that uses the contents of that file to generate a batch file that invokes your editor on each of the files found by the search program.

constants

The concept of constant (expressed by the const keyword) was created to allow the programmer to draw a line between what changes and what doesn't.

This provides safety and control in a C++ programming project. Since its origin, it has taken on a number of different purposes. In the meantime it trickled back into the C language where its meaning was changed. All this can seem a bit confusing at first, and in this chapter you'll learn when, why, and how to use the **const** keyword. At the end there's a discussion of **volatile**, which is a near cousin to **const** (because they both concern change) and has identical syntax.

The first motivation for **const** seems to have been to eliminate the use of preprocessor **#define**s for value substitution. It has since been put to use for pointers, function arguments, and return types, and class objects and member functions. All of these have slightly different but conceptually compatible meanings and will be looked at in separate sections.

value substitution

When programming in C, the preprocessor is liberally used to create macros and to substitute values. Because the preprocessor simply does text replacement and has no concept nor facility for type checking, preprocessor value substitution introduces subtle problems that can be avoided in C++ by using **const** values.

The typical use of the preprocessor to substitute values for names in C looks like this:

```
#define BUFSIZE 100
```

BUFSIZE is a name that doesn't occupy storage and can be placed in a header file to provide a single value for all translation units that use it. It's very important to use value substitution instead of so-called "magic numbers" to support code maintenance. If you use magic numbers in your code, not only does the reader have no idea where the numbers come from or what they represent, but if you decide to change a value, you must perform hand editing, and you have no trail to follow to ensure you don't miss one.

Most of the time, **BUFSIZE** will behave like an ordinary variable, but not all the time. In addition, there's no type information. This can hide bugs that are very difficult to find. C++ uses **const** to eliminate these problems by bringing value substitution into the domain of the compiler. Now you can say

```
const bufsize = 100;
```

or the more explicit form,

```
const int bufsize = 100;
```

You can use **bufsize** anyplace where the compiler must know the value at compile time so it can perform *constant folding*, which means the compiler will reduce a complex constant expression to a simple one by performing the necessary calculations at compile time. This is especially important in array definitions:

```
char buf[bufsize];
```

You can use **const** for all the built-in types (**char**, **int**, **float**, and **double**) and their variants (as well as class objects, as you'll see later in this chapter). You should always use **const** instead of **#define** value substitution.

const in header files

To use **const** instead of **#define**, you must be able to place **const** definitions inside header files as you can with **#define**. This way, you can place the definition for a **const** in a single place and distribute it to a translation unit by including the header file. A **const** in C++ defaults to *internal linkage*; that is, it is visible only within the file where it is defined and cannot be seen at link time by other translation units. You must always assign a value to a **const** when you define it, *except* when you make an explicit declaration using **extern**:

```
extern const bufsize;
```

The C++ compiler avoids creating storage for a **const**, but instead holds the definition in its symbol table, although the above **extern** forces storage to be allocated, as do certain other cases, such as taking the address of a **const**. When the **const** is used, it is folded in at compile time.

Of course, this goal of never allocating storage for a **const** cannot always be achieved, especially with complicated structures. In these cases, the compiler creates storage, which prevents constant folding. This is why **const** must default to internal linkage, that is, linkage only *within* that particular translation unit; otherwise, linker errors would occur with complicated **const**s because they allocate storage in multiple CPP files. The linker sees the same definition in multiple object files, and complains. However, a **const** defaults to internal linkage, so the linker doesn't try to link those definitions across translation units, and there are no collisions. With built-in types, which are used in the majority of cases involving constant expressions, the compiler can always perform constant folding.

safety consts

The use of **const** is not limited to replacing **#define**s in constant expressions. If you initialize a variable with a value that is produced at run time and you know it will not change for the lifetime of that variable, it is good programming practice to make it a **const** so the compiler will give you an error message if you accidentally try to change it. Here's an example:

```
//: SAFECONS.CPP -- Using const for safety
#include <iostream.h>

const int i = 100;  // Typical constant
const int j = i + 10; // Value from const expr
long address = (long)&j; // Forces storage
char buf[j + 10]; // Still a const expression

main() {
  cout << "type a character & CR:";
  const char c = cin.get(); // Can't change
  const char c2 = c + 'a';
  cout << c2;
  // ...
}
```

You can see that **i** is a compile-time **const**, but **j** is calculated from **i**. However, because **i** is a **const**, the calculated value for **j** still comes from a constant expression and is itself a compile-time constant. The very next line requires the address of **j** and therefore forces the compiler to allocate storage for **j**. Yet this doesn't prevent the use of

j in the determination of the size of **buf** because the compiler knows **j** is **const** and that the value is valid even if storage was allocated to hold that value at some point in the program.

In **main( )**, you see a different kind of **const** in the identifier **c** because the value cannot be known at compile time. This means storage is required, and the compiler doesn't attempt to keep anything in its symbol table (the same behavior as in C). The initialization must still happen at the point of definition, and once the initialization occurs, the value cannot be changed. You can see that **c2** is calculated from **c** and also that scoping works for **const**s as it does for any other type — yet another improvement over the use of **#define**.

As a matter of practice, if you think a value shouldn't change, you should make it a **const**. This not only provides insurance against inadvertent changes, it also allows the compiler to generate more efficient code by eliminating storage and memory reads.

aggregates

It's possible to use **const** for aggregates, but you're virtually assured that the compiler will not be sophisticated enough to keep an aggregate in its symbol table, so storage will be allocated. In these situations, **const** means "a piece of storage that cannot be changed." However, the value cannot be used at compile time because the compiler is not required to know the contents of storage at compile time. Thus, you cannot say

```
//: CONSTAG.CPP -- Constants and aggregates

const int i[] = { 1, 2, 3, 4 };

//! float f[i[3]]; // Illegal

struct s { int i, j; };

const s S[] = { { 1, 2 }, { 3, 4 } };
```

```
//! double d[S[1].j]; // Illegal

main() {}
```

In an array definition, the compiler must be able to generate code that moves the stack pointer to accommodate the array. In both of the illegal definitions, the compiler complains because it cannot find a constant expression in the array definition.

differences with C

Constants were introduced in early versions of C++ while the Standard C specification was still being finished. It was then seen as a good idea and included in C. But somehow, **const** in C came to mean "an ordinary variable that cannot be changed." In C, it always occupies storage and its name is global. The C compiler cannot treat a **const** as a compile-time constant. In C, if you say

```
const bufsize = 100;
char buf[bufsize];
```

you will get an error, even though it seems like a rational thing to do. Because **bufsize** occupies storage somewhere, the C compiler cannot know the value at compile time. You can optionally say

```
const bufsize;
```

in C, but not in C++, and the C compiler accepts it as a declaration indicating there is storage allocated elsewhere. Because C defaults to external linkage for **const**s, this makes sense. C++ defaults to internal linkage for **const**s so if you want to accomplish the same thing in C++, you must explicitly change the linkage to external using **extern**:

```
extern const bufsize; // declaration only
```

This line also works in C.

The C approach to **const** is not very useful, and if you want to use a named value inside a constant expression (one that must be evaluated at compile time). C *forces* you to use **#define** in the preprocessor.

pointers

Pointers can be made **const**. The compiler will still endeavor to prevent storage allocation and do constant folding when dealing with **const** pointers, but these features seem less useful in this case. More importantly, the compiler will tell you if you attempt changes using such a pointer later in your code, which adds a great deal of safety.

When using **const** with pointers, you have two options: **const** can be applied to what the pointer is pointing to, or the **const** can be applied to the address stored in the pointer itself. The syntax for these is a little confusing at first but becomes comfortable with practice.

pointer to const

The trick with a pointer definition, as with any complicated definition, is to read it starting at the identifier and working your way out. The **const** specifier binds to the thing it is "closest to." So if you want to prevent any changes to the element you are pointing to, you write a definition like this:

```
const int* x;
```

Starting from the identifier, we read "**x** is a pointer, which points to a **const int**." Here, no initialization is required because you're saying that **x** can point to anything (that is, it is not **const**), but the thing it points to cannot be changed.

Here's the mildly confusing part. You might think that to make the pointer itself unchangeable, that is, to prevent any change to the address contained inside **x**, you would simply move the **const** to the other side of the **int** like this:

```
int const* x;
```

It's not all that crazy to think that this should read "**x** is a **const** pointer to an **int**." However, the way it *actually* reads is "**x** is an ordinary pointer to an **int** that happens to be **const**." That is, the **const** has bound itself to the **int** again, and the effect is the same as the previous definition. The fact that these two definitions are the same is the confusing point; to prevent this confusion on the part of your reader, you should probably stick to the first form.

const pointer

To make the pointer itself a **const**, you must place the **const** specifier to the right of the *****, like this:

```
int d = 1;
int* const x = &d;
```

Now it reads: "**x** is a pointer, which is **const** that points to an **int**." Because the pointer itself is now the **const**, the compiler requires that it be given an initial value that will be unchanged for the life of that pointer. It's OK, however, to change what that value points to by saying ***x = 2;**.

You can also make a **const** pointer to a **const** object using either of two legal forms:

```
int d = 1;
const int* const x = &d;   // (1)
int const* const x2 = &d; // (2)
```

Now neither the pointer nor the object can be changed.

Some people argue that the second form is more consistent because the **const** is always placed to the right of what it modifies. You'll have to decide which is clearer for your particular coding style.

formatting

This book makes a point of only putting one pointer definition on a line, and initializing each pointer at the point of definition whenever possible. Because of this, the formatting style of "attaching" the '*' to the data type is possible:

```
int* u = &w;
```

as if **int*** were a discrete type unto itself. This makes the code easier to understand, but unfortunately that's not actually the way things work. The '*' in fact binds to the identifier, not the type. It can be placed anywhere between the type name and the identifier. So you can do this:

```
int* u = &w, v = 0;
```

which creates an **int* u**, as before, and a nonpointer **int v**. Because readers often find this confusing, it is best to follow the form shown in this book.

assignment and type checking

C++ is very particular about type checking, and this extends to pointer assignments. You can assign the address of a non-**const** object to a **const** pointer because you're simply promising not to change something that is OK to change. However, you can't assign the address of a **const** object to a non-**const** pointer because then you're saying you might change the object via the pointer. Of course, you can always use a cast to force such an assignment, but this is bad programming practice because you are then breaking the **const**ness of the object, along with any safety promised by the **const**. For example:

```
int d = 1;
const int e = 2;
int* u = &d; // OK -- d not const
int* v = &e; // illegal -- e const
int* w = (int*)&e; // legal but bad practice
```

Although C++ helps prevent errors it, does not protect you from yourself if you want to break the safety mechanisms.

string literals

The place where strict **const**ness is not enforced is with string literals. You can say

```
char* cp = "howdy";
```

and the compiler will accept it without complaint. This is technically an error because a string literal (**"howdy"** in this case) is created by the compiler as a constant string, and the result of the quoted string is its starting address in memory.

So string literals are actually constant strings. Of course, the compiler lets you get away with treating them as non-**const** because there's so much existing C code that relies on this. However, if you try to change the values in a string literal, the behavior is undefined, although it will probably work on many machines.

function arguments & return values

The use of **const** to specify function arguments and return values is another place where the concept of constants can be confusing. If you are passing objects *by value*, specifying **const** has no meaning to the client (it means that the passed argument cannot be modified inside the function). If you are returning an object of a user-defined type by value as a **const**, it means the returned value cannot be modified. If you are passing and returning *addresses*, **const** is a promise that the destination of the address will not be changed.

passing by const value

You can specify that function arguments are **const** when passing them by value, such as

```
void f1(const int i) {
  i++; // illegal -- compile-time error
}
```

but what does this mean? You're making a promise that the original value of the variable will not be changed by the function **x( )**. However, because the argument is passed by value, you immediately make a copy of the original variable, so the promise to the client is implicitly kept.

Inside the function, the **const** takes on meaning: the argument cannot be changed. So it's really a tool for the creator of the function, and not the caller.

To avoid confusion to the caller, you can make the argument a **const** *inside* the function, rather than in the argument list. You could do this with a pointer, but a nicer syntax is achieved with the *reference*, a subject that will be fully developed in Chapter 9. Briefly, a reference is like a constant pointer that is automatically dereferenced, so it has the effect of being an alias to an object. To create a reference, you use the **&** in the definition. So the nonconfusing function definition looks like this:

```
void f2(int ic) {
  const int& i = ic;
  i++;  // illegal -- compile-time error
}
```

Again, you'll get an error message, but this time the **const**ness of the local object is not part of the function signature; it only has meaning to the implementation of the function so it's hidden from the client.

---

returning by const value

A similar truth holds for the return value. If you return by value from a function, as a **const**

```
const int g();
```

you are promising that the original variable (inside the function frame) will not be modified. And again, because you're returning it by value, it's copied so the original value is automatically not modified.

At first, this can make the specification of **const** seem meaningless. You can see the apparent lack of effect of returning **const**s by value in this example:

```
//: CONSTVAL.CPP -- Returning consts by value
// Has no meaning for built-in types

int f3() { return 1; }
const int f4() { return 1; }

main() {
  const int j = f3(); // Works fine
  int k = f4(); // But this works fine too!
}
```

For built-in types, it doesn't matter whether you return by value as a **const**, so you should avoid confusing the client programmer by leaving off the **const** when returning a built-in type by value.

Returning by value as a **const** becomes important when you're dealing with user-defined types. If a function returns a class object by value as a **const**, the return value of that function cannot be an lvalue (that is, it cannot be assigned to or otherwise modified). For example:

```
//: CONSTRET.CPP -- Constant return by value
// Result cannot be used as an lvalue
```

```
class X {
  int i;
public:
  X(int I = 0) : i(I) {}
  void modify() { i++; }
};

X f5() {
  return X();
}

const X f6() {
  return X();
}

void f7(X& x) { // Pass by non-const reference
  x.modify();
}

main() {
  f5() = X(1); // OK -- non-const return value
  f5().modify(); // OK
  f7(f5()); // OK
  // Causes compile-time errors:
//!  f6() = X(1);
//!  f6().modify();
//!  f7(f6());
}
```

f5( ) returns a non-**const X** object, while **f6( )** returns a **const X** object. Only the non-**const** return value can be used as an lvalue. Thus, it's important to use **const** when returning an object by value if you want to prevent its use as an lvalue.

The reason **const** has no meaning when you're returning a built-in type by value is that the compiler already prevents it from being an lvalue (because it's always a value, and not a variable). Only when you're returning objects of user-defined types by value does it become an issue.

The function **f7( )** takes its argument as a non-**const** *reference* (an additional way of handling addresses in C++ which is the subject of Chapter 9). This is effectively the same as taking a non-**const** pointer; it's just that the syntax is different.

temporaries

Sometimes, during the evaluation of an expression, the compiler must create *temporary objects*. These are objects like any other: they require storage and they must be constructed and destroyed. The difference is that you never see them — the compiler is responsible for deciding that they're needed and the details of their existence. But there is one thing about temporaries: they're automatically **const**. Because you usually won't be able to get your hands on a temporary object, telling it to do something that will change that temporary is almost certainly a mistake because you won't be able to use that information. By making all temporaries automatically **const**, the compiler informs you when you make that mistake.

The way the constness of class objects is preserved is shown later in the chapter.

passing and returning addresses

If you pass or return a pointer (or a reference), it's possible for the user to take the pointer and modify the original value. If you make the pointer a **const**, you prevent this from happening, which may be an important factor. In fact, whenever you're passing an address into a function, you should make it a **const** if at all possible. If you don't, you're excluding the possibility of using that function with a pointer to a **const**.

The choice of whether to return a pointer to a **const** depends on what you want to allow your user to do with it. Here's an example that demonstrates the use of **const** pointers as function arguments and return values:

```
//: CONSTP.CPP -- Constant pointer arg/return

void t(int*) {}

void u(const int* cip) {
//!  *cip = 2; // Illegal -- modifies value
   int i = *cip; // OK -- copies value
//!  int* ip2 = cip; // Illegal: non-const
}

const char* v() {
   // Returns address of static string:
   return "result of function v()";
}

const int* const w() {
   static int i;
   return &i;
}

main() {
   int x = 0;
   int* ip = &x;
   const int* cip = &x;
   t(ip);  // OK
//!  t(cip); // Not OK
   u(ip);  // OK
   u(cip); // Also OK
//!  char* cp = v(); // Not OK
   const char* ccp = v(); // OK
//!  int* ip2 = w(); // Not OK
   const int* const ccip = w(); // OK
   const int* cip2 = w(); // OK
//!  *w() = 1; // Not OK
```

}

The function **t( )** takes an ordinary non-**const** pointer as an
argument, and **u( )** takes a **const** pointer. Inside **u( )** you can see
that attempting to modify the destination of the **const** pointer is
illegal, but you can of course copy the information out into a non-
const variable. The compiler also prevents you from creating a non-
const pointer using the address stored inside a **const** pointer.

The functions **v( )** and **w( )** test return value semantics. **v( )** returns
a **const char*** that is created from a string literal. This statement
actually produces the address of the string literal, after the compiler
creates it and stores it in the static storage area. As mentioned
earlier, this string is technically a constant, which is properly
expressed by the return value of **v( )**.

The return value of **w( )** requires that both the pointer and what it
points to be a **const**. As with **v( )**, the value returned by **w( )** is valid
after the function returns only because it is **static**. You never want to
return pointers to local stack variables because they will be invalid
after the function returns and the stack is cleaned up. (Another
common pointer you might return is the address of storage
allocated on the heap, which is still valid after the function returns.

In **main( )**, the functions are tested with various arguments. You
can see that **t( )** will accept a non-**const** pointer argument, but if
you try to pass it a pointer to a **const**, there's no promise that **t( )**
will leave the pointer's destination alone, so the compiler gives you
an error message. **u( )** takes a **const** pointer, so it will accept both
types of arguments. Thus, a function that takes a **const** pointer is
more general than one that does not.

As expected, the return value of **v( )** can be assigned only to a
const pointer. You would also expect that the compiler refuses to
assign the return value of **w( )** to a non-**const** pointer, and accepts a
const int* const, but it might be a bit surprising to see that it also
accepts a **const int***, which is not an exact match to the return
type. Once again, because the value (which is the address

contained in the pointer) is being copied, the promise that the original variable is untouched is automatically kept. Thus, the second **const** in **const int* const** is only meaningful when you try to use it as an lvalue, in which case the compiler prevents you.

standard argument passing

In C it's very common to pass by value, and when you want to pass an address your only choice is to use a pointer. However, neither of these approaches is preferred in C++. Instead, your first choice when passing an argument is to pass by reference, and by **const** reference at that. To the client programmer, the syntax is identical to that of passing by value, so there's no confusion about pointers — they don't even have to think about the problem. For the creator of the class, passing an address is virtually always more efficient than passing an entire class object, and if you pass by **const** reference it means your function will not change the destination of that address, so the effect from the client programmer's point of view is exactly the same as pass-by-value.

Because of the syntax of references (it looks like pass-by-value) it's possible to pass a temporary object to a function that takes a reference, whereas you can never pass a temporary object to a function that takes a pointer — the address must be explicitly taken. So passing by reference produces a new situation that never occurs in C: a temporary, which is always **const**, can have its *address* passed to a function. This is why, to allow temporaries to be passed to functions by reference the argument must be a **const** reference. The following example demonstrates this:

```
//: CONSTTMP.CPP -- Temporaries are const

class X {};

X f() { return X(); } // Return by value

void g1(X&) {} // Pass by non-const reference
void g2(const X&) {} // Pass by const reference
```

```
main() {
  // Error: const temporary created by f():
//!  g1(f());
  // OK: g2 takes a const reference:
  g2(f());
}
```

f( ) returns an object of **class X** *by value*. That means when you immediately take the return value of **f( )** and pass it to another function as in the calls to **g1( )** and **g2( )**, a temporary is created and that temporary is **const**. Thus, the call in **g1( )** is an error because **g1( )** doesn't take a **const** reference, but the call to **g2( )** is OK.

classes

This section shows the two ways to use **const** with classes. You may want to create a local **const** in a class to use inside constant expressions that will be evaluated at compile time. However, the meaning of **const** is different inside classes, so you must use an alternate technique with enumerations to achieve the same effect.

You can also make a class object **const** (and as you've just seen, the compiler always makes temporary class objects **const**). But preserving the **const**ness of a class object is more complex. The compiler can ensure the **const**ness of a built-in type but it cannot monitor the intricacies of a class. To guarantee the **const**ness of a class object, the **const** member function is introduced: Only a **const** member function may be called for a **const** object.

const and enum in classes

One of the places you'd like to use a **const** for constant expressions is inside classes. The typical example is when you're creating an array inside a class and you want to use a **const** instead of a **#define** to establish the array size and to use in calculations involving the array. The array size is something you'd like to keep hidden inside the class, so if you used a name like **size**, for example, you could use that name in another class without a clash. The preprocessor treats all **#define**s as global from the point they are defined, so this will not achieve the desired effect.

Initially, you probably assume that the logical choice is to place a **const** inside the class. This doesn't produce the desired result. Inside a class, **const** partially reverts to its meaning in C. It allocates storage within each class object and represents a value that is initialized once and then cannot change. The use of **const** inside a class means "This is constant for the lifetime of the object." However, each different object may contain a different value for that constant.

Thus, when you create a **const** inside a class, you cannot give it an initial value. This initialization must occur in the constructor, of course, but in a special place in the constructor. Because a **const** must be initialized at the point it is created, inside the main body of the constructor the **const** must *already* be initialized. Otherwise you're left with the choice of waiting until some point later in the constructor body, which means the **const** would be un-initialized for a while. Also, there's nothing to keep you from changing the value of the **const** at various places in the constructor body.

the constructor initializer list

The special initialization point is called the *constructor initializer list*, and it was originally developed for use in inheritance (an object-oriented subject of a later chapter). The constructor initializer list — which, as the name implies, occurs only in the definition of the constructor — is a list of "constructor calls" that occur after the function argument list and a colon, but before the opening brace of the constructor body. This is to remind you that the initialization in the list occurs before any of the main constructor code is executed. This is the place to put all **const** initializations, so the proper form for **const** inside a class is

```
class fred {
  const size;
public:
  fred();
};

fred::fred() : size(100) {}
```

The form of the constructor initializer list shown above is at first confusing because you're not used to seeing a built-in type treated as if it has a constructor.

"constructors" for built-in types

As the language developed and more effort was put into making user-defined types look like built-in types, it became apparent that there were times when it was helpful to make built-in types look like user-defined types. In the constructor initializer list, you can treat a built-in type as if it has a constructor, like this:

```
class B {
  int i;
public:
  B(int I);
};

B::B(int I) : i(I) {}
```

This is especially critical when initializing **const** data members because they must be initialized before the function body is entered.

It made sense to extend this "constructor" for built-in types (which simply means assignment) to the general case. Now you can say

```
float pi(3.14159);
```

It's often useful to encapsulate a built-in type inside a class to guarantee initialization with the constructor. For example, here's an **integer** class:

```
class integer {
   int i;
public:
   integer(int I = 0);
};

integer::integer(int I) : i(I) {}
```

Now if you make an array of **integer**s, they are all automatically initialized to zero:

```
integer I[100];
```

This initialization isn't necessarily more costly than a **for** loop or **memset( )**. Many compilers easily optimize this to a very fast process.

compile-time constants in classes

Because storage is allocated in the class object, the compiler cannot know what the contents of the **const** are, so it cannot be used as a compile-time constant. This means that, for constant expressions inside classes, **const** becomes as useless as it is in C. You cannot say

```
class bob {
   const size = 100;  // illegal
   int array[size];   // illegal
//...
```

The meaning of **const** inside a class is "This value is **const** for the lifetime of this particular object, not for the class as a whole." How then do you create a class constant that can be used in constant expressions? A common solution is to use an untagged **enum** with no instances. An enumeration must have all its values established at compile time, it's local to the class, and its values are available for constant expressions. Thus, you will commonly see

```
class bunch {
   enum { size = 1000 };
```

```
  int i[size];
};
```

The use of **enum** here is guaranteed to occupy no storage in the object, and the enumerators are all evaluated at compile time. You can also explicitly establish the values of the enumerators:

```
enum { one = 1, two = 2, three };
```

With integral **enum** types, the compiler will continue counting from the last value, so the enumerator **three** will get the value 3.

Here's an example that shows the use of **enum** inside a container that represents a stack of string pointers:

```
//: SSTACK.CPP -- Enums inside classes
#include <string.h>
#include <iostream.h>

class StringStack {
  enum { size = 100 };
  const char* stack[size];
  int index;
public:
  StringStack();
  void push(const char* s);
  const char* pop();
};

StringStack::StringStack() : index(0) {
  memset(stack, 0, size * sizeof(char*));
}

void StringStack::push(const char* s) {
  if(index < size)
    stack[index++] = s;
}
```

```
const char* StringStack::pop() {
  if(index > 0) {
    const char* rv = stack[--index];
    stack[index] = 0;
    return rv;
  }
  return 0;
}

const char* iceCream[] = {
  "pralines & cream",
  "fudge ripple",
  "jamocha almond fudge",
  "wild mountain blackberry",
  "raspberry sorbet",
  "lemon swirl",
  "rocky road",
  "deep chocolate fudge"
};

const ICsz = sizeof iceCream/sizeof *iceCream;

main() {
  StringStack SS;
  for(int i = 0; i < ICsz; i++)
    SS.push(iceCream[i]);
  const char* cp;
  while((cp = SS.pop()) != 0)
    cout << cp << endl;
}
```

Notice that **push( )** takes a **const char*** as an argument, **pop( )** returns a **const char***, and **stack** holds **const char***. If this were not true, you couldn't use a **StringStack** to hold the pointers in **iceCream**. However, it also prevents you from doing anything that will change the objects contained by **StringStack**. Of course, not all containers are designed with this restriction.

Although you'll often see the **enum** technique in legacy code, C++ also has the **static const** which produces a more flexible compile-time constant inside a class. This is described in Chapter 8.

type checking for enumerations

C's enumerations are fairly primitive, simply associating integral values with names, but providing no type checking. In C++, as you may have come to expect by now, the concept of type is fundamental, and this is true with enumerations. When you create a named enumeration, you effectively create a new type just as you do with a class: The name of your enumeration becomes a reserved word for the duration of that translation unit.

In addition, there's stricter type checking for enumerations in C++ than in C. You'll notice this in particular if you have an instance of an enumeration **color** called **a**. In C you can say **a++** but in C++ you can't. This is because incrementing an enumeration is performing two type conversions, one of them legal in C++ and one of them illegal. First, the value of the enumeration is implicitly cast from a **color** to an **int**, then the value is incremented, then the **int** is cast back into a **color**. In C++ this isn't allowed, because **color** is a distinct type and not equivalent to an **int**. This makes sense because how do you know the increment of **blue** will even be in the list of colors? If you want to increment a **color**, then it should be a class (with an increment operation) and not an **enum**. Any time you write code that assumes an implicit conversion to an **enum** type, the compiler will flag this inherently dangerous activity.

Unions have similar additional type checking.

const objects & member functions

Class member functions can be made **const**. What does this mean? To understand, you must first grasp the concept of **const** objects.

A **const** object is defined the same for a user-defined type as a built-in type. For example:

```
const int i = 1;
const blob B(2);
```

Here, **B** is a **const** object of type **blob**. Its constructor is called with an argument of two. For the compiler to enforce **constness**, it must ensure that no data members of the object are changed during the object's lifetime. It can easily ensure that no public data is modified, but how is it to know which member functions will change the data and which ones are "safe" for a **const** object?

If you declare a member function **const**, you tell the compiler the function can be called for a **const** object. A member function that is not specifically declared **const** is treated as one that will modify data members in an object, and the compiler will not allow you to call it for a **const** object.

It doesn't stop there, however. Just *claiming* a function is **const** inside a class definition doesn't guarantee the member function definition will act that way, so the compiler forces you to reiterate the **const** specification when defining the function. (The **const** becomes part of the function signature, so both the compiler and linker check for **const**ness.) Then it enforces **const**ness during the function definition by issuing an error message if you try to change any members of the object *or* call a non-**const** member function. Thus, any member function you declare **const** is guaranteed to behave that way in the definition.

Preceding the function declaration with **const** means the return value is **const**, so that isn't the proper syntax. You must place the **const** specifier *after* the argument list. For example,

```
class X {
  int i;
public:
  int f() const;
};
```

The **const** keyword must be repeated in the definition using the same form, or the compiler sees it as a different function:

```
int X::f() const { return i; }
```

If **f( )** attempts to change **i** in any way *or* to call another member
function that is not **const**, the compiler flags it as an error.

Any function that doesn't modify member data should be declared
as **const**, so it can be used with **const** objects.

Here's an example that contrasts a **const** and non-**const** member
function:

```
//: QUOTER.CPP -- Random quote selection
#include <iostream.h>
#include <stdlib.h> // Random number generator
#include <time.h> // To seed random generator

class quoter {
  int lastquote;
public:
  quoter();
  int Lastquote() const;
  const char* quote();
};

quoter::quoter(){
  lastquote = -1;
  time_t t;
  srand((unsigned) time(&t)); // Seed generator
}

int quoter::Lastquote() const {
  return lastquote;
}

const char* quoter::quote() {
  static const char* quotes[] = {
    "Are we having fun yet?",
    "Doctors always know best",
```

```
    "Is it ... Atomic?",
    "Fear is obscene",
    "There is no scientific evidence "
    "to support the idea "
    "that life is serious",
  };
  const qsize = sizeof quotes/sizeof *quotes;
  int qnum = rand() % qsize;
  while(lastquote >= 0 && qnum == lastquote)
    qnum = rand() % qsize;
  return quotes[lastquote = qnum];
}

main() {
  quoter q;
  const quoter cq;
  cq.Lastquote(); // OK
//!  cq.quote(); // Not OK; non const function
  for(int i = 0; i < 20; i++)
    cout << q.quote() << endl;
}
```

Neither constructors nor destructors can be **const** member
functions because they virtually always perform some modification
on the object during initialization and cleanup. The **quote( )**
member function also cannot be **const** because it modifies the data
member **lastquote** in the return statement. However, **Lastquote( )**
makes no modifications, and so it can be **const** and can be safely
called for the **const** object **cq**.

mutable: bitwise vs. memberwise const

What if you want to create a **const** member function, but you'd still
like to change some of the data in the object? This is sometimes
referred to as the difference between *bitwise* **const** and
memberwise **const**. Bitwise **const** means that every bit in the
object is permanent, so a bit image of the object will never change.
Memberwise **const** means that, although the entire object is

conceptually constant, there may be changes on a member-by-member basis. However, if the compiler is told that an object is **const**, it will jealously guard that object. There are two ways to change a data member inside a **const** member function.

The first approach is the historical one and is called *casting away constness*. It is performed in a rather odd fashion. You take **this** (the keyword that produces the address of the current object) and you cast it to a pointer to an object of the current type. It would seem that **this** is *already* such a pointer, but it's a **const** pointer, so by casting it to an ordinary pointer, you remove the **const**ness for that operation. Here's an example:

```
//: CASTAWAY.CPP -- "Casting away" constness

class Y {
  int i, j;
public:
  Y() { i = j = 0; }
  void f() const;
};

void Y::f() const {
//!    i++; // Error -- const member function
     ((Y*)this)->j++; //OK: cast away const-ness
}

main() {
  const Y yy;
  yy.f(); // Actually changes it!
}
```

This approach works and you'll see it used in legacy code, but it is not the preferred technique. The problem is that this lack of **const**ness is hidden away in a member function of an object, so the user has no clue that it's happening unless she has access to the source code (and actually goes looking for it). To put everything out in the open, you should use the **mutable** keyword in the class declaration to specify that a particular data member may be changed inside a **const** object:

```
//: MUTABLE.CPP -- The "mutable" keyword

class Y {
  int i;
  mutable int j;
public:
  Y() { i = j = 0; }
  void f() const;
};

void Y::f() const {
//! i++; // Error -- const member function
    j++; // OK: mutable
}

main() {
  const Y yy;
  yy.f(); // Actually changes it!
}
```

Now the user of the class can see from the declaration which members are likely to be modified in a **const** member function.

ROMability

If an object is defined as **const**, it is a candidate to be placed in read-only memory (ROM), which is often an important consideration in embedded systems programming. Simply making an object **const**, however, is not enough — the requirements for ROMability are much more strict. Of course, the object must be bitwise-**const**, rather than memberwise-**const**. This is easy to see if memberwise **const**ness is implemented only through the **mutable** keyword, but probably not detectable by the compiler if **const**ness is cast away inside a **const** member function. In addition,

1. The **class** or **struct** must have no user-defined constructors or destructor.

2. There can be no base classes (covered in the future chapter on inheritance) or member objects with user-defined constructors or destructors.

The effect of a write operation on any part of a **const** object of a ROMable type is undefined. Although a suitably formed object may be placed in ROM, no objects are ever *required* to be placed in ROM.

volatile

The syntax of **volatile** is identical to that for **const**, but **volatile** means "This data may change outside the knowledge of the compiler." Somehow, the environment is changing the data (possibly through multitasking), and **volatile** tells the compiler not to make any assumptions about the data — this is particularly important during optimization. If the compiler says, "I read the data into a register earlier, and I haven't touched that register," normally it wouldn't need to read the data again. But if the data is **volatile**, the compiler cannot make such an assumption because the data may have been changed by another process, and it must reread the data rather than optimizing the code.

You can create **volatile** objects just as you create **const** objects. You can also create **const volatile** objects, which can't be changed by the programmer but instead change through some outside agency. Here is an example that might represent a class to associate with some piece of communication hardware:

```
//: VOLATILE.CPP -- The volatile keyword
```

```
class comm {
  const volatile unsigned char byte;
  volatile unsigned char flag;
  enum { bufsize = 100 };
  unsigned char buf[bufsize];
  int index;
public:
  comm();
  void isr() volatile;
  char read(int Index) const;
};

comm::comm() : index(0), byte(0), flag(0) {}

// Only a demo; won't actually work
// As an interrupt service routine:
void comm::isr() volatile {
  if(flag) flag = 0;
  buf[index++] = byte;
  // Wrap to beginning of buffer:
  if(index >= bufsize) index = 0;
}

char comm::read(int Index) const {
  if(Index < 0 || Index >= bufsize)
    return 0;
  return buf[Index];
}

main() {
  volatile comm Port;
  Port.isr(); // OK
//!  Port.read(0); // Not OK;
                // read() not volatile
}
```

As with **const**, you can use **volatile** for data members, member functions, and objects themselves. You can call only **volatile** member functions for **volatile** objects.

The reason that **isr( )** can't actually be used as an interrupt service routine is that in a member function, the address of the current object (**this**) must be secretly passed, and an ISR generally wants no arguments at all. To solve this problem, you can make **isr( )** a **static** member function, a subject covered in a future chapter.

The syntax of **volatile** is identical to **const**, so discussions of the two are often treated together. To indicate the choice of either one, the two are referred to in combination as the *c-v qualifier*.

summary

The **const** keyword gives you the ability to define objects, function arguments and return values, and member functions as constants, and to eliminate the preprocessor for value substitution without losing any preprocessor benefits. All this provides a significant additional form of type checking and safety in your programming. The use of so-called *const correctness* (the use of **const** anywhere you possibly can) has been a lifesaver for projects.

Although you can ignore **const** and continue to use old C coding practices, it's there to help you. Chapters 9 & 10 begin using references heavily, and there you'll see even more about how critical it is to use **const** with function arguments.

exercises

1. Create a class called **bird** that can **fly( )** and a class **rock** that can't. Create a **rock** object, take its address, and assign that to a **void***. Now take the **void***, assign it to a **bird***, and call **fly( )** through that pointer. Is it clear why C's permission to openly assign via a **void*** is a "hole" in the language?

2. Create a class containing a **const** member that you initialize in the constructor initializer list and an untagged enumeration that you use to determine an array size.

3. Create a class with both **const** and non-**const** member functions. Create **const** and non-**const** objects of this class, and try calling the different types of member functions for the different types of objects.

4. Create a function that takes an argument by value as a **const**; then try to change that argument in the function body.

5. Prove to yourself that the C and C++ compilers really do treat constants differently. Create a global **const** and use it in a constant expression; then compile it under both C and C++.

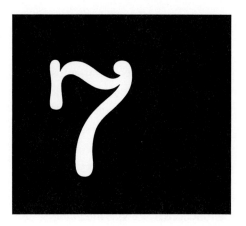

inline functions

One of the important features C++ inherits from C is efficiency. If the efficiency of C++ were dramatically less than C, there would be a significant contingent of programmers who couldn't justify its use.

In C, one of the ways to preserve efficiency is through the use of *macros*, which allow you to make what looks like a function call without the normal overhead of the function call. The macro is implemented with the preprocessor rather than the compiler proper, and the preprocessor replaces all macro calls directly with the macro code, so there's no cost involved from pushing arguments, making an assembly-language CALL, returning arguments, and performing an assembly-language RETURN. All the work is performed by the preprocessor, so you have the convenience and readability of a function call but it doesn't cost you anything.

There are two problems with the use of preprocessor macros in C++. The first is also true with C: A macro looks like a function call, but doesn't always act like one. This can bury difficult-to-find bugs. The second problem is specific to C++: The preprocessor has no permission to access **private** data. This means preprocessor macros are virtually useless as class member functions.

To retain the efficiency of the preprocessor macro, but to add the safety and class scoping of true functions, C++ has the *inline function*. In this chapter, we'll look at the problems of preprocessor macros in C++, how these problems are solved with inline functions, and guidelines and insights on the way inlines work.

preprocessor pitfalls

The key to the problems of preprocessor macros is that you can be fooled into thinking that the behavior of the preprocessor is the same as the behavior of the compiler. Of course, it was intended that a macro look and act like a function call, so it's quite easy to fall into this fiction. The difficulties begin when the subtle differences appear.

As a simple example, consider the following:

```
#define f (x) (x + 1)
```

Now, if a call is made to **f** like this

```
f(1)
```

the preprocessor expands it, somewhat unexpectedly, to the following:

```
(x) (x + 1)(1)
```

The problem occurs because of the gap between **f** and its opening parenthesis in the macro definition. When this gap is removed, you can actually *call* the macro with the gap

```
f (1)
```

and it will still expand properly, to

```
(1 + 1)
```

The above example is fairly trivial and the problem will make itself evident right away. The real difficulties occur when using expressions as arguments in macro calls.

There are two problems. The first is that expressions may expand inside the macro so that their evaluation precedence is different from what you expect. For example,

```
#define floor(x,b) x>=b?0:1
```

Now, if expressions are used for the arguments

```
if(floor(a&0x0f,0x07)) // ...
```

the macro will expand to

```
if(a&0x0f>=0x07?0:1)
```

The precedence of **&** is lower than that of **>=**, so the macro evaluation will surprise you. Once you discover the problem (and as a general practice when creating preprocessor macros) you can solve it by putting parentheses around everything in the macro definition. Thus,

```
#define floor(x,b) ((x)>=(b)?0:1)
```

Discovering the problem may be difficult, however, and you may not find it until after you've taken the proper macro behavior for granted. In the unparenthesized version of the preceding example, *most* expressions will work correctly, because the precedence of **>=** is lower than most of the operators like +, /, – –, and even the bitwise shift operators. So you can easily begin to think that it works with all expressions, including those using bitwise logical operators.

The preceding problem can be solved with careful programming practice: Parenthesize everything in a macro. The second difficulty is more subtle. Unlike a normal function, every time you use an argument in a macro, that argument is evaluated. As long as the macro is called only with ordinary variables, this evaluation is benign, but if the evaluation of an argument has side effects, then the results can be surprising and will definitely not mimic function behavior.

For example, this macro determines whether its argument falls within a certain range:

```
#define band(x)  (((x)>5 && (x)<10) ? (x) : 0)
```

As long as you use an "ordinary" argument, the macro works very much like a real function. But as soon as you relax and start believing it *is* a real function, the problems start. Thus,

```
//: MACRO.CPP -- Side effects with macros
#include <fstream.h>
#define band(x)  (((x)>5 && (x)<10) ? (x) : 0)

main() {
  ofstream out("macro.out");
  for(int i = 4; i < 11; i++) {
    int a = i;
    out << "a = " << a << endl << '\t';
    out << "band(++a)=" << band(++a) << endl;
    out << "\t a = " << a << endl;
  }
}
```

Here's the output produced by the program, which is not at all what you would have expected from a true function:

```
a = 4
```

```
          band(++a)=0
            a = 5
a = 5
          band(++a)=8
            a = 8
a = 6
          band(++a)=9
            a = 9
a = 7
          band(++a)=10
            a = 10
a = 8
          band(++a)=0
            a = 10
a = 9
          band(++a)=0
            a = 11
a = 10
          band(++a)=0
            a = 12
```

When **a** is four, only the first part of the conditional occurs, so the expression is evaluated only once, and the side effect of the macro call is that **a** becomes five, which is what you would expect from a normal function call in the same situation. However, when the number is within the band, both conditionals are tested, which results in two increments. The result is produced by evaluating the argument again, which results in a third increment. Once the number gets out of the band, both conditionals are still tested so you get two increments. The side effects are different, depending on the argument.

This is clearly not the kind of behavior you want from a macro that looks like a function call. In this case, the obvious solution is to make it a true function, which of course adds the extra overhead and may reduce efficiency if you call that function a lot. Unfortunately, the problem may not always be so obvious, and you can unknowingly get a library that contains functions and macros mixed together, so a problem like this can hide some very difficult-to-find bugs. For example, the **putc( )** macro in STDIO.H may evaluate its second argument twice. This is specified in Standard C. Also, careless implementations of **toupper( )** as a macro may evaluate the argument more than once, which will give you unexpected results with **toupper(*p++)**.[1]

macros and access

Of course, careful coding and use of preprocessor macros are required with C, and we could certainly get away with the same thing in C++ if it weren't for one problem: A macro has no concept of the scoping required with member functions. The preprocessor simply performs text substitution, so you cannot say something like

```
class X {
  int i;
public:
#define val (X::i) // Error
```

or anything even close. In addition, there would be no indication of which object you were referring to. There is simply no way to express class scope in a macro. Without some alternative to preprocessor macros, programmers will be tempted to make some data members **public** for the sake of efficiency, thus exposing the underlying implementation and preventing changes in that implementation.

inline functions

In solving the C++ problem of a macro with access to private class members, *all* the problems associated with preprocessor macros

---

[1]Andrew Koenig goes into more detail in his book *C Traps & Pitfalls* (Addison-Wesley, 1989).

were eliminated. This was done by bringing macros under the control of the compiler, where they belong. In C++, the concept of a macro is implemented as an *inline function*, which is a true function in every sense. Any behavior you expect from an ordinary function, you get from an inline function. The only difference is that an inline function is expanded in place, like a preprocessor macro, so the overhead of the function call is eliminated. Thus, you should (almost) never use macros, only inline functions.

Any function defined within a class body is automatically inline, but you can also make a nonclass function inline by preceding it with the **inline** keyword. However, for it to have any effect, you must include the function body with the declaration; otherwise the compiler will treat it as an ordinary function declaration. Thus,

```
inline int PlusOne(int x);
```

has no effect at all other than declaring the function (which may or may not get an inline definition sometime later). The successful approach is

```
inline int PlusOne(int x) { return ++x; }
```

Notice that the compiler will check (as it always does) for the proper use of the function argument list and return value (performing any necessary conversions), something the preprocessor is incapable of. Also, if you try to write the above as a preprocessor macro, you get an unwanted side effect.

You'll almost always want to put inline definitions in a header file. When the compiler sees such a definition, it puts the function type (signature + return value) *and* the function body in its symbol table. When you use the function, the compiler checks to ensure the call is correct and the return value is being used correctly, and then substitutes the function body for the function call, thus eliminating the overhead. The inline code does occupy space, but if the function is small, this can actually take less space than the code generated to do an ordinary function call (pushing arguments on the stack and doing the CALL).

An inline function in a header file defaults to *internal linkage* — that is, it is **static** and can only be seen in translation units where it is included. Thus, as long as they aren't declared in the same translation unit, there will be no clash at link time between an inline function and a global function with the same signature. (Remember the return value is not included in the resolution of function overloading.

inlines inside classes

To define an inline function, you must ordinarily precede the function definition with the **inline** keyword. However, this is not necessary inside a class definition. Any function you define inside a class definition is automatically an inline. Thus,

```
//: INLINE.CPP -- Inlines inside classes
#include <iostream.h>

class point {
  int i, j, k;
public:
  point() { i = j = k = 0; }
  point(int I, int J, int K) {
    i = I;
    j = J;
    k = K;
  }
  void print(const char* msg = "") const {
    if(*msg) cout << msg << endl;
    cout << "i = " << i << ", "
         << "j = " << j << ", "
         << "k = " << k << endl;
  }
};

main() {
  point p, q(1,2,3);
```

```
    p.print("value of p");
    q.print("value of q");
}
```

Of course, the temptation is to use inlines everywhere inside class
declarations because they save you the extra step of making the
external member function definition. Keep in mind, however, that
the idea of an inline is to reduce the overhead of a function call. If
the function body is large, chances are you'll spend a much larger
percentage of your time inside the body versus. going in and out of
the function, so the gains will be small. But inlining a big function
will cause that code to be duplicated everywhere the function is
called, producing code bloat with little or no speed benefit.

access functions

One of the most important uses of inlines inside classes is the
access function. This is a small function that allows you to read or
change part of the state of an object — that is, an internal variable
or variables. The reason inlines are so important with access
functions can be seen in the following example:

```
//: ACCESS.CPP -- Inline access functions

class access {
   int i;
public:
   int read() const { return i; }
   void set(int I) { i = I; }
};

main() {
   access A;
   A.set(100);
   int x = A.read();
}
```

Here, the class user never has direct contact with the state variables inside the class, and they can be kept **private**, under the control of the class designer. All the access to the **private** data members can be controlled through the member function interface. In addition, access is remarkably efficient. Consider the **read( )**, for example. Without inlines, the code generated for the call to **read( )** would include pushing **this** on the stack and making an assembly language CALL. With most machines, the size of this code would be larger than the code created by the inline, and the execution time would certainly be longer.

Without inline functions, an efficiency-conscious class designer will be tempted to simply make **i** a public member, eliminating the overhead by allowing the user to directly access **i**. From a design standpoint, this is disastrous because **i** then becomes part of the public interface, which means the class designer can never change it. You're stuck with an **int** called **i**. This is a problem because you may learn sometime later that it would be much more useful to represent the state information as a **float** rather than an **int**, but because **int i** is part of the public interface, you can't change it. If, on the other hand, you've always used member functions to read and change the state information of an object, you can modify the underlying representation of the object to your heart's content (and permanently remove from your mind the idea that you are going to perfect your design before you code it and try it out).

accessors and mutators

Some people further divide the concept of access functions into *accessors* (to read state information from an object) and *mutators* (to change the state of an object). In addition, function overloading may be used to provide the same function name for both the accessor and mutator; how you call the function determines whether you're reading or modifying state information. Thus,

```
//: RECTANGL.CPP -- Accessors & mutators

class rectangle {
```

```
    int Width, Height;
public:
  rectangle(int W = 0, int H = 0)
    : Width(W), Height(H) {}
  int width() const { return Width; } // Read
  void width(int W) { Width = W; } // Set
  int height() const { return Height; } // Read
  void height(int H) { Height = H; } // Set
};

main() {
  rectangle R(19, 47);
  // Change width & height:
  R.height(2 * R.width());
  R.width(2 * R.height());
}
```

The constructor uses the constructor initializer list (briefly
introduced in Chapter 6 and covered fully in Chapter 12) to initialize
the values of **Width** and **Height** (using the pseudoconstructor-call
form for built-in types).

Of course, accessors and mutators don't have to be simple
pipelines to an internal variable. Sometimes they can perform some
sort of calculation. The following example uses the Standard C
library time functions to produce a simple **Time** class:

```
//: CPPTIME.H -- A simple time class
#ifndef CPPTIME_H_
#define CPPTIME_H_
#include <time.h>
#include <string.h>

class Time {
  time_t T;
  tm local;
  char Ascii[26];
```

```
      unsigned char lflag, aflag;
      void updateLocal() {
        if(!lflag) {
          local = *localtime(&T);
          lflag++;
        }
      }
      void updateAscii() {
        if(!aflag) {
          updateLocal();
          strcpy(Ascii, asctime(&local));
          aflag++;
        }
      }
    public:
      Time() { mark(); }
      void mark() {
        lflag = aflag = 0;
        time(&T);
      }
      const char* ascii() {
        updateAscii();
        return Ascii;
      }
      // Difference in seconds:
      int delta(Time* dt) const {
        return difftime(T, dt->T);
      }
      int DaylightSavings() {
        updateLocal();
        return local.tm_isdst;
      }
      int DayOfYear() { // Since January 1
        updateLocal();
        return local.tm_yday;
      }
      int DayOfWeek() { // Since Sunday
```

```
      updateLocal();
      return local.tm_wday;
    }
    int Since1900() { // Years since 1900
      updateLocal();
      return local.tm_year;
    }
    int Month() { // Since January
      updateLocal();
      return local.tm_mon;
    }
    int DayOfMonth() {
      updateLocal();
      return local.tm_mday;
    }
    int Hour() { // Since midight, 24-hour clock
      updateLocal();
      return local.tm_hour;
    }
    int Minute() {
      updateLocal();
      return local.tm_min;
    }
    int Second() {
      updateLocal();
      return local.tm_sec;
    }
};
#endif // CPPTIME_H_
```

The Standard C library functions have multiple representations for time, and these are all part of the **Time** class. However, it isn't necessary to update all of them all the time, so instead the **time_t T** is used as the base representation, and the **tm local** and ASCII character representation **Ascii** each have flags to indicate if they've been updated to the current **time_t**. The two **private** functions

updateLocal( ) and **updateAscii( )** check the flags and conditionally perform the update.

The constructor calls the **mark( )** function (which the user can also call to force the object to represent the current time), and this clears the two flags to indicate that the local time and ASCII representation are now invalid. The **ascii( )** function calls **updateAscii( )**, which copies the result of the Standard C library function **asctime( )** into a local buffer because **asctime( )** uses a static data area that is overwritten if the function is called elsewhere. The return value is the address of this local buffer.

In the functions starting with **DaylightSavings( )**, all use the **updateLocal( )** function, which causes the composite inline to be fairly large. This doesn't seem worthwhile, especially considering you probably won't call the functions very much. However, this doesn't mean all the functions should be made out of line. If you leave **updateLocal( )** as an inline, its code will be duplicated in all the out-of-line functions, eliminating the extra overhead.

Here's a small test program:

```
//: CPPTIME.CPP -- Testing a simple time class
#include "..\7\cpptime.h"
#include <iostream.h>

main() {
  Time start;
  for(int i = 1; i < 1000; i++) {
    cout << i << ' ';
    if(i%10 == 0) cout << endl;
  }
  Time end;
  cout << endl;
  cout << "start = " << start.ascii();
  cout << "end = " << end.ascii();
  cout << "delta = " << end.delta(&start);
}
```

A **Time** object is created, then some time-consuming activity is performed, then a second **Time** object is created to mark the ending time. These are used to show starting, ending, and elapsed times.

inlines & the compiler

To understand when inlining is effective, it's helpful to understand what the compiler does when it encounters an inline. As with any function, the compiler holds the function *type* (that is, the function prototype including the name and argument types, in combination with the function return value) in its symbol table. In addition, when the compiler sees the inline function body *and* the function body parses without error, the code for the function body is also brought into the symbol table. Whether the code is stored in source form or as compiled assembly instructions is up to the compiler.

When you make a call to an inline function, the compiler first ensures that the call can be correctly made; that is, all the argument types must be the proper types, or the compiler must be able to make a type conversion to the proper types, and the return value must be the correct type (or convertible to the correct type) in the destination expression. This, of course, is exactly what the compiler does for any function and is markedly different from what the preprocessor does because the preprocessor cannot check types or make conversions.

If all the function type information fits the context of the call, then the inline code is substituted directly for the function call, eliminating the call overhead. Also, if the inline is a member function, the address of the object (**this**) is put in the appropriate place(s), which of course is another thing the preprocessor is unable to perform.

limitations

There are two situations when the compiler cannot perform inlining. In these cases, it simply reverts to the ordinary form of a function by taking the inline definition and creating storage for the function just as it does for a non-inline. If it must do this in multiple translation units (which would normally cause a multiple definition error), the linker is told to ignore the multiple definitions.

The compiler cannot perform inlining if the function is too complicated. This depends upon the particular compiler, but at the point most compilers give up, the inline probably wouldn't gain you any efficiency. Generally, any sort of looping is considered too complicated to expand as an inline, and if you think about it, looping probably entails much more time inside the function than embodied in the calling overhead. If the function is just a collection of simple statements, the compiler probably won't have any trouble inlining it, but if there are a lot of statements, the overhead of the function call will be much less than the cost of executing the body. And remember, every time you call a big inline function, the entire function body is inserted in place of each call, so you can easily get code bloat without any noticeable performance improvement. Some of the examples in this book may exceed reasonable inline sizes in favor of conserving screen real estate.

The compiler also cannot perform inlining if the address of the function is taken, implicitly or explicitly. If the compiler must produce an address, then it will allocate storage for the function code and use the resulting address. However, where an address is not required, the compiler will probably still inline the code.

It is important to understand that an inline is just a suggestion to the compiler; the compiler is not forced to inline anything at all. A good compiler will inline small, simple functions while intelligently ignoring inlines that are too complicated. This will give you the results you want — the true semantics of a function call with the efficiency of a macro.

order of evaluation

If you're imagining what the compiler is doing to implement inlines, you can confuse yourself into thinking there are more limitations than actually exist. In particular, if an inline makes a forward reference to a function that hasn't yet been declared in the class, it can seem like the compiler won't be able to handle it:

```
//: EVORDER.CPP -- Inline evaluation order

class forward {
  int i;
public:
  forward() : i(0) {}
  // Call to undeclared function:
  int f() const { return g() + 1; }
  int g() const { return i; }
};

main() {
  forward F;
  F.f();
}
```

In **f( )**, a call is made to **g( )**, although **g( )** has not yet been declared. This works because the language definition states that no inline functions in a class shall be evaluated until the closing brace of the class declaration.

Of course, if **g( )** in turn called **f( )**, you'd end up with a set of recursive calls, which are too complicated for the compiler to inline. (Also, you'd have to perform some test in **f( )** or **g( )** to force one of them to "bottom out," or the recursion would be infinite.)

hidden activities in constructors & destructors

Constructors and destructors are two places where you can be fooled into thinking that an inline is more efficient than it actually is. Both constructors and destructors may have hidden activities, because the class can contain subobjects whose constructors and destructors must be called. These sub-objects may be member objects, or they may exist because of inheritance (which hasn't been introduced yet). As an example of a class with member objects

```
//: HIDDEN.CPP -- Hidden activites in inlines
#include <iostream.h>

class member {
  int i, j, k;
public:
  member(int x = 0) { i = j = k = x; }
  ~member() { cout << "~member" << endl; }
};

class withMembers {
  member Q, R, S; // Have constructors
  int i;
public:
  withMembers(int I) : i(I) {} // Trivial?
  ~withMembers() {
    cout << "~withMembers" << endl;
  }
};

main() {
  withMembers WM(1);
}
```

In **class withMembers**, the inline constructor and destructor look straightforward and simple enough, but there's more going on than meets the eye. The constructors and destructors for the member objects **Q**, **R**, and **S** are being called automatically, and *those* constructors and destructors are also inline, so the difference is significant from normal member functions. This doesn't necessarily mean that you should always make constructor and destructor definitions out-of-line. When you're making an initial "sketch" of a program by quickly writing code, it's often more convenient to use inlines. However, if you're concerned about efficiency, it's a place to look.

reducing clutter

In a book like this, the simplicity and terseness of putting inline definitions inside classes is very useful because more fits on a page or screen (in a seminar). However, Dan Saks[2] has pointed out that in a real project this has the effect of needlessly cluttering the class interface and thereby making the class harder to use. He refers to member functions defined within classes using the Latin *in situ* (in place) and maintains that all definitions should be placed outside the class to keep the interface clean. Optimization, he argues, is a separate issue. If you want to optimize, use the **inline** keyword. Using this approach, the earlier RECTANGL.CPP example (page 314) becomes

```
//: NOINSITU.CPP -- Removing in situ functions

class rectangle {
  int Width, Height;
public:
  rectangle(int W = 0, int H = 0);
```

[2] Co-author with Tom Plum of *C++ Programming Guidelines*, Plum Hall, 1991.

```
      int width() const; // Read
      void width(int W); // Set
      int height() const; // Read
      void height(int H); // Set
};

inline rectangle::rectangle(int W, int H)
    : Width(W), Height(H) {
}

inline int rectangle::width() const {
    return Width;
}

inline void rectangle::width(int W) {
    Width = W;
}

inline int rectangle::height() const {
    return Height;
}

inline void rectangle::height(int H) {
    Height = H;
}

main() {
    rectangle R(19, 47);
    // Transpose width & height:
    R.height(R.width());
    R.width(R.height());
}
```

Now if you want to compare the effect of inlining with out-of-line functions, you can simply remove the **inline** keyword. (Inline functions should normally be put in header files, however, while non-inline functions must reside in their own translation unit.) If you want to put the functions into documentation, it's a simple cut-and-paste operation. *In situ* functions require more work and have greater potential for errors. Another argument for this approach is that you can always produce a consistent formatting style for function definitions, something that doesn't always occur with *in situ* functions.

preprocessor features

Earlier, I said you *almost* always want to use **inline** functions instead of preprocessor macros. The exceptions are when you need to use three special features in the Standard C preprocessor (which is, by inheritance, the C++ preprocessor): stringizing, string concatenation, and token pasting. Stringizing, performed with the **#** directive, allows you to take an identifier and turn it into a string, whereas string concatenation takes place when two adjacent strings have no intervening punctuation, in which case the strings are combined. These two features are exceptionally useful when writing debug code. Thus,

```
#define DEBUG(X) cout << #X " = " << X << endl
```

This prints the value of any variable. You can also get a trace that prints out the statements as they execute:

```
#define TRACE(S) cout << #S << endl; S
```

The **#S** stringizes the statement for output, and the second **S** reiterates the statement so it is executed. Of course, this kind of thing can cause problems, especially in one-line **for** loops:

```
for(int i = 0; i < 100; i++)
  TRACE(f(i));
```

Because there are actually two statements in the **TRACE( )** macro, the one-line **for** loop executes only the first one. The solution is to replace the semicolon with a comma in the macro.

token pasting

Token pasting is very useful when you are manufacturing code. It allows you to take two identifiers and paste them together to automatically create a new identifier. For example,

```
#define FIELD(A) char* A##_string; int A##_size
class record {
  FIELD(one);
  FIELD(two);
  FIELD(three);
  // ...
};
```

Each call to the **FIELD( )** macro creates an identifier to hold a string and another to hold the length of that string. Not only is it easier to read, it can eliminate coding errors and make maintenance easier. Notice, however, the use of all upper-case characters in the name of the macro. This is a helpful practice because it tells the reader this is a macro and not a function, so if there are problems, it acts as a little reminder.

improved error checking

It's convenient to improve the error checking for the rest of the book; with inline functions you can simply include the file and not worry about what to link. Up until now, the **assert( )** macro has been used for "error checking," but it's really for debugging and should be replaced with something that provides useful information at run-time. In addition, exceptions (presented in Chapter 16) provide a much more effective way of handling these kinds of errors.

This is another example where the preprocessor is still useful because the __FILE__ and __LINE__ directives only work with the preprocessor, and they're used in **assert( )**. If **assert( )** is called within an error function, it will only report the line number and file

---

name where the error function exists, not where the error function is called. The approach shown here uses a function in conjunction with a macro (much the way **assert( )** does), followed by a call to **assert( )** (which is eliminated by a **#define NDEBUG** for the shipping product).

The following header file will be placed in the book's root directory so it's easily accessed from all chapters. "Allege" is a synonym for assert:

```
//: ALLEGE.H -- Error checking
#ifndef ALLEGE_H_
#define ALLEGE_H_
#include <stdio.h>
#include <stdlib.h>
#include <assert.h>

inline void
allege_error(int val, const char * msg){
  if(!val) {
     fprintf(stderr, "error: %s\n", msg);
#ifdef NDEBUG
     exit(1);
#endif
  }
}

#define allege(expr, msg) \
{  allege_error((expr) ? 1 : 0, msg); \
   assert(expr); }

#define allegemem(expr) \
  allege(expr, "out of memory")

#define allegefile(expr) \
  allege(expr, "could not open file")
```

```
#endif // ALLEGE_H_
```

The **allege_error( )** function takes a value produced by the evaluation of an integral expression, and a message to print if that expression evaluates to false. **fprintf( )** is used instead of iostreams because there are a small number of error situations where it works better. If this is not a build for debugging, **exit(1)** is called to end the program.

The **allege( )** macro uses the ternary if-then-else to force an evaluation of the expression **expr**. This is used in a call to **allege_error( )**, followed by an **assert( )**, so you'll get the benefits of **assert( )** during debugging — some environments closely integrate their debuggers with **assert( )**.

The **allegefile( )** and **allegemem( )** macros are specific versions of **allege( )** for checking files and memory, respectively. This code provides the minimum information necessary for error reporting, but you can add to it from this framework.

Here's a simple program to test ALLEGE.H:

```cpp
//: ERRTEST.CPP -- Testing the allege() macro
// #define NDEBUG // turn off asserts
#include "..\allege.h"
#include <fstream.h>

main() {
  int i = 1;
  allege(i, "value must be nonzero");
  void* m = malloc(100);
  allegemem(m);
  ifstream nofile("nofile.xxx");
  allegefile(nofile);
}
```

You can see what happens for the "shipping" program by un-commenting the line:

```
// #define NDEBUG // turn off asserts
```

For the rest of the book, the **allege( )** macros will be used instead of **assert( )**, except where the check is only necessary for debugging and not needed at run-time.

summary

It's critical that you be able to hide the underlying implementation of a class because you may want to change that implementation sometime later. You'll do this for efficiency, or because you get a better understanding of the problem, or because some new class becomes available that you want to use in the implementation. Anything that jeopardizes the privacy of the underlying implementation reduces the flexibility of the language. Thus, the inline function is very important because it virtually eliminates the need for preprocessor macros and their attendant problems. With inlines, member functions can be as efficient as preprocessor macros.

The inline function can be overused in class definitions, of course. The programmer is tempted to do so because it's easier, so it will happen. However, it's not that big an issue because later, when looking for size reductions, you can always move the functions out of line with no effect on their functionality. The development guideline should be "First make it work, then optimize it."

exercises

1. Take Exercise 2 from Chapter 6, and add an inline constructor, and an inline member function called **print( )** to print out all the values in the array.

2. Take the NESTFRND.CPP example from Chapter 2 and replace all the member functions with inlines. Make them non-*in situ* inline functions. Also change the **initialize( )** functions to constructors.

---

2. Take the NESTFRND.CPP example from Chapter 2 and replace all the member functions with inlines. Make them non-*in situ* inline functions. Also change the **initialize( )** functions to constructors.

3. Take the NL.CPP example from Chapter 5 and turn **nl** into an **inline** function in its own header file.

4. Create a class **A** with a default constructor that announces itself. Now make a new class **B** and put an object of **A** as a member of **B**, and give **B** an inline constructor. Create an array of **B** objects and see what happens.

5. Create a large quantity of the objects from Exercise 4, and use the **Time** class to time the difference between a non-inline constructor and an inline constructor. (If you have a profiler, also try using that.)

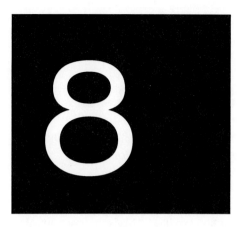

name control

Creating names is a fundamental activity in programming, and when a project gets large the number of names can easily be overwhelming. C++ allows you a great deal of control over both the creation and visibility of names, where storage for those names is placed, and linkage for names.

The **static** keyword was overloaded in C before people knew what the term "overload" meant, and C++ has added yet another meaning. The underlying concept with all uses of **static** seems to be "something that holds its position" (like static electricity), whether that means a physical location in memory or visibility within a file.

In this chapter, you'll learn how **static** controls storage and visibility, and an improved way to control access to names via C++'s *namespace* feature. You'll also find out how to use functions that were written and compiled in C.

static elements from C

In both C and C++ the keyword **static** has two basic meanings, which unfortunately often step on each other's toes:

1. Allocated once at a fixed address; that is, the object is created in a special *static data area* rather than on the stack each time a function is called. This is the concept of *static storage*.

2. Local to a particular translation unit (and class scope in C++, as you will see later). Here, **static** controls the *visibility* of a name, so that name cannot be seen outside the translation unit or class. This also describes the concept of *linkage*, which determines what names the linker will see.

This section will look at the above meanings of **static** as they were inherited from C.

static variables inside functions

Normally, when you create a variable inside a function, the compiler allocates storage for that variable each time the function is called by moving the stack pointer down an appropriate amount. If there is an initializer for the variable, the initialization is performed each time that sequence point is passed.

Sometimes, however, you want to retain a value between function calls. You could accomplish this by making a global variable, but that variable would not be under the sole control of the function. C and C++ allow you to create a **static** object inside a function; the storage for this object is not on the stack but instead in the program's static storage area. This object is initialized once the first time the function is called and then retains its value between function invocations. For example, the following function returns the next character in the string each time the function is called:

```cpp
//: STATFUN.CPP -- Static vars inside functions
#include <iostream.h>
#include "..\allege.h"

char onechar(const char* string = 0) {
  static const char* s;
  if(string) {
    s = string;
    return *s;
  }
  else
    allege(s, "un-initialized s");
  if(*s == '\0')
    return 0;
  return *s++;
}

char* a = "abcdefghijklmnopqrstuvwxyz";

main() {
  // Onechar(); // causes allege()
  onechar(a); // Initializes s to a
  char c;
  while((c = onechar()) != 0)
    cout << c << endl;
}
```

The **static char* s** holds its value between calls of **onechar( )** because its storage is not part of the stack frame of the function, but is in the static storage area of the program. When you call **onechar( )** with a **char*** argument, **s** is assigned to that argument, and the first character of the string is returned. Each subsequent call to **onechar( )** *without* an argument produces the default value of zero for **string**, which indicates to the function that you are still extracting characters from the previously initialized value of **s**. The function will continue to produce characters until it reaches the null terminator of the string, at which point it stops incrementing the pointer so it doesn't overrun the end of the string.

But what happens if you call **onechar( )** with no arguments and without previously initializing the value of **s**? In the definition for **s**, you could have provided an initializer,

```
static char* s = 0;
```

but if you do not provide an initializer for a static variable of a built-in type, the compiler guarantees that variable will be initialized to zero (converted to the proper type) at program start-up. So in **onechar( )**, the first time the function is called, **s** is zero. In this case, the **if(!s)** conditional will catch it.

The above initialization for **s** is very simple, but initialization for static objects (like all other objects) can be arbitrary expressions involving constants and previously declared variables and functions.

static class objects inside functions

The rules are the same for static objects of user-defined types, including the fact that some initialization is required for the object. However, assignment to zero has meaning only for built-in types; user-defined types must be initialized with constructor calls. Thus, if you don't specify constructor arguments when you define the static object, the class must have a default constructor. For example,

```
//: FUNOBJ.CPP -- Static objects in functions
#include <iostream.h>

class X {
  int i;
public:
  X(int I = 0) : i(I) {} // Default
  ~X() { cout << "X::~X()" << endl; }
};
```

```
void f() {
  static X x1(47);
  static X x2; // Default constructor required
}

main() {
  f();
}
```

The static objects of type **X** inside **f( )** can be initialized either with
the constructor argument list or with the default constructor. This
construction occurs the first time control passes through the
definition, and only the first time.

static object destructors

Destructors for static objects (all objects with static storage, not just
local static objects as in the above example) are called when
main( ) exits or when the Standard C library function **exit( )** is
explicitly called, **main( )** in most implementations calls **exit( )**
when it terminates. This means that it can be dangerous to call
exit( ) inside a destructor because you can end up with infinite
recursion. Static object destructors are *not* called if you exit the
program using the Standard C library function **abort( )**.

You can specify actions to take place when leaving **main( )** (or
calling **exit( )**) by using the Standard C library function **atexit( )**. In
this case, the functions registered by **atexit( )** may be called before
the destructors for any objects constructed before leaving **main( )**
(or calling **exit( )**).

Destruction of static objects occurs in the reverse order of
initialization. However, only objects that have been constructed are
destroyed. Fortunately, the programming system keeps track of
initialization order and the objects that have been constructed.
Global objects are always constructed before **main( )** is entered, so
this last statement applies only to static objects that are local to
functions. If a function containing a local static object is never

called, the constructor for that object is never executed, so the destructor is also not executed. For example,

```cpp
//: STATDEST.CPP -- Static object destructors
#include <fstream.h>
ofstream out("statdest.out"); // Trace file

class obj {
  char c; // Identifier
public:
  obj(char C) : c(C) {
    out << "obj::obj() for " << c << endl;
  }
  ~obj() {
    out << "obj::~obj() for " << c << endl;
  }
};

obj A('A'); // Global (static storage)
// Constructor & destructor always called

void f() {
  static obj B('B');
}

void g() {
  static obj C('C');
}

main() {
  out << "inside main()" << endl;
  f(); // Calls static constructor for B
  // g() not called
  out << "leaving main()" << endl;
}
```

Thinking in C++ *Bruce Eckel*

In **obj**, the **char c** acts as an identifier so the constructor and destructor can print out information about the object they're working on. The **obj A** is a global object, so the constructor is always called for it before **main( )** is entered, but the constructors for the **static obj B** inside **f( )** and the **static obj C** inside **g( )** are called only if those functions are called.

To demonstrate which constructors and destructors are called, inside **main( )** only **f( )** is called. The output of the program is

```
obj::obj() for A
inside main()
obj::obj() for B
leaving main()
obj::~obj() for B
obj::~obj() for A
```

The constructor for **A** is called before **main( )** is entered, and the constructor for **B** is called only because **f( )** is called. When **main( )** exits, the destructors for the objects that have been constructed are called in reverse order of their construction. This means that if **g( )** *is* called, the order in which the destructors for **B** and **C** are called depends on whether **f( )** or **g( )** is called first.

Notice that the trace file **ofstream** object **out** is also a static object. It is important that its definition (as opposed to an **extern** declaration) appear at the beginning of the file, before there is any possible use of **out**. Otherwise you'll be using an object before it is properly initialized.

In C++ the constructor for a global static object is called before **main( )** is entered, so you now have a simple and portable way to execute code before entering **main( )** and to execute code with the destructor after exiting **main( )**. In C this was always a trial that required you to root around in the compiler vendor's assembly-language startup code.

controlling linkage

Ordinarily, any name at *file scope* (that is, not nested inside a class or function) is visible throughout all translation units in a program. This is often called *external linkage* because at link time the name is visible to the linker everywhere, external to that translation unit. Global variables and ordinary functions have external linkage.

There are times when you'd like to limit the visibility of a name. You might like to have a variable at file scope so all the functions in that file can use it, but you don't want functions outside that file to see or access that variable, or to inadvertently cause name clashes with identifiers outside the file.

An object or function name at file scope that is explicitly declared **static** is local to its translation unit (in the terms of this book, the .CPP file where the declaration occurs); that name has *internal linkage*. This means you can use the same name in other translation units without a name clash.

One advantage to internal linkage is that the name can be placed in a header file without worrying that there will be a clash at link time. Names that are commonly placed in header files, such as **const** definitions and **inline** functions, default to internal linkage. (However, **const** defaults to internal linkage only in C++; in C it defaults to external linkage.) Note that linkage refers only to elements that have addresses at link/load time; thus, class declarations and local variables have no linkage.

confusion

Here's an example of how the two meanings of **static** can cross over each other. All global objects implicitly have static storage class, so if you say (at file scope),

```
int a = 0;
```

then storage for **a** will be in the program's static data area, and the initialization for **a** will occur once, before **main( )** is entered. In addition, the visibility of **a** is global, across all translation units. In

---

terms of visibility, the opposite of **static** (visible only in this translation unit) is **extern**, which explicitly states that the visibility of the name is across all translation units. So the above definition is equivalent to saying

```
extern int a = 0;
```

But if you say instead,

```
static int a = 0;
```

all you've done is change the visibility, so **a** has internal linkage. The storage class is unchanged — the object resides in the static data area whether the visibility is **static** or **extern**.

Once you get into local variables, **static** stops altering the visibility (and **extern** has no meaning) and instead alters the storage class.

With function names, **static** and **extern** can only alter visibility, so if you say,

```
extern void f();
```

it's the same as the unadorned declaration

```
void f();
```

and if you say,

```
static void f();
```

it means **f( )** is visible only within this translation unit; this is sometimes called *file static*.

other storage class specifiers

You will see **static** and **extern** used commonly. There are two other storage class specifiers that occur less often. The **auto** specifier is almost never used because it tells the compiler that this is a local variable. The compiler can always determine this fact from the context in which the variable is defined, so **auto** is redundant.

A **register** variable is a local (**auto**) variable, along with a hint to the compiler that this particular variable will be heavily used, so the compiler ought to keep it in a register if it can. Thus, it is an optimization aid. Various compilers respond differently to this hint; they have the option to ignore it. If you take the address of the variable, the **register** specifier will almost certainly be ignored. You should avoid using **register** because the compiler can usually do a better job at of optimization than you.

namespaces

Although names can be nested inside classes, the names of global functions, global variables, and classes are still in a single global name space. The **static** keyword gives you some control over this by allowing you to give variables and functions internal linkage (make them file static). But in a large project, lack of control over the global name space can cause problems. To solve these problems for classes, vendors often create long complicated names that are unlikely to clash, but then you're stuck typing those names. (A **typedef** is often used to simplify this.) It's not an elegant, language-supported solution.

You can subdivide the global name space into more manageable pieces using the *namespace* feature of C++.[1] The **namespace** keyword, like **class**, **struct**, **enum**, and **union**, puts the names of its members in a distinct space. While the other keywords have additional purposes, the creation of a new name space is the only purpose for **namespace**.

---

[1] Your compiler may not have implemented this feature yet; check your local documentation.

creating a namespace

The creation of a namespace is notably similar to the creation of a **class**:

```
namespace MyLib {
  // Declarations
}
```

This produces a new **namespace** containing the enclosed declarations. There are significant differences with **class**, **struct**, **union** and **enum**, however:

1. A **namespace** definition can only appear at the global scope, but namespaces can be nested within each other.

2. No terminating semicolon is necessary after the closing brace of a **namespace** definition.

3. A **namespace** definition can be "continued" over multiple header files using a syntax that would appear to be a redefinition for a class:

```
//: HEADER1.H
namespace MyLib {
  extern int X;
  void f();
  // ...
}
//: HEADER2.H
// Add more names to MyLib
namespace MyLib { // NOT a redefinition!
  extern int Y;
  void g();
  // ...
}
```

4. A namespace name can be *aliased* to another name, so you don't have to type an unwieldy name created by a library vendor:

```
namespace BobsSuperDuperLibrary {
  class widget { /* ... */ };
  class poppit { /* ... */ };
  // ...
}
// Too much to type! I'll alias it:
namespace Bob = BobsSuperDuperLibrary;
```

5. You cannot create an instance of a namespace as you can with a class.

unnamed namespaces

Each translation unit contains an unnamed namespace that you can add to by saying **namespace** without an identifier:

```
namespace {
  class arm  { /* ... */ };
  class leg  { /* ... */ };
  class head { /* ... */ };
  class robot {
    arm Arm[4];
    leg Leg[16];
    head Head[3];
    // ...
  } Xanthan;
  int i, j, k;
}
```

The names in this space are automatically available in that translation unit without qualification. It is guaranteed that an unnamed space is unique for each translation unit. If you put local names in an unnamed namespace, you don't need to give them internal linkage by making them **static**.

friends

You can *inject* a **friend** declaration into a namespace by declaring it within an enclosed class:

```
namespace me {
  class us {
    //...
    friend you();
  };
}
```

Now the function **you( )** is a member of the namespace **me**.

using a namespace

You can refer to a name within a namespace in two ways: one name at a time, using the scope resolution operator, and more expediently with the **using** keyword.

scope resolution

Any name in a namespace can be explicitly specified using the scope resolution operator, just like the names within a class:

```
namespace X {
  class Y {
    static int i;
  public:
    void f();
  };
  class Z;
  void foo();
}

int X::Y::i = 9;

class X::Z {
  int u, v, w;
public:
  Z(int I);
  int g();
};
```

```
X::Z::Z(int I) { u = v = w = I; }
int X::Z::g() { return u = v = w = 0; }

void X::foo() {
  X::Z a(1);
  a.g();
}
```

So far, namespaces look very much like classes.

the using directive

Because it can rapidly get tedious to type the full qualification for an identifier in a namespace, the **using** keyword allows you to import an entire namespace at once. When used in conjunction with the **namespace** keyword, this is called a *using directive*. The **using** directive declares all the names of a namespace to be in the current scope, so you can conveniently use the unqualified names:

```
namespace math {
  enum sign { positive, negative };
  class integer {
    int i;
    sign s;
  public:
    integer(int I = 0)
      : i(I),
        s(i >= 0 ? positive : negative)
    {}
    sign Sign() { return s; }
    void Sign(sign S) { s = S; }
    // ...
  };
  integer A, B, C;
  integer divide(integer, integer);
  // ...
}
```

Now you can declare all the names in **math** inside a function, but leave those names nested within the function:

```
void arithmetic() {
  using namespace math;
  integer X;
  X.Sign(positive);
}
```

Without the **using** directive, all the names in the namespace would need to be fully qualified.

One aspect of the **using** directive may seem slightly counterintuitive at first. The visibility of the names introduced with a **using** directive is the scope where the directive is made. But you can override the names from the **using** directive as if they've been declared globally to that scope!

```
void q() {
  using namespace math;
  integer A; // Hides math::A;
  A.Sign(negative);
  math::A.Sign(positive);
}
```

If you have a second namespace:

```
namespace calculation {
  class integer {};
  integer divide(integer, integer);
  // ...
}
```

And this namespace is also introduced with a **using** directive, you have the possibility of a collision. However, the ambiguity appears at the point of *use* of the name, not at the **using** directive:

```
void s() {
  using namespace math;
  using namespace calculation;
```

```
  // Everything's ok until:
  divide(1, 2); // Ambiguity
}
```

Thus it's possible to write **using** directives to introduce a number of namespaces with conflicting names without ever producing an ambiguity.

the using declaration

You can introduce names one at a time into the current scope with a *using declaration*. Unlike the **using** directive, which treats names as if they were declared globally to the scope, a **using** declaration is a declaration within the current scope. This means it can override names from a **using** directive:

```
namespace U {
  void f();
  void g();
}

namespace V {
  void f();
  void g();
}

void func() {
  using namespace U; // Using directive
  using V::f; // Using declaration
  f(); // Calls V::f();
  U::f(); // Must fully qualify to call
}
```

The **using** declaration just gives the fully specified name of the identifier, but no type information. This means that if the namespace contains a set of overloaded functions with the same name, the **using** declaration declares all the functions in the overloaded set.

You can put a **using** declaration anywhere a normal declaration can occur. A **using** declaration works like a normal declaration in all ways but one: it's possible for a **using** declaration to cause the overload of a function with the same argument types (which isn't allowed with normal overloading). This ambiguity, however, doesn't show up until the point of use, rather than the point of declaration.

A using declaration can also appear within a namespace, and it has the same effect as anywhere else: that name is declared within the space:

```
namespace Q {
  using U::f;
  using V::g;
  // ...
}

void m() {
  using namespace Q;
  f(); // calls U::f();
  g(); // calls V::g();
}
```

A using declaration is an alias, and it allows you to declare the same function in separate namespaces. If you end up redeclaring the same function by importing different namespaces, it's OK — there won't be any ambiguities or duplications.

static members in C++

There are times when you need a single storage space to be used by all objects of a class. In C, you would use a global variable, but this is not very safe. Global data can be modified by anyone, and its name can clash with other identical names in a large project. It would be ideal if the data could be stored as if it were global, but be hidden inside a class, and clearly associated with that class.

This is accomplished with **static** data members inside a class. There is a single piece of storage for a **static** data member, regardless of how many objects of that class you create. All objects share the same **static** storage space for that data member, so it is a way for them to "communicate" with each other. But the **static** data belongs to the class; its name is scoped inside the class and it can be **public**, **private**, or **protected**.

defining storage for static data members

Because **static** data has a single piece of storage regardless of how many objects are created, that storage must be defined in a single place. The compiler will not allocate storage for you, although this was once true, with some compilers. The linker will report an error if a **static** data member is declared but not defined.

The definition must occur outside the class (no inlining is allowed), and only one definition is allowed. Thus it is usual to put it in the implementation file for the class. The syntax sometimes gives people trouble, but it is actually quite logical. For example,

```
class A {
  static int i;
public:
  //...
};
```

and later, in the definition file,

```
int A::i = 1;
```

If you were to define an ordinary global variable, you would say

```
int i = 1;
```

but here, the scope resolution operator and the class name are used to specify **A::i**.

Some people have trouble with the idea that **A::i** is **private**, and yet here's something that seems to be manipulating it right out in the open. Doesn't this break the protection mechanism? It's a completely safe practice for two reasons. First, the only place this initialization is legal is in the definition. Indeed, if the **static** data were an object with a constructor, you would call the constructor instead of using the = operator. Secondly, once the definition has been made, the end-user cannot make a second definition — the linker will report an error. And the class creator is forced to create the definition, or the code won't link during testing. This ensures that the definition happens only once and that it's in the hands of the class creator.

The entire initialization expression for a static member is in the scope of the class. For example,

```
//: STATINIT.CPP -- Scope of static initializer
#include <iostream.h>

int x = 100;

class withStatic {
  static int x;
  static int y;
public:
  void print() const {
    cout << "withStatic::x = " << x << endl;
    cout << "withStatic::y = " << y << endl;
  }
};

int withStatic::x = 1;
int withStatic::y = x + 1;
// WithStatic::x NOT ::x

main() {
  withStatic WS;
  WS.print();
}
```

Here, the qualification **withStatic::** extends the scope of **withStatic** to the entire definition.

static array initialization

It's possible to create **static const** objects as well as arrays of **static** objects, both **const** and non-**const**. Here's the syntax you use to initialize such elements:

```
//: STATARRY.CPP -- Initializing static arrays

class Values {
  static const int size;
  static const float table[4];
  static char letters[10];
};

const int Values::size = 100;

const float Values::table[4] = {
  1.1, 2.2, 3.3, 4.4
};

char Values::letters[10] = {
  'a', 'b', 'c', 'd', 'e',
  'f', 'g', 'h', 'i', 'j'
};

main() {}
```

As with all **static** member data, you must provide a single external definition for the member. These definitions have internal linkage, so they can be placed in header files. The syntax for initializing static arrays is the same as any aggregate, but you cannot use automatic counting. With the exception of the above paragraph, the compiler must have enough knowledge about the class to create an object by the end of the class declaration, including the exact sizes of all the components.

compile-time constants inside classes

In Chapter 6 enumerations were introduced as a way to create a compile-time constant (one that can be evaluated by the compiler in a constant expression, such as an array size) that's local to a class. This practice, although commonly used, is often referred to as the "enum hack" because it uses enumerations in a way they were not originally intended.

To accomplish the same thing using a better approach, you can use a **static const** inside a class.[2] Because it's both **const** (it won't change) and **static** (there's only one definition for the whole class), a **static const** inside a class can be used as a compile-time constant, like this:

```
class X {
  static const int size;
  int array[size];
public:
  // ...
};

const int X::size = 100; // definition
```

If you're using it in a constant expression inside a class, the definition of the **static const** member must appear before any instances of the class or member function definitions (presumably in the header file). As with an ordinary global **const** used with a built-in type, no storage is allocated for the **const,** and it has internal linkage so no clashes occur.

---

[2] Your compiler may not have implemented this feature yet; check your local documentation.

An additional advantage to this approach is that any built-in type may be made a member **static const**. With **enum**, you're limited to integral values.

nested and local classes

You can easily put static data members in that are nested inside other classes. The definition of such members is an intuitive and obvious extension — you simply use another level of scope resolution. However, you cannot have static data members inside local classes (classes defined inside functions). Thus,

```
//: LOCAL.CPP -- Static members & local classes
#include <iostream.h>

// Nested class CAN have static data members:
class outer {
  class inner {
    static int i; // OK
  };
};

int outer::inner::i = 47;

// Local class cannot have static data members:
void f() {
  class foo {
  public:
//! static int i;   // Error
    // (how would you define i?)
  } x;
}

main() {}
```

You can see the immediate problem with a static member in a local class: How do you describe the data member at file scope in order to define it? In practice, local classes are used very rarely.

static member functions

You can also create **static** member functions that, like **static** data members, work for the class as a whole rather than for a particular object of a class. Instead of making a global function that lives in and "pollutes" the global or local namespace, you bring the function inside the class. When you create a **static** member function, you are expressing an association with a particular class.

A **static** member function cannot access ordinary data members, only **static** data members. It can call only other **static** member functions. Normally, the address of the current object (**this**) is quietly passed in when any member function is called, but a **static** member has no **this**, which is the reason it cannot access ordinary members. Thus, you get the tiny increase in speed afforded by a global function, which doesn't have the extra overhead of passing **this**, but the benefits of having the function inside the class.

Using **static** to indicate that only one piece of storage for a class member exists for all objects of a class parallels its use with functions, to mean that only one copy of a local variable is used for all calls of a function.

Here's an example showing **static** data members and **static** member functions used together:

```
//: SFUNC.CPP -- Static member functions

class X {
  int i;
  static int j;
public:
  X(int I = 0) : i(I) {
      // Non-static member function can access
      // Static member function or data:
```

```
      j = i;
    }
    int val() const { return i; }
    static int incr() {
      //! i++; // Error: static member function
      // Cannot access non-static member data
      return ++j;
    }
    static int f() {
      //! val(); // Error: static member function
      // Cannot access non-static member function
      return incr(); // OK -- calls static
    }
};

int X::j = 0;

main() {
  X x;
  X* xp = &x;
  x.f();
  xp->f();
  X::f(); // Only works with static members
}
```

Because they have no **this** pointer, **static** member functions can neither access non**static** data members nor call non**static** member functions. (Those functions require a **this** pointer.)

Notice in **main( )** that a **static** member can be selected using the usual dot or arrow syntax, associating that function with an object, but also with no object (because a **static** member is associated with a class, not a particular object), using the class name and scope resolution operator.

Here's an interesting feature: Because of the way initialization happens for **static** member objects, you can put a **static** data member of the same class *inside* that class. Here's an example that allows only a single object of type **egg** to exist by making the constructor private. You can access that object, but you can't create any new **egg** objects:

```
//: SELFMEM.CPP -- Static member of same type
// Ensures only one object of this type exists.
// Also referred to as a "singleton" pattern.
#include <iostream.h>

class egg {
  static egg E;
  int i;
  egg(int I) : i(I) {}
public:
  static egg* instance() { return &E; }
  int val() { return i; }
};

egg egg::E(47);

main() {
//!  egg x(1); // error -- can't create an egg
  // You can access the single instance:
  cout << egg::instance()->val() << endl;
}
```

The initialization for **E** happens after the class declaration is complete, so the compiler has all the information it needs to allocate storage and make the constructor call.

static initialization dependency

Within a specific translation unit, the order of initialization of static objects is guaranteed to be the order in which the object definitions appear in that translation unit. The order of destruction is guaranteed to be the reverse of the order of initialization.

However, there is no guarantee concerning the order of initialization of static objects *across* translation units, and there's no way to specify this order. This can cause significant problems. As an example of an instant disaster (which will halt primitive operating systems, and kill the process on sophisticated ones), if one file contains

```
// first file
#include <fstream.h>
ofstream out("out.txt");
```

and another file uses the **out** object in one of its initializers

```
// second file
#include <fstream.h>
extern ofstream out;
class oof {
public:
  oof() { out << "barf"; }
} OOF;
```

the program may work, and it may not. If the programming environment builds the program so that the first file is initialized before the second file, then there will be no problem. However, if the second file is initialized before the first, the constructor for **oof** relies upon the existence of **out**, which hasn't been constructed yet and this causes chaos. This is only a problem with static object initializers *that depend on each other*, because by the time you get into **main( )**, all constructors for static objects have already been called.

A more subtle example can be found in the ARM.[3] In one file,

```
extern int y;
int x = y + 1;
```

and in a second file,

```
extern int x;
int y = x + 1;
```

For all static objects, the linking-loading mechanism guarantees a static initialization to zero before the dynamic initialization specified by the programmer takes place. In the previous example, zeroing of the storage occupied by the **fstream out** object has no special meaning, so it is truly undefined until the constructor is called. However, with built-in types, initialization to zero *does* have meaning, and if the files are initialized in the order they are shown above, **y** begins as statically initialized to zero, so **x** becomes one, and **y** is dynamically initialized to two. However, if the files are initialized in the opposite order, **x** is statically initialized to zero, **y** is dynamically initialized to one, and **x** then becomes two.

Programmers must be aware of this because they can create a program with static initialization dependencies and get it working on one platform, but move it to another compiling environment where it suddenly, mysteriously, doesn't work.

what to do

There are three approaches to dealing with this problem:

---

[3]Bjarne Stroustrup and Margaret Ellis, *The Annotated C++ Reference Manual*, Addison-Wesley, 1990, pp. 20-21.

1. Don't do it. Avoiding static initializer dependencies is the best solution.

2. If you must do it, put the critical static object definitions in a single file, so you can portably control their initialization by putting them in the correct order.

3. If you're convinced it's unavoidable to scatter static objects across translation units — as in the case of a library, where you can't control the programmer who uses it — there is a technique pioneered by Jerry Schwarz while creating the iostream library (because the definitions for **cin**, **cout**, and **cerr** live in a separate file).

This technique requires an additional class in your library header file. This class is responsible for the dynamic initialization of your library's static objects. Here is a simple example:

```
//: DEPEND.H -- Static initialization technique
#ifndef DEPEND_H_
#define DEPEND_H_
#include <iostream.h>
extern int x; // Delarations, not definitions
extern int y;

class initializer {
  static int init_count;
public:
  initializer() {
    cout << "initializer()" << endl;
    // Initialize first time only
    if(init_count++ == 0) {
      cout << "performing initialization"
          << endl;
      x = 100;
      y = 200;
    }
  }
}
```

```
    ~initializer() {
      cout << "~initializer()" << endl;
      // Clean up last time only
      if(--init_count == 0) {
        cout << "performing cleanup" << endl;
        // Any necessary cleanup here
      }
    }
};


// The following creates one object in each
// file where DEPEND.H is included, but that
// object is only visible within that file:
static initializer init;

#endif // DEPEND_H_
```

The declarations for **x** and **y** announce only that these objects exist, but don't allocate storage for them. However, the definition for the **initializer init** allocates storage for that object in every file where the header is included, but because the name is **static** (controlling visibility this time, not the way storage is allocated because that is at file scope by default), it is only visible within that translation unit, so the linker will not complain about multiple definition errors.

Here is the file containing the definitions for **x**, **y**, and **init_count**:

```
//: DEPDEFS.CPP -- Definitions for DEPEND.H
#include "depend.h"
// Static initialization will force
// all these values to zero:
int x;
int y;
int initializer::init_count;
```

(Of course, a file static instance of **init** is also placed in this file.)
Suppose that two other files are created by the library user:

```
//: DEPEND.CPP -- Static initialization
#include "depend.h"
```

and

```
//: DEPEND2.CPP -- Static initialization
#include "depend.h"

main() {
  cout << "inside main()" << endl;
  cout << "leaving main()" << endl;
}
```

Now it doesn't matter which translation unit is initialized first. The first time a translation unit containing DEPEND.H is initialized, **init_count** will be zero so the initialization will be performed. (This depends heavily on the fact that global objects of built-in types are set to zero before any dynamic initialization takes place.) For all the rest of the translation units, the initialization will be skipped. Cleanup happens in the reverse order, and **~initializer( )** ensures that it will happen only once.

This example used built-in types as the global static objects. The technique also works with classes, but those objects must then be dynamically initialized by the **initializer** class. One way to do this is to create the classes without constructors and destructors, but instead with initialization and cleanup member functions using different names. A more common approach, however, is to have pointers to objects and to create them dynamically on the heap inside **initializer( )**. This requires the use of two C++ keywords, **new** and **delete**, which will be explored in Chapter 11.

alternate linkage specifications

What happens if you're writing a program in C++ and you want to use a C library? If you make the C function declaration,

```
float f(int a, char b);
```

the C++ compiler will mangle (decorate) this name to something like **_f_int_int** to support function overloading (and type-safe linkage). However, the C compiler that compiled your C library has most definitely *not* mangled the name, so its internal name will be **_f**. Thus, the linker will not be able to resolve your C++ calls to **f( )**.

The escape mechanism provided in C++ is the *alternate linkage specification*, which was produced in the language by overloading the **extern** keyword. The **extern** is followed by a string that specifies the linkage you want for the declaration, followed by the declaration itself:

```
extern "C" float f(int a, char b);
```

This tells the compiler to give C linkage to **f( )**; that is, don't mangle the name. The only two types of linkage specifications supported by the standard are **"C"** and **"C++,"** but compiler vendors have the option of supporting other languages in the same way.

If you have a group of declarations with alternate linkage, put them inside braces, like this:

```
extern "C" {
  float f(int a, char b);
  double d(int a, char b);
}
```

Or, for a header file,

```
extern "C" {
#include "myheader.h"
}
```

Most C++ compiler vendors handle the alternate linkage specifications inside their header files that work with both C and C++, so you don't have to worry about it.

The only alternate linkage specification strings that are standard are "C" and "C++" but implementations can support other languages using the same mechanism.

summary

The **static** keyword can be confusing because in some situations it controls the location of storage, and in others it controls visibility and linkage of a name.

With the introduction of C++ namespaces, you have an improved and more flexible alternative to control the proliferation of names in large projects.

The use of **static** inside classes is one more way to control names in a program. The names do not clash with global names, and the visibility and access is kept within the program, giving you greater control in the maintenance of your code.

exercises

1. Create a class that holds an array of **int**s. Set the size of the array using an untagged enumeration inside the class. Add a **const int** variable, and initialize it in the constructor initializer list. Add a **static int** member variable and initialize it to a specific value. Add a **static** member function that prints the **static** data member. Add an **inline** constructor and an **inline** member function called **print( )** to print

out all the values in the array, and to call the static member function.

2. In STATDEST.CPP, experiment with the order of constructor and destructor calls by calling **f( )** and **g( )** inside **main( )** in different orders. Does your compiler get it right?

3. In STATDEST.CPP, test the default error handling of your implementation by turning the original definition of **out** into an **extern** declaration and putting the actual definition after the definition of **A** (whose **obj** constructor sends information to **out**). Make sure there's nothing else important running on your machine when you run the program or that your machine will handle faults robustly.

4. Create a class with a destructor that prints a message and then calls **exit( )**. Create a global static object of this class and see what happens.

5. Modify VOLATILE.CPP from Chapter 6 to make **comm::isr( )** something that would actually work as an interrupt service routine.

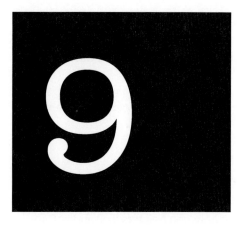

references & the copy-constructor

References are a C++ feature that are like constant pointers automatically dereferenced by the compiler.

Although references also exist in Pascal, the C++ version was taken from the Algol language. They are essential in C++ to support the syntax of operator overloading (see Chapter 10), but are also a general convenience to control the way arguments are passed into and out of functions.

This chapter will first look briefly at the differences between pointers in C and C++, then introduce references. But the bulk of the chapter will delve into a rather confusing issue for the new C++ programmer: the copy-constructor, a special constructor (requiring references) that makes a new object from an existing object of the same type. The copy-constructor is used by the compiler to pass and return objects *by value* into and out of functions.

Finally, the somewhat obscure C++ *pointer-to-member* feature is illuminated.

pointers in C++

The most important difference between pointers in C and in C++ is that C++ is a more strongly typed language. This stands out where **void*** is concerned. C doesn't let you casually assign a pointer of one type to another, but it *does* allow you to quietly accomplish this through a **void***. Thus,

```
bird* b;
rock* r;
void* v;
v = r;
b = v;
```

C++ doesn't allow this because it leaves a big hole in the type system. The compiler gives you an error message, and if you really want to do it, you must make it explicit, both to the compiler and to the reader, using a cast. (See Chapter 17 for C++'s improved casting syntax.)

references in C++

A *reference* (**&**) is like a constant pointer that is automatically dereferenced. It is usually used for function argument lists and function return values. But you can also make a free-standing reference. For example,

```
int x;
int & r = x;
```

When a reference is created, it must be initialized to a live object. However, you can also say

```
int & q = 12;
```

Here, the compiler allocates a piece of storage, initializes it with the value 12, and ties the reference to that piece of storage. The point is that any reference must be tied to someone *else's* piece of storage. When you access a reference, you're accessing that storage. Thus if you say,

```
int x = 0;
int & a = x;
a++;
```

incrementing **a** is actually incrementing **x**. Again, the easiest way to think about a reference is as a fancy pointer. One advantage of this pointer is you never have to wonder whether it's been initialized (the compiler enforces it) and how to dereference it (the compiler does it).

There are certain rules when using references:

1. A reference must be initialized when it is created. (Pointers can be initialized at any time.)

2. Once a reference is initialized to an object, it cannot be changed to refer to another object. (Pointers can be pointed to another object at any time.)

3. You cannot have NULL references. You must always be able to assume that a reference is connected to a legitimate piece of storage.

references in functions

The most common place you'll see references is in function arguments and return values. When a reference is used as a function argument, any modification to the reference *inside* the function will cause changes to the argument *outside* the function. Of course, you could do the same thing by passing a pointer, but a reference has much cleaner syntax. (You can think of a reference as nothing more than a syntax convenience, if you want.)

If you return a reference from a function, you must take the same care as if you return a pointer from a function. Whatever the reference is connected to shouldn't go away when the function returns; otherwise you'll be referring to unknown memory.

Here's an example:

```
//: REFRNCE.CPP -- Simple C++ references

int* f(int* x) {
  (*x)++;
  return x; // Safe; x is outside this scope
}

int& g(int& x) {
  x++; // Same effect as in f()
  return x; // Safe; outside this scope
}

int& h() {
  int q;
//!  return q;   // Error
  static int x;
  return x; // Safe; x lives outside scope
}

main() {
  int A = 0;
```

```
    f(&A); // Ugly (but explicit)
    g(A);  // Clean (but hidden)
}
```

The call to **f( )** doesn't have the convenience and cleanliness of using references, but it's clear that an address is being passed. In the call to **g( )**, an address is being passed (via a reference), but you don't see it.

const references

The reference argument in REFRNCE.CPP works only when the argument is a non-**const** object. If it is a **const** object, the function **g( )** will not accept the argument, which is actually a good thing, because the function *does* modify the outside argument. If you know the function will respect the **const**ness of an object, making the argument a **const** reference will allow the function to be used in all situations. This means that, for built-in types, the function will not modify the argument, and for user-defined types the function will call only **const** member functions, and won't modify any **public** data members.

The use of **const** references in function arguments is especially important because your function may receive a temporary object, created as a return value of another function or explicitly by the user of your function. Temporary objects are always **const**, so if you don't use a **const** reference, that argument won't be accepted by the compiler. As a very simple example,

```
//: PASCONST.CPP -- Passing references as const

void f(int&) {}
void g(const int&) {}

main() {
//!  f(1); // Error
    g(1);      .
}
```

The call to **f(1)** produces a compiler error because the compiler must first create a reference. It does so by allocating storage for an **int**, initializing it to one and producing the address to bind to the reference. The storage *must* be a **const** because changing it would make no sense — you can never get your hands on it again. With all temporary objects you must make the same assumption, that they're inaccessible. It's valuable for the compiler to tell you when you're changing such data because the result would be lost information.

pointer references

In C, if you wanted to modify the *contents* of the pointer rather than what it points to, your function declaration would look like

```
void f(int**);
```

and you'd have to take the address of the pointer when passing it in:

```
int I = 47;
int* ip = &I;
f(&ip);
```

With references in C++, the syntax is cleaner. The function argument becomes a reference to a pointer, and you no longer have to take the address of that pointer. Thus,

```
//: REFPTR.CPP -- Reference to pointer
#include <iostream.h>

void increment(int*& i) { i++; }

main() {
  int* i = 0;
  cout << "i = " << i << endl;
  increment(i);
  cout << "i = " << i << endl;
}
```

By running this program, you'll prove to yourself that the pointer itself is incremented, not what it points to.

argument-passing guidelines

Your normal habit when passing an argument to a function should be to pass by **const** reference. Although this may at first seem like only an efficiency concern (and you normally don't want to concern yourself with efficiency tuning while you're designing and assembling your program), there's more at stake: as you'll see in the remainder of the chapter, a copy-constructor is required to pass an object by value, and this isn't always available.

The efficiency savings can be substantial for such a simple habit: to pass an argument by value requires a constructor and destructor call, but if you're not going to modify the argument then passing by **const** reference only needs an address pushed on the stack.

In fact, virtually the only time passing an address *isn't* preferable is when you're going to do such damage to an object that passing by value is the only safe approach (rather than modifying the outside object, something the caller doesn't usually expect). This is the subject of the next section.

the copy-constructor

Now that you understand the basics of the reference in C++, you're ready to tackle one of the more confusing concepts in the language: the copy-constructor, often called **X(X&)** ("X of X ref"). This constructor is essential to control passing and returning of user-defined types by value during function calls.

passing & returning by value

To understand the need for the copy-constructor, consider the way C handles passing and returning variables by value during function calls. If you declare a function and make a function call,

---

```
int f(int x, char c);
int g = f(a, b);
```

how does the compiler know how to pass and return those
variables? It just knows! The range of the types it must deal with is
so small — **char**, **int**, **float**, and **double** and their variations — that
this information is built into the compiler.

If you figure out how to generate assembly code with your compiler
and determine the statements generated by the function call to **f( )**,
you'll get the equivalent of,

```
push   b
push   a
call   f()
add    sp,4
mov    g, register a
```

This code has been cleaned up significantly to make it generic —
the expressions for **b** and **a** will be different depending on whether
the variables are global (in which case they will be **_b** and **_a**) or
local (the compiler will index them off the stack pointer). This is
also true for the expression for **g**. The appearance of the call to **f( )**
will depend on your name-mangling scheme, and "register a"
depends on how the CPU registers are named within your
assembler. The logic behind the code, however, will remain the
same.

In C and C++, arguments are pushed on the stack from right to left,
the function call is made, then the calling code is responsible for
cleaning the arguments off the stack (which accounts for the **add
sp,4**). But notice that to pass the arguments by value, the compiler
simply pushes copies on the stack — it knows how big they are and
that pushing those arguments makes accurate copies of them.

The return value of **f( )** is placed in a register. Again, the compiler
knows everything there is to know about the return value type
because it's built into the language, so the compiler can return it by

placing it in a register. The simple act of copying the bits of the value is equivalent to copying the object.

passing & returning large objects

But now consider user-defined types. If you create a class and you want to pass an object of that class by value, how is the compiler supposed to know what to do? This is no longer a built-in type the compiler writer knows about; it's a type someone has created since then.

To investigate this, you can start with a simple structure that is clearly too large to return in registers:

```
//: PASSTRUC.CPP -- Passing a big structure

struct big {
  char buf[100];
  int i;
  long d;
} B, B2;

big bigfun(big b) {
  b.i = 100; // Do something to the argument
  return b;
}

main() {
  B2 = bigfun(B);
}
```

Decoding the assembly output is a little more complicated here because most compilers use "helper" functions rather than putting all functionality inline. In **main( )**, the call to **bigfun( )** starts as you might guess — the entire contents of **B** is pushed on the stack. (Here, you might see some compilers load registers with the address of **B** and its size, then call a helper function to push it onto the stack.)

In the previous example, pushing the arguments onto the stack was all that was required before making the function call. In PASSTRUC.CPP, however, you'll see an additional action: The address of **B2** is pushed before making the call, even though it's obviously not an argument. To comprehend what's going on here, you need to understand the constraints on the compiler when it's making a function call.

function-call stack frame

When the compiler generates code for a function call, it first pushes all the arguments on the stack, then makes the call. Inside the function itself, code is generated to move the stack pointer down even further to provide storage for the function's local variables. ("Down" is relative here; your machine may increment or decrement the stack pointer during a push.) But during the assembly-language CALL, the CPU pushes the address in the program code where the function call *came from*, so the assembly-language RETURN can use that address to return to the calling point. This address is of course sacred, because without it your program will get completely lost. Here's what the stack frame looks like after the CALL and the allocation of local variable storage in the function:

function arguments
return address
local variables

The code generated for the rest of the function expects the memory to be laid out exactly this way, so it can carefully pick from the function arguments and local variables without touching the return address. I shall call this block of memory, which is everything used by a function in the process of the function call, the *function frame*.

You might think it reasonable to try to return values on the stack. The compiler could simply push it, and the function could return an offset to indicate how far down in the stack the return value begins.

re-entrancy

The problem occurs because functions in C and C++ support interrupts; that is, the languages are *re-entrant*. They also support recursive function calls. This means that at any point in the execution of a program an interrupt can occur without disturbing the program. Of course, the person who writes the interrupt service routine (ISR) is responsible for saving and restoring all the registers he uses, but if the ISR needs to use any memory that's further down on the stack, that must be a safe thing to do. (You can think of an ISR as an ordinary function with no arguments and **void** return value that saves and restores the CPU state. An ISR function call is triggered by some hardware event rather than an explicit call from within a program.)

Now imagine what would happen if the called function tried to return values on the stack from an ordinary function. You can't touch any part of the stack that's above the return address, so the function would have to push the values below the return address. But when the assembly-language RETURN is executed, the stack pointer must be pointing to the return address (or right below it, depending on your machine), so right before the RETURN, the function must move the stack pointer up, thus clearing off all its local variables. If you're trying to return values on the stack below the return address, you become vulnerable at that moment because an interrupt could come along. The ISR would move the stack pointer down to hold its return address and its local variables and overwrite your return value.

To solve this problem, the caller could be responsible for allocating the extra storage on the stack for the return values *before* calling the function. However, C was not designed this way, and C++ must be compatible. As you'll see shortly, the C++ compiler uses a more efficient scheme.

Your next idea might be to return the value in some global data area, but this doesn't work either. Re-entrancy means that any function can interrupt any other function, *including the same function you're currently inside*. Thus, if you put the return value in a global area, you might return into the same function, which would overwrite that return value. The same logic applies to recursion.

The only safe place to return values is in the registers, so you're back to the problem of what to do when the registers aren't large enough to hold the return value. The answer is to push the address of the return value's destination on the stack as one of the function arguments, and let the function copy the return information directly into the destination. This not only solves all the problems, it's more efficient. It's also the reason that, in PASSTRUC.CPP, the compiler pushes the address of **B2** before the call to **bigfun( )** in **main( )**. If you look at the assembly output for **bigfun( )**, you can see it expects this hidden argument and performs the copy to the destination *inside* the function.

bitcopy versus initialization

So far, so good. There's a workable process for passing and returning large simple structures. But notice that all you have is a way to copy the bits from one place to another, which certainly works fine for the primitive way that C looks at variables. But in C++ objects can be much more sophisticated than a patch of bits; they have meaning. This meaning may not respond well to having its bits copied.

Consider a simple example: a class that knows how many objects of its type exist at any one time. From Chapter 8, you know the way to do this is by including a **static** data member:

```
//: HOWMANY.CPP -- Class counts its objects
#include <fstream.h>
ofstream out("howmany.out");

class howmany {
  static int object_count;
```

```
public:
  howmany() {
    object_count++;
  }
  static void print(const char* msg = 0) {
    if(msg) out << msg << ": ";
    out << "object_count = "
        << object_count << endl;
  }
  ~howmany() {
    object_count--;
    print("~howmany()");
  }
};

int howmany::object_count = 0;

// Pass and return BY VALUE:
howmany f(howmany x) {
  x.print("x argument inside f()");
  return x;
}

main() {
  howmany h;
  howmany::print("after construction of h");
  howmany h2 = f(h);
  howmany::print("after call to f()");
}
```

The class **howmany** contains a **static int** and a **static** member
function **print( )** to report the value of that **int**, along with an
optional message argument. The constructor increments the count
each time an object is created, and the destructor decrements it.

The output, however, is not what you would expect:

```
after construction of h: object_count = 1
x argument inside f(): object_count = 1
~howmany(): object_count = 0
after call to f(): object_count = 0
~howmany(): object_count = -1
~howmany(): object_count = -2
```

After **h** is created, the object count is one, which is fine. But after the call to **f( )** you would expect to have an object count of two, because **h2** is now in scope as well. Instead, the count is zero, which indicates something has gone horribly wrong. This is confirmed by the fact that the two destructors at the end make the object count go negative, something that should never happen.

Look at the point inside **f( )**, which occurs after the argument is passed by value. This means the original object **h** exists outside the function frame, and there's an additional object *inside* the function frame, which is the copy that has been passed by value. However, the argument has been passed using C's primitive notion of bitcopying, whereas the C++ **howmany** class requires true initialization to maintain its integrity, so the default bitcopy fails to produce the desired effect.

When the local object goes out of scope at the end of the call to **f( )**, the destructor is called, which decrements **object_count**, so outside the function, **object_count** is zero. The creation of **h2** is also performed using a bitcopy, so the constructor isn't called there, either, and when **h** and **h2** go out of scope, their destructors cause the negative values of **object_count**.

copy-construction

The problem occurs because the compiler makes an assumption about how to create *a new object from an existing object*. When you pass an object by value, you create a new object, the passed object inside the function frame, from an existing object, the original object outside the function frame. This is also often true when returning an object from a function. In the expression

Thinking in C++   *Bruce Eckel*

```
howmany h2 = f(h);
```

h2, a previously unconstructed object, is created from the return value of **f( )**, so again a new object is created from an existing one.

The compiler's assumption is that you want to perform this creation using a bitcopy, and in many cases this may work fine but in **howmany** it doesn't fly because the meaning of initialization goes beyond simply copying. Another common example occurs if the class contains pointers — what do they point to, and should you copy them or should they be connected to some new piece of memory?

Fortunately, you can intervene in this process and prevent the compiler from doing a bitcopy. You do this by defining your own function to be used whenever the compiler needs to make a new object from an existing object. Logically enough, you're making a new object, so this function is a constructor, and also logically enough, the single argument to this constructor has to do with the object you're constructing from. But that object can't be passed into the constructor by value because you're trying to define the function that handles passing by value, and syntactically it doesn't make sense to pass a pointer because, after all, you're creating the new object from an existing *object*. Here, references come to the rescue, so you take the reference of the source object. This function is called the *copy-constructor* and is often referred to as **X(X&)**, which is its appearance for a class called **X**.

If you create a copy-constructor, the compiler will not perform a bitcopy when creating a new object from an existing one. It will always call your copy-constructor. So, if you don't create a copy-constructor, the compiler will do something sensible, but you have the choice of taking over complete control of the process.

Now it's possible to fix the problem in HOWMANY.CPP:

```
//: HOWMANY2.CPP -- The copy-constructor
#include <fstream.h>
#include <string.h>
```

```
ofstream out("howmany2.out");

class howmany2 {
  enum { bufsize = 30 };
  char id[bufsize]; // Object identifier
  static int object_count;
public:
  howmany2(const char* ID = 0) {
    if(ID) strncpy(id, ID, bufsize);
    else *id = 0;
    ++object_count;
    print("howmany2()");
  }
  // The copy-constructor:
  howmany2(const howmany2& h) {
    strncpy(id, h.id, bufsize);
    strncat(id, " copy", bufsize - strlen(id));
    ++object_count;
    print("howmany2(howmany2&)");
  }
  // Can't be static (printing id):
  void print(const char* msg = 0) const {
    if(msg) out << msg << endl;
    out << '\t' << id << ": "
        << "object_count = "
        << object_count << endl;
  }
  ~howmany2() {
    --object_count;
    print("~howmany2()");
  }
};

int howmany2::object_count = 0;

// Pass and return BY VALUE:
howmany2 f(howmany2 x) {
```

```
      x.print("x argument inside f()");
      out << "returning from f()" << endl;
      return x;
    }

    main() {
      howmany2 h("h");
      out << "entering f()" << endl;
      howmany2 h2 = f(h);
      h2.print("h2 after call to f()");
      out << "call f(), no return value" << endl;
      f(h);
      out << "after call to f()" << endl;
    }
```

There are a number of new twists thrown in here so you can get a better idea of what's happening. First, the character buffer **id** acts as an object identifier so you can figure out which object the information is being printed about. In the constructor, you can put an identifier string (usually the name of the object) that is copied to **id** using the Standard C library function **strncpy( )**, which only copies a certain number of characters, preventing overrun of the buffer.

Next is the copy-constructor, **howmany2(howmany2&)**. The copy-constructor can create a new object only from an existing one, so the existing object's name is copied to **id**, followed by the word "copy" so you can see where it came from. Note the use of the Standard C library function **strncat( )** to copy a maximum number of characters into **id**, again to prevent overrunning the end of the buffer.

Inside the copy-constructor, the object count is incremented just as it is inside the normal constructor. This means you'll now get an accurate object count when passing and returning by value.

The **print( )** function has been modified to print out a message, the object identifier, and the object count. It must now access the **id** data of a particular object, so it can no longer be a **static** member function.

Inside **main( )**, you can see a second call to **f( )** has been added. However, this call uses the common C approach of ignoring the return value. But now that you know how the value is returned (that is, code *inside* the function handles the return process, putting the result in a destination whose address is passed as a hidden argument), you might wonder what happens when the return value is ignored. The output of the program will throw some illumination on this.

Before showing the output, here's a little program that uses iostreams to add line numbers to any file:

```
//: LINENUM.CPP -- Add line numbers
#include <fstream.h>
#include <strstrea.h>
#include <stdlib.h>
#include "..\allege.h"

main(int argc, char* argv[]) {
  if(argc < 2) {
    cerr << "usage: linenum file\n"
         << "adds line numbers to file"
         << endl;
    exit(1);
  }
  strstream text;
  {
    ifstream in(argv[1]);
    allegefile(in);
    text << in.rdbuf(); // Read in whole file
  } // Close file
  ofstream out(argv[1]); // Overwrite file
  const bsz = 100;
  char buf[bsz];
  int line = 0;
```

```
    while(text.getline(buf, bsz)) {
      out.setf(ios::right, ios::adjustfield);
      out.width(2);
      out << ++line << ") " << buf << endl;
    }
}
```

The entire file is read into a **strstream** (which can be both written
to and read from) and the **ifstream** is closed with scoping. Then an
ofstream is created for the same file, overwriting it. **getline( )**
fetches a line at a time from the **strstream** and line numbers are
added as the line is written back into the file.

The line numbers are printed right-aligned in a field width of two, so
the output still lines up in its original configuration. You can change
the program to add an optional second command-line argument
that allows the user to select a field width, *or* you can be more
clever and count all the lines in the file to determine the field width
automatically.

When LINENUM.CPP is applied to HOWMANY2.OUT, the result is

```
 1) howmany2()
 2)   h: object_count = 1
 3) entering f()
 4) howmany2(howmany2&)
 5)   h copy: object_count = 2
 6) x argument inside f()
 7)   h copy: object_count = 2
 8) returning from f()
 9) howmany2(howmany2&)
10)   h copy copy: object_count = 3
11) ~howmany2()
12)   h copy: object_count = 2
13) h2 after call to f()
14)   h copy copy: object_count = 2
15) call f(), no return value
16) howmany2(howmany2&)
```

```
17)    h copy: object_count = 3
18) x argument inside f()
19)    h copy: object_count = 3
20) returning from f()
21) howmany2(howmany2&)
22)    h copy copy: object_count = 4
23) ~howmany2()
24)    h copy: object_count = 3
25) ~howmany2()
26)    h copy copy: object_count = 2
27) after call to f()
28) ~howmany2()
29)    h copy copy: object_count = 1
30) ~howmany2()
31)    h: object_count = 0
```

As you would expect, the first thing that happens is the normal constructor is called for **h**, which increments the object count to one. But then, as **f( )** is entered, the copy-constructor is quietly called by the compiler to perform the pass-by-value. A new object is created, which is the copy of **h** (thus the name "h copy") inside the function frame of **f( )**, so the object count becomes two, courtesy of the copy-constructor.

Line eight indicates the beginning of the return from **f( )**. But before the local variable "h copy" can be destroyed (it goes out of scope at the end of the function), it must be copied into the return value, which happens to be **h2**. A previously unconstructed object (**h2**) is created from an existing object (the local variable inside **f( )**), so of course the copy-constructor is used again in line nine. Now the name becomes "h copy copy" for **h2**'s identifier because it's being copied from the copy that is the local object inside **f( )**. After the object is returned, but before the function ends, the object count becomes temporarily three, but then the local object "h copy" is destroyed. After the call to **f( )** completes in line 13, there are only two objects, **h** and **h2**, and you can see that **h2** did indeed end up as "h copy copy."

Thinking in C++

temporary objects

Line 15 begins the call to **f(h)**, this time ignoring the return value. You can see in line 16 that the copy-constructor is called just as before to pass the argument in. And also, as before, line 21 shows the copy-constructor is called for the return value. But the copy-constructor must have an address to work on as its destination (a **this** pointer). Where is the object returned to?

It turns out the compiler can create a temporary object whenever it needs one to properly evaluate an expression. In this case it creates one you don't even see to act as the destination for the ignored return value of **f( )**. The lifetime of this temporary object is as short as possible so the landscape doesn't get cluttered up with temporaries waiting to be destroyed, taking up valuable resources. In some cases, the temporary might be immediately passed to another function, but in this case it isn't needed after the function call, so as soon as the function call ends by calling the destructor for the local object (lines 23 and 24), the temporary object is destroyed (lines 25 and 26).

Now, in lines 28-31, the **h2** object is destroyed, followed by **h**, and the object count goes correctly back to zero.

default copy-constructor

Because the copy-constructor implements pass and return by value, it's important that the compiler will create one for you in the case of simple structures — effectively, the same thing it does in C. However, all you've seen so far is the default primitive behavior: a bitcopy.

When more complex types are involved, the C++ compiler will still automatically create a copy-constructor if you don't make one. Again, however, a bitcopy doesn't make sense, because it doesn't necessarily implement the proper meaning.

Here's an example to show the more intelligent approach the compiler takes. Suppose you create a new class composed of objects of several existing classes. This is called, appropriately enough, *composition*, and it's one of the ways you can make new classes from existing classes. Now take the role of a naive user who's trying to solve a problem quickly by creating the new class this way. You don't know about copy-constructors, so you don't create one. The example demonstrates what the compiler does while creating the default copy-constructor for your new class:

```cpp
//: AUTOCC.CPP -- Automatic copy-constructor
#include <iostream.h>
#include <string.h>

class withCC { // With copy-constructor
public:
  // Explicit default constructor required:
  withCC() {}
  withCC(const withCC&) {
    cout << "withCC(withCC&)" << endl;
  }
};

class woCC { // Without copy-constructor
  enum { bsz = 30 };
  char buf[bsz];
public:
  woCC(const char* msg = 0 ) {
    memset(buf, 0, bsz);
    if(msg) strncpy(buf, msg, bsz);
  }
  void print(const char* msg = 0) const {
    if(msg) cout << msg << ": ";
    cout << buf << endl;
  }
};

class composite {
  withCC WITHCC; // Embedded objects
```

```
  woCC WOCC;
public:
  composite() : WOCC("composite()") {}
  void print(const char* msg = 0) {
    WOCC.print(msg);
  }
};

main() {
  composite c;
  c.print("contents of c");
  cout << "calling composite copy-constructor"
       << endl;
  composite c2 = c;  // Calls copy-constructor
  c2.print("contents of c2");
}
```

The class **withCC** contains a copy-constructor, which simply announces it has been called, and this brings up an interesting issue. In the class **composite**, an object of **withCC** is created using a default constructor. If there were no constructors at all in **withCC**, the compiler would automatically create a default constructor, which would do nothing in this case. However, if you add a copy-constructor, you've told the compiler you're going to handle constructor creation, so it no longer creates a default constructor for you and will complain unless you explicitly create a default constructor as was done for **withCC**.

The class **woCC** has no copy-constructor, but its constructor will store a message in an internal buffer that can be printed out using **print( )**. This constructor is explicitly called in **composite**'s constructor initializer list (briefly introduced in Chapter 6 and covered fully in Chapter 12). The reason for this becomes apparent later.

The class **composite** has member objects of both **withCC** and **woCC** (note the embedded object **WOCC** is initialized in the

---

constructor-initializer list, as it must be), and no explicitly defined copy-constructor. However, in **main( )** an object is created using the copy-constructor in the definition:

```
composite c2 = c;
```

The copy-constructor for **composite** is created automatically by the compiler, and the output of the program reveals how it is created.

To create a copy-constructor for a class that uses composition (and inheritance, which is introduced in Chapter 12), the compiler recursively calls the copy-constructors for all the member objects and base classes. That is, if the member object also contains another object, its copy-constructor is also called. So in this case, the compiler calls the copy-constructor for **withCC**. The output shows this constructor being called. Because **woCC** has no copy-constructor, the compiler creates one for it, which is the default behavior of a bitcopy, and calls that inside the **composite** copy-constructor. The call to **composite::print( )** in main shows that this happens because the contents of **c2.WOCC** are identical to the contents of **c.WOCC**. The process the compiler goes through to synthesize a copy-constructor is called *memberwise initialization*.

It's best to always create your own copy-constructor rather than letting the compiler do it for you. This guarantees it will be under your control.

alternatives to copy-construction

At this point your head may be swimming, and you might be wondering how you could have possibly written a functional class without knowing about the copy-constructor. But remember: You need a copy-constructor only if you're going to pass an object of your class *by value*. If that never happens, you don't need a copy-constructor.

preventing pass-by-value

"But," you say, "if I don't make a copy-constructor, the compiler will create one for me. So how do I know that an object will never be passed by value?"

There's a simple technique for preventing pass-by-value: Declare a **private** copy-constructor. You don't even need to create a definition, unless one of your member functions or a **friend** function needs to perform a pass-by-value. If the user tries to pass or return the object by value, the compiler will produce an error message because the copy-constructor is **private**. It can no longer create a default copy-constructor because you've explicitly stated you're taking over that job.

Here's an example:

```cpp
//: STOPCC.CPP -- Preventing copy-construction

class noCC {
  int i;
  noCC(const noCC&); // No definition
public:
  noCC(int I = 0) : i(I) {}
};

void f(noCC);

main() {
  noCC n;
//! f(n); // Error: copy-constructor called
//! noCC n2 = n; // Error: c-c called
//! noCC n3(n); // Error: c-c called
}
```

Notice the use of the more general form

```cpp
noCC(const noCC&);
```

using the **const**.

functions that modify outside objects

Reference syntax is nicer to use than pointer syntax, yet it clouds the meaning for the reader. For example, in the iostreams library one overloaded version of the **get( )** function takes a **char&** as an argument, and the whole point of the function is to modify its argument by inserting the result of the **get( )**. However, when you read code using this function it's not immediately obvious to you the outside object is being modified:

```
char c;
cin.get(c);
```

Instead, the function call looks like a pass-by-value, which suggests the outside object is *not* modified.

Because of this, it's probably safer from a code maintenance standpoint to use pointers when you're passing the address of an argument to modify. If you *always* pass addresses as **const** references *except* when you intend to modify the outside object via the address, where you pass by non-**const** pointer, then your code is far easier for the reader to follow.

pointers to members

A pointer is a variable that holds the address of some location, which can be either data or a function, so you can change what a pointer selects at run-time. The C++ *pointer-to-member* follows this same concept, except that what it selects is a location inside a class. The dilemma here is that all a pointer needs is an address, but there is no "address" inside a class; selecting a member of a class means offsetting into that class. You can't produce an actual address until you combine that offset with the starting address of a particular object. The syntax of pointers to members requires that you select an object at the same time you're dereferencing the pointer to member.

To understand this syntax, consider a simple structure:

```
struct simple { int a; };
```

If you have a pointer **sp** and an object **so** for this structure, you can select members by saying

```
sp->a;
so.a;
```

Now suppose you have an ordinary pointer to an integer, **ip**. To access what **ip** is pointing to, you dereference the pointer with a *:

```
*ip = 4;
```

Finally, consider what happens if you have a pointer that happens to point to something inside a class object, even if it does in fact represent an offset into the object. To access what it's pointing at, you must dereference it with *. But it's an offset into an object, so you must also refer to that particular object. Thus, the * is combined with the object dereferencing. As an example using the **simple** class,

```
sp->*pm = 47;
so.*pm = 47;
```

So the new syntax becomes **–>*** for a pointer to an object, and **.*** for the object or a reference. Now, what is the syntax for defining **pm**? Like any pointer, you have to say what type it's pointing at, and you use a * in the definition. The only difference is you must say what class of objects this pointer-to-member is used with. Of course, this is accomplished with the name of the class and the scope resolution operator. Thus,

```
int simple::*pm;
```

You can also initialize the pointer-to-member when you define it (or any other time):

```
int simple::*pm = &simple::a;
```

There is actually no "address" of **simple::a** because you're just referring to the class and not an object of that class. Thus, **&simple::a** can be used only as pointer-to-member syntax.

functions

A similar exercise produces the pointer-to-member syntax for member functions. A pointer to a function is defined like this:

```
int (*fp)(float);
```

The parentheses around **(*fp)** are necessary to force the compiler to evaluate the definition properly. Without them this would appear to be a function that returns an **int***.

To define and use a pointer to a member function, parentheses play a similarly important role. If you have a function inside a structure:

```
struct simple2 { int f(float); };
```

you define a pointer to that member function by inserting the class name and scope resolution operator into an ordinary function pointer definition:

```
int (simple2::*fp)(float);
```

You can also initialize it when you create it, or at any other time:

```
int (simple2::*fp)(float) = &simple2::f;
```

As with normal functions, the **&** is optional; you can give the function identifier without an argument list to mean the address:

```
fp = simple2::f;
```

an example

The value of a pointer is that you can change what it points to at run-time, which provides an important flexibility in your programming because through a pointer you can select or change *behavior* at run-time. A pointer-to-member is no different; it allows you to choose a member at run-time. Typically, your classes will have only member functions publicly visible (data members are usually considered part of the underlying implementation), so the following example selects member functions at run-time.

```
//: PMEM.CPP -- Pointers to members

class widget {
public:
  void f(int);
  void g(int);
  void h(int);
  void i(int);
};

void widget::h(int) {}

main() {
  widget w;
  widget* wp = &w;
  void (widget::*pmem)(int) = &widget::h;
  (w.*pmem)(1);
  (wp->*pmem)(2);
}
```

Of course, it isn't particularly reasonable to expect the casual user to create such complicated expressions. If the user must directly manipulate a pointer-to-member, then a **typedef** is in order. To really clean things up, you can use the pointer-to-member as part of the internal implementation mechanism. Here's the preceding example using a pointer-to-member *inside* the class. All the user needs to do is pass a number in to select a function.[1]

```
//: PMEM2.CPP -- Pointers to members
#include <iostream.h>
```

---

[1] Thanks to Owen Mortensen for this example

```
class widget {
  void f(int) const {cout << "widget::f()\n";}
  void g(int) const {cout << "widget::g()\n";}
  void h(int) const {cout << "widget::h()\n";}
  void i(int) const {cout << "widget::i()\n";}
  enum { count = 4 };
  void (widget::*fptr[count])(int) const;
public:
  widget() {
    fptr[0] = &widget::f; // Full spec required
    fptr[1] = &widget::g;
    fptr[2] = &widget::h;
    fptr[3] = &widget::i;
  }
  void select(int I, int J) {
    if(I < 0 || I >= count) return;
    (this->*fptr[I])(J);
  }
  int Count() { return count; }
};

main() {
  widget w;
  for(int i = 0; i < w.Count(); i++)
    w.select(i, 47);
}
```

In the class interface and in **main( )**, you can see that the entire
implementation, including the functions themselves, has been
hidden away. The code must even ask for the **Count( )** of functions.
This way, the class implementor can change the quantity of
functions in the underlying implementation without affecting the
code where the class is used.

The initialization of the pointers-to-members in the constructor may
seem overspecified. Shouldn't you be able to say

```
fptr[1] = &g;
```

because the name **g** occurs in the member function, which is automatically in the scope of the class? The problem is this doesn't conform to the pointer-to-member syntax, which is required so everyone, especially the compiler, can figure out what's going on. Similarly, when the pointer-to-member is dereferenced, it seems like

```
(this->*fptr[i])(j);
```

is also over-specified; **this** looks redundant. Again, the syntax requires that a pointer-to-member always be bound to an object when it is dereferenced.

summary

Pointers in C++ are remarkably similar to pointers in C, which is good. Otherwise a lot of C code wouldn't compile properly under C++. The only compiler errors you will produce is where dangerous assignments occur. If these are in fact what are intended, the compiler errors can be removed with a simple (and explicit!) cast.

C++ also adds the *reference* from Algol and Pascal, which is like a constant pointer that is automatically dereferenced by the compiler. A reference holds an address, but you treat it like an object. References are essential for clean syntax with operator overloading (the subject of the next chapter), but they also add syntactic convenience for passing and returning objects for ordinary functions.

The copy-constructor takes a reference to an existing object of the same type as its argument, and it is used to create a new object from an existing one. The compiler automatically calls the copy-constructor when you pass or return an object by value. Although the compiler will automatically create a copy-constructor for you, if you think one will be needed for your class you should always define it yourself to ensure that the proper behavior occurs. If you don't want the object passed or returned by value, you should create a private copy-constructor.

Pointers-to-members have the same functionality as ordinary pointers: You can choose a particular region of storage (data or function) at run-time. Pointers-to-members just happen to work with class members rather than global data or functions. You get the programming flexibility that allows you to change behavior at run-time.

exercises

1. Create a function that takes a **char&** argument and modifies that argument. In **main( )**, print out a **char** variable, call your function for that variable, and print it out again to prove to yourself it has been changed. How does this affect program readability?

2. Write a class with a copy-constructor that announces itself to **cout**. Now create a function that passes an object of your new class in by value and another one that creates a local object of your new class and returns it by value. Call these functions to prove to yourself that the copy-constructor is indeed quietly called when passing and returning objects by value.

3. Discover how to get your compiler to generate assembly language, and produce assembly for PASSTRUC.CPP. Trace through and demystify the way your compiler generates code to pass and return large structures.

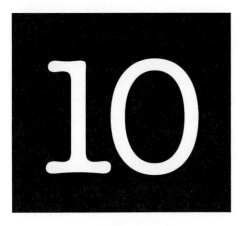

operator overloading

Operator overloading is just "syntactic sugar," which means it is simply another way for you to make a function call.

The difference is the arguments for this function don't appear inside parentheses, but instead surrounding or next to characters you've always thought of as immutable operators.

But in C++, it's possible to define new operators that work with classes. This definition is just like an ordinary function definition except the name of the function begins with the keyword **operator** and ends with the operator itself. That's the only difference, and it becomes a function like any other function, which the compiler calls when it sees the appropriate pattern.

warning & reassurance

It's very tempting to become overenthusiastic with operator overloading. It's a fun toy, at first. But remember it's *only* syntactic sugar, another way of calling a function. Looking at it this way, you have no reason to overload an operator except that it will make the code involving your class easier to write and especially *read*. (Remember, code is read much more than it is written.) If this isn't the case, don't bother.

Another common response to operator overloading is panic: Suddenly, C operators have no familiar meaning anymore. "Everything's changed and all my C code will do different things !" This isn't true. All the operators used in expressions that contain only built-in data types cannot be changed. You can never overload operators such that

```
1 << 4;
```

behaves differently, or

```
1.414 << 2;
```

has meaning. Only an expression containing a user-defined type can have an overloaded operator.

syntax

Defining an overloaded operator is like defining a function, but the name of that function is **operator@**, where @ represents the operator. The number of arguments in the function argument list depends on two factors:

1. Whether it's a unary (one argument) or binary (two argument) operator.

2. Whether the operator is defined as a global function (one argument for unary, two for binary) or a member function (zero arguments for unary, one for binary — the object becomes the left-hand argument).

Here's a small class that shows the syntax for operator overloading:

```
//: OPOVER.CPP -- Operator overloading syntax
#include <iostream.h>

class integer {
  int i;
public:
  integer(int I) { i = I; }
  const integer
  operator+(const integer& rv) const {
    cout << "operator+" << endl;
    return integer(i + rv.i);
  }
  integer&
  operator+=(const integer& rv) {
    cout << "operator+=" << endl;
    i += rv.i;
    return *this;
  }
};

main() {
  cout << "built-in types:" << endl;
  int i = 1, j = 2, k = 3;
  k += i + j;
  cout << "user-defined types:" << endl;
  integer I(1), J(2), K(3);
  K += I + J;
}
```

The two overloaded operators are defined as inline member functions that announce when they are called. The single argument is what appears on the right-hand side of the operator for binary operators. Unary operators have no arguments when defined as member functions. The member function is called for the object on the left-hand side of the operator.

For nonconditional operators (conditionals usually return a Boolean value) you'll almost always want to return an object or reference of the same type you're operating on if the two arguments are the same type. If they're not, the interpretation of what it should produce is up to you. This way complex expressions can be built up:

```
K += I + J;
```

The **operator+** produces a new **integer** (a temporary) that is used as the **rv** argument for the **operator+=**. This temporary is destroyed as soon as it is no longer needed.

overloadable operators

Although you can overload almost all the operators available in C, the use is fairly restrictive. In particular, you cannot combine operators that currently have no meaning in C (such as ** to represent exponentiation), you cannot change the evaluation precedence of operators, and you cannot change the number of arguments an operator takes. This makes sense — all these actions would produce operators that confuse meaning rather than clarify it.

The next two subsections give examples of all the "regular" operators, overloaded in the form that you'll most likely use.

unary operators

The following example shows the syntax to overload all the unary operators, both in the form of global functions and member functions. These will expand upon the **integer** class shown previously and add a new **byte** class. The meaning of your particular operators will depend on the way you want to use them, but consider the client programmer before doing something unexpected.

```
//: UNARY.CPP -- Overloading unary operators
#include <iostream.h>
class integer {
  long i;
  integer* This() { return this; }
public:
  integer(long I = 0) : i(I) {}
  // No side effects takes const& argument:
  friend const integer&
    operator+(const integer& a);
  friend const integer
    operator-(const integer& a);
  friend const integer
    operator~(const integer& a);
  friend integer*
    operator&(integer& a);
  friend int
    operator!(const integer& a);
  // Side effects don't take const& argument:
  // Prefix:
  friend const integer&
    operator++(integer& a);
  // Postfix:
  friend const integer
    operator++(integer& a, int);
  // Prefix:
  friend const integer&
    operator--(integer& a);
  // Postfix:
  friend const integer
    operator--(integer& a, int);
```

```
};

// Global operators:
const integer& operator+(const integer& a) {
  cout << "+integer\n";
  return a; // Unary + has no effect
}
const integer operator-(const integer& a) {
  cout << "-integer\n";
  return integer(-a.i);
}
const integer operator~(const integer& a) {
  cout << "~integer\n";
  return integer(~a.i);
}
integer* operator&(integer& a) {
  cout << "&integer\n";
  return a.This(); // &a is recursive!
}
int operator!(const integer& a) {
  cout << "!integer\n";
  return !a.i;
}
// Prefix; return incremented value
const integer& operator++(integer& a) {
  cout << "++integer\n";
  a.i++;
  return a;
}
// Postfix; return the value before increment:
const integer operator++(integer& a, int) {
  cout << "integer++\n";
  integer r(a.i);
  a.i++;
  return r;
}
// Prefix; return decremented value
```

```cpp
const integer& operator--(integer& a) {
  cout << "--integer\n";
  a.i--;
  return a;
}
// Postfix; return the value before decrement:
const integer operator--(integer& a, int) {
  cout << "integer--\n";
  integer r(a.i);
  a.i--;
  return r;
}

void f(integer a) {
  +a;
  -a;
  ~a;
  integer* ip = &a;
  !a;
  ++a;
  a++;
  --a;
  a--;
}

// Member operators (implicit "this"):
class byte {
  unsigned char b;
public:
  byte(unsigned char B = 0) : b(B) {}
  // No side effects: const member function:
  const byte& operator+() const {
    cout << "+byte\n";
    return *this;
  }
  const byte operator-() const {
    cout << "-byte\n";
```

```
    return byte(-b);
  }
  const byte operator~() const {
    cout << "~byte\n";
    return byte(~b);
  }
  byte operator!() const {
    cout << "!byte\n";
    return byte(!b);
  }
  byte* operator&() {
    cout << "&byte\n";
    return this;
  }
  // Side effects: non-const member function:
  const byte& operator++() { // Prefix
    cout << "++byte\n";
    b++;
    return *this;
  }
  const byte operator++(int) { // Postfix
    cout << "byte++\n";
    byte before(b);
    b++;
    return before;
  }
  const byte& operator--() { // Prefix
    cout << "--byte\n";
    --b;
    return *this;
  }
  const byte operator--(int) { // Postfix
    cout << "byte--\n";
    byte before(b);
    --b;
    return before;
  }
```

```
};

void g(byte b) {
   +b;
   -b;
   ~b;
   byte* bp = &b;
   !b;
   ++b;
   b++;
   --b;
   b--;
}

main() {
   integer a;
   f(a);
   byte b;
   g(b);
}
```

The functions are grouped according to the way their arguments
are passed. Guidelines for how to pass and return arguments are
given later. The above forms (and the ones that follow in the next
section) are typically what you'll use, so start with them as a pattern
when overloading your own operators.

increment & decrement

The overloaded **++** and **– –** operators present a dilemma because
you want to be able to call different functions depending on
whether they appear before (prefix) or after (postfix) the object
they're acting upon. The solution is simple, but some people find it
a bit confusing at first. When the compiler sees, for example, **++a**
(a preincrement), it generates a call to **operator++(a)**; but when it
sees **a++**, it generates a call to **operator++(a, int)**. That is, the
compiler differentiates between the two forms by making different
function calls. In UNARY.CPP for the member function versions, if

---

the compiler sees **++b**, it generates a call to **B::operator++( )**; and if it sees **b++** it calls **B::operator++(int)**.

The user never sees the result of her action except that a different function gets called for the prefix and postfix versions. Underneath, however, the two functions calls have different signatures, so they link to two different function bodies. The compiler passes a dummy constant value for the **int** argument (which is never given an identifier because the value is never used) to generate the different signature for the postfix version.

binary operators

The following listing repeats the example of UNARY.CPP for binary operators. Both global versions and member function versions are shown.

```
//: BINARY.CPP -- Overloading binary operators
#include <fstream.h>
#include "..\allege.h"
ofstream out("binary.out");

class integer { // Combine this with UNARY.CPP
  long i;
public:
  integer(long I = 0) : i(I) {}
  // Operators that create new, modified value:
  friend const integer
    operator+(const integer& left,
              const integer& right);
  friend const integer
    operator-(const integer& left,
              const integer& right);
  friend const integer
    operator*(const integer& left,
              const integer& right);
  friend const integer
    operator/(const integer& left,
```

```
                          const integer& right);
    friend const integer
      operator%(const integer& left,
                    const integer& right);
    friend const integer
      operator^(const integer& left,
                    const integer& right);
    friend const integer
      operator&(const integer& left,
                    const integer& right);
    friend const integer
      operator|(const integer& left,
                    const integer& right);
    friend const integer
      operator<<(const integer& left,
                    const integer& right);
    friend const integer
      operator>>(const integer& left,
                    const integer& right);
    // Assignments modify & return lvalue:
    friend integer&
      operator+=(integer& left,
                    const integer& right);
    friend integer&
      operator-=(integer& left,
                    const integer& right);
    friend integer&
      operator*=(integer& left,
                    const integer& right);
    friend integer&
      operator/=(integer& left,
                    const integer& right);
    friend integer&
      operator%=(integer& left,
                    const integer& right);
    friend integer&
      operator^=(integer& left,
```

```
                const integer& right);
  friend integer&
    operator&=(integer& left,
                const integer& right);
  friend integer&
    operator|=(integer& left,
                const integer& right);
  friend integer&
    operator>>=(integer& left,
                 const integer& right);
  friend integer&
    operator<<=(integer& left,
                 const integer& right);
  // Conditional operators return true/false:
  friend int
    operator==(const integer& left,
                const integer& right);
  friend int
    operator!=(const integer& left,
                const integer& right);
  friend int
    operator<(const integer& left,
               const integer& right);
  friend int
    operator>(const integer& left,
               const integer& right);
  friend int
    operator<=(const integer& left,
                const integer& right);
  friend int
    operator>=(const integer& left,
                const integer& right);
  friend int
    operator&&(const integer& left,
                const integer& right);
  friend int
    operator||(const integer& left,
```

```cpp
                        const integer& right);
    // Write the contents to an ostream:
    void print(ostream& os) const { os << i; }
};

const integer
  operator+(const integer& left,
            const integer& right) {
    return integer(left.i + right.i);
}
const integer
  operator-(const integer& left,
            const integer& right) {
    return integer(left.i - right.i);
}
const integer
  operator*(const integer& left,
            const integer& right) {
    return integer(left.i * right.i);
}
const integer
  operator/(const integer& left,
            const integer& right) {
    allege(right.i != 0, "divide by zero");
    return integer(left.i / right.i);
}
const integer
  operator%(const integer& left,
            const integer& right) {
    allege(right.i != 0, "modulo by zero");
    return integer(left.i % right.i);
}
const integer
  operator^(const integer& left,
            const integer& right) {
    return integer(left.i ^ right.i);
}
```

```cpp
const integer
  operator&(const integer& left,
            const integer& right) {
  return integer(left.i & right.i);
}
const integer
  operator|(const integer& left,
            const integer& right) {
  return integer(left.i | right.i);
}
const integer
  operator<<(const integer& left,
             const integer& right) {
  return integer(left.i << right.i);
}
const integer
  operator>>(const integer& left,
             const integer& right) {
  return integer(left.i >> right.i);
}
// Assignments modify & return lvalue:
integer& operator+=(integer& left,
                    const integer& right) {
  if(&left == &right) {/* self-assignment */}
  left.i += right.i;
  return left;
}
integer& operator-=(integer& left,
                    const integer& right) {
  if(&left == &right) {/* self-assignment */}
  left.i -= right.i;
  return left;
}
integer& operator*=(integer& left,
                    const integer& right) {
  if(&left == &right) {/* self-assignment */}
  left.i *= right.i;
```

```
      return left;
   }
   integer& operator/=(integer& left,
                       const integer& right) {
      allege(right.i != 0, "divide by zero");
      if(&left == &right) {/* self-assignment */}
      left.i /= right.i;
      return left;
   }
   integer& operator%=(integer& left,
                       const integer& right) {
      allege(right.i != 0, "modulo by zero");
      if(&left == &right) {/* self-assignment */}
      left.i %= right.i;
      return left;
   }
   integer& operator^=(integer& left,
                       const integer& right) {
      if(&left == &right) {/* self-assignment */}
      left.i ^= right.i;
      return left;
   }
   integer& operator&=(integer& left,
                       const integer& right) {
      if(&left == &right) {/* self-assignment */}
      left.i &= right.i;
      return left;
   }
   integer& operator|=(integer& left,
                       const integer& right) {
      if(&left == &right) {/* self-assignment */}
      left.i |= right.i;
      return left;
   }
   integer& operator>>=(integer& left,
                        const integer& right) {
      if(&left == &right) {/* self-assignment */}
```

```
    left.i >>= right.i;
    return left;
}
integer& operator<<=(integer& left,
                     const integer& right) {
    if(&left == &right) {/* self-assignment */}
    left.i <<= right.i;
    return left;
}
// Conditional operators return true/false:
int operator==(const integer& left,
               const integer& right) {
    return left.i == right.i;
}
int operator!=(const integer& left,
               const integer& right) {
    return left.i != right.i;
}
int operator<(const integer& left,
              const integer& right) {
    return left.i < right.i;
}
int operator>(const integer& left,
              const integer& right) {
    return left.i > right.i;
}
int operator<=(const integer& left,
               const integer& right) {
    return left.i <= right.i;
}
int operator>=(const integer& left,
               const integer& right) {
    return left.i >= right.i;
}
int operator&&(const integer& left,
               const integer& right) {
    return left.i && right.i;
```

```
}
int operator||(const integer& left,
               const integer& right) {
   return left.i || right.i;
}

void h(integer& c1, integer& c2) {
  // A complex expression:
  c1 += c1 * c2 + c2 % c1;
  #define TRY(op) \
  out << "c1 = "; c1.print(out); \
  out << ", c2 = "; c2.print(out); \
  out << ";  c1 " #op " c2 produces ";\
  (c1 op c2).print(out); \
  out << endl;
  TRY(+) TRY(-) TRY(*) TRY(/)
  TRY(%) TRY(^) TRY(&) TRY(|)
  TRY(<<) TRY(>>) TRY(+=) TRY(-=)
  TRY(*=) TRY(/=) TRY(%=) TRY(^=)
  TRY(&=) TRY(|=) TRY(>>=) TRY(<<=)
  // Conditionals:
  #define TRYC(op) \
  out << "c1 = "; c1.print(out); \
  out << ", c2 = "; c2.print(out); \
  out << ";  c1 " #op " c2 produces ";\
  out << (c1 op c2); \
  out << endl;
  TRYC(<) TRYC(>) TRYC(==) TRYC(!=) TRYC(<=)
  TRYC(>=) TRYC(&&) TRYC(||)
}

// Member operators (implicit "this"):
class byte { // Combine this with UNARY.CPP
  unsigned char b;
public:
  byte(unsigned char B = 0) : b(B) {}
  // No side effects: const member function:
```

```cpp
const byte
  operator+(const byte& right) const {
  return byte(b + right.b);
}
const byte
  operator-(const byte& right) const {
  return byte(b - right.b);
}
const byte
  operator*(const byte& right) const {
  return byte(b * right.b);
}
const byte
  operator/(const byte& right) const {
  allege(right.b != 0, "divide by zero");
  return byte(b / right.b);
}
const byte
  operator%(const byte& right) const {
  allege(right.b != 0, "modulo by zero");
  return byte(b % right.b);
}
const byte
  operator^(const byte& right) const {
  return byte(b ^ right.b);
}
const byte
  operator&(const byte& right) const {
  return byte(b & right.b);
}
const byte
  operator|(const byte& right) const {
  return byte(b | right.b);
}
const byte
  operator<<(const byte& right) const {
  return byte(b << right.b);
```

```
    }
    const byte
      operator>>(const byte& right) const {
      return byte(b >> right.b);
    }
    // Assignments modify & return lvalue.
    // operator= can only be a member function:
    byte& operator=(const byte& right) {
      // Handle self-assignment:
      if(this == &right) return *this;
      b = right.b;
      return *this;
    }
    byte& operator+=(const byte& right) {
      if(this == &right) {/* self-assignment */}
      b += right.b;
      return *this;
    }
    byte& operator-=(const byte& right) {
      if(this == &right) {/* self-assignment */}
      b -= right.b;
      return *this;
    }
    byte& operator*=(const byte& right) {
      if(this == &right) {/* self-assignment */}
      b *= right.b;
      return *this;
    }
    byte& operator/=(const byte& right) {
      allege(right.b != 0, "divide by zero");
      if(this == &right) {/* self-assignment */}
      b /= right.b;
      return *this;
    }
    byte& operator%=(const byte& right) {
      allege(right.b != 0, "modulo by zero");
      if(this == &right) {/* self-assignment */}
```

```
    b %= right.b;
    return *this;
  }
  byte& operator^=(const byte& right) {
    if(this == &right) {/* self-assignment */}
    b ^= right.b;
    return *this;
  }
  byte& operator&=(const byte& right) {
    if(this == &right) {/* self-assignment */}
    b &= right.b;
    return *this;
  }
  byte& operator|=(const byte& right) {
    if(this == &right) {/* self-assignment */}
    b |= right.b;
    return *this;
  }
  byte& operator>>=(const byte& right) {
    if(this == &right) {/* self-assignment */}
    b >>= right.b;
    return *this;
  }
  byte& operator<<=(const byte& right) {
    if(this == &right) {/* self-assignment */}
    b <<= right.b;
    return *this;
  }
  // Conditional operators return true/false:
  int operator==(const byte& right) const {
      return b == right.b;
  }
  int operator!=(const byte& right) const {
      return b != right.b;
  }
  int operator<(const byte& right) const {
      return b < right.b;
```

```cpp
  }
  int operator>(const byte& right) const {
      return b > right.b;
  }
  int operator<=(const byte& right) const {
      return b <= right.b;
  }
  int operator>=(const byte& right) const {
      return b >= right.b;
  }
  int operator&&(const byte& right) const {
      return b && right.b;
  }
  int operator||(const byte& right) const {
      return b || right.b;
  }
  // Write the contents to an ostream:
  void print(ostream& os) const {
    os << "0x" << hex << int(b) << dec;
  }
};

void k(byte& b1, byte& b2) {
  b1 = b1 * b2 + b2 % b1;

  #define TRY2(op) \
  out << "b1 = "; b1.print(out); \
  out << ", b2 = "; b2.print(out); \
  out << ";   b1 " #op " b2 produces ";\
  (b1 op b2).print(out); \
  out << endl;

  b1 = 9; b2 = 47;
  TRY2(+)  TRY2(-)  TRY2(*)  TRY2(/)
  TRY2(%)  TRY2(^)  TRY2(&)  TRY2(|)
  TRY2(<<)  TRY2(>>)  TRY2(+=)  TRY2(-=)
  TRY2(*=)  TRY2(/=)  TRY2(%=)  TRY2(^=)
```

```
TRY2(&=)  TRY2(|=)  TRY2(>>=)  TRY2(<<=)
TRY2(=) // Assignment operator

// Conditionals:
#define TRYC2(op) \
out << "b1 = "; b1.print(out); \
out << ", b2 = "; b2.print(out); \
out << ";  b1 " #op " b2 produces ";\
out << (b1 op b2); \
out << endl;

b1 = 9; b2 = 47;
TRYC2(<)  TRYC2(>)  TRYC2(==)  TRYC2(!=)  TRYC2(<=)
TRYC2(>=)  TRYC2(&&)  TRYC2(||)

// Chained assignment:
byte b3 = 92;
b1 = b2 = b3;
}

main() {
  integer c1(47), c2(9);
  h(c1, c2);
  out << "\n member functions:" << endl;
  byte b1(47), b2(9);
  k(b1, b2);
}
```

You can see that **operator=** is only allowed to be a member function. This is explained later.

Notice that all the assignment operators have code to check for self-assignment in operator overloading, as a general guideline. In some cases this is not necessary; for example, with **operator+=** you may *want* to say **A+=A** and have it add **A** to itself. The most important place to check for self-assignment is **operator=** because with complicated objects disastrous results may occur (in some cases it's OK, but you should always keep it in mind when writing **operator=**.)

All of the operators shown in the previous two examples are overloaded to handle a single type. It's also possible to overload operators to handle mixed types, so you can add apples to oranges, for example. Before you start on an exhaustive overloading of operators, however, you should look at the section on automatic type conversion later in this chapter. Often, a type conversion in the right place can save you a lot of overloaded operators.

arguments & return values

It may seem a little confusing at first when you look at UNARY.CPP and BINARY.CPP and see all the different ways that arguments are passed and returned. Although you *can* pass and return arguments any way you want to, the choices in these examples were not selected at random. They follow a very logical pattern, the same one you'll want to use in most of your choices.

1. As with any function argument, if you only need to read from the argument and not change it, default to passing it as a **const** reference. Ordinary arithmetic operations (like **+** and **–**, etc.) and Booleans will not change their arguments, so pass by **const** reference is predominantly what you'll use. When the function is a class member, this translates to making it a **const** member function. Only with the operator-assignments (like **+=**) and the **operator=**, which change the left-hand argument, is the left argument *not* a constant, but it's still passed in as an address because it will be changed.

2. The type of return value you should select depends on the expected meaning of the operator. (Again, you can do anything you want with the arguments and return values.) If the effect of the operator is to produce a new value, you will need to generate a new object as the return value. For example, **integer::operator+** must produce an **integer** object that is the sum of the operands. This object is

returned by value as a **const**, so the result cannot be modified as an lvalue.

3. All the assignment operators modify the lvalue. To allow the result of the assignment to be used in chained expressions, like **A=B=C**, it's expected that you will return a reference to that same lvalue that was just modified. But should this reference be a **const** or non**const**? Although you read **A=B=C** from left to right, the compiler parses it from right to left, so you're not forced to return a non**const** to support assignment chaining. However, people do sometimes expect to be able to perform an operation on the thing that was just assigned to, such as **(A=B).foo( );** to call **foo( )** on **A** after assigning **B** to it. Thus the return value for all the assignment operators should be a non**const** reference to the lvalue.

4. For the logical operators, everyone expects to get at worst an **int** back, and at best a **bool**. (Libraries developed before most compilers supported C++'s built-in **bool** will use **int** or an equivalent **typedef**).

5. The increment and decrement operators present a dilemma because of the pre- and postfix versions. Both versions change the object and so cannot treat the object as a **const**. The prefix version returns the value of the object after it was changed, so you expect to get back the object that was changed. Thus, with prefix you can just return ***this** as a reference. The postfix version is supposed to return the value *before* the value is changed, so you're forced to create a separate object to represent that value and return it. Thus, with postfix you must return by value if you want to preserve the expected meaning. (Note that you'll often find the increment and decrement operators returning an **int** or **bool** to indicate, for example, whether an iterator is at the end of a list). Now the question is: Should these be returned as **const** or non**const**? If you allow the object to be modified and someone writes **(++A).foo( );**, **foo( )** will be operating on **A** itself, but with **(A++).foo( );**, **foo( )** operates on the temporary object returned by the postfix **operator++**. Temporary objects are automatically **const**, so this would be flagged by the compiler, but for consistency's sake it may

make more sense to make them both **const**, as was done here. Because of the variety of meanings you may want to give the increment and decrement operators, they will need to be considered on a case-by-case basis.

return by value as const

Returning by value as a const can seem a bit subtle at first, and so deserves a bit more explanation. Consider the binary **operator+**. If you use it in an expression such as **f(A+B)**, the result of **A+B** becomes a temporary object that is used in the call to **f( )**. Because it's a temporary, it's automatically **const**, so whether you explicitly make the return value const or not has no effect.

However, it's also possible for you to send a message to the return value of **A+B**, rather than just passing it to a function. For example, you can say **(A+B).g( )**, where **g( )** is some member function of **integer**, in this case. By making the return value **const**, you state that only a **const** member function can be called for that return value. This is **const**-correct, because it prevents you from storing potentially valuable information in an object that will most likely be lost.

return efficiency

When new objects are created to return by value, notice the form used. In **operator+**, for example:

```
return integer(left.i + right.i);
```

This may look at first like a "function call to a constructor," but it's not. The syntax is that of a temporary object; the statement says "make a temporary **integer** object and return it." Because of this, you might think that the result is the same as creating a named local object and returning that. However, it's quite different. If you were to say instead:

```
integer tmp(left.i + right.i);
return tmp;
```

three things will happen. First, the **tmp** object is created including its constructor call. Then, the copy-constructor copies the **tmp** to the location of the outside return value. Finally, the destructor is called for **tmp** at the end of the scope.

In contrast, the "returning a temporary" approach works quite differently. When the compiler sees you do this, it knows that you have no other need for the object it's creating than to return it so it builds the object *directly* into the location of the outside return value. This requires only a single ordinary constructor call (no copy-constructor is necessary) and there's no destructor call because you never actually create a local object. Thus, while it doesn't cost anything but programmer awareness, it's significantly more efficient.

unusual operators

Several additional operators have a slightly different syntax for overloading.

The subscript, **operator[]**, must be a member function and it requires a single argument. Because it implies that the object acts like an array, you will often return a reference from this operator, so it can be used conveniently on the left-hand side of an equal sign. This operator is commonly overloaded; you'll see examples in the rest of the book.

The comma operator is called when it appears next to an object of the type the comma is defined for. However, **operator,** is *not* called for function argument lists, only for objects that are out in the open, separated by commas. There doesn't seem to be a lot of practical uses for this operator; it's in the language for consistency. Here's an example showing how the comma function can be called when the comma appears *before* an object, as well as after:

```
//: COMMA.CPP -- Overloading operator,
#include <iostream.h>

class after {
```

```
public:
  const after& operator,(const after&) const {
    cout << "after::operator,()" << endl;
    return *this;
  }
};

class before {};

before& operator,(int, before& b) {
  cout << "before::operator,()" << endl;
  return b;
}

main() {
  after a, b;
  a, b;  // Operator comma called

  before c;
  1, c;  // Operator comma called
}
```

The global function allows the comma to be placed before the object in question. The usage shown is fairly obscure and questionable. Although you would probably use a comma-separated list as part of a more complex expression, it's too subtle to use in most situations.

The *function call* **operator( )** must be a member function, and it is unique in that it allows any number of arguments. It makes your object look like it's actually a function name, so it's probably best used for types that only have a single operation, or at least an especially prominent one.

The operators **new** and **delete** control dynamic storage allocation, and can be overloaded. This very important topic is covered in the next chapter.

The **operator–>*** is a binary operator that behaves like all the other binary operators. It is provided for those situations when you want to mimic the behavior provided by the built-in *pointer-to-member* syntax, described in the previous chapter.

The *smart pointer* **operator–>** is designed to be used when you want to make an object appear to be a pointer. This is especially useful if you want to "wrap" a class around a pointer to make that pointer safe, or in the common usage of an *iterator*, which is an object that moves through a *collection* or *container* of other objects and selects them one at a time, without providing direct access to the implementation of the container. (You'll often find containers and iterators in class libraries.)

A smart pointer must be a member function. It has additional, atypical constraints: It must return either an object (or reference to an object) that also has a smart pointer or a pointer that can be used to select what the smart pointer arrow is pointing at. Here's a simple example:

```
//: SMARTP.CPP -- Smart pointer example
#include <iostream.h>
#include <string.h>

class obj {
  static int i, j;
public:
  void f() { cout << i++ << endl; }
  void g() { cout << j++ << endl; }
};

// Static member definitions:
int obj::i = 47;
int obj::j = 11;

// Container:
class obj_container {
  enum { sz = 100 };
```

```
  obj* a[sz];
  int index;
public:
  obj_container() {
    index = 0;
    memset(a, 0, sz * sizeof(obj*));
  }
  void add(obj* OBJ) {
    if(index >= sz) return;
    a[index++] = OBJ;
  }
  friend class sp;
};

// Iterator:
class sp {
  obj_container* oc;
  int index;
public:
  sp(obj_container* OC) {
    index = 0;
    oc = OC;
  }
  // Return value indicates end of list:
  int operator++() { // Prefix
    if(index >= oc->sz) return 0;
    if(oc->a[++index] == 0) return 0;
    return 1;
  }
  int operator++(int) { // Postfix
    return operator++(); // Use prefix version
  }
  obj* operator->() const {
    if(oc->a[index]) return oc->a[index];
    static obj dummy;
    return &dummy;
  }
```

```
};

main() {
  const sz = 10;
  obj o[sz];
  obj_container OC;
  for(int i = 0; i < sz; i++)
    OC.add(&o[i]); // Fill it up
  sp SP(&OC); // Create an iterator
  do {
    SP->f(); // Smart pointer calls
    SP->g();
  } while(SP++);
}
```

The class **obj** defines the objects that are manipulated in this program. The functions **f( )** and **g( )** simply print out interesting values using **static** data members. Pointers to these objects are stored inside containers of type **obj_container** using its **add( )** function. **obj_container** looks like an array of pointers, but you'll notice there's no way to get the pointers back out again. However, **sp** is declared as a **friend** class, so it has permission to look inside the container. The **sp** class looks very much like an intelligent pointer — you can move it forward using **operator++** (you can also define an **operator– –**), it won't go past the end of the container it's pointing to, and it returns (via the smart pointer operator) the value it's pointing to. Notice that an iterator is a custom fit for the container it's created for — unlike a pointer, there isn't a "general purpose" iterator. Containers and iterators are covered in more depth in Chapter 14.

In **main( )**, once the container **OC** is filled with **obj** objects, an iterator **SP** is created. The smart pointer calls happen in the expressions:

```
SP->f(); // Smart pointer calls
SP->g();
```

Thinking in C++   *Bruce Eckel*

Here, even though **SP** doesn't actually have **f( )** and **g( )** member functions, the smart pointer mechanism calls those functions for the **obj*** that is returned by **sp::operator–>**. The compiler performs all the checking to make sure the function call works properly.

Although the underlying mechanics of the smart pointer are more complex than the other operators, the goal is exactly the same — to provide a more convenient syntax for the users of your classes.

operators you can't overload

There are certain operators in the available set that cannot be overloaded. The general reason for the restriction is safety: If these operators were overloadable, it would somehow jeopardize or break safety mechanisms. Often it makes things harder, or confuses existing practice.

The member selection **operator.**. Currently, the dot has a meaning for any member in a class, but if you allow it to be overloaded, then you couldn't access members in the normal way; instead you'd have to use a pointer and the arrow operator **–>**.

The pointer to member dereference **operator.***. For the same reason as **operator.**.

There's no exponentiation operator. The most popular choice for this was **operator**** from Fortran, but this raised difficult parsing questions. Also, C has no exponentiation operator, so C++ didn't seem to need one either because you can always perform a function call. An exponentiation operator would add a convenient notation, but no new language functionality, to account for the added complexity of the compiler.

There are no user-defined operators. That is, you can't make up new operators that aren't currently in the set. Part of the problem is how to determine precedence, and part of the problem is an insufficient need to account for the necessary trouble.

You can't change the precedence rules. They're hard enough to remember as it is, without letting people play with them.

nonmember operators

In some of the previous examples, the operators may be members or nonmembers, and it doesn't seem to make much difference. This usually raises the question, "Which should I choose?" In general, if it doesn't make any difference, they should be members, to emphasize the association between the operator and its class. When the left-hand operand is an object of the current class, it works fine.

This isn't always the case — sometimes you want the left-hand operand to be an object of some other class. A very common place to see this is when the operators **<<** and **>>** are overloaded for iostreams:

```
//: IOSOP.CPP -- Iostream operator overloading
// Example of non-member overloaded operators
#include <iostream.h>
#include <strstrea.h>
#include <string.h>
#include "..\allege.h"

class intarray {
  enum { sz = 5 };
  int i[sz];
public:
  intarray() {
    memset(i, 0, sz* sizeof(*i));
  }
  int& operator[](int x) {
    allege(x >= 0 && x < sz,
           "operator[] out of range");
    return i[x];
```

Thinking in C++ *Bruce Eckel*

```
  }
  friend ostream&
    operator<<(ostream& os,
               const intarray& ia);
  friend istream&
    operator>>(istream& is, intarray& ia);
};

ostream& operator<<(ostream& os,
                    const intarray& ia){
  for(int j = 0; j < ia.sz; j++) {
    os << ia.i[j];
    if(j != ia.sz -1)
      os << ", ";
  }
  os << endl;
  return os;
}

istream& operator>>(istream& is, intarray& ia){
  for(int j = 0; j < ia.sz; j++)
    is >> ia.i[j];
  return is;
}

main() {
  istrstream input("47 34 56 92 103");
  intarray I;
  input >> I;
  I[4] = -1; // Use overloaded operator[]
  cout << I;
}
```

This class also contains an overloaded **operator[]**, which returns a reference to a legitimate value in the array. A reference is returned, so the expression

```
I[4] = -1;
```

not only looks much more civilized than if pointers were used, it also accomplishes the desired effect.

The overloaded shift operators pass and return by reference, so the actions will affect the external objects. In the function definitions, expressions like

```
os << ia.i[j];
```

cause *existing* overloaded operator functions to be called (that is, those defined in IOSTREAM.H). In this case, the function called is **ostream& operator<<(ostream&, int)** because **ia.i[j]** resolves to an **int**.

Once all the actions are performed on the **istream** or **ostream**, it is returned so it can be used in a more complicated expression.

The form shown in this example for the inserter and extractor is standard. If you want to create a set for your own class, copy the function signatures and return types and follow the form of the body.

basic guidelines

Murray[1] suggests these guidelines for choosing between members and nonmembers:

Operator	Recommended use
All unary operators	member
= ( ) [] ->	*must* be member

---

[1] Rob Murray, C++ *Strategies & Tactics*, Addison-Wesley, 1993, page 47.

Operator	Recommended use
+= -= /= *= ^= &= |= %= >>= <<=	member
All other binary operators	nonmember

overloading assignment

A common source of confusion with new C++ programmers is assignment. This is no doubt because the = sign is such a fundamental operation in programming, right down to copying a register at the machine level. In addition, the copy-constructor (from the previous chapter) can also be invoked when using the = sign:

```
foo B;
foo A = B;
A = B;
```

In the second line, the object **A** is being *defined*. A new object is being created where one didn't exist before. Because you know by now how defensive the C++ compiler is about object initialization, you know that a constructor must always be called at the point where an object is defined. But which constructor? **A** is being created from an existing **foo** object, so there's only one choice: the copy-constructor. So even though an equal sign is involved, the copy-constructor is called.

In the third line, things are different. On the left side of the equal sign, there's a previously initialized object. Clearly, you don't call a constructor for an object that's already been created. In this case **foo::operator=** is called for **A**, taking as an argument whatever appears on the right-hand side. (You can have multiple **operator=** functions to take different right-hand arguments.)

This behavior is not restricted to the copy-constructor. Any time you're initializing an object using an = instead of the ordinary function-call form of the constructor, the compiler will look for a constructor that accepts whatever is on the right-hand side:

```
//: FEEFI.CPP -- Copying vs. initialization

class fi {
public:
  fi() {}
};

class fee {
public:
  fee(int) {}
  fee(const fi&) {}
};

main() {
  fee f = 1; // fee(int)
  fi FI;
  fee fum = FI; // fee(fi)
}
```

When dealing with the = sign, it's important to keep this distinction in mind: If the object hasn't been created yet, initialization is required; otherwise the assignment **operator=** is used.

It's even better to avoid writing code that uses the = for initialization; instead, always use the explicit constructor form; the last line becomes

```
fee fum(FI);
```

This way, you'll avoid confusing your readers.

behavior of operator=

In BINARY.CPP, you saw that **operator=** can be only a member function. It is intimately connected to the object on the left side of the **=**, and if you could define **operator=** globally, you could try to redefine the built-in **=** sign:

```
int operator=(int, foo); // global = not allowed!
```

The compiler skirts this whole issue by forcing you to make **operator=** a member function.

When you create an **operator=**, you must copy all the necessary information from the right-hand object into yourself to perform whatever you consider "assignment" for your class. For simple objects, this is obvious:

```
//: SIMPCOPY.CPP -- Simple operator=()
#include <iostream.h>

class value {
  int a, b;
  float c;
public:
  value(int A = 0, int B = 0, float C = 0.0) {
    a = A;
    b = B;
    c = C;
  }
  value& operator=(const value& rv) {
    a = rv.a;
    b = rv.b;
    c = rv.c;
    return *this;
  }
  friend ostream&
    operator<<(ostream& os, const value& rv) {
      return os << "a = " << rv.a << ", b = "
        << rv.b << ", c = " << rv.c;
```

```
        }
};

main() {
  value A, B(1, 2, 3.3);
  cout << "A: " << A << endl;
  cout << "B: " << B << endl;
  A = B;
  cout << "A after assignment: " << A << endl;
}
```

Here, the object on the left side of the **=** copies all the elements of the object on the right, then returns a reference to itself, so a more complex expression can be created.

A common mistake was made in this example. When you're assigning two objects of the same type, you should always check first for self-assignment: Is the object being assigned to itself? In some cases, such as this one, it's harmless if you perform the assignment operations anyway, but if changes are made to the implementation of the class it, can make a difference, and if you don't do it as a matter of habit, you may forget and cause hard-to-find bugs.

pointers in classes

What happens if the object is not so simple? For example, what if the object contains pointers to other objects? Simply copying a pointer means you'll end up with two objects pointing to the same storage location. In situations like these, you need to do bookkeeping of your own.

There are two common approaches to this problem. The simplest technique is to copy whatever the pointer refers to when you do an assignment or a copy-constructor. This is very straightforward:

```
//: COPYMEM.CPP -- Duplicate during assignment
#include <stdlib.h>
#include <string.h>
```

```
#include "..\allege.h"

class withPointer {
  char* p;
  enum { blocksz = 100 };
public:
  withPointer() {
    p = (char*)malloc(blocksz);
    allegemem(p);
    memset(p, 1, blocksz);
  }
  withPointer(const withPointer& wp) {
    p = (char*)malloc(blocksz);
    allegemem(p);
    memcpy(p, wp.p, blocksz);
  }
  withPointer&
  operator=(const withPointer& wp) {
    // Check for self-assignment:
    if(&wp != this)
      memcpy(p, wp.p, blocksz);
    return *this;
  }
  ~withPointer() {
    free(p);
  }
};

main() {}
```

This shows the four functions you will always need to define when your class contains pointers: all necessary ordinary constructors, the copy-constructor, **operator=** (either define it or disallow it), and a destructor. The **operator=** checks for self-assignment as a matter of course, even though it's not strictly necessary here. This virtually eliminates the possibility that you'll forget to check for self-assignment if you *do* change the code so that it matters.

Here, the constructors allocate the memory and initialize it, the **operator=** copies it, and the destructor frees the memory. However, if you're dealing with a lot of memory or a high overhead to initialize that memory, you may want to avoid this copying. A very common approach to this problem is called *reference counting*. You make the block of memory smart, so it knows how many objects are pointing to it. Then copy-construction or assignment means attaching another pointer to an existing block of memory and incrementing the reference count. Destruction means reducing the reference count and destroying the object if the reference count goes to zero.

But what if you want to write to the block of memory? More than one object may be using this block, so you'd be modifying someone else's block as well as yours, which doesn't seem very neighborly. To solve this problem, an additional technique called *copy-on-write* is often used. Before writing to a block of memory, you make sure no one else is using it. If the reference count is greater than one, you must make yourself a personal copy of that block before writing it, so you don't disturb someone else's turf. Here's a simple example of reference counting and copy-on-write:

```
//: REFCOUNT.CPP -- Reference count, copy-on-write
#include <string.h>
#include <assert.h>

class counted {
  class memblock {
    enum { size = 100 };
    char c[size];
    int refcount;
  public:
    memblock() {
      memset(c, 1, size);
      refcount = 1;
    }
    memblock(const memblock& rv) {
```

```
      memcpy(c, rv.c, size);
      refcount = 1;
    }
    void attach() { ++refcount; }
    void detach() {
      assert(refcount != 0);
      // Destroy object if no one is using it:
      if(--refcount == 0) delete this;
    }
    int count() const { return refcount; }
    void set(char x) { memset(c, x, size); }
    // Conditionally copy this memblock.
    // Call before modifying the block; assign
    // resulting pointer to your block;
    memblock* unalias() {
      // Don't duplicate if not aliased:
      if(refcount == 1) return this;
      --refcount;
      // Use copy-constructor to duplicate:
      return new memblock(*this);
    }
  } * block;
public:
  counted() {
    block = new memblock; // Sneak preview
  }
  counted(const counted& rv) {
    block = rv.block; // Pointer assignment
    block->attach();
  }
  void unalias() { block = block->unalias(); }
  counted& operator=(const counted& rv) {
    // Check for self-assignment:
    if(&rv == this) return *this;
    // Clean up what you're using first:
    block->detach();
    block = rv.block; // Like copy-constructor
```

```
    block->attach();
    return *this;
  }
  // Decrement refcount, conditionally destroy
  ~counted() { block->detach(); }
  // Copy-on-write:
  void write(char value) {
    // Do this before any write operation:
    unalias();
    // It's safe to write now.
    block->set(value);
  }
};

main() {
  counted A, B;
  counted C(A);
  B = A;
  C = C;
  C.write('x');
}
```

The nested class **memblock** is the block of memory pointed to. (Notice the pointer **block** defined at the end of the nested class.) It contains a reference count and functions to control and read the reference count. There's a copy-constructor so you can make a new **memblock** from an existing one.

The **attach( )** function increments the reference count of a **memblock** to indicate there's another object using it. **detach( )** decrements the reference count. If the reference count goes to zero, then no one is using it anymore, so the member function destroys its own object by saying **delete this**.

You can modify the memory with the **set( )** function, but before you make any modifications, you should ensure that you aren't walking on a **memblock** that some other object is using. You do this by calling **counted::unalias( )**, which in turn calls **memblock::unalias( )**. The latter function will return the **block** pointer if the reference count is one (meaning no one else is pointing to that block), but will duplicate the block if the reference count is more than one.

This example includes a sneak preview of the next chapter. Instead of C's **malloc( )** and **free( )** to create and destroy the objects, the special C++ operators **new** and **delete** are used. For this example, you can think of **new** and **delete** just like **malloc( )** and **free( )**, except **new** calls the constructor after allocating memory, and **delete** calls the destructor before freeing the memory.

The copy-constructor, instead of creating its own memory, assigns **block** to the **block** of the source object. Then, because there's now an additional object using that block of memory, it increments the reference count by calling **memblock::attach( )**.

The **operator=** deals with an object that has already been created on the left side of the **=**, so it must first clean that up by calling **detach( )** for that **memblock**, which will destroy the old **memblock** if no one else is using it. Then **operator=** repeats the behavior of the copy-constructor. Notice that it first checks to detect whether you're assigning the same object to itself.

The destructor calls **detach( )** to conditionally destroy the **memblock**.

To implement copy-on-write, you must control all the actions that write to your block of memory. This means you can't ever hand a raw pointer to the outside world. Instead you say, "Tell me what you want done and I'll do it for you!" For example, the **write( )** member function allows you to change the values in the block of memory. But first, it uses **unalias( )** to prevent the modification of an aliased block (a block with more than one **counted** object using it).

main( ) tests the various functions that must work correctly to implement reference counting: the constructor, copy-constructor, **operator=**, and destructor. It also tests the copy-on-write by calling the **write( )** function for object **C**, which is aliased to **A**'s memory block.

tracing the output

To verify that the behavior of this scheme is correct, the best approach is to add information and functionality to the class to generate a trace output that can be analyzed. Here's REFCOUNT.CPP with added trace information:

```
//: RCTRACE.CPP -- REFCOUNT.CPP w/ trace info
#include <string.h>
#include <fstream.h>
#include <assert.h>
ofstream out("rctrace.out");

class counted {
  class memblock {
    enum { size = 100 };
    char c[size];
    int refcount;
    static int blockcount;
    int blocknum;
  public:
    memblock() {
      memset(c, 1, size);
      refcount = 1;
      blocknum = blockcount++;
    }
    memblock(const memblock& rv) {
      memcpy(c, rv.c, size);
      refcount = 1;
      blocknum = blockcount++;
      print("copied block");
      out << endl;
      rv.print("from block");
    }
    ~memblock() {
```

```
          out << "\tdestroying block "
              << blocknum << endl;
      }
      void print(const char* msg = "") const {
        if(*msg) out << msg << ", ";
        out << "blocknum:" << blocknum;
        out << ", refcount:" << refcount;
      }
      void attach() { ++refcount; }
      void detach() {
        assert(refcount != 0);
        // Destroy object if no one is using it:
        if(--refcount == 0) delete this;
      }
      int count() const { return refcount; }
      void set(char x) { memset(c, x, size); }
      // Conditionally copy this memblock.
      // Call before modifying the block; assign
      // resulting pointer to your block;
      memblock* unalias() {
        // Don't duplicate if not aliased:
        if(refcount == 1) return this;
        --refcount;
        // Use copy-constructor to duplicate:
        return new memblock(*this);
      }
    } * block;
    enum { sz = 30 };
    char id[sz];
  public:
    counted(const char* ID = "tmp") {
      block = new memblock; // Sneak preview
      strncpy(id, ID, sz);
    }
    counted(const counted& rv) {
      block = rv.block; // Pointer assignment
      block->attach();
```

```
    strncpy(id, rv.id, sz);
    strncat(id, " copy", sz - strlen(id));
  }
  void unalias() { block = block->unalias(); }
  void addname(const char* nm) {
    strncat(id, nm, sz - strlen(id));
  }
  counted& operator=(const counted& rv) {
    print("inside operator=\n\t");
    if(&rv == this) {
      out << "self-assignment" << endl;
      return *this;
    }
    // Clean up what you're using first:
    block->detach();
    block = rv.block; // Like copy-constructor
    block->attach();
    return *this;
  }
  // Decrement refcount, conditionally destroy
  ~counted() {
    out << "preparing to destroy: " << id
        << endl << "\tdecrementing refcount ";
    block->print();
    out << endl;
    block->detach();
  }
  // Copy-on-write:
  void write(char value) {
    unalias();
    block->set(value);
  }
  void print(const char* msg = "") {
    if(*msg) out << msg << " ";
    out << "object " << id << ": ";
    block->print();
    out << endl;
```

```
      }
  };

  int counted::memblock::blockcount = 0;

  main() {
    counted A("A"), B("B");
    counted C(A);
    C.addname(" (C) ");
    A.print();
    B.print();
    C.print();
    B = A;
    A.print("after assignment\n\t");
    B.print();
    out << "Assigning C = C" << endl;
    C = C;
    C.print("calling C.write('x')\n\t");
    C.write('x');
    out << endl << "exiting main()" << endl;
  }
```

Now **memblock** contains a **static** data member **blockcount** to keep track of the number of blocks created, and to create a unique number (stored in **blocknum**) for each block so you can tell them apart. The destructor announces which block is being destroyed, and the **print( )** function displays the block number and reference count.

The **counted** class contains a buffer **id** to keep track of information about the object. The **counted** constructor creates a **new memblock** object and assigns the result (a pointer to the **memblock** object on the heap) to **block**. The identifier, copied from the argument, has the word "copy" appended to show where it's copied from. Also, the **addname( )** function lets you put additional information about the object in **id** (the actual identifier, so you can see what it is as well as where it's copied from).

Here's the output:

```
object A: blocknum:0, refcount:2
object B: blocknum:1, refcount:1
object A copy (C) : blocknum:0, refcount:2
inside operator=
        object B: blocknum:1, refcount:1
        destroying block 1
after assignment
        object A: blocknum:0, refcount:3
object B: blocknum:0, refcount:3
Assigning C = C
inside operator=
        object A copy (C) : blocknum:0, refcount:3
self-assignment
calling C.write('x')
        object A copy (C) : blocknum:0, refcount:3
copied block, blocknum:2, refcount:1
from block, blocknum:0, refcount:2
exiting main()
preparing to destroy: A copy (C)
        decrementing refcount blocknum:2, refcount:1
        destroying block 2
preparing to destroy: B
        decrementing refcount blocknum:0, refcount:2
preparing to destroy: A
        decrementing refcount blocknum:0, refcount:1
        destroying block 0
```

By studying the output, tracing through the source code, and experimenting with the program, you'll deepen your understanding of these techniques.

automatic operator= creation

Because assigning an object to another object *of the same type* is an activity most people expect to be possible, the compiler will automatically create a **type::operator=(type)** if you don't make one. The behavior of this operator mimics that of the automatically

---

Thinking in C++   *Bruce Eckel*

created copy-constructor: If the class contains objects (or is inherited from another class), the **operator=** for those objects is called recursively. This is called *memberwise assignment*. For example,

```
//: AUTOEQ.CPP -- Automatic operator=()
#include <iostream.h>

class bar {
public:
  bar& operator=(const bar&) {
    cout << "inside bar::operator=()" << endl;
    return *this;
  }
};

class foo {
  bar B;
};

main() {
  foo a, b;
  a = b; // Prints: "inside bar::operator=()"
}
```

The automatically generated **operator=** for **foo** calls **bar::operator=**.

Generally you don't want to let the compiler do this for you. With classes of any sophistication (especially if they contain pointers!) you want to explicitly create an **operator=**. If you really don't want people to perform assignment, declare **operator=** as a **private** function. (You don't need to define it unless you're using it inside the class.)

automatic type conversion

In C and C++, if the compiler sees an expression or function call using a type that isn't quite the one it needs, it can often perform an automatic type conversion from the type it has to the type it wants. In C++, you can achieve this same effect for user-defined types by defining automatic type-conversion functions. These functions come in two flavors: a particular type of constructor and an overloaded operator.

constructor conversion

If you define a constructor that takes as its single argument an object (or reference) of another type, that constructor allows the compiler to perform an automatic type conversion. For example,

```
//: AUTOCNST.CPP -- Type conversion constructor

class one {
public:
  one() {}
};

class two {
public:
  two(const one&) {}
};

void f(two) {}

main() {
  one One;
  f(One); // Wants a two, has a one
}
```

When the compiler sees **f( )** called with a **one** object, it looks at the declaration for **f( )** and notices it wants a **two**. Then it looks to see if there's any way to get a **two** from a **one**, and it finds the constructor **two::two(one)**, which it quietly calls. The resulting **two** object is handed to **f( )**.

In this case, automatic type conversion has saved you from the trouble of defining two overloaded versions of **f( )**. However, the cost is the hidden constructor call to **two**, which may matter if you're concerned about the efficiency of calls to **f( )**.

preventing constructor conversion

There are times when automatic type conversion via the constructor can cause problems. To turn it off, you modify the constructor by prefacing with the keyword **explicit**[2] (which only works with constructors). Used to modify the constructor of class **two** in the above example:

```
class one {
public:
  one() {}
};

class two {
public:
  explicit two(const one&) {}
};

void f(two) {}

main() {
  one One;
```

---

[2] At the time of this writing, **explicit** was a new keyword in the language. Your compiler may not support it yet.

```
//!  f(One); // no auto conversion allowed
   f(two(One)); // OK -- user performs conversion
}
```

By making **two**'s constructor explicit, the compiler is told not to
perform any automatic conversion using that particular constructor
(other non-**explicit** constructors in that class can still perform
automatic conversions). If the user wants to make the conversion
happen, the code must be written out. In the above code,
f(two(One)) creates a temporary object of type **two** from **One**, just
like the compiler did in the previous version.

operator conversion

The second way to effect automatic type conversion is through
operator overloading. You can create a member function that takes
the current type and converts it to the desired type using the
operator keyword followed by the type you want to convert to. This
form of operator overloading is unique because you don't appear to
specify a return type — the return type is the *name* of the operator
you're overloading. Here's an example:

```
//: OPCONV.CPP -- Op overloading conversion

class three {
  int i;
public:
  three(int I = 0, int = 0) : i(I) {}
};

class four {
  int x;
public:
  four(int X) : x(X) {}
  operator three() const { return three(x); }
};

void g(three) {}
```

```
main() {
  four Four(1);
  g(Four);
  g(1);  // Calls three(1,0)
}
```

With the constructor technique, the destination class is performing the conversion, but with operators, the source class performs the conversion. The value of the constructor technique is you can add a new conversion path to an existing system as you're creating a new class. However, creating a single-argument constructor *always* defines an automatic type conversion (even if it's got more than one argument, if the rest of the arguments are defaulted), which may not be what you want. In addition, there's no way to use a constructor conversion from a user-defined type to a built-in type; this is possible only with operator overloading.

reflexivity

One of the most convenient reasons to use global overloaded operators rather than member operators is that in the global versions, automatic type conversion may be applied to either operand, whereas with member objects, the left-hand operand must already be the proper type. If you want both operands to be converted, the global versions can save a lot of coding. Here's a small example:

```
//: REFLEX.CPP -- Reflexivity in overloading

class number {
  int i;
public:
  number(int I = 0) { i = I; }
  const number
  operator+(const number& n) const {
    return number(i + n.i);
  }
```

```
    friend const number
      operator-(const number&, const number&);
};

const number
  operator-(const number& n1,
            const number& n2) {
    return number(n1.i - n2.i);
}

main() {
  number a(47), b(11);
  a + b; // OK
  a + 1; // 2nd arg converted to number
//! 1 + a; // Wrong! 1st arg not of type number
  a - b; // OK
  a - 1; // 2nd arg converted to number
  1 - a; // 1st arg converted to number
}
```

Class **number** has a member **operator+** and a friend **operator–**. Because there's a constructor that takes a single **int** argument, an **int** can be automatically converted to a **number**, but only under the right conditions. In **main( )**, you can see that adding a **number** to another **number** works fine because it's an exact match to the overloaded operator. Also, when the compiler sees a **number** followed by a **+** and an **int**, it can match to the member function **number::operator+** and convert the **int** argument to a **number** using the constructor. But when it sees an **int** and a **+** and a **number**, it doesn't know what to do because all it has is **number::operator+**, which requires that the left operand already be a **number** object. Thus the compiler issues an error.

With the **friend operator–**, things are different. The compiler needs to fill in both its arguments however it can; it isn't restricted to having a **number** as the left-hand argument. Thus, if it sees **1 – a**, it can convert the first argument to a **number** using the constructor.

Thinking in C++   *Bruce Eckel*

Sometimes you want to be able to restrict the use of your operators by making them members. For example, when multiplying a matrix by a vector, the vector must go on the right. But if you want your operators to be able to convert either argument, make the operator a friend function.

Fortunately, the compiler will not take **1 – 1** and convert both arguments to **number** objects and then call **operator–**. That would mean that existing C code might suddenly start to work differently. The compiler matches the "simplest" possibility first, which is the built-in operator for the expression **1 – 1**.

a perfect example: strings

An example where automatic type conversion is extremely helpful occurs with a **string** class. Without automatic type conversion, if you wanted to use all the existing string functions from the Standard C library, you'd have to create a member function for each one, like this:

```
//: STRINGS1.CPP -- No auto type conversion
#include <string.h>
#include <stdlib.h>
#include "..\allege.h"

class string {
  char* s;
public:
  string(const char* S = "") {
    s = (char*)malloc(strlen(S) + 1);
    allegemem(s);
    strcpy(s, S);
  }
  ~string() { free(s); }
  int Strcmp(const string& S) const {
    return ::strcmp(s, S.s);
  }
  // ... etc., for every function in string.h
```

```
};

main() {
  string s1("hello"), s2("there");
  s1.Strcmp(s2);
}
```

Here, only the **strcmp( )** function is created, but you'd have to
create a corresponding function for every one in STRING.H that
might be needed. Fortunately, you can provide an automatic type
conversion allowing access to all the functions in STRING.H:

```
//: STRINGS2.CPP -- With auto type conversion
#include <string.h>
#include <stdlib.h>
#include "..\allege.h"

class string {
  char* s;
public:
  string(const char* S = "") {
    s = (char*)malloc(strlen(S) + 1);
    allegemem(s);
    strcpy(s, S);
  }
  ~string() { free(s); }
  operator const char*() const { return s; }
};

main() {
  string s1("hello"), s2("there");
  strcmp(s1, s2); // Standard C function
  strspn(s1, s2); // Any string function!
}
```

Now any function that takes a **char*** argument can also take a **string** argument because the compiler knows how to make a **char*** from a **string**.

pitfalls in automatic type conversion

Because the compiler must choose how to quietly perform a type conversion, it can get into trouble if you don't design your conversions correctly. A simple and obvious situation occurs with a class **X** that can convert itself to an object of class **Y** with an **operator Y( )**. If class **Y** has a constructor that takes a single argument of type **X**, this represents the identical type conversion. The compiler now has two ways to go from **X** to **Y**, so it will generate an ambiguity error when that conversion occurs:

```
//: AMBIG.CPP -- Ambiguity in type conversion

class Y; // Class declaration

class X {
public:
  operator Y() const; // Convert X to Y
};

class Y {
public:
  Y(X); // Convert X to Y
};

void f(Y);

main() {
  X x;
//! f(x); // Error: ambiguous conversion
}
```

The obvious solution to this problem is not to do it: Just provide a single path for automatic conversion from one type to another.

A more difficult problem to spot occurs when you provide automatic conversion to more than one type. This is sometimes called *fan-out*:

```
//: FANOUT.CPP -- Type conversion fanout

class A {};
class B {};

class C {
public:
  operator A() const;
  operator B() const;
};

// Overloaded h():
void h(A);
void h(B);

main() {
  C c;
//! h(c); // Error: C -> A or C -> B ???
}
```

Class **C** has automatic conversions to both **A** and **B**. The insidious thing about this is that there's no problem until someone innocently comes along and creates two overloaded versions of **h( )**. (With only one version, the code in **main( )** works fine.)

Again, the solution — and the general watchword with automatic type conversion — is to only provide a single automatic conversion from one type to another. You can have conversions to other types; they just shouldn't be *automatic*. You can create explicit function calls with names like **make_A( )** and **make_B( )**.

hidden activities

Automatic type conversion can introduce more underlying activities than you may expect. As a little brain teaser, look at this modification of FEEFI.CPP(from page 432):

```
//: FEEFI2.CPP -- Copying vs. initialization

class fi {};

class fee {
public:
  fee(int) {}
  fee(const fi&) {}
};

class fo {
  int i;
public:
  fo(int x = 0) { i = x; }
  operator fee() const { return fee(i); }
};

main() {
  fo FO;
  fee fiddle = FO;
}
```

There is no constructor to create the **fee fiddle** from a **fo** object. However, **fo** has an automatic type conversion to a **fee**. There's no copy-constructor to create a **fee** from a **fee**, but this is one of the special functions the compiler can create for you. (The default constructor, copy-constructor, **operator=**, and destructor can be created automatically.) So for the relatively innocuous statement

```
fee fiddle = FO;
```

the automatic type conversion operator is called, and a copy-constructor is created.

Chapter 10: Operator Overloading   *455*

Automatic type conversion should be used carefully. It's excellent when it significantly reduces a coding task, but it's usually not worth using gratuitously.

summary

The whole reason for the existence of operator overloading is for those situations when it makes life easier. There's nothing particularly magical about it; the overloaded operators are just functions with funny names, and the function calls happen to be made for you by the compiler when it spots the right pattern. But if operator overloading doesn't provide a significant benefit to you (the creator of the class) or the user of the class, don't confuse the issue by adding it.

exercises

1. Create a simple class with an overloaded **operator++**. Try calling this operator in both pre- and postfix form and see what kind of compiler warning you get.

2. Create a class that contains a single **private char**. Overload the iostream operators **<<** and **>>** (as in IOSOP.CPP) and test them. You can test them with **fstreams**, **strstreams**, and **stdiostreams** (**cin** and **cout**).

3. Write a **number** class with overloaded operators for **+, –, *, /**, and assignment. Choose the return values for these functions so that expressions can be chained together, and for efficiency. Write an automatic type conversion **operator int( )**.

4. Combine the classes in UNARY.CPP and BINARY.CPP.

5. Fix FANOUT.CPP by creating an explicit function to call to perform the type conversion, instead of one of the automatic conversion operators.

dynamic object
creation

Sometimes you know the exact quantity,
type, and lifetime of the objects in your
program. But not always.

How many planes will an air-traffic system have to handle? How
many shapes will a CAD system need? How many nodes will there
be in a network?

To solve the general programming problem, it's essential that you
be able to create and destroy objects at run-time. Of course, C has
always provided the *dynamic memory allocation* functions
malloc( )and **free( )**(along with variants of **malloc( )**) that allocate
storage from the *heap* (also called the *free store*) at run-time.

However, this simply won't work in C++. The constructor doesn't allow you to hand it the address of the memory to initialize, and for good reason: If you could do that, you might

1. Forget. Then guaranteed initialization of objects in C++ wouldn't be guaranteed.

2. Accidentally do something to the object before you initialize it, expecting the right thing to happen.

3. Hand it the wrong-sized object.

And of course, even if you did everything correctly, anyone who modifies your program is prone to the same errors. Improper initialization is responsible for a large portion of programming errors, so it's especially important to guarantee constructor calls for objects created on the heap.

So how does C++ guarantee proper initialization and cleanup, but allow you to create objects dynamically, on the heap?

The answer is, "by bringing dynamic object creation into the core of the language." **malloc( )** and **free( )** are library functions, and thus outside the control of the compiler. However, if you have an *operator* to perform the combined act of dynamic storage allocation and initialization and another to perform the combined act of cleanup and releasing storage, the compiler can still guarantee that constructors and destructors will be called for all objects.

In this chapter, you'll learn how C++'s **new** and **delete** elegantly solve this problem by safely creating objects on the heap.

object creation

When a C++ object is created, two events occur:

1. Storage is allocated for the object.

2. The constructor is called to initialize that storage.

   By now you should believe that step two *always* happens. C++ enforces it because uninitialized objects are a major source of program bugs. It doesn't matter where or how the object is created — the constructor is always called.

   Step one, however, can occur in several ways, or at alternate times:

1. Storage can be allocated before the program begins, in the *static storage area*. This storage exists for the life of the program.

2. Storage can be created on the stack whenever a particular execution point is reached (an opening brace). That storage is released automatically at the complementary execution point (the closing brace). These stack-allocation operations are built into the instruction set of the processor and are very efficient. However, you have to know exactly how much storage you need when you're writing the program so the compiler can generate the right code.

3. Storage can be allocated from a pool of memory called the *heap* (also known as the *free store*). This is called *dynamic memory allocation*. To allocate this memory, a function is called at run-time; this means you can decide at any time that you want some memory and how much you need. You are also responsible for determining when to release the memory, which means the lifetime of that memory can be as long as you choose — it isn't determined by scope.

   Often these three regions are placed in a single contiguous piece of physical memory: the static area, the stack, and the heap (in an order determined by the compiler writer). However, there are no rules. The stack may be in a special place, and the heap may be implemented by making calls for chunks of memory from the operating system. As a programmer, these things are normally shielded from you, so all you need to think about is that the memory is there when you call for it.

C's approach to the heap

To allocate memory dynamically at run-time, C provides functions in its standard library: **malloc( )** and its variants **calloc( )** and **realloc( )** to produce memory from the heap, and **free( )** to release the memory back to the heap. These functions are pragmatic but primitive and require understanding and care on the part of the programmer. To create an instance of a class on the heap using C's dynamic memory functions, you'd have to do something like this:

```
//: MALCLASS.CPP -- Malloc with class objects
// What you'd have to do if not for "new"
#include <stdlib.h> // Malloc() & free()
#include <string.h> // Memset()
#include "..\allege.h"
#include <iostream.h>

class obj {
  int i, j, k;
  enum { sz = 100 };
  char buf[sz];
public:
  void initialize() { // Can't use constructor
    cout << "initializing obj" << endl;
    i = j = k = 0;
    memset(buf, 0, sz);
  }
  void destroy() { // Can't use destructor
    cout << "destroying obj" << endl;
  }
};

main() {
  obj* Obj = (obj*)malloc(sizeof(obj));
  allegemem(Obj);
  Obj->initialize();
  // ... sometime later:
```

```
    Obj->destroy();
    free(Obj);
}
```

You can see the use of **malloc( )** to create storage for the object in the line:

```
obj* Obj = (obj*)malloc(sizeof(obj));
```

Here, the user must determine the size of the object (one place for an error). **malloc( )** returns a **void*** because it's just a patch of memory, not an object. C++ doesn't allow a **void*** to be assigned to any other pointer, so it must be cast.

Because **malloc( )** may fail to find any memory (in which case it returns zero), you must check the returned pointer to make sure it was successful.

But the worst problem is this line:

```
Obj->initialize();
```

If they make it this far correctly, users must remember to initialize the object before it is used. Notice that a constructor was not used because the constructor cannot be called explicitly — it's called for you by the compiler when an object is created. The problem here is that the user now has the option to forget to perform the initialization before the object is used, thus reintroducing a major source of bugs.

It also turns out that many programmers seem to find C's dynamic memory functions too confusing and complicated; it's not uncommon to find C programmers who use virtual memory machines allocating huge arrays of variables in the static storage area to avoid thinking about dynamic memory allocation. Because C++ is attempting to make library use safe and effortless for the casual programmer, C's approach to dynamic memory is unacceptable.

operator new

The solution in C++ is to combine all the actions necessary to create an object into a single operator called **new**. When you create an object with **new** (using a *new-expression*), it allocates enough storage on the heap to hold the object, and calls the constructor for that storage. Thus, if you say

```
foo *fp = new foo(1,2);
```

at run-time, the equivalent of **malloc(sizeof(foo))** is called (often, it is literally a call to **malloc( )**), and the constructor for **foo** is called with the resulting address as the **this** pointer, using **(1,2)** as the argument list. By the time the pointer is assigned to **fp**, it's a live, initialized object — you can't even get your hands on it before then. It's also automatically the proper **foo** type so no cast is necessary.

The default **new** also checks to make sure the memory allocation was successful before passing the address to the constructor, so you don't have to explicitly determine if the call was successful. Later in the chapter you'll find out what happens if there's no memory left.

You can create a new-expression using any constructor available for the class. If the constructor has no arguments, you can make the new-expression without the constructor argument list:

```
foo *fp = new foo;
```

Notice how simple the process of creating objects on the heap becomes — a single expression, with all the sizing, conversions, and safety checks built in. It's as easy to create an object on the heap as it is on the stack.

operator delete

The complement to the new-expression is the *delete-expression*, which first calls the destructor and then releases the memory (often with a call to **free( )**). Just as a new-expression returns a

---

pointer to the object, a delete-expression requires the address of an object.

```
delete fp;
```

cleans up the dynamically allocated **foo** object created earlier.

delete can be called only for an object created by **new**. If you **malloc( )** (or **calloc( )** or **realloc( )**) an object and then **delete** it, the behavior is undefined. Because most default implementations of **new** and **delete** use **malloc( )** and **free( )**, you'll probably release the memory without calling the destructor.

If the pointer you're deleting is zero, nothing will happen. For this reason, people often recommend setting a pointer to zero immediately after you delete it, to prevent deleting it twice. Deleting an object more than once is definitely a bad thing to do, and will cause problems.

a simple example

This example shows that the initialization takes place:

```
//: NEWDEL.CPP -- Simple demo of new & delete
#include <iostream.h>

class tree {
  int height;
public:
  tree(int Height) {
    height = Height;
  }
  ~tree() { cout << "*"; }
  friend ostream&
  operator<<(ostream& os, const tree* t) {
    return os << "tree height is: "
              << t->height << endl;
  }
};
```

```
main() {
  tree* T = new tree(40);
  cout << T;
  delete T;
}
```

We can prove that the constructor is called by printing out the value of the **tree**. Here, it's done by overloading the **operator<<** to use with an **ostream**. Note, however, that even though the function is declared as a **friend**, it is defined as an inline! This is a mere convenience — defining a **friend** function as an inline to a class doesn't change the **friend** status or the fact that it's a global function and not a class member function. Also notice that the return value is the result of the entire output expression, which is itself an **ostream&** (which it must be, to satisfy the return value type of the function).

memory manager overhead

When you create auto objects on the stack, the size of the objects and their lifetime is built right into the generated code, because the compiler knows the exact quantity and scope. Creating objects on the heap involves additional overhead, both in time and in space. Here's a typical scenario. (You can replace **malloc( )** with **calloc( )** or **realloc( )**.)

1. You call **malloc( )**, which requests a block of memory from the pool. (This code may actually be part of **malloc( )**.)

2. The pool is searched for a block of memory large enough to satisfy the request. This is done by checking a map or directory of some sort that shows which blocks are currently in use and which blocks are available. It's a quick process, but it may take several tries so it might not be deterministic — that is, you can't necessarily count on **malloc( )** always taking exactly the same amount of time.

3. Before a pointer to that block is returned, the size and location of the block must be recorded so further calls to **malloc( )** won't use it, and so that when you call **free( )**, the system knows how much memory to release.

The way all this is implemented can vary widely. For example, there's nothing to prevent primitives for memory allocation being implemented in the processor. If you're curious, you can write test programs to try to guess the way your **malloc( )** is implemented. You can also read the library source code, if you have it.

early examples redesigned

Now that **new** and **delete** have been introduced (as well as many other subjects), the **stash** and **stack** examples from the early part of this book can be rewritten using all the features discussed in the book so far. Examining the new code will also give you a useful review of the topics.

heap-only string class

At this point in the book, neither the **stash** nor **stack** classes will "own" the objects they point to; that is, when the **stash** or **stack** object goes out of scope, it will not call **delete** for all the objects it points to. The reason this is not possible is because, in an attempt to be generic, they hold **void** pointers. If you **delete** a **void** pointer, the only thing that happens is the memory gets released, because there's no type information and no way for the compiler to know what destructor to call. When a pointer is returned from the **stash** or **stack** object, you must cast it to the proper type before using it. These problems will be dealt with in the next chapter, and in Chapter 14.

Because the container doesn't own the pointer, the user must be responsible for it. This means there's a serious problem if you add pointers to objects created on the stack *and* objects created on the heap to the same container because a delete-expression is unsafe for a pointer that hasn't been allocated on the heap. (And when you fetch a pointer back from the container, how will you know where its object has been allocated?) To solve this problem in the following version of a simple **String** class, steps have been taken to prevent the creation of a **String** anywhere but on the heap:

```cpp
//: STRINGS.H -- Simple string class
// Can only be built on the heap
#ifndef STRINGS_H_
#define STRINGS_H_
#include <string.h>
#include <iostream.h>

class String {
  char* s;
  String(const char* S) {
    s = new char[strlen(S) + 1];
    strcpy(s, S);
  }
  // Prevent copying:
  String(const String&);
  void operator=(String&);
public:
  // Only make Strings on the heap:
  friend String* makeString(const char* S) {
    return new String(S);
  }
  // Alternate approach:
  static String* make(const char* S) {
    return new String(S);
  }
  ~String() { delete s; }
  operator char*() const { return s;}
```

```
    char* str() const { return s; }
    friend ostream&
      operator<<(ostream& os, const String& S) {
        return os << S.s;
    }
};
#endif // STRINGS_H_
```

To restrict what the user can do with this class, the main constructor is made **private**, so no one can use it but you. In addition, the copy-constructor is declared **private** but never defined, because you want to prevent anyone from using it, and the same goes for the **operator=**. The only way for the user to create an object is to call a special function that creates a **String** on the heap (so you know all **String** objects are created on the heap) and returns its pointer.

There are two approaches to this function. For ease of use, it can be a global **friend** function (called **makeString( )**), but if you don't want to pollute the global name space, you can make it a **static** member function (called **make( )**) and call it by saying **String::make( )**. The latter form has the benefit of more explicitly belonging to the class.

In the constructor, note the expression:

```
s = new char[strlen(S) + 1];
```

The square brackets mean that an array of objects is being created (in this case, an array of **char**), and the number inside the brackets is the number of objects to create. This is how you create an array at run-time.

The automatic type conversion to **char*** means that you can use a **String** object anywhere you need a **char***. In addition, an iostream output operator extends the iostream library to handle **String** objects.

stash for pointers

This version of the **stash** class, which you last saw in Chapter 4, is changed to reflect all the new material introduced since Chapter 4. In addition, the new **pstash** holds *pointers* to objects that exist by themselves on the heap, whereas the old **stash** in Chapter 4 and earlier copied the *objects* into the **stash** container. With the introduction of **new** and **delete**, it's easy and safe to hold pointers to objects that have been created on the heap.

Here's the header file for the "pointer stash":

```
//: PSTASH.H -- Holds pointers instead of objects
#ifndef PSTASH_H_
#define PSTASH_H_

class pstash {
  int quantity; // Number of storage spaces
  int next; // Next empty space
   // Pointer storage:
  void** storage;
  void inflate(int increase);
public:
  pstash() {
    quantity = 0;
    storage = 0;
    next = 0;
  }
  // No ownership:
  ~pstash() { delete storage; }
  int add(void* element);
  void* operator[](int index) const; // Fetch
  // Number of elements in stash:
  int count() const { return next; }
};
#endif // PSTASH_H_
```

The underlying data elements are fairly similar, but now **storage** is an array of **void** pointers, and the allocation of storage for that array is performed with **new** instead of **malloc( )**. In the expression

```
storage = new void*[quantity = Quantity];
```

the type of object allocated is a **void***, so the expression allocates an array of **void** pointers.

The destructor deletes the storage where the **void** pointers are held, rather than attempting to delete what they point at (which, as previously noted, will release their storage and not call the destructors because a **void** pointer has no type information).

The other change is the replacement of the **fetch( )** function with **operator[]**, which makes more sense syntactically. Again, however, a **void*** is returned, so the user must remember what types are stored in the container and cast the pointers when fetching them out (a problem which will be repaired in future chapters).

Here are the member function definitions:

```
//: PSTASH.CPP -- Pointer stash definitions
#include "..\11\pstash.h"
#include <iostream.h>
#include <string.h> // Mem functions

int pstash::add(void* element) {
  const InflateSize = 10;
  if(next >= quantity)
    inflate(InflateSize);
  storage[next++] = element;
  return(next - 1); // Index number
}

// Operator overloading replacement for fetch
void* pstash::operator[](int index) const {
  if(index >= next || index < 0)
```

```
      return 0;  // Out of bounds
  // Produce pointer to desired element:
  return storage[index];
}

void pstash::inflate(int increase) {
  const psz = sizeof(void*);
  // realloc() is cleaner than this:
  void** st = new void*[quantity + increase];
  memset(st, 0, (quantity + increase) * psz);
  memcpy(st, storage, quantity * psz);
  quantity += increase;
  delete storage; // Old storage
  storage = st; // Point to new memory
}
```

The **add( )** function is effectively the same as before, except that
the pointer is stored instead of a copy of the whole object, which,
as you've seen, actually requires a copy-constructor for normal
objects.

The **inflate( )** code is actually more complicated and less efficient
than in the earlier version. This is because **realloc( )**, which was
used before, can resize an existing chunk of memory, or failing that,
automatically copy the contents of your old chunk to a bigger piece.
In either event you don't have to worry about it, *and* it's potentially
faster if memory doesn't have to be moved. There's no equivalent
of **realloc( )** with **new**, however, so in this example you always
have to allocate a bigger chunk, perform a copy, and delete the old
chunk. In this situation it might make sense to use **malloc( )**,
realloc( ), and **free( )** in the underlying implementation rather than
new and **delete**. Fortunately, the implementation is hidden so the
client programmer will remain blissfully ignorant of these kinds of
changes; also the **malloc( )** family of functions is guaranteed to
interact safely in parallel with **new** and **delete**, as long as you don't
mix calls with the same chunk of memory, so this is a completely
plausible thing to do.

a test

Here's the old test program for **stash** rewritten for the **pstash**:

```
//: PSTEST.CPP -- Test of pointer stash
#include "..\11\pstash.h"
#include "..\11\strings.h"
#include <fstream.h>
#include "..\allege.h"

main() {
  pstash intStash;
  // new works with built-in types, too:
  for(int i = 0; i < 25; i++)
    intStash.add(new int(i)); // Pseudo-constr.
  for(int u = 0; u < intStash.count(); u++)
    cout << "intStash[" << u << "] = "
         << *(int*)intStash[u] << endl;

  ifstream infile("pstest.cpp");
  allegefile(infile);
  const bufsize = 80;
  char buf[bufsize];
  pstash stringStash;
  // Use global function makeString:
  for(int j = 0; j < 10; j++)
    if(infile.getline(buf, bufsize))
      stringStash.add(makeString(buf));
  // Use static member make:
  while(infile.getline(buf, bufsize))
    stringStash.add(String::make(buf));
  // Print out the strings:
  for(int v = 0; stringStash[v]; v++) {
    char* p = *(String*)stringStash[v];
    cout << "stringStash[" << v << "] = "
         << p << endl;
  }
}
```

As before, stashes are created and filled with information, but this time the information is the pointers resulting from new-expressions. In the first case, note the line:

```
intStash.add(new int(i));
```

The expression **new int(i)** uses the pseudoconstructor form, so storage for a new **int** object is created on the heap, and the **int** is initialized to the value **i**.

Note that during printing, the value returned by **pstash::operator[]** must be cast to the proper type; this is repeated for the rest of the **pstash** objects in the program. It's an undesirable effect of using **void** pointers as the underlying representation and will be fixed in later chapters.

The second test opens the source code file and reads it into another **pstash**, converting each line into a **String** object. You can see that both **makeString( )** and **String::make( )** are used to show the difference between the two. The **static** member is probably the better approach because it's more explicit.

When fetching the pointers back out, you see the expression:

```
char* p = *(String*)stringStash[i];
```

The pointer returned from **operator[]** must be cast to a **String*** to give it the proper type. Then the **String*** is dereferenced so the expression evaluates to an object, at which point the compiler sees a **String** object when it wants a **char***, so it calls the automatic type conversion operator in **String** to produce a **char***.

In this example, the objects created on the heap are never destroyed. This is not harmful here because the storage is released when the program ends, but it's not something you want to do in practice. It will be fixed in later chapters.

the stack

The **stack** benefits greatly from all the features introduced since Chapter 3. Here's the new header file:

```
//: STACK11.H -- New version of stack
#ifndef STACK11_H_
#define STACK11_H_

class stack {
  struct link {
    void* data;
    link* next;
    link(void* Data, link* Next) {
      data = Data;
      next = Next;
    }
  } * head;
public:
  stack() { head = 0; }
  ~stack();
  void push(void* Data) {
    head = new link(Data,head);
  }
  void* peek() const { return head->data; }
  void* pop();
};
#endif // STACK11_H_
```

The nested **struct link** can now have its own constructor because in **stack::push( )** the use of **new** safely calls that constructor. (And notice how much cleaner the syntax is, which reduces potential bugs.) The **link::link( )** constructor simply initializes the **data** and **next** pointers, so in **stack::push( )** the line

```
head = new link(Data,head);
```

not only allocates a new link, but neatly initializes the pointers for that link.

The rest of the logic is virtually identical to what it was in Chapter 3. Here is the implementation of the two remaining (non-inline) functions:

```
//: STACK11.CPP -- New version of stack
#include <stdlib.h>
#include "..\11\stack11.h"

void* stack::pop() {
  if(head == 0) return 0;
  void* result = head->data;
  link* oldHead = head;
  head = head->next;
  delete oldHead;
  return result;
}

stack::~stack() {
  link* cursor = head;
  while(head) {
    cursor = cursor->next;
    delete head;
    head = cursor;
  }
}
```

The only difference is the use of **delete** instead of **free( )** in the destructor.

As with the **stash**, the use of **void** pointers means that the objects created on the heap cannot be destroyed by the **stack**, so again there is the possibility of an undesirable memory leak if the user doesn't take responsibility for the pointers in the **stack**. You can see this in the test program:

```
//: STKTST11.CPP -- Test new stack
#include "..\11\stack11.h"
#include "..\11\strings.h"
#include <fstream.h>
#include "..\allege.h"

main() {
  // Could also use command-line argument:
  ifstream file("stktst11.cpp");
  allegefile(file);
  const bufsize = 100;
  char buf[bufsize];
  stack textlines;
  // Read file and store lines in the stack:
  while(file.getline(buf,bufsize))
    textlines.push(String::make(buf));
  // Pop lines from the stack and print them:
  String* s;
  while((s = (String*)textlines.pop()) != 0)
    cout << *s << endl;
}
```

As with the **stash** example, a file is opened and each line is turned into a **String** object, which is stored in a **stack** and then printed. This program doesn't **delete** the pointers in the **stack** and the **stack** itself doesn't do it, so that memory is lost.

new & delete for arrays

In C++, you can create arrays of objects on the stack or on the heap with equal ease, and (of course) the constructor is called for each object in the array. There's one constraint, however: There must be a default constructor, except for aggregate initialization on the stack (see Chapter 3), because a constructor with no arguments must be called for every object.

When creating arrays of objects on the heap using **new**, there's something else you must do. An example of such an array is

```
foo* fp = new foo[100];
```

This allocates enough storage on the heap for 100 **foo** objects and calls the constructor for each one. Now, however, you simply have a **foo***, which is exactly the same as you'd get if you said

```
foo* fp2 = new foo;
```

to create a single object. Because you wrote the code, you know that **fp** is actually the starting address of an array, so it makes sense to select array elements with **fp[2]**. But what happens when you destroy the array? The statements

```
delete fp2; // OK
delete fp;  // Not the desired effect
```

look exactly the same, and their effect will be the same: The destructor will be called for the **foo** object pointed to by the given address, and then the storage will be released. For **fp2** this is fine, but for **fp** this means the other 99 destructor calls won't be made. The proper amount of storage will still be released, however, because it is allocated in one big chunk, and the size of the whole chunk is stashed somewhere by the allocation routine.

The solution requires you to give the compiler the information that this is actually the starting address of an array. This is accomplished with the following syntax:

```
delete []fp;
```

The empty brackets tell the compiler to generate code that fetches the number of objects in the array, stored somewhere when the array is created, and calls the destructor for that many array objects. This is actually an improved syntax from the earlier form, which you may still occasionally see in old code:

```
delete [100]fp;
```

which forced the programmer to include the number of objects in the array and introduced the possibility that the programmer would get it wrong. The additional overhead of letting the compiler handle it was very low, and it was considered better to specify the number of objects in one place rather than two.

making a pointer more like an array

As an aside, the **fp** defined above can be changed to point to anything, which doesn't make sense for the starting address of an array. It makes more sense to define it as a constant, so any attempt to modify the pointer will be flagged as an error. To get this effect, you might try

```
int const* q = new int[10];
```

or

```
const int* q = new int[10];
```

but in both cases the **const** will bind to the **int**, that is, what is being pointed *to*, rather than the quality of the pointer itself. Instead, you must say

```
int* const q = new int[10];
```

Now the array elements in **q** can be modified, but any change to **q** itself (like **q++**) is illegal, as it is with an ordinary array identifier.

running out of storage

What happens when the **operator new** cannot find a contiguous block of storage large enough to hold the desired object? A special function called the *new-handler* is called. Or rather, a pointer to a function is checked, and if the pointer is nonzero, then the function it points to is called.

The default behavior for the new-handler is to *throw an exception*, the subject covered in Chapter 16. However, if you're using heap allocation in your program, it's wise to at least replace the new-handler with a message that says you've run out of memory and then aborts the program. That way, during debugging, you'll have a clue about what happened. For the final program you'll want to use more robust recovery.

You replace the new-handler by including NEW.H and then calling **set_new_handler( )** with the address of the function you want installed:

```
//: NEWHANDL.CPP -- Changing the new-handler
#include <iostream.h>
#include <stdlib.h>
#include <new.h>

void out_of_memory() {
  cerr << "memory exhausted!" << endl;
  exit(1);
}

main() {
  set_new_handler(out_of_memory);
  while(1)
    new int[1000]; // Exhausts memory
}
```

The new-handler function must take no arguments and have **void** return value. The **while** loop will keep allocating **int** objects (and throwing away their return addresses) until the free store is exhausted. At the very next call to **new**, no storage can be allocated, so the new-handler will be called.

Of course, you can write more sophisticated new-handlers, even one to try to reclaim memory (commonly known as a *garbage collector*). This is not a job for the novice programmer.

overloading new & delete

When you create a new-expression, two things occur: First, storage is allocated using the **operator new**, then the constructor is called. In a delete-expression, the destructor is called, then storage is deallocated using the **operator delete**. The constructor and destructor calls are never under your control (otherwise you might accidentally subvert them), but you *can* change the storage allocation functions **operator new** and **operator delete**.

The memory allocation system used by **new** and **delete** is designed for general-purpose use. In special situations, however, it doesn't serve your needs. The most common reason to change the allocator is efficiency: You might be creating and destroying so many objects of a particular class that it has become a speed bottleneck. C++ allows you to overload **new** and **delete** to implement your own storage allocation scheme, so you can handle problems like this.

Another issue is heap fragmentation: By allocating objects of different sizes it's possible to break up the heap so that you effectively run out of storage. That is, the storage might be available, but because of fragmentation no piece is big enough to satisfy your needs. By creating your own allocator for a particular class, you can ensure this never happens.

In embedded and real-time systems, a program may have to run for a very long time with restricted resources. Such a system may also require that memory allocation always take the same amount of time, and there's no allowance for heap exhaustion or fragmentation. A custom memory allocator is the solution; otherwise programmers will avoid using **new** and **delete** altogether in such cases and miss out on a valuable C++ asset.

When you overload **operator new** and **operator delete**, it's important to remember that you're changing only the way *raw storage is allocated*. The compiler will simply call your **new** instead of the default version to allocate storage, then call the constructor for that storage. So, although the compiler allocates storage *and* calls the constructor when it sees **new**, all you can change when you overload **new** is the storage allocation portion. (**delete** has a similar limitation.)

When you overload **operator new**, you also replace the behavior when it runs out of memory, so you must decide what to do in your **operator new**: return zero, write a loop to call the new-handler and retry allocation, or (typically) throw a **bad_alloc** exception (discussed in Chapter 16).

Overloading **new** and **delete** is like overloading any other operator. However, you have a choice of overloading the global allocator or using a different allocator for a particular class.

overloading global new & delete

This is the drastic approach, when the global versions of **new** and **delete** are unsatisfactory for the whole system. If you overload the global versions, you make the defaults completely inaccessible — you can't even call them from inside your redefinitions.

The overloaded **new** must take an argument of **size_t** (the Standard C standard type for sizes). This argument is generated and passed to you by the compiler and is the size of the object you're responsible for allocating. You must return a pointer either to an object of that size (or bigger, if you have some reason to do so), or to zero if you can't find the memory (in which case the constructor is *not* called!). However, if you can't find the memory, you should probably do something more drastic than just returning zero, like calling the new-handler or throwing an exception, to signal that there's a problem.

The return value of **operator new** is a **void***, *not* a pointer to any particular type. All you've done is produce memory, not a finished object — that doesn't happen until the constructor is called, an act the compiler guarantees and which is out of your control.

The **operator delete** takes a **void*** to memory that was allocated by **operator new**. It's a **void*** because you get that pointer *after* the destructor is called, which removes the object-ness from the piece of storage. The return type is **void**.

Here's a very simple example showing how to overload the global **new** and **delete**:

```
//: GLOBLNEW.CPP -- Overload global new/delete
#include <stdio.h>
#include <stdlib.h>

void* operator new(size_t sz) {
  printf("operator new: %d bytes\n", sz);
  void* m = malloc(sz);
  if(!m) puts("out of memory");
  return m;
}

void operator delete(void* m) {
  puts("operator delete");
  free(m);
}

class s {
  int i[100];
public:
  s() { puts("s::s()"); }
  ~s() { puts("s::~s()"); }
};

main() {
  puts("creating & destroying an int");
  int* p = new int(47);
  delete p;
  puts("creating & destroying an s");
  s* S = new s;
```

```
  delete S;
  puts("creating & destroying s[3]");
  s* SA = new s[3];
  delete []SA;
}
```

Here you can see the general form for overloading **new** and **delete**. These use the Standard C library functions **malloc( )** and **free( )** for the allocators (which is probably what the default **new** and **delete** use, as well!). However, they also print out messages about what they are doing. Notice that **printf( )** and **puts( )** are used rather than **iostreams**. Thus, when an **iostream** object is created (like the global **cin**, **cout**, and **cerr**), they call **new** to allocate memory. With **printf( )**, you don't get into a deadlock because it doesn't call **new** to initialize itself.

In **main( )**, objects of built-in types are created to prove that the overloaded **new** and **delete** are also called in that case. Then a single object of type **s** is created, followed by an array. For the array, you'll see that extra memory is requested to put information about the number of objects in the array. In all cases, the global overloaded versions of **new** and **delete** are used.

overloading new & delete for a class

Although you don't have to explicitly say **static**, when you overload **new** and **delete** for a class, you're creating **static** member functions. Again, the syntax is the same as overloading any other operator. When the compiler sees you use **new** to create an object of your class, it chooses the member **operator new** over the global version. However, the global versions of **new** and **delete** are used for all other types of objects (unless they have their own **new** and **delete**).

In the following example, a very primitive storage allocation system is created for the class **framis**. A chunk of memory is set aside in the static data area at program start-up, and that memory is used to allocate space for objects of type **framis**. To determine which blocks have been allocated, a simple array of bytes is used, one byte for each block:

```
//: FRAMIS.CPP -- Local overloaded new & delete
#include <stddef.h> // Size_t
#include <fstream.h>
ofstream out("framis.out");

class framis {
  char c[10];
  static unsigned char pool[];
  static unsigned char alloc_map[]; // Alloc map
public:
  enum { psize = 100 };  // # of frami allowed
  framis() { out << "framis()\n"; }
  ~framis() { out << "~framis() ... "; }
  void* operator new(size_t);
  void operator delete(void*);
};
unsigned char framis::pool[psize * sizeof(framis)];
unsigned char framis::alloc_map[psize] = {0};

// Size is ignored -- assume a framis object
void* framis::operator new(size_t) {
  for(int i = 0; i < psize; i++)
    if(!alloc_map[i]) {
      out << "using block " << i << " ... ";
      alloc_map[i] = 1; // Mark it used
      return pool + (i * sizeof(framis));
    }
  out << "out of memory" << endl;
  return 0;
}

void framis::operator delete(void* m) {
  if(!m) return; // Check for null pointer
  // Assume it was created in the pool
```

```
  // Calculate which block number it is:
  unsigned long block = (unsigned long)m
    - (unsigned long)pool;
  block /= sizeof(framis);
  out << "freeing block " << block << endl;
  // Mark it free:
  alloc_map[block] = 0;
}

main() {
  framis* f[framis::psize];
  for(int i = 0; i < framis::psize; i++)
    f[i] = new framis;
  new framis; // Out of memory
  delete f[10];
  f[10] = 0;
  // Use released memory:
  framis* x = new framis;
  delete x;
  for(int j = 0; j < framis::psize; j++)
    delete f[j]; // Delete f[10] OK
}
```

The pool of memory for the **framis** heap is created by allocating an
array of bytes large enough to hold **psize framis** objects. The
allocation map is **psize** bytes long, so there's one byte for every
block. All the bytes in the allocation map are initialized to zero using
the aggregate initialization trick of setting the first element to zero so
the compiler automatically initializes all the rest.

The local **operator new** has the same form as the global one. All it
does is search through the allocation map looking for a zero byte,
then sets that byte to one to indicate it's been allocated and returns
the address of that particular block. If it can't find any memory, it
issues a message and returns zero (Notice that the new-handler is
not called and no exceptions are thrown because the behavior
when you run out of memory is now under your control.) In this

example, it's OK to use iostreams because the global **operator new** and **delete** are untouched.

The **operator delete** assumes the **framis** address was created in the pool. This is a fair assumption, because the local **operator new** will be called whenever you create a single **framis** object on the heap — but not an array. Global **new** is used in that case. So the user might accidentally have called **operator delete** without using the empty bracket syntax to indicate array destruction. This would cause a problem. Also, the user might be deleting a pointer to an object created on the stack. If you think these things could occur, you might want to add a line to make sure the address is within the pool and on a correct boundary.

operator delete calculates which block in the pool this pointer represents, and then sets the allocation map's flag for that block to zero to indicate the block has been released.

In **main( )**, enough **framis** objects are dynamically allocated to run out of memory; this checks the out-of-memory behavior. Then one of the objects is freed, and another one is created to show that the released memory is reused.

Because this allocation scheme is specific to **framis** objects, it's probably much faster than the general-purpose memory allocation scheme used for the default **new** and **delete**.

overloading new & delete for arrays

If you overload operator **new** and **delete** for a class, those operators are called whenever you create an object of that class. However, if you create an *array* of those class objects, the global **operator new( )** is called to allocate enough storage for the array all at once, and the global **operator delete( )** is called to release that storage. You can control the allocation of arrays of objects by overloading the special array versions of **operator new[]** and **operator delete[]** for the class. Here's an example that shows when the two different versions are called:

```
//: NEWARRY.CPP -- Operator new for arrays
#include <new.h> // Size_t definition
#include <fstream.h>
ofstream trace("newarry.out");

class widget {
  int i[10];
public:
  widget() { trace << "*"; }
  ~widget() { trace << "~"; }
  void* operator new(size_t sz) {
    trace << "widget::new: "
          << sz << " bytes" << endl;
    return ::new char[sz];
  }
  void operator delete(void* p) {
    trace << "widget::delete" << endl;
    ::delete []p;
  }
  void* operator new[](size_t sz) {
    trace << "widget::new[]: "
          << sz << " bytes" << endl;
    return ::new char[sz];
  }
  void operator delete[](void* p) {
    trace << "widget::delete[]" << endl;
    ::delete []p;
  }
};

main() {
  trace << "new widget" << endl;
  widget* w = new widget;
  trace << "\ndelete widget" << endl;
  delete w;
  trace << "\nnew widget[25]" << endl;
  widget* wa = new widget[25];
```

```
     trace << "\ndelete []widget" << endl;
     delete []wa;
};
```

Here, the global versions of **new** and **delete** are called so the effect is the same as having no overloaded versions of **new** and **delete** except that trace information is added. Of course, you can use any memory allocation scheme you want in the overloaded **new** and **delete**.

You can see that the array versions of **new** and **delete** are the same as the individual-object versions with the addition of the brackets. In both cases you're handed the size of the memory you must allocate. The size handed to the array version will be the size of the entire array. It's worth keeping in mind that the *only* thing the overloaded operator **new** is required to do is hand back a pointer to a large enough memory block. Although you may perform initialization on that memory, normally that's the job of the constructor that will automatically be called for your memory by the compiler.

The constructor and destructor simply print out characters so you can see when they've been called. Here's what the trace file looks like for one compiler:

```
new widget
widget::new: 20 bytes
*
delete widget
~widget::delete

new widget[25]
widget::new[]: 504 bytes
************************
delete []widget
~~~~~~~~~~~~~~~~~~~~~~~~~widget::delete[]
```

Creating an individual object requires 20 bytes, as you might expect (this machine uses two bytes for an **int**). The **operator new** is called, then the constructor (indicated by the *). In a complementary fashion, calling **delete** causes the destructor to be called, then the **operator delete**.

When an array of **widget** objects is created, the array version of **operator new** is used, as promised. But notice that the size requested is four more bytes than expected. This extra four bytes is where the system keeps information about the array, in particular, the number of objects in the array. That way, when you say

```
delete []widget;
```

the brackets tell the compiler it's an array of objects, so the compiler generates code to look for the number of objects in the array and to call the destructor that many times.

You can see that, even though the array **operator new** and **operator delete** are only called once for the entire array chunk, the default constructor and destructor are called for each object in the array.

constructor calls

Considering that

```
foo* f = new foo;
```

calls **new** to allocate a **foo**-sized piece of storage, then invokes the **foo** constructor on that storage, what happens if all the safeguards fail and the value returned by **operator new** is zero? The constructor is not called in that case, so although you still have an unsuccessfully created object, at least you haven't invoked the constructor and handed it a zero pointer. Here's an example to prove it:

```
//: NOMEMORY.CPP -- Constructor isn't called
// If new returns 0
#include <iostream.h>
#include <new.h> // size_t definition
```

```
void my_new_handler() {
  cout << "new handler called" << endl;
}

class nomemory {
public:
  nomemory() {
    cout << "nomemory::nomemory()" << endl;
  }
  void* operator new(size_t sz) {
    cout << "nomemory::operator new" << endl;
    return 0; // "Out of memory"
  }
};

main() {
  set_new_handler(my_new_handler);
  nomemory* nm = new nomemory;
  cout << "nm = " << nm << endl;
}
```

When the program runs, it prints only the message from **operator new**. Because **new** returns zero, the constructor is never called so its message is not printed.

object placement

There are two other, less common, uses for overloading **operator new**.

1. You may want to place an object in a specific location in memory. This is especially important with hardware-oriented embedded systems where an object may be synonymous with a particular piece of hardware.

2. You may want to be able to choose from different allocators when calling **new**.

Both of these situations are solved with the same mechanism: The overloaded **operator new** can take more than one argument. As you've seen before, the first argument is always the size of the object, which is secretly calculated and passed by the compiler. But the other arguments can be anything you want: the address you want the object placed at, a reference to a memory allocation function or object, or anything else that is convenient for you.

The way you pass the extra arguments to **operator new** during a call may seem slightly curious at first: You put the argument list (*without* the **size_t** argument, which is handled by the compiler) after the keyword **new** and before the class name of the object you're creating. For example,

```
X* xp = new(a) X;
```

will pass **a** as the second argument to **operator new**. Of course, this can work only if such an **operator new** has been declared.

Here's an example showing how you can place an object at a particular location:

```
//: PLACEMNT.CPP -- Placement with operator new
#include <stddef.h> // Size_t
#include <iostream.h>

class X {
  int i;
public:
  X(int I = 0) { i = I; }
  ~X() {
    cout << "X::~X()" << endl;
  }
  void* operator new(size_t, void* loc) {
    return loc;
  }
};
```

```
main() {
  int 1[10];
  X* xp = new(1) X(47); // X at location 1
  xp->X::~X(); // Explicit destructor call
  // ONLY use with placement!
}
```

Notice that **operator new** only returns the pointer that's passed to it. Thus, the caller decides where the object is going to sit, and the constructor is called for that memory as part of the new-expression.

A dilemma occurs when you want to destroy the object. There's only one version of **operator delete**, so there's no way to say, "Use my special deallocator for this object." You want to call the destructor, but you don't want the memory to be released by the dynamic memory mechanism because it wasn't allocated on the heap.

The answer is a very special syntax: You can explicitly call the destructor, as in

```
xp->X::~X(); // explicit destructor call
```

A stern warning is in order here. Some people see this as a way to destroy objects at some time before the end of the scope, rather than either adjusting the scope or (more correctly) using dynamic object creation if they want the object's lifetime to be determined at run-time. You will have serious problems if you call the destructor this way for an object created on the stack because the destructor will be called again at the end of the scope. If you call the destructor this way for an object that was created on the heap, the destructor will execute, but the memory won't be released, which probably isn't what you want. The only reason that the destructor can be called explicitly this way is to support the placement syntax for **operator new**.

Although this example shows only one additional argument, there's nothing to prevent you from adding more if you need them for other purposes.

summary

It's convenient and optimally efficient to create automatic objects on the stack, but to solve the general programming problem you must be able to create and destroy objects at any time during a program's execution, particularly to respond to information from outside the program. Although C's dynamic memory allocation will get storage from the heap, it doesn't provide the ease of use and guaranteed construction necessary in C++. By bringing dynamic object creation into the core of the language with **new** and **delete**, you can create objects on the heap as easily as making them on the stack. In addition, you get a great deal of flexibility. You can change the behavior of **new** and **delete** if they don't suit your needs, particularly if they aren't efficient enough. Also, you can modify what happens when the heap runs out of storage. (However, *exception handling*, described in Chapter 16, also comes into play here.)

exercises

1. Prove to yourself that **new** and **delete** always call the constructors and destructors by creating a class with a constructor and destructor that announce themselves through **cout**. Create an object of that class with **new**, and destroy it with **delete**. Also create and destroy an array of these objects on the heap.

2. Create a **pstash** object, and fill it with **new** objects from Exercise 1. Observe what happens when this **pstash** object goes out of scope and its destructor is called.

3. Create a class with an overloaded operator **new** and **delete**, both the single-object versions and the array versions. Demonstrate that both versions work.

4. Devise a test for FRAMIS.CPP to show yourself approximately how much faster the custom **new** and **delete** run than the global **new** and **delete**.

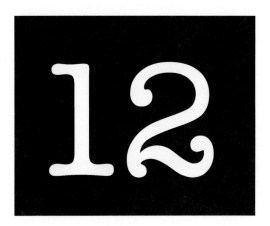

12: inheritance & composition

One of the most compelling features about C++ is code reuse. But to be revolutionary, you've got to be able to do a lot more than copy code and change it.

That's the C approach, and it hasn't worked very well. As with most everything in C++, the solution revolves around the class. You reuse code by creating new classes, but instead of creating them from scratch, you use existing classes that someone else has built and debugged.

The trick is to use the classes without soiling the existing code. In this chapter you'll see two ways to accomplish this. The first is quite straightforward: You simply create objects of your existing class inside the new class. This is called *composition* because the new class is composed of objects of existing classes.

The second approach is more subtle. You create a new class as a *type of* an existing class. You literally take the form of the existing class and add code to it, without modifying the existing class. This magical act is called *inheritance*, and most of the work is done by the compiler. Inheritance is one of the cornerstones of object-oriented programming and has additional implications that will be explored in the next chapter.

It turns out that much of the syntax and behavior are similar for both composition and inheritance (which makes sense; they are both ways of making new types from existing types). In this chapter, you'll learn about these code reuse mechanisms.

composition syntax

Actually, you've been using composition all along to create classes. You've just been composing classes using built-in types. It turns out to be almost as easy to use composition with user-defined types.

Consider an existing class that is valuable for some reason:

```
//: USEFUL.H -- A class to reuse
#ifndef USEFUL_H_
#define USEFUL_H_

class X {
  int i;
  enum { factor = 11 };
public:
  X() { i = 0; }
  void set(int I) { i = I; }
  int read() const { return i; }
  int permute() { return i = i * factor; }
};
```

```
#endif // USEFUL_H_
```

The data members are **private** in this class, so it's completely safe to embed an object of type **X** as a **public** object in a new class, which makes the interface straightforward:

```
//: COMPOSE.CPP -- Reuse code with composition
#include "..\12\useful.h"

class Y {
  int i;
public:
  X x; // Embedded object
  Y() { i = 0; }
  void f(int I) { i = I; }
  int g() const { return i; }
};

main() {
  Y y;
  y.f(47);
  y.x.set(37); // Access the embedded object
}
```

Accessing the member functions of the embedded object (referred to as a *subobject*) simply requires another member selection.

It's probably more common to make the embedded objects **private**, so they become part of the underlying implementation (which means you can change the implementation if you want). The **public** interface functions for your new class then involve the use of the embedded object, but they don't necessarily mimic the object's interface:

```
//: COMPOSE2.CPP -- Private embedded objects
#include "..\12\useful.h"
```

```
class Y {
  int i;
  X x; // Embedded object
public:
  Y() { i = 0; }
  void f(int I) { i = I; x.set(I); }
  int g() const { return i * x.read(); }
  void permute() { x.permute(); }
};

main() {
  Y y;
  y.f(47);
  y.permute();
}
```

Here, the **permute( )** function is carried through to the new class interface, but the other member functions of **X** are used within the members of **Y**.

inheritance syntax

The syntax for composition is obvious, but to perform inheritance there's a new and different form.

When you inherit, you are saying, "This new class is like that old class." You state this in code by giving the name of the class, as usual, but before the opening brace of the class body, you put a colon and the name of the *base class* (or classes, for multiple inheritance). When you do this, you automatically get all the data members and member functions in the base class. Here's an example:

```
//: INHERIT.CPP -- Simple inheritance
#include "..\12\useful.h"
#include <iostream.h>
```

```
class Y : public X {
  int i; // Different from X's i
public:
  Y() { i = 0; }
  int change() {
    i = permute(); // Different name call
    return i;
  }
  void set(int I) {
    i = I;
    X::set(I); // Same-name function call
  }
};

main() {
  cout << "sizeof(X) = " << sizeof(X) << endl;
  cout << "sizeof(Y) = "
       << sizeof(Y) << endl;
  Y D;
  D.change();
  // X function interface comes through:
  D.read();
  D.permute();
  // Redefined functions hide base versions:
  D.set(12);
}
```

In **Y** you can see inheritance going on, which means that **Y** will contain all the data elements in **X** and all the member functions in **X**. In fact, **Y** contains a subobject of **X** just as if you had created a member object of **X** inside **Y** instead of inheriting from **X**. Both member objects and base class storage are referred to as subobjects.

In **main( )** you can see that the data elements are added because the **sizeof(Y)** is twice as big as **sizeof(X)**.

You'll notice that the base class is preceded by **public**. During inheritance, everything defaults to **private**, which means all the **public** members of the base class are **private** in the derived class. This is almost never what you want; the desired result is to keep all the **public** members of the base class **public** in the derived class. You do this by using the **public** keyword during inheritance.

In **change( )**, the base-class **permute( )** function is called. The derived class has direct access to all the **public** base-class functions.

The **set( )** function in the derived class *redefines* the **set( )** function in the base class. That is, if you call the functions **read( )** and **permute( )** for an object of type **Y**, you'll get the base-class versions of those functions (you can see this happen inside **main( )**), but if you call **set( )** for a **Y** object, you get the redefined version. This means that if you don't like the version of a function you get during inheritance, you can change what it does. (You can also add completely new functions like **change( )**.)

However, when you're redefining a function, you may still want to call the base-class version. If, inside **set( )**, you simply call **set( )** you'll get the local version of the function — a recursive function call. To call the base-class version, you must explicitly name it, using the base-class name and the scope resolution operator.

the constructor initializer list

You've seen how important it is in C++ to guarantee proper initialization, and it's no different during composition and inheritance. When an object is created, the compiler guarantees that constructors for all its subobjects are called. In the examples so far, all the subobjects have default constructors, and that's what the compiler automatically calls. But what happens if your subobjects don't have default constructors, or if you want to change a default argument in a constructor? This is a problem because the new class constructor doesn't have permission to access the **private** data elements of the subobject, so it can't initialize them directly.

The solution is simple: Call the constructor for the subobject. C++ provides a special syntax for this, the *constructor initializer list*. The form of the constructor initializer list echoes the act of inheritance. With inheritance, you put the base classes after a colon and before the opening brace of the class body. In the constructor initializer list, you put the calls to subobject constructors after the constructor argument list and a colon, but before the opening brace of the function body. For a class **foo**, inherited from **bar**, this might look like

```
foo::foo(int i) : bar(i) { // ...
```

if **bar** has a constructor that takes a single **int** argument.

member object initialization

It turns out that you use this very same syntax for member object initialization when using composition. For composition, you give the names of the objects rather than the class names. If you have more than one constructor call in the initializer list, you separate the calls with commas:

```
foo2:foo2(int I) : bar(i), memb(i+1) { // ...
```

This is the beginning of a constructor for class **foo2**, which is inherited from **bar** and contains a member object called **memb**. Note that while you can see the type of the base class in the constructor initializer list, you only see the member object identifier.

built-in types in the initializer list

The constructor initializer list allows you to explicitly call the constructors for member objects. In fact, there's no other way to call those constructors. The idea is that the constructors are all called before you get into the body of the new class's constructor. That way, any calls you make to member functions of subobjects will always go to initialized objects. There's no way to get to the opening brace of the constructor without *some* constructor being called for all the member objects and base-class objects, even if the compiler must make a hidden call to a default constructor. This is a further enforcement of the C++ guarantee that no object (or part of an object) can get out of the starting gate without its constructor being called.

This idea that all the member objects are initialized by the opening brace of the constructor is a convenient programming aid, as well. Once you hit the opening brace, you can assume all subobjects are properly initialized and focus on specific tasks you want to accomplish in the constructor. However, there's a hitch: What about embedded objects of built-in types, which don't *have* constructors?

To make the syntax consistent, you're allowed to treat built-in types as if they have a single constructor, which takes a single argument: a variable of the same type as the variable you're initializing. Thus, you can say

```
class X {
  int i;
  float f;
  char c;
  char* s;
public:
  X() : i(7), f(1.4), c('x'), s("howdy") {}
  // ...
```

The action of these "pseudoconstructor calls" is to perform a simple assignment. It's a convenient technique and a good coding style, so you'll often see it used.

It's even possible to use the pseudoconstructor syntax when creating a variable of this type outside of a class:

```
int i(100);
```

This makes built-in types act a little bit more like objects.
Remember, though, that these are not real constructors. In
particular, if you don't explicitly make a pseudo-constructor call, no
initialization is performed.

combining composition & inheritance

Of course, you can use the two together. The following example
shows the creation of a more complex class, using both inheritance
and composition.

```
//: COMBINED.CPP -- Inheritance & composition

class A {
  int i;
public:
  A(int I) { i = I; }
  ~A() {}
  void f() const {}
};

class B {
  int i;
public:
  B(int I) { i = I; }
  ~B() {}
  void f() const {}
};

class C : public B {
  A a;
public:
```

```
    C(int I) : B(I), a(I) {}
    ~C() {} // Calls ~A() and ~B()
    void f() const {  // Redefinition
      a.f();
      B::f();
    }
};

main() {
  C c(47);
}
```

C inherits from **B** and has a member object ("is composed of ") **A**. You can see the constructor initializer list contains calls to both the base-class constructor and the member-object constructor.

The function **C::f( )** redefines **B::f( )** that it inherits, and also calls the base-class version. In addition, it calls **a.f( )**. Notice that the only time you can talk about redefinition of functions is during inheritance; with a member object you can only manipulate the public interface of the object, not redefine it. In addition, calling **f( )** for an object of class **C** would not call **a.f( )** if **C::f( )** had not been defined, whereas it *would* call **B::f( )**.

automatic destructor calls

Although you are often required to make explicit constructor calls in the initializer list, you never need to make explicit destructor calls because there's only one destructor for any class, and it doesn't take any arguments. However, the compiler still ensures that all destructors are called, and that means all the destructors in the entire hierarchy, starting with the most-derived destructor and working back to the root.

It's worth emphasizing that constructors and destructors are quite unusual in that every one in the hierarchy is called, whereas with a normal member function only that function is called, but not any of the base-class versions. If you also want to call the base-class version of a normal member function that you're overriding, you must do it explicitly.

order of constructor & destructor calls

It's interesting to know the order of constructor and destructor calls when an object has many subobjects. The following example shows exactly how it works:

```
//: ORDER.CPP -- Constructor/destructor order
#include <fstream.h>
ofstream out("order.out");

#define CLASS(ID) class ID { \
public: \
  ID(int) { out << #ID " constructor\n"; } \
  ~ID() { out << #ID " destructor\n"; } \
};

CLASS(base1);
CLASS(member1);
CLASS(member2);
CLASS(member3);
CLASS(member4);

class derived1 : public base1 {
  member1 m1;
  member2 m2;
public:
  derived1(int) : m2(1), m1(2), base1(3) {
    out << "derived1 constructor\n";
  }
  ~derived1() {
    out << "derived1 destructor\n";
  }
};
```

```
class derived2 : public derived1 {
  member3 m3;
  member4 m4;
public:
  derived2() : m3(1), derived1(2), m4(3) {
    out << "derived2 constructor\n";
  }
  ~derived2() {
    out << "derived2 destructor\n";
  }
};

main() { derived2 d2; }
```

First, an **ofstream** object is created to send all the output to a file. Then, to save some typing and demonstrate a macro technique that will be replaced by a much improved technique in Chapter 17, a macro is created to build some of the classes, which are then used in inheritance and composition. Each of the constructors and destructors report themselves to the trace file. Note that the constructors are not default constructors; they each have an **int** argument. The argument itself has no identifier; its only job is to force you to explicitly call the constructors in the initializer list. (Eliminating the identifier prevents compiler warning messages.)

The output of this program is

```
base1 constructor
member1 constructor
member2 constructor
derived1 constructor
member3 constructor
member4 constructor
derived2 constructor
derived2 destructor
member4 destructor
member3 destructor
```

```
derived1 destructor
member2 destructor
member1 destructor
base1 destructor
```

You can see that construction starts at the very root of the class hierarchy, and that at each level the base class constructor is called first, followed by the member object constructors. The destructors are called in exactly the reverse order of the constructors — this is important because of potential dependencies.

It's also interesting that the order of constructor calls for member objects is completely unaffected by the order of the calls in the constructor initializer list. The order is determined by the order that the member objects are declared in the class. If you could change the order of constructor calls via the constructor initializer list, you could have two different call sequences in two different constructors, but the poor destructor wouldn't know how to properly reverse the order of the calls for destruction, and you could end up with a dependency problem.

name hiding

If a base class has a function name that's overloaded several times, redefining that function name in the derived class will hide *all* the base-class versions. That is, they become unavailable in the derived class:

```
//: HIDE.CPP -- Name hiding during inheritance

class homer {
public:
  int doh(int) const { return 1; }
  char doh(char) const { return 'd';}
  float doh(float) const { return 1.0; }
};

class bart : public homer {
```

```
public:
  class milhouse {};
  void doh(milhouse) const {}
};

main() {
  bart b;
//! b.doh(1); // Error
//! b.doh('x'); // Error
//! b.doh(1.0); // Error
}
```

Because **bart** redefines **doh( )**, none of the base-class versions can be called for a **bart** object. In each case, the compiler attempts to convert the argument into a **milhouse** object and complains because it can't find a conversion.

As you'll see in the next chapter, it's far more common to redefine functions using exactly the same signature and return type as in the base class.

functions that don't automatically inherit

Not all functions are automatically inherited from the base class into the derived class. Constructors and destructors deal with the creation and destruction of an object, and they can know what to do with the aspects of the object only for their particular level, so all the constructors and destructors in the entire hierarchy must be called. Thus, constructors and destructors don't inherit.

In addition, the **operator=** doesn't inherit because it performs a constructor-like activity. That is, just because you know how to initialize all the members of an object on the left-hand side of the = from an object on the right-hand side doesn't mean that initialization will still have meaning after inheritance.

In lieu of inheritance, these functions are synthesized by the compiler if you don't create them yourself. (With constructors, you can't create *any* constructors for the default constructor and the copy-constructor to be automatically created.) This was briefly described in Chapter 10. The synthesized constructors use memberwise initialization and the synthesized **operator=** uses memberwise assignment. Here's an example of the functions that are created by the compiler rather than inherited:

```cpp
//: NINHERIT.CPP -- Non-inherited functions
#include <fstream.h>
ofstream out("ninherit.out");

class root {
public:
  root() { out << "root()\n"; }
  root(root&) { out << "root(root&)\n"; }
  root(int) { out << "root(int)\n"; }
  root& operator=(const root&) {
    out << "root::operator=()\n";
    return *this;
  }
  class other {};
  operator other() const {
    out << "root::operator other()\n";
    return other();
  }
  ~root() { out << "~root()\n"; }
};

class derived : public root {};

void f(root::other) {}

main() {
  derived d1;  // Default constructor
  derived d2 = d1; // Copy-constructor
```

```
//! derived d3(1); // Error: no int constructor
  d1 = d2; // Operator= not inherited
  f(d1); // Type-conversion IS inherited
}
```

All the constructors and the **operator=** announce themselves so
you can see when they're used by the compiler. In addition, the
operator other( ) performs automatic type conversion from a **root**
object to an object of the nested class **other**. The class **derived**
simply inherits from **root** and creates no functions (to see how the
compiler responds). The function **f( )** takes an **other** object to test
the automatic type conversion function.

In **main( )**, the default constructor and copy-constructor are
created and the **root** versions are called as part of the constructor-
call hierarchy. Even though it looks like inheritance, new
constructors are actually created. As you might expect, no
constructors with arguments are automatically created because
that's too much for the compiler to intuit.

The **operator=( )** is also synthesized as a new function in **derived**
using memberwise assignment because that function was not
explicitly written in the new class.

Because of all these rules about rewriting functions that handle
object creation, it may seem a little strange at first that the
automatic type conversion operator *is* inherited. But it's not too
unreasonable — if there are enough pieces in **root** to make an
other object, those pieces are still there in anything derived from
root and the type conversion operator is still valid (even though you
may in fact want to redefine it).

choosing composition vs. inheritance

Both composition and inheritance place subobjects inside your new class. Both use the constructor initializer list to construct these subobjects. You may now be wondering what the difference is between the two, and when to choose one over the other.

Composition is generally used when you want the features of an existing class inside your new class, but not its interface. That is, you embed an object that you're planning on using to implement features of your new class, but the user of your new class sees the interface you've defined rather than the interface from the original class. For this effect, you embed **private** objects of existing classes inside your new class.

Sometimes it makes sense to allow the class user to directly access the composition of your new class, that is, to make the member objects **public**. The member objects use implementation hiding themselves, so this is a safe thing to do and when the user knows you're assembling a bunch of parts it, makes the interface easier for him to understand. A **car** object is a good example:

```
//: CAR.CPP -- Public composition

class engine {
public:
  void start() const {}
  void rev() const {}
  void stop() const {}
};

class wheel {
public:
  void inflate(int psi) const {}
```

```
};

class window {
public:
  void rollup() const {}
  void rolldown() const {}
};

class door {
public:
  window Window;
  void open() const {}
  void close() const {}
};

class car {
public:
  engine Engine;
  wheel Wheel[4];
  door left, right; // 2-door
};

main() {
  car Car;
  Car.left.Window.rollup();
  Car.Wheel[0].inflate(72);
}
```

Because the composition of a car is part of the analysis of the problem (and not simply part of the underlying design), making the members public assists the client programmer's understanding of how to use the class and requires less code complexity for the creator of the class.

With a little thought, you'll also see that it would make no sense to compose a car using a vehicle object — a car doesn't contain a vehicle, it *is* a vehicle. The *is-a* relationship is expressed with inheritance, and the *has-a* relationship is expressed with composition.

subtyping

Now suppose you want to create a type of **ifstream** object that not only opens a file but also keeps track of the name of the file. You can use composition and embed both an **ifstream** and a **strstream** into the new class:

```
//: FNAME1.CPP -- An fstream with a file name
#include <fstream.h>
#include <strstrea.h>
#include "..\allege.h"

class fname1 {
  ifstream File;
  enum { bsize = 100 };
  char buf[bsize];
  ostrstream Name;
  int nameset;
public:
  fname1() : Name(buf, bsize), nameset(0) {}
  fname1(const char* filename)
    : File(filename), Name(buf, bsize) {
      allegefile(File);
      Name << filename << ends;
      nameset = 1;
  }
  const char* name() const { return buf; }
  void name(const char* newname) {
    if(nameset) return; // Don't overwrite
    Name << newname << ends;
    nameset = 1;
  }
  operator ifstream&() { return File; }
};
```

```
main() {
  fname1 file("fname1.cpp");
  cout << file.name() << endl;
  // Error: rdbuf() not a member:
//!  cout << file.rdbuf() << endl;
}
```

There's a problem here, however. An attempt is made to allow the use of the **fname1** object anywhere an **ifstream** object is used, by including an automatic type conversion operator from **fname1** to an **ifstream&**. But in main, the line

```
cout << file.rdbuf() << endl;
```

will not compile because automatic type conversion happens only in function calls, not during member selection. So this approach won't work.

A second approach is to add the definition of **rdbuf( )** to **fname1**:

```
filebuf* rdbuf() { return File.rdbuf(); }
```

This will work if there are only a few functions you want to bring through from the **ifstream** class. In that case you're only using part of the class, and composition is appropriate.

But what if you want everything in the class to come through? This is called *subtyping* because you're making a new type from an existing type, and you want your new type to have exactly the same interface as the existing type (plus any other member functions you want to add), so you can use it everywhere you'd use the existing type. This is where inheritance is essential. You can see that subtyping solves the problem in the preceding example perfectly:

```
//: FNAME2.CPP -- Subtyping solves the problem
#include <fstream.h>
#include <strstrea.h>
#include "..\allege.h"
```

```
class fname2 : public ifstream {
  enum { bsize = 100 };
  char buf[bsize];
  ostrstream Name;
  int nameset;
public:
  fname2() : Name(buf, bsize), nameset(0) {}
  fname2(const char* filename)
    : ifstream(filename), Name(buf, bsize) {
      Name << filename << ends;
      nameset = 1;
  }
  const char* name() const { return buf; }
  void name(const char* newname) {
    if(nameset) return; // Don't overwrite
    Name << newname << ends;
    nameset = 1;
  }
};

main() {
  fname2 file("fname2.cpp");
  allegefile(file);
  cout << "name: " << file.name() << endl;
  const bsize = 100;
  char buf[bsize];
  file.getline(buf, bsize); // This works too!
  file.seekg(-200, ios::end);
  cout << file.rdbuf() << endl;
}
```

Now any member function that works with an **ofstream** object also works with an **fname2** object. That's because an **fname2** *is* a type of **ofstream**; it doesn't simply contain one. This is a very important issue that will be explored at the end of this chapter and in Chapter 13.

specialization

When you inherit, you take an existing class and make a special version of it. Generally, this means you're taking a general-purpose class and specializing it for a particular need.

For example, consider the **stack** class from the previous chapter. One of the problems with that class is that you had to perform a cast every time you fetched a pointer from the container. This is not only tedious, it's unsafe — you could cast the pointer to anything you want.

A better approach is to specialize the general **stack** class using inheritance. Here's an example that uses the class from the previous chapter:

```
//: INHSTAK.CPP -- Specializing the stack class
#include "..\11\stack11.h"
#include "..\11\strings.h"
#include <fstream.h>
#include "..\allege.h"

class Stringlist : public stack {
public:
  void push(String* str) {
    stack::push(str);
  }
  String* peek() const {
    return (String*)stack::peek();
  }
  String* pop() {
    return (String*)stack::pop();
  }
};

main() {
  ifstream file("inhlist.cpp");
  allegefile(file);
```

```
    const bufsize = 100;
    char buf[bufsize];
    Stringlist textlines;
    while(file.getline(buf,bufsize))
      textlines.push(String::make(buf));
    String* s;
    while((s = textlines.pop()) != 0) // No cast!
      cout << *s << endl;
}
```

Both the STRINGS.H (page 468) and STACK11.H (page 475) header files are brought in from Chapter 11. (The STACK11.OBJ file must be linked in as well.)

Stringlist specializes **stack** so that **push( )** will accept only **String** pointers. Before, **stack** would accept **void** pointers, so the user had no type checking to make sure the proper pointers were inserted. In addition, **peek( )** and **pop( )** now return **String** pointers rather than **void** pointers, so no cast is necessary to use the pointer.

Amazingly enough, this extra type-checking safety is free! The compiler is being given extra type information, that it uses at compile-time, but the functions are inline and no extra code is generated.

Unfortunately, inheritance doesn't solve all the problems with this container class. The destructor still causes trouble. You'll remember from Chapter 11 that the **stack::~stack( )** destructor moves through the list and calls **delete** for all the pointers. The problem is, **delete** is called for **void** pointers, which only releases the memory and doesn't call the destructors (because **void*** has no type information). If a **Stringlist::~Stringlist( )** destructor is created to move through the list and call **delete** for all the **String** pointers in the list, the problem is solved *if*

1. The **stack** data members are made **protected** so the **Stringlist** destructor can access them. (**protected** is described a bit later in the chapter.)

---

2. The **stack** base class destructor is removed so the memory isn't released twice.

3. No more inheritance is performed, because you'd end up with the same dilemma again: multiple destructor calls versus an incorrect destructor call (to a **String** object rather than what the class derived from **Stringlist** might contain).

This issue will be revisited in the next chapter, but will not be fully solved until templates are introduced in Chapter 14.

private inheritance

You can inherit a base class privately by leaving off the **public** in the base-class list, or by explicitly saying **private** (probably a better policy because it is clear to the user that you mean it). When you inherit privately, you're "implementing in terms of"; that is, you're creating a new class that has all the data and functionality of the base class, but that functionality is hidden, so it's only part of the underlying implementation. The class user has no access to the underlying functionality, and an object cannot be treated as a member of the base class (as it was in FNAME2.CPP on page 516).

You may wonder what the purpose of **private** inheritance is, because the alternative of creating a **private** object in the new class seems more appropriate. **private** inheritance is included in the language for completeness, but if for no other reason than to reduce confusion, you'll usually want to use a **private** member rather than **private** inheritance. However, there may occasionally be situations where you want to produce part of the same interface as the base class *and* disallow the treatment of the object as if it were a base-class object. **private** inheritance provides this ability.

publicizing privately inherited members

When you inherit privately, all the **public** members of the base class become **private**. If you want any of them to be visible, just say their names (no arguments or return values) in the **public** section of the derived class:

```
//: PRIVINH.CPP -- Private inheritance

class base1 {
public:
  char f() const { return 'a'; }
  int g() const { return 2; }
  float h() const { return 3.0; }
};

class derived : base1 { // Private inheritance
public:
  base1::f; // Name publicizes member
  base1::h;
};

main() {
  derived d;
  d.f();
  d.h();
//! d.g(); // Error -- private function
}
```

Thus, **private** inheritance is useful if you want to hide part of the functionality of the base class.

You should think carefully before using **private** inheritance instead of member objects; **private** inheritance has particular complications when combined with run-time type identification (the subject of Chapter 17).

protected

Now that you've been introduced to inheritance, the keyword **protected** finally has meaning. In an ideal world, **private** members would always be hard-and-fast **private**, but in real projects there are times when you want to make something hidden from the world at large and yet allow access for members of derived classes. The **protected** keyword is a nod to pragmatism; it says, "This is **private** as far as the class user is concerned, but available to anyone who inherits from this class."

The best tact to take is to leave the data members **private** — you should always preserve your right to change the underlying implementation. You can then allow controlled access to inheritors of your class through **protected** member functions:

```cpp
//: PROTECT.CPP -- The protected keyword
#include <fstream.h>

class base {
  int i;
protected:
  int read() const { return i; }
  void set(int I) { i = I; }
public:
  base(int I = 0) : i(I) {}
  int value(int m) const { return m*i; }
};

class derived : public base {
  int j;
public:
  derived(int J = 0) : j(J) {}
  void change(int x) { set(x); }
};

main() {}
```

You can see an excellent example of the need for **protected** in the SSHAPE examples in Appendix C.

protected inheritance

When you're inheriting, the base class defaults to **private**, which means that all the public member functions are **private** to the user of the new class. Normally, you'll make the inheritance **public** so the interface of the base class is also the interface of the derived class. However, you can also use the **protected** keyword during inheritance.

Protected derivation means "implemented-in-terms-of" to other classes but "is-a" for derived classes and friends. It's something you don't use very often, but it's in the language for completeness.

multiple inheritance

You can inherit from one class, so it would seem to make sense to inherit from more than one class at a time. Indeed you can, but whether it makes sense as part of a design is a subject of continuing debate. One thing is generally agreed upon: You shouldn't try this until you've been programming quite a while and understand the language thoroughly. By that time, you'll probably realize that no matter how much you think you absolutely must use multiple inheritance, you can almost always get away with single inheritance.

Initially, multiple inheritance seems simple enough: You add more classes in the base-class list during inheritance, separated by commas. However, multiple inheritance introduces a number of possibilities for ambiguity, which is why Chapter 15 is devoted to the subject.

incremental development

One of the advantages of inheritance is that it supports *incremental development* by allowing you to introduce new code without

---

causing bugs in existing code and isolating new bugs to the new code. By inheriting from an existing, functional class and adding data members and member functions (and redefining existing member functions) you leave the existing code — that someone else may still be using — untouched and unbugged. If a bug happens, you know it's in your new code, which is much shorter and easier to read than if you had modified the body of existing code.

It's rather amazing how cleanly the classes are separated. You don't even need the source code for the member functions to reuse the code, just the header file describing the class and the object file or library file with the compiled member functions. (This is true for both inheritance and composition.)

It's important to realize that program development is an incremental process, just like human learning. You can do as much analysis as you want, but you still won't know all the answers when you set out on a project. You'll have much more success — and more immediate feedback — if you start out to "grow" your project as an organic, evolutionary creature, rather than constructing it all at once like a glass-box skyscraper.

Although inheritance for experimentation is a useful technique, at some point after things stabilize you need to take a new look at your class hierarchy with an eye to collapsing it into a sensible structure. Remember that underneath it all, inheritance is meant to express a relationship that says, "This new class is a *type of* that old class." Your program should not be concerned with pushing bits around, but instead with creating and manipulating objects of various types to express a model in the terms given you by the problem's space.

upcasting

Earlier in the chapter, you saw how an object of a class derived from **ofstream** has all the characteristics and behaviors of an ofstream object. In FNAME2.CPP on page 516, any **ofstream** member function could be called for an **fname2** object.

The most important aspect of inheritance is not that it provides member functions for the new class, however. It's the relationship expressed between the new class and the base class. This relationship can be summarized by saying, "The new class *is a type of* the existing class."

This description is not just a fanciful way of explaining inheritance — it's supported directly by the compiler. As an example, consider a base class called **instrument** that represents musical instruments and a derived class called **wind**. Because inheritance means that all the functions in the base class are also available in the derived class, any message you can send to the base class can also be sent to the derived class. So if the **instrument** class has a **play( )** member function, so will **wind** instruments. This means we can accurately say that a **wind** object is also a type of **instrument**. The following example shows how the compiler supports this notion:

```
//: WIND.CPP -- Inheritance & upcasting
enum note { middleC, Csharp, Cflat }; // Etc.

class instrument {
public:
  void play(note) const {}
};

// Wind objects are instruments
// because they have the same interface:
class wind : public instrument {};

void tune(instrument& i) {
  // ...
  i.play(middleC);
}

main() {
```

```
wind flute;
tune(flute); // Upcasting
}
```

What's interesting in this example is the **tune( )** function, which accepts an **instrument** reference. However, in **main( )** the **tune( )** function is called by giving it a **wind** object. Given that C++ is very particular about type checking, it seems strange that a function that accepts one type will readily accept another type, until you realize that a **wind** object is also an **instrument** object, and there's no function that **tune( )** could call for an **instrument** that isn't also in **wind**. Inside **tune( )**, the code works for **instrument** and anything derived from **instrument**, and the act of converting a **wind** object, reference, or pointer into an **instrument** object, reference, or pointer is called *upcasting*.

why "upcasting"?

The reason for the term is historical and is based on the way class inheritance diagrams have traditionally been drawn: with the root at the top of the page, growing downward. (Of course, you can draw your diagrams any way you find helpful.) The inheritance diagram for WIND.CPP is then:

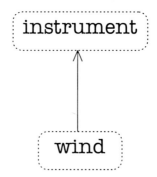

Casting from derived to base moves *up* on the inheritance diagram, so it's commonly referred to as upcasting. Upcasting is always safe because you're going from a more specific type to a more general type — the only thing that can occur to the class interface is that it lose member functions, not gain them. This is why the compiler allows upcasting without any explicit casts or other special notation.

downcasting

You can also perform the reverse of upcasting, called *downcasting*, but this involves a dilemma that is the subject of Chapter 17.

composition vs. inheritance (revisited)

One of the clearest ways to determine whether you should be using composition or inheritance is by asking whether you'll ever need to upcast from your new class. Earlier in this chapter, the **stack** class was specialized using inheritance. However, chances are the **Stringlist** objects will be used only as **String** containers, and never upcast, so a more appropriate alternative might be composition:

```
//: INHSTAK2.CPP -- Composition vs inheritance
#include "..\11\stack11.h"
#include "..\11\strings.h"
#include <fstream.h>
#include "..\allege.h"

class Stringlist {
  stack Stack; // Embed instead of inherit
public:
  void push(String* str) {
    Stack.push(str);
  }
  String* peek() const {
    return (String*)Stack.peek();
  }
  String* pop() {
    return (String*)Stack.pop();
  }
};

main() {
  ifstream file("inhlst2.cpp");
```

```
      allegefile(file);
      const bufsize = 100;
      char buf[bufsize];
      Stringlist textlines;
      while(file.getline(buf,bufsize))
        textlines.push(String::make(buf));
      String* s;
      while((s = textlines.pop()) != 0) // No cast!
        cout << *s << endl;
}
```

The file is identical to INHSTACK.CPP (page 518), except that a **stack** object is embedded in **Stringlist**, and member functions are called for the embedded object. There's still no time or space overhead because the subobject takes up the same amount of space, and all the additional type checking happens at compile time.

You can also use **private** inheritance to express "implemented in terms of." The method you use to create the **Stringlist** class is not critical in this situation — they all solve the problem adequately. One place it becomes important, however, is when multiple inheritance might be warranted. In that case, if you can detect a class where composition can be used instead of inheritance, you may be able to eliminate the need for multiple inheritance.

pointer & reference upcasting

In WIND.CPP (page 525), the upcasting occurs during the function call — a **wind** object outside the function has its reference taken and becomes an **instrument** reference inside the function. Upcasting can also occur during a simple assignment to a pointer or reference:

```
wind w;
instrument* ip = &w; // upcast
instrument& ir = w;  // upcast
```

Like the function call, neither of these cases require an explicit cast.

a crisis

Of course, any upcast loses type information about an object. If you say

```
wind w;
instrument* ip = &w;
```

the compiler can deal with **ip** only as an **instrument** pointer and nothing else. That is, it cannot know that **ip** *actually* happens to point to a **wind** object. So when you call the **play( )** member function by saying

```
ip->play(middleC);
```

the compiler can know only that it's calling **play( )** for an **instrument** pointer, and call the base-class version of **instrument::play( )** instead of what it should do, which is call **wind::play( )**. Thus you won't get the correct behavior.

This is a significant problem; it is solved in the next chapter by introducing the third cornerstone of object-oriented programming: polymorphism (implemented in C++ with **virtual** functions).

summary

Both inheritance and composition allow you to create a new type from existing types, and both embed subobjects of the existing types inside the new type. Typically, however, you use composition to reuse existing types as part of the underlying implementation of the new type and inheritance when you want to reuse the interface as well as the implementation. If the derived class has the base-class interface, it can be *upcast* to the base, which is critical for polymorphism as you'll see in the next chapter.

Although code reuse through composition and inheritance is very helpful for rapid project development, you'll generally want to redesign your class hierarchy before allowing other programmers to become dependent on it. Your goal is a hierarchy where each class has a specific use and is neither too big (encompassing so much functionality that it's unwieldy to reuse) nor annoyingly small (you can't use it by itself or without adding functionality). Your finished classes should themselves be easily reused.

exercises

1. Modify CAR.CPP so it also inherits from a class called **vehicle**, placing appropriate member functions in **vehicle** (that is, make up some member functions). Add a nondefault constructor to **vehicle**, which you must call, inside **car**'s constructor.

2. Create two classes, **A** and **B**, with default constructors that announce themselves. Inherit a new class called **C** from **A**, and create a member object of **B** in **C**, but do not create a constructor for **C**. Create an object of class **C** and observe the results.

3. Use inheritance to specialize the **pstash** class in Chapter 11 (PSTASH.H & PSTASH.CPP) so it accepts and returns **String** pointers. Also modify PSTEST.CPP and test it. Change the class so **pstash** is a member object.

4. Use **private** and **protected** inheritance to create two new classes from a base class. Then attempt to upcast objects of the derived class to the base class. Explain what happens.

polymorphism & virtual functions

Polymorphism (implemented in C++ with virtual functions) is the third essential feature of an object-oriented programming language, after data abstraction and inheritance.

It provides another dimension of separation of interface from implementation, to decouple *what* from *how*. Polymorphism allows improved code organization and readability as well as the creation of *extensible* programs that can be "grown" not only during the original creation of the project, but also when new features are desired.

Encapsulation creates new data types by combining characteristics and behaviors. Implementation hiding separates the interface from the implementation by making the details **private**. This sort of mechanical organization makes ready sense to someone with a procedural programming background. But virtual functions deal with decoupling in terms of *types*. In the last chapter, you saw how inheritance allows the treatment of an object as its own type *or* its base type. This ability is critical because it allows many types (derived from the same base type) to be treated as if they were one type, and a single piece of code to work on all those different types equally. The virtual function allows one type to express its distinction from another, similar type, as long as they're both derived from the same base type. This distinction is expressed through differences in behavior of the functions you can call through the base class.

In this chapter, you'll learn about virtual functions starting from the very basics, with simple examples that strip away everything but the "virtualness" of the program.

evolution of C++ programmers

C programmers seem to acquire C++ in three steps. First, as simply a "better C," because C++ forces you to declare all functions before using them and is much pickier about how variables are used. You can often find the errors in a C program simply by compiling it with a C++ compiler.

The second step is "object-based" C++. This means that you easily see the code organization benefits of grouping a data structure together with the functions that act upon it, the value of constructors and destructors, and perhaps some simple inheritance. Most programmers who have been working with C for a while quickly see the usefulness of this because, whenever they create a library, this is exactly what they try to do. With C++, you have the aid of the compiler.

You can get stuck at the object-based level because it's very easy to get to and you get a lot of benefit without much mental effort. It's also easy to feel like you're creating data types — you make classes, and objects, and you send messages to those objects, and everything is nice and neat.

But don't be fooled. If you stop here, you're missing out on the greatest part of the language, which is the jump to true object-oriented programming. You can do this only with virtual functions.

Virtual functions enhance the concept of type rather than just encapsulating code inside structures and behind walls, so they are without a doubt the most difficult concept for the new C++ programmer to fathom. However, they're also the turning point in the understanding of object-oriented programming. If you don't use virtual functions, you don't understand OOP yet.

Because the virtual function is intimately bound with the concept of type, and type is at the core of object-oriented programming, there is no analog to the virtual function in a traditional procedural language. As a procedural programmer, you have no referent with which to think about virtual functions, as you do with almost every other feature in the language. Features in a procedural language can be understood on an algorithmic level, but virtual functions can be understood only from a design viewpoint.

upcasting

In the last chapter you saw how an object can be used as its own type or as an object of its base type. In addition, it can be manipulated through an address of the base type. Taking the address of an object (either a pointer or a reference) and treating it as the address of the base type is called *upcasting* because of the way inheritance trees are drawn with the base class at the top.

You also saw a problem arise, which is embodied in the following code:

```
//: WIND2.CPP -- Inheritance & upcasting
#include <iostream.h>
enum note { middleC, Csharp, Cflat }; // Etc.

class instrument {
public:
  void play(note) const {
    cout << "instrument::play" << endl;
  }
};

// Wind objects are instruments
// because they have the same interface:
class wind : public instrument {
public:
  // Redefine interface function:
  void play(note) const {
    cout << "wind::play" << endl;
  }
};

void tune(instrument& i) {
  // ...
  i.play(middleC);
}

main() {
  wind flute;
  tune(flute); // Upcasting
}
```

The function **tune( )** accepts (by reference) an **instrument**, but also without complaint anything derived from **instrument**. In **main( )**, you can see this happening as a **wind** object is passed to **tune( )**, with no cast necessary. This is acceptable; the interface in **instrument** must exist in **wind**, because **wind** is publicly inherited from **instrument**. Upcasting from **wind** to **instrument** may "narrow" that interface, but it cannot make it any less than the full interface to **instrument**.

The same arguments are true when dealing with pointers; the only difference is that the user must explicitly take the addresses of objects as they are passed into the function.

the problem

The problem with WIND2.CPP can be seen by running the program. The output is **instrument::play**. This is clearly not the desired output, because you happen to know that the object is actually a **wind** and not just an **instrument**. The call should resolve to **wind::play**. For that matter, any object of a class derived from **instrument** should have its version of **play** used, regardless of the situation.

However, the behavior of WIND2.CPP is not surprising, given C's approach to functions. To understand the issues, you need to be aware of the concept of *binding*.

function call binding

Connecting a function call to a function body is called *binding*. When binding is performed before the program is run (by the compiler and linker), it's called *early binding*. You may not have heard the term before because it's never been an option with procedural languages: C compilers have only one kind of function call, and that's early binding.

The problem in the above program is caused by early binding because the compiler cannot know the correct function to call when it has only an **instrument** address.

The solution is called *late binding*, which means the binding occurs at run-time, based on the type of the object. Late binding is also called *dynamic binding* or *run-time binding*. When a language implements late binding, there must be some mechanism to

---

determine the type of the object at run time and call the appropriate member function. That is, the compiler still doesn't know the actual object type, but it inserts code that finds out and calls the correct function body. The late-binding mechanism varies from language to language, but you can imagine that some sort of type information must be installed in the objects themselves. You'll see how this works later.

virtual functions

To cause late binding to occur for a particular function, C++ requires that you use the **virtual** keyword when declaring the function in the base class. Late binding occurs only with **virtual** functions, and only when you're using an address of the base class where those **virtual** functions exist, although they may also be defined in an earlier base class.

To create a member function as **virtual**, you simply precede the declaration of the function with the keyword **virtual**. You don't repeat it for the function definition, and you don't *need* to repeat it in any of the derived-class function redefinitions (though it does no harm to do so). If a function is declared as **virtual** in the base class, it is **virtual** in all the derived classes. The redefinition of a **virtual** function in a derived class is often called *overriding.*

To get the desired behavior from WIND2.CPP, simply add the **virtual** keyword in the base class before **play( )**:

```
//: WIND3.CPP -- Late binding with virtual
#include <iostream.h>
enum note { middleC, Csharp, Cflat }; // Etc.

class instrument {
public:
  virtual void play(note) const {
    cout << "instrument::play" << endl;
  }
```

```
};

// Wind objects are instruments
// because they have the same interface:
class wind : public instrument {
public:
  // Redefine interface function:
  void play(note) const {
    cout << "wind::play" << endl;
  }
};

void tune(instrument& i) {
  // ...
  i.play(middleC);
}

main() {
  wind flute;
  tune(flute); // Upcasting
}
```

This file is identical to WIND2.CPP except for the addition of the **virtual** keyword, and yet the behavior is significantly different: Now the output is **wind::play**.

extensibility

With **play( )** defined as **virtual** in the base class, you can add as many new types as you want to the system without changing the **tune( )** function. In a well-designed OOP program, most or all of your functions will follow the model of **tune( )** and communicate only with the base-class interface. Such a program is *extensible* because you can add new functionality by inheriting new data types from the common base class. The functions that manipulate the base-class interface will not need to be changed at all to accommodate the new classes.

Here's the instrument example with more virtual functions and a number of new classes, all of which work correctly with the old, unchanged **tune( )** function:

```
//: WIND4.CPP -- Extensibility in OOP
#include <iostream.h>
enum note { middleC, Csharp, Cflat }; // Etc.

class instrument {
public:
  virtual void play(note) const {
    cout << "instrument::play" << endl;
  }
  virtual char* what() const {
    return "instrument";
  }
  // Assume this will modify the object:
  virtual void adjust(int) {}
};

class wind : public instrument {
public:
  void play(note) const {
    cout << "wind::play" << endl;
  }
  char* what() const { return "wind"; }
  void adjust(int) {}
};

class percussion : public instrument {
public:
  void play(note) const {
    cout << "percussion::play" << endl;
  }
  char* what() const { return "percussion"; }
  void adjust(int) {}
};
```

```
class string : public instrument {
public:
  void play(note) const {
    cout << "string::play" << endl;
  }
  char* what() const { return "string"; }
  void adjust(int) {}
};

class brass : public wind {
public:
  void play(note) const {
    cout << "brass::play" << endl;
  }
  char* what() const { return "brass"; }
};

class woodwind : public wind {
public:
  void play(note) const {
    cout << "woodwind::play" << endl;
  }
  char* what() const { return "woodwind"; }
};

// Identical function from before:
void tune(instrument& i) {
  // ...
  i.play(middleC);
}

// New function:
void f(instrument& i) { i.adjust(1); }

// Upcasting during array initialization:
instrument* A[] = {
```

```
    new wind,
    new percussion,
    new string,
    new brass
};

main() {
  wind flute;
  percussion drum;
  string violin;
  brass flugelhorn;
  woodwind recorder;
  tune(flute);
  tune(drum);
  tune(violin);
  tune(flugelhorn);
  tune(recorder);
  f(flugelhorn);
}
```

You can see that another inheritance level has been added beneath **wind**, but the **virtual** mechanism works correctly no matter how many levels there are. The **adjust( )** function is *not* redefined for **brass** and **woodwind**. When this happens, the previous definition is automatically used — the compiler guarantees there's always *some* definition for a virtual function, so you'll never end up with a call that doesn't bind to a function body. (This would spell disaster.)

The array **A[]** contains pointers to the base class instrument, so upcasting occurs during the process of array initialization. This array and the function **f( )** will be used in later discussions.

In the call to **tune( )**, upcasting is performed on each different type of object, yet the desired behavior always takes place. This can be described as "sending a message to an object and letting the object worry about what to do with it." The **virtual** function is the lens to use when you're trying to analyze a project: Where should the base classes occur, and how might you want to extend the program? However, even if you don't discover the proper base class interfaces and virtual functions at the initial creation of the program, you'll often discover them later, even much later, when you set out to extend or otherwise maintain the program. This is not an analysis or design error; it simply means you didn't have all the information the first time. Because of the tight class modularization in C++, it isn't a large problem when this occurs because changes you make in one part of a system tend not to propagate to other parts of the system as they do in C.

how C++ implements late binding

How can late binding happen? All the work goes on behind the scenes by the compiler, which installs the necessary late-binding mechanism when you ask it to (you ask by creating virtual functions). Because programmers often benefit from understanding the mechanism of virtual functions in C++, this section will elaborate on the way the compiler implements this mechanism.

The keyword **virtual** tells the compiler it should not perform early binding. Instead, it should automatically install all the mechanisms necessary to perform late binding. This means that if you call **play( )** for a **brass** object *through an address for the base-class* **instrument**, you'll get the proper function.

To accomplish this, the compiler creates a single table (called the VTABLE) for each class that contains **virtual** functions. The compiler places the addresses of the virtual functions for that particular class in the VTABLE. In each class with virtual functions, it secretly places a pointer, called the *vpointer* (abbreviated as VPTR), which points to the VTABLE for that object. When you make a virtual function call through a base-class pointer (that is, when you make a polymorphic call), the compiler quietly inserts code to fetch the VPTR and look up the function address in the VTABLE, thus calling the right function and causing late binding to take place.

All of this — setting up the VTABLE for each class, initializing the VPTR, inserting the code for the virtual function call — happens automatically, so you don't have to worry about it. With virtual functions, the proper function gets called for an object, even if the compiler cannot know the specific type of the object.

The following sections go into this process in more detail.

storing type information

You can see that there is no explicit type information stored in any of the classes. But the previous examples, and simple logic, tell you that there must be some sort of type information stored in the objects; otherwise the type could not be established at run-time. This is true, but the type information is hidden. To see it, here's an example to examine the sizes of classes that use virtual functions compared with those that don't:

```
//: SIZES.CPP -- Object sizes vs. virtual funcs
#include <iostream.h>

class no_virtual {
  int a;
public:
  void x() const {}
  int i() const { return 1; }
};

class one_virtual {
  int a;
public:
  virtual void x() const {}
  int i() const { return 1; }
};
```

```
class two_virtuals {
  int a;
public:
  virtual void x() const {}
  virtual int i() const { return 1; }
};

main() {
  cout << "int: " << sizeof(int) << endl;
  cout << "no_virtual: "
       << sizeof(no_virtual) << endl;
  cout << "void* : " << sizeof(void*) << endl;
  cout << "one_virtual: "
       << sizeof(one_virtual) << endl;
  cout << "two_virtuals: "
       << sizeof(two_virtuals) << endl;
}
```

With no virtual functions, the size of the object is exactly what you'd expect: the size of a single **int**. With a single virtual function in **one_virtual**, the size of the object is the size of **no_virtual** plus the size of a **void** pointer. It turns out that the compiler inserts a single pointer (the VPTR) into the structure if you have one *or more* virtual functions. There is no size difference between **one_virtual** and **two_virtuals**. That's because the VPTR points to a table of function addresses. You need only one because all the virtual function addresses are contained in that single table.

This example required at least one data member. If there had been no data members, the C++ compiler would have forced the objects to be a nonzero size because each object must have a distinct address. If you imagine indexing into an array of zero-sized objects, you'll understand. A "dummy" member is inserted into objects that would otherwise be zero-sized. When the type information is inserted because of the **virtual** keyword, this takes the place of the "dummy" member. Try commenting out the **int a** in all the classes in the above example to see this.

picturing virtual functions

To understand exactly what's going on when you use a virtual function, it's helpful to visualize the activities going on behind the curtain. Here's a drawing of the array of pointers **A[]** in WIND4.CPP (page 538):

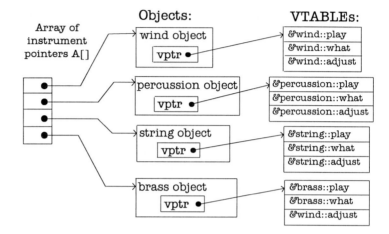

The array of **instrument** pointers has no specific type information; they each point to an object of type **instrument. wind, percussion, string,** and **brass** all fit into this category because they are derived from **instrument** (and thus have the same interface as **instrument,** and can respond to the same messages), so their addresses can also be placed into the array. However, the compiler doesn't know they are anything more than **instrument** objects, so left to its own devices, it would normally call the base-class versions of all the functions. But in this case, all those functions have been declared with the **virtual** keyword, so something different happens.

Each time you create a class that contains virtual functions, or you derive from a class that contains virtual functions, the compiler creates a VTABLE for that class, seen on the right of the diagram. In that table it places the addresses of all the functions that are declared virtual in this class or in the base class. If you don't redefine a function that was declared virtual in the base class, the compiler uses the address of the base-class version in the derived class. (You can see this in the **adjust** entry in the **brass** VTABLE.) Then it places the VPTR (discovered in SIZES.CPP) into the class. There is only one VPTR for each object when using simple inheritance like this. The VPTR must be initialized to point to the starting address of the appropriate VTABLE. (This happens in the constructor, which you'll see later in more detail.)

Once the VPTR is initialized to the proper VTABLE, the object in effect "knows" what type it is. But this self-knowledge is worthless unless it is used at the point a virtual function is called.

When you call a virtual function through a base class address (the situation when the compiler doesn't have all the information necessary to perform early binding), something special happens. Instead of performing a typical function call, which is simply an assembly-language **CALL** to a particular address, the compiler generates different code to perform the function call. Here's what a call to **adjust( )** for a **brass** object it looks like, if made through an **instrument** pointer. An **instrument** reference produces the same result:

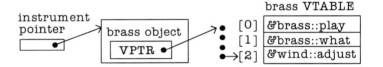

The compiler starts with the **instrument** pointer, which points to the starting address of the object. All **instrument** objects or objects derived from **instrument** have their VPTR in the same place (often at the beginning of the object), so the compiler can pick the VPTR out of the object. The VPTR points to the starting address of the VTABLE. All the VTABLEs are laid out in the same order, regardless of the specific type of the object. **play( )** is first, **what( )** is second, and **adjust( )** is third. The compiler knows that regardless of the specific object type, the **adjust( )** function is at the location

---

VPTR+2. Thus instead of saying, "Call the function at the absolute location **instrument::adjust**" (early binding; the wrong action), it generates code that says, in effect, "Call the function at VPTR+2." Because the fetching of the VPTR and the determination of the actual function address occur at run-time, you get the desired late binding. You send a message to the object, and the object figures out what to do with it.

under the hood

It can be helpful to see the assembly-language code generated by a virtual function call, so you can see that late-binding is indeed taking place. Here's the output from one compiler for the call

```
i.adjust(1);
```

inside the function **f(instrument& i)**:

```
push   1
push   si
mov    bx,word ptr [si]
call   word ptr [bx+4]
add    sp,4
```

The arguments of a C++ function call, like a C function call, are pushed on the stack from right to left (this order is required to support C's variable argument lists), so the argument **1** is pushed on the stack first. At this point in the function, the register **si** (part of the Intel X86 processor architecture) contains the address of **i**. This is also pushed on the stack because it is the starting address of the object of interest. Remember that the starting address corresponds to the value of **this**, and **this** is quietly pushed on the stack as an argument before every member function call, so the member function knows which particular object it is working on. Thus you'll always see the number of arguments plus one pushed on the stack before a member function call (except for **static** member functions, which have no **this**).

Now the actual virtual function call must be performed. First, the VPTR must be produced, so the VTABLE can be found. For this compiler the VPTR is inserted at the beginning of the object, so the contents of **this** correspond to the VPTR. The line

```
mov    bx,word ptr [si]
```

fetches the word that **si** (that is, **this**) points to, which is the VPTR. It places the VPTR into the register **bx**.

The VPTR contained in **bx** points to the starting address of the VTABLE, but the function pointer to call isn't at the zeroth location of the VTABLE, but instead the second location (because it's the third function in the list). For this memory model each function pointer is two bytes long, so the compiler adds four to the VPTR to calculate where the address of the proper function is. Note that this is a constant value, established at compile time, so the only thing that matters is that the function pointer at location number two is the one for **adjust( )**. Fortunately, the compiler takes care of all the bookkeeping for you and ensures that all the function pointers in all the VTABLEs occur in the same order.

Once the address of the proper function pointer in the VTABLE is calculated, that function is called. So the address is fetched and called all at once in the statement

```
call   word ptr [bx+4]
```

Finally, the stack pointer is moved back up to clean off the arguments that were pushed before the call. In C and C++ assembly code you'll often see the caller clean off the arguments but this may vary depending on processors and compiler implementations.

installing the vpointer

Because the VPTR determines the virtual function behavior of the object, you can see how it's critical that the VPTR always be pointing to the proper VTABLE. You don't ever want to be able to

---

make a call to a virtual function before the VPTR is properly initialized. Of course, the place where initialization can be guaranteed is in the constructor, but none of the WIND examples has a constructor.

This is where creation of the default constructor is essential. In the WIND examples, the compiler creates a default constructor that does nothing except initialize the VPTR. This constructor, of course, is automatically called for all **instrument** objects before you can do anything with them, so you know that it's always safe to call virtual functions.

The implications of the automatic initialization of the VPTR inside the constructor are discussed in a later section.

objects are different

It's important to realize that upcasting deals only with addresses. If the compiler has an object, it knows the exact type and therefore (in C++) will not use late binding for any function calls — or at least, the compiler doesn't *need* to use late binding. For efficiency's sake, most compilers will perform early binding when they are making a call to a virtual function for an object because they know the exact type. Here's an example:

```
//: EARLY.CPP -- Early binding & virtuals
#include <iostream.h>

class base {
public:
  virtual int f() const { return 1; }
};

class derived : public base {
public:
  int f() const { return 2; }
};
```

```
main() {
  derived d;
  base* b1 = &d;
  base& b2 = d;
  base b3;
  // Late binding for both:
  cout << "b1->f() = " << b1->f() << endl;
  cout << "b2.f() = " << b2.f() << endl;
  // Early binding (probably):
  cout << "b3.f() = " << b3.f() << endl;
}
```

In **b1–>f( )** and **b2.f( )** addresses are used, which means the information is incomplete: **b1** and **b2** can represent the address of a **base** *or* something derived from base, so the virtual mechanism must be used. When calling **b3.f( )** there's no ambiguity. The compiler knows the exact type and that it's an object, so it can't possibly be an object derived from **base** — it's *exactly* a **base**. Thus early binding is probably used. However, if the compiler doesn't want to work so hard, it can still use late binding and the same behavior will occur.

why virtual functions?

At this point you may have a question: "If this technique is so important, and if it makes the 'right' function call all the time, why is it an option? Why do I even need to know about it?"

This is a good question, and the answer is part of the fundamental philosophy of C++: "Because it's not quite as efficient." You can see from the previous assembly-language output that instead of one simple CALL to an absolute address, there are two more sophisticated assembly instructions required to set up the virtual function call. This requires both code space and execution time.

Some object-oriented languages have taken the approach that late binding is so intrinsic to object-oriented programming that it should always take place, that it should not be an option, and the user shouldn't have to know about it. This is a design decision when creating a language, and that particular path is appropriate for many languages.[1] However, C++ comes from the C heritage, where efficiency is critical. After all, C was created to replace assembly language for the implementation of an operating system (thereby rendering that operating system — Unix — far more portable than its predecessors). One of the main reasons for the invention of C++ was to make C programmers more efficient.[2] And the first question asked when C programmers encounter C++ is "What kind of size and speed impact will I get?" If the answer were, "Everything's great except for function calls when you'll always have a little extra overhead," many people would stick with C rather than make the change to C++. In addition, inline functions would not be possible, because virtual functions must have an address to put into the VTABLE. So the virtual function is an option, *and* the language defaults to nonvirtual, which is the fastest configuration. Stroustrup stated that his guideline was "If you don't use it, you don't pay for it."

Thus the **virtual** keyword is provided for efficiency tuning. When designing your classes, however, you shouldn't be worrying about efficiency tuning. If you're going to use polymorphism, use virtual functions everywhere. You only need to look for functions to make non-virtual when looking for ways to speed up your code (and there are usually much bigger gains to be had in other areas).

---

[1]Smalltalk, for instance, uses this approach with great success.

[2]At Bell labs, where C++ was invented, there are a *lot* of C programmers. Making them all more efficient, even just a bit, saves the company many millions.

Anecdotal evidence suggests that the size and speed impacts of going to C++ are within 10% of the size and speed of C, and often much closer to the same. The reason you might get better size and speed efficiency is because you may design a C++ program in a smaller, faster way than you would using C.

abstract base classes and pure virtual functions

In all the instrument examples, the functions in the base class **instrument** were always "dummy" functions. If these functions are ever called, they indicate you've done something wrong. That's because the intent of **instrument** is to create a *common interface* for all the classes derived from it, as seen on the diagram on the following page.

The dashed lines indicate a class (a class is only a description and not a physical item — the dashed lines suggest its "nonphysical" nature), and the arrows from the derived classes to the base class indicate the inheritance relationship.

The only reason to establish the common interface is so it can be expressed differently for each different subtype. It establishes a basic form, so you can say what's in common with all the derived classes. Nothing else. Another way of saying this is to call **instrument** an *abstract base class* (or simply an *abstract class*). You create an abstract class when you want to manipulate a set of classes through this common interface.

Notice you are only required to declare a function as **virtual** in the base class. All derived-class functions that match the signature of the base-class declaration will be called using the virtual mechanism. You *can* use the **virtual** keyword in the derived-class declarations (and some people do, for clarity), but it is redundant.

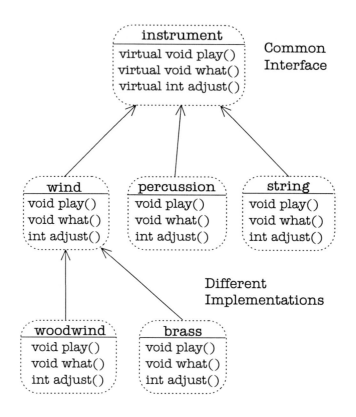

If you have a genuine abstract class (like **instrument**), objects of that class almost always have no meaning. That is, **instrument** is meant to express only the interface, and not a particular implementation, so creating an **instrument** object makes no sense, and you'll probably want to prevent the user from doing it. This can be accomplished by making all the virtual functions in **instrument** print error messages, but this delays the information until run-time and requires reliable exhaustive testing on the part of the user. It is much better to catch the problem at compile time.

C++ provides a mechanism for doing this called the *pure virtual function*. Here is the syntax used for a declaration:

```
virtual void X() = 0;
```

By doing this, you tell the compiler to reserve a slot for a function in the VTABLE, but not to put an address in that particular slot. If only one function in a class is declared as pure virtual, the VTABLE is incomplete. A class containing pure virtual functions is called a *pure abstract base class*.

If the VTABLE for a class is incomplete, what is the compiler supposed to do when someone tries to make an object of that class? It cannot safely create an object of a pure abstract class, so you get an error message from the compiler if you try to make an object of a pure abstract class. Thus, the compiler ensures the purity of the abstract class, and you don't have to worry about misusing it.

Here's WIND4.CPP (page 538) modified to use pure virtual functions:

```
//: WIND5.CPP -- Pure abstract base classes
#include <iostream.h>
enum note { middleC, Csharp, Cflat }; // Etc.

class instrument {
public:
  // Pure virtual functions:
  virtual void play(note) const = 0;
  virtual char* what() const = 0;
  // Assume this will modify the object:
  virtual void adjust(int) = 0;
};
// Rest of the file is the same ...

class wind : public instrument {
public:
  void play(note) const {
    cout << "wind::play" << endl;
  }
  char* what() const { return "wind"; }
  void adjust(int) {}
```

```cpp
};

class percussion : public instrument {
public:
  void play(note) const {
    cout << "percussion::play" << endl;
  }
  char* what() const { return "percussion"; }
  void adjust(int) {}
};

class string : public instrument {
public:
  void play(note) const {
    cout << "string::play" << endl;
  }
  char* what() const { return "string"; }
  void adjust(int) {}
};

class brass : public wind {
public:
  void play(note) const {
    cout << "brass::play" << endl;
  }
  char* what() const { return "brass"; }
};

class woodwind : public wind {
public:
  void play(note) const {
    cout << "woodwind::play" << endl;
  }
  char* what() const { return "woodwind"; }
};

// Identical function from before:
```

```
void tune(instrument& i) {
  // ...
  i.play(middleC);
}

// New function:
void f(instrument& i) { i.adjust(1); }

main() {
  wind flute;
  percussion drum;
  string violin;
  brass flugelhorn;
  woodwind recorder;
  tune(flute);
  tune(drum);
  tune(violin);
  tune(flugelhorn);
  tune(recorder);
  f(flugelhorn);
}
```

Pure virtual functions are very helpful because they make explicit the abstractness of a class and tell both the user and the compiler how it was intended to be used.

Note that pure virtual functions prevent a function call with the pure abstract class being passed in by value. Thus it is also a way to prevent object slicing from accidentally upcasting by value. This way you can ensure that a pointer or reference is always used during upcasting.

Because one pure virtual function prevents the VTABLE from being generated doesn't mean you don't want function bodies for some of the others. Often you will want to call a base-class version of a function, even if it is virtual. It's always a good idea to put common code as close as possible to the root of your hierarchy. Not only does this save code space, it allows easy propagation of changes.

pure virtual definitions

It's possible to provide a definition for a pure virtual function in the base class. You're still telling the compiler not to allow objects of that pure abstract base class, and the pure virtual functions must be defined in derived classes in order to create objects. However, there may be a piece of code you want some or all the derived class definitions to use in common, and you don't want to duplicate that code in every function. Here's what it looks like:

```cpp
//: PVDEF.CPP -- Pure virtual base definition
#include <iostream.h>

class base {
public:
  virtual void v() const = 0;
  // In situ:
  virtual void f() const = 0 {
    cout << "base::f()\n";
  }
};

void base::v() const { cout << "base::v()\n";}

class d : public base {
public:
  // Use the common base code:
  void v() const { base::v(); }
  void f() const { base::f(); }
};

main() {
  d D;
  D.v();
```

```
    D.f();
}
```

The slot in the **base** VTABLE is still empty, but there happens to be a function by that name you can call in the derived class.

The other benefit to this feature is that it allows you to change to a pure virtual without disturbing the existing code. (This is a way for you to locate classes that don't redefine that virtual function).

inheritance and the VTABLE

You can imagine what happens when you perform inheritance and redefine some of the virtual functions. The compiler creates a new VTABLE for your new class, and it inserts your new function addresses, using the base-class function addresses for any virtual functions you don't redefine. One way or another, there's always a full set of function addresses in the VTABLE, so you'll never be able to make a call to an address that isn't there (which would be disastrous).

But what happens when you inherit and add new virtual functions in the *derived* class? Here's a simple example:

```
//: ADDV.CPP -- Adding virtuals in derivation
#include <iostream.h>

class base {
  int i;
public:
  base(int I) : i(I) {}
  virtual int value() const { return i; }
};
```

```
class derived : public base {
public:
  derived(int I) : base(I) {}
  int value() const {
    return base::value() * 2;
  }
  // New virtual function in the derived class:
  virtual int shift(int x) const {
    return base::value() << x;
  }
};

main() {
  base* B[] = { new base(7), new derived(7) };
  cout << "B[0]->value() = "
       << B[0]->value() << endl;
  cout << "B[1]->value() = "
       << B[1]->value() << endl;
//! cout << "B[1]->shift(3) = "
//!      << B[1]->shift(3) << endl; // Illegal
}
```

The class **base** contains a single virtual function **value( )**, and **derived** adds a second one called **shift( )**, as well as redefining the meaning of **value( )**. A diagram will help visualize what's happening. Here are the VTABLEs created by the compiler for **base** and **derived**:

base vtable   derived vtable

| &base::value | | &derived::value |
                      | &derived::shift |

Notice the compiler maps the location of the **value** address into exactly the same spot in the **derived** VTABLE as it is in the **base** VTABLE. Similarly, if a class is inherited from **derived**, its version of **shift** would be placed in its VTABLE in exactly the same spot as it is in **derived**. This is because (as you saw with the assembly-language example) the compiler generates code that uses a simple numerical offset into the VTABLE to select the virtual function. Regardless of what specific subtype the object belongs to, its VTABLE is laid out the same way, so calls to the virtual functions will always be made the same way.

In this case, however, the compiler is working only with a pointer to a base-class object. The base class has only the **value( )** function, so that is the only function the compiler will allow you to call. How could it possibly know that you are working with a **derived** object, if it has only a pointer to a base-class object? That pointer might point to some other type, which doesn't have a **shift** function. It may or may not have some other function address at that point in the VTABLE, but in either case, making a virtual call to that VTABLE address is not what you want to do. So it's fortunate and logical that the compiler protects you from making virtual calls to functions that exist only in derived classes.

There are some less-common cases where you may know that the pointer actually points to an object of a specific subclass. If you want to call a function that only exists in that subclass, then you must cast the pointer. You can remove the error message produced by the previous program like this:

```
((derived*)B[1])->shift(3)
```

Here, you happen to know that **B[1]** points to a **derived** object, but generally you don't know that. If your problem is set up so that you must know the exact types of all objects, you should rethink it, because you're probably not using virtual functions properly. However, there are some situations where the design works best (or you have no choice) if you know the exact type of all objects kept in a generic container. This is the problem of *run-time type identification* (RTTI).

Run-time type identification is all about casting base-class pointers *down* to derived-class pointers ("up" and "down" are relative to a typical class diagram, with the base class at the top). Casting *up* happens automatically, with no coercion, because it's completely safe. Casting *down* is unsafe because there's no compile-time information about the actual types, so you must know exactly what type the object really is. If you cast it into the wrong type, you'll be in trouble.

Chapter 17 describes the way C++ provides run-time type information.

object slicing

There is a distinct difference between passing addresses and passing values when treating objects polymorphically. All the examples you've seen here, and virtually all the examples you should see, pass addresses and not values. This is because addresses all have the same size,[3] so passing the address of an object of a derived type (which is usually bigger) is the same as passing the address of an object of the base type (which is usually smaller). As explained before, this is the goal when using polymorphism — code that manipulates objects of a base type can transparently manipulate derived-type objects as well.

If you use an object instead of a pointer or reference as the recipient of your upcast, something will happen that may surprise you: The object is "sliced" until all that remains is the subobject that corresponds to your destination. In the following example you can see what's left after slicing by examining the size of the objects:

```
//: SLICE.CPP -- Object slicing
#include <iostream.h>

class base {
  int i;
public:
```

---

[3]Actually, not all pointers are the same size on all machines. In the context of this discussion, however, they can be considered to be the same.

```
    base(int I = 0) : i(I) {}
    virtual int sum() const { return i; }
};

class derived : public base {
   int j;
public:
   derived(int I = 0, int J = 0)
      : base(I), j(J) {}
   int sum() const { return base::sum() + j; }
};

void call(base b) {
   cout << "sum = " << b.sum() << endl;
}

main() {
   base b(10);
   derived d(10, 47);
   call(b);
   call(d);
}
```

The function **call( )** is passed an object of type **base** *by value*. It then calls the virtual function **sum( )** for the **base** object. In **main( )**, you might expect the first call to produce 10, and the second to produce 57. In fact, both calls produce 10.

Two things are happening in this program. First, **call( )** accepts only a **base** object, so all the code inside the function body will manipulate only members associated with **base**. Any calls to **call( )** will cause an object the size of **base** to be pushed on the stack and cleaned up after the call. This means that if an object of a class inherited from **base** is passed to **call( )**, the compiler accepts it, but it copies only the **base** portion of the object. It *slices* the derived portion off of the object, like this:

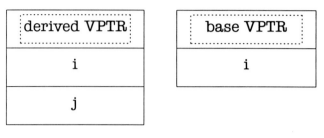

before slice   after slice

Now you may wonder about the virtual function call. Here, the virtual function makes use of portions of both **base** (which still exists) and **derived**, which no longer exists because it was sliced off! So what happens when the virtual function is called?

You're saved from disaster precisely because the object is being passed by value. Because of this, the compiler thinks it knows the precise type of the object (and it does, here, because any information that contributed extra features to the objects has been lost). In addition, when passing by value, it uses the copy-constructor for a **base** object, which initializes the VPTR to the **base** VTABLE and copies only the **base** parts of the object. There's no explicit copy-constructor here, so the compiler synthesizes one. Under all interpretations, the object truly becomes a **base** during slicing.

Object slicing actually removes part of the object rather than simply changing the meaning of an address as when using a pointer or reference. Because of this, upcasting into an object is not often done; in fact, it's usually something to watch out for and prevent. You can explicitly prevent object slicing by putting pure virtual functions in the base class; this will cause a compile-time error message for an object slice.

virtual functions & constructors

When an object containing virtual functions is created, its VPTR must be initialized to point to the proper VTABLE. This must be done before there's any possibility of calling a virtual function. As you might guess, because the constructor has the job of bringing an object into existence, it is also the constructor's job to set up the VPTR. The compiler secretly inserts code into the beginning of the constructor that initializes the VPTR. In fact, even if you don't explicitly create a constructor for a class, the compiler will create one for you with the proper VPTR initialization code (if you have virtual functions). This has several implications.

The first concerns efficiency. The reason for **inline** functions is to reduce the calling overhead for small functions. If C++ didn't provide **inline** functions, the preprocessor might be used to create these "macros." However, the preprocessor has no concept of access or classes, and therefore couldn't be used to create member function macros. In addition, with constructors that must have hidden code inserted by the compiler, a preprocessor macro wouldn't work at all.

You must be aware when hunting for efficiency holes that the compiler is inserting hidden code into your constructor function. Not only must it initialize the VPTR, it must also check the value of **this** (in case the **operator new** returns zero) and call base-class constructors. Taken together, this code can impact what you thought was a tiny inline function call. In particular, the size of the constructor can overwhelm the savings you get from reduced function-call overhead. If you make a lot of inline constructor calls, your code size can grow without any benefits in speed.

Of course, you probably won't make all tiny constructors non-inline right away, because they're much easier to write as inlines. But

---

when you're tuning your code, remember to remove inline constructors.

order of constructor calls

The second interesting facet of constructors and virtual functions concerns the order of constructor calls and the way virtual calls are made within constructors.

All base-class constructors are always called in the constructor for an inherited class. This makes sense because the constructor has a special job: to see that the object is built properly. A derived class has access only to its own members, and not those of the base class; only the base-class constructor can properly initialize its own elements. Therefore it's essential that all constructors get called; otherwise the entire object wouldn't be constructed properly. That's why the compiler enforces a constructor call for every portion of a derived class. It will call the default constructor if you don't explicitly call a base-class constructor in the constructor initializer list. If there is no default constructor, the compiler will complain. (In this example, **class X** has no constructors so the compiler can automatically make a default constructor.)

The order of the constructor calls is important. When you inherit, you know all about the base class and can access any **public** and **protected** members of the base class. This means you must be able to assume that all the members of the base class are valid when you're in the derived class. In a normal member function, construction has already taken place, so all the members of all parts of the object have been built. Inside the constructor, however, you must be able to assume that all members that you use have been built. The only way to guarantee this is for the base-class constructor to be called first. Then when you're in the derived-class constructor, all the members you can access in the base class have been initialized. "Knowing all members are valid" inside the constructor is also the reason that, whenever possible, you should initialize all member objects (that is, objects placed in the class using composition) in the constructor initializer list. If you follow this practice, you can assume that all base class members *and* member objects of the current object have been initialized.

behavior of virtual functions inside constructors

The hierarchy of constructor calls brings up an interesting dilemma. What happens if you're inside a constructor and you call a virtual function? Inside an ordinary member function you can imagine what will happen — the virtual call is resolved at run-time because the object cannot know whether it belongs to the class the member function is in, or some class derived from it. For consistency, you might think this is what should happen inside constructors.

This is not the case. If you call a virtual function inside a constructor, only the local version of the function is used. That is, the virtual mechanism doesn't work within the constructor.

This behavior makes sense for two reasons. Conceptually, the constructor's job is to bring the object into existence (which is hardly an ordinary feat). Inside any constructor, the object may only be partially formed — you can only know that the base-class objects have been initialized, but you cannot know which classes are inherited from you. A virtual function call, however, reaches "forward" or "outward" into the inheritance hierarchy. It calls a function in a derived class. If you could do this inside a constructor, you'd be calling a function that might manipulate members that hadn't been initialized yet, a sure recipe for disaster.

The second reason is a mechanical one. When a constructor is called, one of the first things it does is initialize its VPTR. However, it can only know that it is of the "current" type. The constructor code is completely ignorant of whether or not the object is in the base of another class. When the compiler generates code for that constructor, it generates code for a constructor of that class, not a base class and not a class derived from it (because a class can't know who inherits it). So the VPTR it uses must be for the VTABLE of that class. The VPTR remains initialized to that VTABLE for the

---

rest of the object's lifetime *unless* this isn't the last constructor call. If a more-derived constructor is called afterwards, that constructor sets the VPTR to *its* VTABLE, and so on, until the last constructor finishes. The state of the VPTR is determined by the constructor that is called last. This is another reason why the constructors are called in order from base to most-derived.

But while all this series of constructor calls is taking place, each constructor has set the VPTR to its own VTABLE. If it uses the virtual mechanism for function calls, it will produce only a call through its own VTABLE, not the most-derived VTABLE (as would be the case after *all* the constructors were called). In addition, many compilers recognize that a virtual function call is being made inside a constructor, and perform early binding because they know that late-binding will produce a call only to the local function. In either event, you won't get the results you might expect from a virtual function call inside a constructor.

destructors and virtual destructors

Constructors cannot be made explicitly virtual (and the technique in Appendix B only simulates virtual constructors), but destructors can and often must be virtual.

The constructor has the special job of putting an object together piece-by-piece, first by calling the base constructor, then the more derived constructors in order of inheritance. Similarly, the destructor also has a special job — it must disassemble an object that may belong to a hierarchy of classes. To do this, it must call all the destructors, but in the *reverse* order that they are called by the constructor. That is, the destructor starts at the most-derived class and works its way down to the base class. This is the safe and desirable thing to do: The current destructor always knows that the base-class members are alive and active because it knows what it is derived from. Thus, the destructor can perform its own cleanup, then call the next-down destructor, which will perform *its* own cleanup, knowing what it is derived from, but not what is derived from it.

You should keep in mind that constructors and destructors are the only places where this hierarchy of calls must happen. In all other functions, only *that* function will be called, whether it's virtual or not. The only way for base-class versions of the same function to be called in ordinary functions (virtual or not) is if you *explicitly* call that function.

Normally, the action of the destructor is quite adequate. But what happens if you want to manipulate an object through a pointer to its base class (that is, manipulate the object through its generic interface)? This is certainly a major objective in object-oriented programming. The problem occurs when you want to **delete** a pointer of this type for an object that has been created on the stack with **new**. If the pointer is to the base class, the compiler can only know to call the base-class version of the destructor during **delete**. Sound familiar? This is the same problem that virtual functions were created to solve for the general case. Fortunately virtual functions work for destructors as they do for all other functions except constructors.

Even though the destructor, like the constructor, is an "exceptional" function, it is possible for the destructor to be virtual because the object already knows what type it is (whereas it doesn't during construction). Once an object has been constructed, its VPTR is initialized, so virtual function calls can take place.

If you create a pure virtual destructor, you must provide a function body because (unlike ordinary functions) all destructors in a class hierarchy are always called. Thus, the body for your pure virtual destructor ends up being called. Here's an example:

```
//: PVDEST.CPP -- Pure virtual destructors
// require a function body.
```

```
#include <iostream.h>

class base {
public:
  virtual ~base() = 0 {
    cout << "~base()" << endl;
  }
};

class derived : public base {
public:
  ~derived() {
    cout << "~derived()" << endl;
  }
};

main() {
  base* bp = new derived; // Upcast
  delete bp; // Virtual destructor call
}
```

The pureness of the virtual destructor in the base class has the effect of forcing an inheritor to redefine the destructor, but the base class body is still called as part of destruction.

As a guideline, any time you have a virtual function in a class, you should immediately add a virtual destructor (even if it does nothing). This way, you ensure against any surprises later.

virtuals in destructors

There's something that happens during destruction that you might not immediately expect. If you're inside an ordinary member function and you call a virtual function, that function is called using the late-binding mechanism. This is not true with destructors, virtual or not. Inside a destructor, only the "local" version of the member function is called; the virtual mechanism is ignored.

Why is this? Suppose the virtual mechanism *were* used inside the destructor. Then it would be possible for the virtual call to resolve to a function that was "further out" (more derived) on the inheritance hierarchy than the current destructor. But destructors are called from the "outside in" (from the most-derived destructor down to the base destructor), so the actual function called would rely on portions of an object that has *already been destroyed*! Thus, the compiler resolves the calls at compile-time and calls only the "local" version of the function. Notice that the same is true for the constructor (as described earlier), but in the constructor's case the information wasn't available, whereas in the destructor the information (that is, the VPTR) is there, but is isn't reliable.

summary

Polymorphism — implemented in C++ with virtual functions — means "different forms." In object-oriented programming, you have the same face (the common interface in the base class) and different forms using that face: the different versions of the virtual functions.

You've seen in this chapter that it's impossible to understand, or even create, an example of polymorphism without using data abstraction and inheritance. Polymorphism is a feature that cannot be viewed in isolation (like **const** or a **switch** statement, for example), but instead works only in concert, as part of a "big picture" of class relationships. People are often confused by other, non-object-oriented features of C++, like overloading and default arguments, which are sometimes presented as object-oriented. Don't be fooled: If it isn't late binding, it isn't polymorphism.

To use polymorphism, and thus object-oriented techniques, effectively in your programs you must expand your view of programming to include not just members and messages of an individual class, but also the commonality among classes and their relationships with each other. Although this requires significant effort, it's a worthy struggle, because the results are faster program development, better code organization, extensible programs, and easier code maintenance.

Polymorphism completes the object-oriented features of the language, but there are two more major features in C++: templates (Chapter 14), and exception handling (Chapter 16). These features provide you as much increase in programming power as each of the object-oriented features: abstract data typing, inheritance, and polymorphism.

exercises

1. Create a very simple "shape" hierarchy: a base class called **shape** and derived classes called **circle**, **square**, and **triangle**. In the base class, make a virtual function called **draw( ),** and redefine this in the derived classes. Create an array of pointers to **shape** objects you create on the heap (and thus perform upcasting of the pointers), and call **draw( )** through the base-class pointers, to verify the behavior of the virtual function. If your debugger supports it, single-step through the example.

2. Modify Exercise 1 so **draw( )** is a pure virtual function. Try creating an object of type **shape**. Try to call the pure virtual function inside the constructor and see what happens. Give **draw( )** a definition.

3. Write a small program to show the difference between calling a virtual function inside a normal member function and calling a virtual function inside a constructor. The program should prove that the two calls produce different results.

4. In EARLY.CPP, how can you tell whether the compiler makes the call using early or late binding? Determine the case for your own compiler.

5. (Intermediate) Create a base **class X** with no members and no constructor, but with a **virtual** function. Create a **class Y** that

inherits from **X**, but without an explicit constructor. Generate assembly code and examine it to determine if a constructor is created and called for **X**, and if so, what the code does. Explain what you discover. **X** has no default constructor, so why doesn't the compiler complain?

6. (Intermediate) Modify Exercise 5 so each constructor calls a virtual function. Generate assembly code. Determine where the VPTR is being assigned inside each constructor. Is the virtual mechanism being used by your compiler inside the constructor? Establish why the local version of the function is still being called.

7. (Advanced) If function calls to an object passed by value *weren't* early-bound, a virtual call might access parts that didn't exist. Is this possible? Write some code to force a virtual call, and see if this causes a crash. To explain the behavior, examine what happens when you pass an object by value.

8. (Advanced) Find out exactly how much more time is required for a virtual function call by going to your processor's assembly-language information or other technical manual and finding out the number of clock states required for a simple call versus the number required for the virtual function instructions.

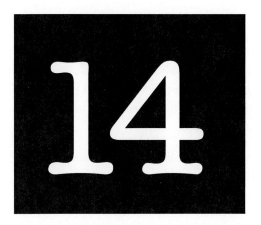

14

templates & container classes

A container class is a building block used to create object-oriented programs — it makes the internals of the program much easier to construct.

A container class describes an object that holds other objects. You can think of it as a scratch pad or an intelligent patch of memory that allows you to store objects and fetch them out later.

Container classes are so important that they were considered fundamental to early object-oriented languages. In Smalltalk, for example, programmers think of the language as the program translator together with the class library, and a critical part of that library is the container classes. So it became natural that C++ compiler vendors also include a container class library.

Like many other early C++ libraries, early container class libraries followed Smalltalk's *object-based hierarchy*, which worked well for Smalltalk, but turned out to be awkward and difficult to use in C++. Another approach was required.

A container class represents a different kind of code reuse problem. Inheritance and composition provide a way to reuse object code. The *template* feature in C++ provides a way to reuse *source* code.

Although C++ templates are a general-purpose programming tool, when they were introduced in the language, they seemed to discourage the use of object-based container-class hierarchies. Later versions of container-class libraries are built exclusively with templates and are much easier for the programmer to use.

This chapter begins with an introduction to containers and the way they are implemented with templates, followed by examples of container classes and how to use them.

containers & iterators

Suppose you want to create a stack. In C, you would make a data structure and associated functions, but of course in C++ you package the two together into an abstract data type. This **stack** class hold will **int**s, to keep it simple:

```
//: ISTACK.CPP -- Simple integer stack
#include <assert.h>
#include <iostream.h>

class istack {
  enum { ssize = 100 };
  int stack[ssize];
  int top;
```

```
public:
  istack() : top(0) { stack[top] = 0; }
  void push(int i) {
    if(top < ssize) stack[top++] = i;
  }
  int pop() {
    return stack[top > 0 ? --top : top];
  }
  friend class istackIter;
};

// An iterator is a "super-pointer":
class istackIter {
  istack& S;
  int index;
public:
  istackIter(istack& is)
    : S(is), index(0) {}
  int operator++() { // Prefix form
    if (index < S.top - 1) index++;
    return S.stack[index];
  }
  int operator++(int) { // Postfix form
    int returnval = S.stack[index];
    if (index < S.top - 1) index++;
    return returnval;
  }
};
// For interest, generate Fibonacci numbers:
int fibonacci(int N) {
  const sz = 100;
  assert(N < sz);
  static F[sz]; // Initialized to zero
  F[0] = F[1] = 1;
  // Scan for unfilled array elements:
  int i;
  for(i = 0; i < sz; i++)
```

```
      if(F[i] == 0) break;
    while(i <= N) {
      F[i] = F[i-1] + F[i-2];
      i++;
    }
    return F[N];
}

main() {
    istack is;
    for(int i = 0; i < 20; i++)
      is.push(fibonacci(i));
    // Traverse with an iterator:
    istackIter it(is);
    for(int j = 0; j < 20; j++)
      cout << it++ << endl;
    for(int k = 0; k < 20; k++)
      cout << is.pop() << endl;
}
```

The class **istack** is an almost trivial example of a push-down stack. For simplicity it has been created here with a fixed size, but you can also modify it to automatically expand by allocating memory off the heap. (This will be demonstrated in later examples.)

The second class, **istackIter**, is an example of an *iterator*, which you can think of as a superpointer that has been customized to work only with an **istack**. Notice that **istackIter** is a **friend** of **istack**, which gives it access to all the **private** elements of **istack**.

Like a pointer, **istackIter**'s job is to move through an **istack** and retrieve values. In this simple example, the **istackIter** can move only forward (using both the pre- and postfix forms of the **operator++**) and it can fetch only values. However, there is no boundary to the way an iterator can be defined. It is perfectly acceptable for an iterator to move around any way within its associated container and to cause the contained values to be modified. However, it is customary that an iterator is created with a constructor that attaches it to a single container object and that it is not reattached during its lifetime. (Most iterators are small, so you can easily make another one.)

To make the example more interesting, the **fibonacci( )** function generates the traditional rabbit-reproduction numbers. This is a fairly efficient implementation, because it never generates the numbers more than once. (Although if you've been out of school awhile, you've probably figured out that you don't spend your days researching more efficient implementations of algorithms, as textbooks might lead you to believe.)

In **main( )** you can see the creation and use of the stack and its associated iterator. Once you have the classes built, they're quite simple to use.

the need for containers

Obviously an integer stack isn't a crucial tool. The real need for containers comes when you start making objects on the heap using **new** and destroying them with **delete**. In the general programming problem, you don't know how many objects you're going to need while you're writing the program. For example, in an air-traffic control system you don't want to limit the number of planes your system can handle. You don't want the program to abort just because you exceed some number. In a computer-aided design system, you're dealing with lots of shapes, but only the user determines (at run-time) exactly how many shapes you're going to need. Once you notice this tendency, you'll discover lots of examples in your own programming situations.

C programmers who rely on virtual memory to handle their "memory management" often find the idea of **new**, **delete,** and container classes disturbing. Apparently, one practice in C is to create a huge global array, larger than anything the program would appear to need. This may not require much thought (or awareness of **malloc( )** and **free( )**), but it produces programs that don't port well and can hide subtle bugs.

In addition, if you create a huge global array of objects in C++, the constructor and destructor overhead can slow things down significantly. The C++ approach works much better: When you need an object, create it with **new,** and put its pointer in a container. Later on, fish it out and do something to it. This way, you create only the objects you absolutely need. And generally you don't have all the initialization conditions at the start-up of the program; you have to wait until something happens in the environment before you can actually create the object.

So in the most common situation, you'll create a container that holds pointers to some objects of interest. You will create those objects using **new** and put the resulting pointer in the container (potentially upcasting it in the process), fishing it out later when you want to do something with the object. This technique produces the most flexible, general sort of program.

overview of templates

Now a problem arises. You have an **istack**, which holds integers. But you want a stack that holds shapes or airliners or plants or something else. Reinventing your source-code every time doesn't seem like a very intelligent approach with a language that touts reusability. There must be a better way.

There are three techniques for source-code reuse: the C way, presented here for contrast; the Smalltalk approach, which significantly affected C++; and the C++ approach: templates.

the C approach

Of course you're trying to get away from the C approach because it's messy and error prone and completely inelegant. You copy the source code for a **stack** and make modifications by hand, introducing new errors in the process. This is certainly not a very productive technique.

the Smalltalk approach

Smalltalk took a simple and straightforward approach: You want to reuse code, so use inheritance. To implement this, each container class holds items of the generic base class **object**. But, as mentioned before, the library in Smalltalk is of fundamental importance, so fundamental, in fact, that you don't ever create a class from scratch. Instead, you must always inherit it from an existing class. You find a class as close as possible to the one you want, inherit from it, and make a few changes. Obviously this is a benefit because it minimizes your effort (and explains why you spend a lot of time learning the class library before becoming an effective Smalltalk programmer).

But it also means that all classes in Smalltalk end up being part of a single inheritance tree. You must inherit from a branch of this tree when creating a new class. Most of the tree is already there (it's the Smalltalk class library), and at the root of the tree is a class called **object** — the same class that each Smalltalk container holds.

This is a neat trick because it means that every class in the Smalltalk class hierarchy is derived from **object**, so every class can be held in every container, including that container itself. This type of single-tree hierarchy based on a fundamental generic type (often named **object**) is referred to as an "object-based hierarchy." You may have heard this term before and assumed it was some new fundamental concept in OOP, like polymorphism. It just means a class tree with **object** (or some similar name) at its root and container classes that hold **object**.

Because the Smalltalk class library had a much longer history and experience behind it than C++, and the original C++ compilers had *no* container class libraries, it seemed like a good idea to duplicate the Smalltalk library in C++. This was done as an experiment with a very early C++ implementation,[1] and because it represented a significant body of code, many people began using it. In the process of trying to use the container classes, they discovered a problem.

The problem was that in Smalltalk, you could force people to derive everything from a single hierarchy, but in C++ you can't. You might have your nice object-based hierarchy with its container classes, but then you might buy a set of shape classes or airline classes from another vendor who didn't use that hierarchy. (For one thing, the hierarchy imposes overhead, which C programmers eschew.) How do you shoehorn a separate class tree into the container class in your object-based hierarchy? Here's what the problem looks like:

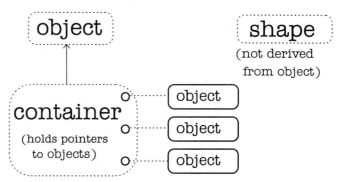

Because C++ supports multiple independent hierarchies, Smalltalk's object-based hierarchy does not work so well.

The solution seemed obvious. If you can have many inheritance hierarchies, then you should be able to inherit from more than one class: Multiple inheritance will solve the problem. So you do the following:

---

[1] The OOPS library, by Keith Gorlen while he was at NIH. Generally available from public sources.

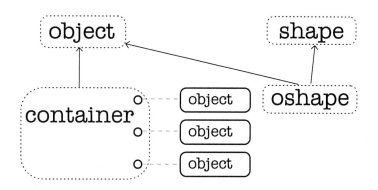

Now **oshape** has **shape**'s characteristics and behaviors, but because it is also derived from **object** it can be placed in **container**.

But multiple inheritance wasn't originally part of C++. Once the container problem was seen, there came a great deal of pressure to add the feature. Other programmers felt (and still feel) multiple inheritance wasn't a good idea and that it adds unneeded complexity to the language. An oft-repeated statement at that time was, "C++ is not Smalltalk," which, if you knew enough to translate it, meant "Don't use object based hierarchies for container classes." But in the end[2] the pressure persisted, and multiple inheritance was added to the language. Compiler vendors followed suit by including object-based container-class hierarchies, most of which have since been replaced by template versions. You can argue that multiple inheritance is needed for solving general programming problems, but you'll see in the next chapter that its complexity is best avoided except in special cases.

the template approach

Although an object-based hierarchy with multiple inheritance is conceptually straightforward, it turns out to be painful to use. In his

---

[2] We'll probably never know the full story because control of the language was still within AT&T at the time.

original book[3] Stroustrup demonstrated what he considered a preferable alternative to the object-based hierarchy. Container classes were created as large preprocessor macros for parameterized types, instead of templates with arguments that could be substituted for your desired type. When you wanted to create a container to hold a particular type, you made a couple of macro calls.

Unfortunately, this approach was confused by all the existing Smalltalk literature, and it was a bit unwieldy. Basically, nobody got it.

In the meantime, Stroustrup and the C++ team at Bell Labs had modified his original macro approach, simplifying it and moving it from the domain of the preprocessor into the compiler itself. This new code-substitution device is called a **template**[4], and it represents a completely different way to reuse code: Instead of reusing object code, as with inheritance and composition, a template reuses *source code*. The container no longer holds a generic base class called **object**, but instead an unspecified parameter. When you use a template, the parameter is substituted *by the compiler*, much like the old macro approach, but cleaner and easier to use.

Now, instead of worrying about inheritance or composition when you want to use a container class, you take the template version of the container and stamp out a specific version for your particular problem, like this:

---

[3] *The C++ Programming Language* by Bjarne Stroustrup (1st edition, Addison-Wesley, 1986).

[4] The inspiration for templates appears to be ADA generics.

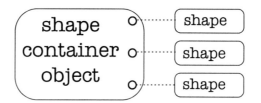

The compiler does the work for you, and you end up with exactly the container you need to do your job, rather than an unwieldy inheritance hierarchy. In C++, the template implements the concept of a *parameterized type*. Another benefit of the template approach is that the novice programmer who may be unfamiliar or uncomfortable with inheritance can still use canned container classes right away.

template syntax

The **template** keyword tells the compiler that the following class definition will manipulate one or more unspecified types. At the time the object is defined, those types must be specified so the compiler can substitute them.

Here's a small example to demonstrate the syntax:

```
//: STEMP.CPP -- Simple template example
#include <iostream.h>
#include <assert.h>

template<class T>
class array {
  enum { size = 100 };
  T A[size];
public:
  T& operator[](int index) {
    assert(index >= 0 && index < size);
    return A[index];
  }
};
```

```
main() {
  array<int> ia;
  array<float> fa;
  for(int i = 0; i < 20; i++) {
    ia[i] = i * i;
    fa[i] = float(i) * 1.414;
  }
  for(int j = 0; j < 20; j++)
    cout << j << ": " << ia[j]
         << ", " << fa[j] << endl;
}
```

You can see that it looks like a normal class except for the line

```
template<class T>
```

which says that **T** is the substitution parameter, and it represents a type name. Also, you see **T** used everywhere in the class where you would normally see the specific type the container holds.

In **array**, elements are inserted *and* extracted with the same function, the overloaded **operator[]**. It returns a reference, so it can be used on both sides of an equal sign. Notice that if the index is out of bounds, the Standard C library macro **assert( )** is used to print a message (**assert( )** is used instead of **allege( )** because you'll probably want to completely remove the test code once it's debugged). This is actually a case where throwing an exception is more appropriate, because then the class user can recover from the error, but that topic is not covered until Chapter 16.

In **main( )**, you can see how easy it is to create **array**s that hold different types of objects. When you say

```
array<int> ia;
array<float> fa;
```

the compiler expands the **array** template (this is called *instantiation*) twice, to create two new *generated classes*, which you can think of as **array_int** and **array_float.** (Different compilers may decorate the names in different ways.) These are classes just like the ones you would have produced if you had performed the substitution by hand, except that the compiler creates them for you as you define the objects **ia** and **fa**. Also note that duplicate class definitions are either avoided by the compiler or merged by the linker.

non-inline function definitions

Of course, there are times when you'll want to have non-inline member function definitions. In this case, the compiler needs to see the **template** declaration before the member function definition. Here's the above example, modified to show the non-inline member definition:

```
//: STEMP2.CPP -- Non-inline template example
#include <assert.h>

template<class T>
class array {
  enum { size = 100 };
  T A[size];
public:
  T& operator[](int index);
};

template<class T>
T& array<T>::operator[](int index) {
  assert(index >= 0 && index < size);
  return A[index];
}

main() {
  array<float> fa;
  fa[0] = 1.414;
}
```

Notice that in the member function definition the class name is now qualified with the template argument type: **array<T>**. You can imagine that the compiler does indeed carry both the name and the argument type(s) in some mangled form.

header files

Even if you create non-inline function definitions, you'll generally want to put all declarations *and* definitions for a template in a header file. This may seem to violate the normal header file rule of "Don't put in anything that allocates storage" to prevent multiple definition errors at link time, but template definitions are special. Anything preceded by **template<...>** means the compiler won't allocate storage for it at that point, but will instead wait until it's told to (by a template instantiation), and that somewhere in the compiler and linker there's a mechanism for removing multiple definitions of an identical template. So you'll almost always put the entire template declaration *and* definition in the header file, for ease of use.

There are times when you may need to place the template definitions in a separate CPP file to satisfy special needs (for example, forcing template instantiations to exist in only a single Windows DLL file). Most compilers have some mechanism to allow this; you'll have to investigate your particular compiler's documentation to use it.

the stack as a template

Here is the container and iterator in ISTACK.CPP (page 574), implemented as a generic container class using templates:

```
//: STACKT.H -- Simple stack template
#ifndef STACKT_H_
#define STACKT_H_
template<class T> class stacktIter; // declare

template<class T>
class stackt {
```

```
  enum { ssize = 100 };
  T stack[ssize];
  int top;
public:
  stackt() : top(0) { stack[top] = 0; }
  void push(const T& i) {
    if(top < ssize) stack[top++] = i;
  }
  T pop() {
    return stack[top > 0 ? --top : top];
  }
  friend class stacktIter<T>;
};

template<class T>
class stacktIter {
  stackt<T>& S;
  int index;
public:
  stacktIter(stackt<T>& is)
    : S(is), index(0) {}
  T& operator++() { // Prefix form
    if (index < S.top - 1) index++;
    return S.stack[index];
  }
  T& operator++(int) { // Postfix form
    int returnIndex = index;
    if (index < S.top - 1) index++;
    return S.stack[returnIndex];
  }
};
#endif // STACKT_H_
```

Notice that anywhere a template's class name is referred to, it must be accompanied by its template argument list, as in **stackt<T>& S**. You can imagine that internally, the arguments in the template argument list are also being mangled to produce a unique class name for each template instantiation.

Also notice that a template makes certain assumptions about the objects it is holding. For example, **stackt** assumes there is some sort of assignment operation for **T** inside the **push( )** function.

Here's the revised example to test the template:

```
//: STACKT.CPP -- Test simple stack template
#include <assert.h>
#include <iostream.h>
#include "..\14\stackt.h"
// For interest, generate Fibonacci numbers:
int fibonacci(int N) {
  const sz = 100;
  assert(N < sz);
  static F[sz]; // Initialized to zero
  F[0] = F[1] = 1;
  // Scan for unfilled array elements:
  int i;
  for(i = 0; i < sz; i++)
    if(F[i] == 0) break;
  while(i <= N) {
    F[i] = F[i-1] + F[i-2];
    i++;
  }
  return F[N];
}

main() {
  stackt<int> is;
  for(int i = 0; i < 20; i++)
    is.push(fibonacci(i));
  // Traverse with an iterator:
  stacktIter<int> it(is);
  for(int j = 0; j < 20; j++)
    cout << it++ << endl;
```

```
  for(int k = 0; k < 20; k++)
    cout << is.pop() << endl;
}
```

The only difference is in the creation of **is** and **it**: You specify the
type of object the stack and iterator should hold inside the template
argument list.

constants in templates

Template arguments are not restricted to class types; you can also
use built-in types. The values of these arguments then become
compile-time constants for that particular instantiation of the
template. You can even use default values for these arguments:

```
//: MBLOCK.CPP -- Built-in types in templates
#include <assert.h>
#include <iostream.h>

template<class T, int size = 100>
class mblock {
  T array[size];
public:
  T& operator[](int index) {
    assert(index >= 0 && index < size);
    return array[index];
  }
};

class number {
  float f;
public:
  number(float F = 0.0f) : f(F) {}
  number& operator=(const number& n) {
    f = n.f;
    return *this;
  }
```

```
    operator float() const { return f; }
    friend ostream&
      operator<<(ostream& os, const number& x) {
        return os << x.f;
    }
};

template<class T, int sz = 20>
class holder {
  mblock<T, sz>* np;
public:
  holder() : np(0) {}
  number& operator[](int i) {
    assert(i >= 0 && i < sz);
    if(!np) np = new mblock<T, sz>;
    return np->operator[](i);
  }
};

main() {
  holder<number, 20> H;
  for(int i = 0; i < 20; i++)
    H[i] = i;
  for(int j = 0; j < 20; j++)
    cout << H[j] << endl;
}
```

Class **mblock** is a checked array of objects; you cannot index out of bounds. (Again, the exception approach in Chapter 16 may be more appropriate than **assert( )** in this situation.)

The class **holder** is much like **mblock** except that it has a pointer to an **mblock** instead of an embedded object of type **mblock**. This pointer is not initialized in the constructor; the initialization is delayed until the first access. You might use a technique like this if you are creating a lot of objects, but not accessing them all, and want to save storage.

stash & stack as templates

It turns out that the **stash** and **stack** classes that have been updated periodically throughout this book are actually container classes, so it makes sense to convert them to templates. But first, one other important issue arises with container classes: When a container releases a pointer to an object, does it destroy that object? For example, when a container object goes out of scope, does it destroy all the objects it points to?

the ownership problem

This issue is commonly referred to as *ownership*. Containers that hold entire objects don't usually worry about ownership because they clearly own the objects they contain. But if your container holds pointers (which is more common with C++, especially with polymorphism), then it's very likely those pointers may also be used somewhere else in the program, and you don't necessarily want to delete the object because then the other pointers in the program would be referencing a destroyed object. To prevent this from happening, you must consider ownership when designing and using a container.

Many programs are very simple, and one container holds pointers to objects that are used only by that container. In this case ownership is very straightforward: The container owns its objects. Generally, you'll want this to be the default case for a container because it's the most common situation.

The best approach to handling the ownership problem is to give the client programmer the choice. This is often accomplished by a constructor argument that defaults to indicating ownership (typically desired for simple programs). In addition there may be read and set functions to view and modify the ownership of the container. If the container has functions to remove an object, the ownership state usually affects that removal, so you may also find options to control destruction in the removal function. You could conceivably also add ownership data for every element in the container, so each position would know whether it needed to be destroyed; this is a variant of reference counting where the container and not the object knows the number of references pointing to an object.

stash as a template

The "stash" class that has been evolving throughout the book (last seen in Chapter 11) is an ideal candidate for a template. Now an iterator has been added along with ownership operations:

```
//: TSTASH.H -- PSTASH using templates
#ifndef TSTASH_H_
#define TSTASH_H_
#include <stdlib.h>
#include "..\allege.h"
// More convenient than nesting in tstash:
enum owns { no = 0, yes = 1, Default };
// Declaration required:
template<class Type, int sz> class tstashIter;

template<class Type, int chunksize = 20>
class tstash {
  int quantity;
  int next;
  owns own; // Flag
  void inflate(int increase = chunksize);
protected:
  Type** storage;
public:
  tstash(owns Owns = yes);
  ~tstash();
  int Owns() const { return own; }
```

```
    void Owns(owns newOwns) { own = newOwns; }
    int add(Type* element);
    int remove(int index, owns d = Default);
    Type* operator[](int index);
    int count() const { return next; }
    friend class tstashIter<Type, chunksize>;
};

template<class Type, int sz = 20>
class tstashIter {
  tstash<Type, sz>& ts;
  int index;
public:
  tstashIter(tstash<Type, sz>& TS)
    : ts(TS), index(0) {}
  tstashIter(const tstashIter& rv)
    : ts(rv.ts), index(rv.index) {}
  // Jump interator forward or backward:
  void forward(int amount) {
    index += amount;
    if(index >= ts.next) index = ts.next -1;
  }
  void backward(int amount) {
    index -= amount;
    if(index < 0) index = 0;
  }
  // Return value of ++ and -- to be
  // used inside conditionals:
  int operator++() {
    if(++index >= ts.next) return 0;
    return 1;
  }
  int operator++(int) { return operator++(); }
  int operator--() {
    if(--index < 0) return 0;
    return 1;
  }
```

```cpp
  int operator--(int) { return operator--(); }
  operator int() {
    return index >= 0 && index < ts.next;
  }
  Type* operator->() {
    Type* t = ts.storage[index];
    if(t) return t;
    allege(0,"tstashIter::operator->return 0");
    return 0; // To allow inlining
  }
  // Remove the current element:
  int remove(owns d = Default){
    return ts.remove(index, d);
  }
};

template<class Type, int sz>
tstash<Type, sz>::tstash(owns Owns) : own(Owns) {
  quantity = 0;
  storage = 0;
  next = 0;
}

// Destruction of contained objects:
template<class Type, int sz>
tstash<Type, sz>::~tstash() {
  if(!storage) return;
  if(own == yes)
    for(int i = 0; i < count(); i++)
      delete storage[i];
  free(storage);
}

template<class Type, int sz>
int tstash<Type, sz>::add(Type* element) {
  if(next >= quantity)
    inflate();
```

```
    storage[next++] = element;
    return(next - 1); // Index number
}

template<class Type, int sz>
int tstash<Type, sz>::remove(int index,owns d){
  if(index >= next || index < 0)
    return 0;
  switch(d) {
    case Default:
      if(own != yes) break;
    case yes:
      delete storage[index];
    case no:
      storage[index] = 0; // Position is empty
  }
  return 1;
}

template<class Type, int sz> inline
Type* tstash<Type, sz>::operator[](int index) {
  // No check in shipping application:
  assert(index >= 0 && index < next);
  return storage[index];
}

template<class Type, int sz>
void tstash<Type, sz>::inflate(int increase) {
  void* v =
    realloc(storage,
(quantity+increase)*sizeof(Type*));
  allegemem(v);  // Was it successful?
  storage = (Type**)v;
  quantity += increase;
}
#endif // TSTASH_H_
```

The **enum owns** is global, although you'd normally want to nest it inside the class. Here it's more convenient to use, but you can try moving it if you want to see the effect.

The **storage** pointer is made **protected** so inherited classes can directly access it. This means that the inherited classes may become dependent on the specific implementation of **tstash**, but as you'll see in the SORTED.CPP example (page 622), it's worth it.

The **own** flag indicates whether the container defaults to owning its objects. If so, in the destructor each object whose pointer is in the container is destroyed. This is straightforward; the container knows the type it contains. You can also change the default ownership in the constructor or read and modify it with the overloaded **Owns( )** function.

You should be aware that if the container holds pointers to a base-class type, that type should have a **virtual** destructor to ensure proper cleanup of derived objects whose addresses have been upcast when placing them in the container.

The **tstashIter** follows the iterator model of bonding to a single container object for its lifetime. In addition, the copy-constructor allows you to make a new iterator pointing at the same location as the existing iterator you create it from, effectively making a bookmark into the container. The **forward( )** and **backward( )** member functions allow you to jump an iterator by a number of spots, respecting the boundaries of the container. The overloaded increment and decrement operators move the iterator by one place. The smart pointer is used to operate on the element the iterator is referring to, and **remove( )** destroys the current object by calling the container's **remove( )**.

The following example creates and tests two different kinds of **stash** objects, one for a new class called **Int** that announces its construction and destruction and one that holds objects of the class **String** from Chapter 11.

```
//: TSTEST.CPP -- Test TSTASH
```

```
#include <fstream.h>
#include "..\allege.h"
#include "..\14\tstash.h"
#include "..\11\strings.h"
const bufsize = 80;
ofstream out("tstest.out");

class Int {
  int i;
public:
  Int(int I = 0) : i(I) {
    out << ">" << i << endl;
  }
  ~Int() { out << "~" << i << endl; }
  operator int() const { return i; }
  friend ostream&
    operator<<(ostream& os, const Int& x) {
      return os << x.i;
  }
};

main() {
  tstash<Int> intStash; // Instantiate for int
  for(int i = 0; i < 30; i++)
    intStash.add(new Int(i));
  tstashIter<Int> Intit(intStash);
  Intit.forward(5);
  for(int j = 0; j < 20; j++, Intit++)
    Intit.remove(); // Default removal
  for(int k = 0; k < intStash.count(); k++)
    if(intStash[k]) // Remove() causes "holes"
      out << *intStash[k] << endl;

  ifstream file("tstest.cpp");
  allegefile(file);
  char buf[bufsize];
  // Instantiate for String:
```

```
tstash<String> stringStash;
while(file.getline(buf, bufsize))
  stringStash.add(makeString(buf));
for(int u = 0; u < stringStash.count(); u++)
  if(stringStash[u])
    out << *stringStash[u] << endl;
tstashIter<String> it(stringStash);
int j = 25;
it.forward(j);
while(it) {
  out << j++ << ": " << it->str() << endl;
  it++;
}
}
```

In both cases an iterator is created and used to move through the container. Notice the elegance produced by using these constructs: You aren't assailed with the implementation details of using an array. You tell the container and iterator objects *what* to do, not how. This makes the solution easier to conceptualize, to build, and to modify.

stack as a template

The **stack** class, last seen in Chapter 12, is also a container and is also best expressed as a template with an associated iterator. Here's the new header file:

```
//: TSTACK.H -- Stack using templates
#ifndef TSTACK_H_
#define TSTACK_H_

// Declaration required:
template<class T> class tstackIterator;

template<class T>
class tstack {
```

```
     struct link {
       T* data;
       link* next;
       link(T* Data, link* Next) {
         data = Data;
         next = Next;
       }
     } * head;
     int owns;
public:
     tstack(int Owns = 1) : head(0), owns(Owns) {}
     ~tstack();
     void push(T* Data) {
       head = new link(Data,head);
     }
     T* peek() const { return head->data; }
     T* pop();
     int Owns() const { return owns; }
     void Owns(int newownership) {
       owns = newownership;
     }
     friend class tstackIterator<T>;
};

template<class T>
T* tstack<T>::pop() {
   if(head == 0) return 0;
   T* result = head->data;
   link* oldHead = head;
   head = head->next;
   delete oldHead;
   return result;
}

template<class T>
tstack<T>::~tstack() {
   link* cursor = head;
```

```
  while(head) {
    cursor = cursor->next;
    // Conditional cleanup of data:
    if(owns) delete head->data;
    delete head;
    head = cursor;
  }
}

template<class T>
class tstackIterator {
  tstack<T>::link* p;
public:
  tstackIterator(const tstack<T>& tl)
    : p(tl.head) {}
  tstackIterator(const tstackIterator& tl)
    : p(tl.p) {}
  // operator++ returns boolean indicating end:
  int operator++() {
    if(p->next)
      p = p->next;
    else p = 0; // Indicates end of list
    return int(p);
  }
  int operator++(int) { return operator++(); }
  // Smart pointer:
  T* operator->() const {
    if(!p) return 0;
    return p->data;
  }
  T* current() const {
    if(!p) return 0;
    return p->data;
  }
  // int conversion for conditional test:
  operator int() const { return p ? 1 : 0; }
};
```

```
#endif // TSTACK_H_
```

You'll also notice the class has been changed to support ownership, which works now because the class knows the exact type (or at least the base type, which will work assuming virtual destructors are used). As with **tstash**, the default is for the container to destroy its objects but you can change this by either modifying the constructor argument or using the **Owns( )** read/write member functions.

The iterator is very simple and very small — the size of a single pointer. When you create a **tstackIterator**, it's initialized to the head of the linked list, and you can only increment it forward through the list. If you want to start over at the beginning, you create a new iterator, and if you want to remember a spot in the list, you create a new iterator from the existing iterator pointing at that spot (using the copy-constructor).

To call functions for the object referred to by the iterator, you can use the smart pointer (a very common sight in iterators) or a function called **current( )** that *looks* identical to the smart pointer because it returns a pointer to the current object, but is different because the smart pointer performs the extra levels of dereferencing (see Chapter 10). Finally, the **operator int( )** indicates whether or not you are at the end of the list and allows the iterator to be used in conditional statements.

The entire implementation is contained in the header file, so there's no separate CPP file. Here's a small test that also exercises the iterator:

```
//: TSTKTST.CPP -- Use template list & iterator
#include "..\14\tstack.h"
#include "..\11\strings.h"
#include <fstream.h>
#include "..\allege.h"

main() {
```

```
ifstream file("tstktst.cpp");
allegefile(file);
const bufsize = 100;
char buf[bufsize];
tstack<String> textlines;
// Read file and store lines in the list:
while(file.getline(buf,bufsize))
  textlines.push(String::make(buf));
int i = 0;
// Use iterator to print lines from the list:
tstackIterator<String> it(textlines);
tstackIterator<String>* it2 = 0;
while(it) {
  cout << *it.current() << endl;
  it++;
  if(++i == 10) // Remember 10th line
    it2 = new tstackIterator<String>(it);
}
cout << *(it2->current()) << endl;
delete it2;
}
```

A **tstack** is instantiated to hold **String** objects and filled with lines
from a file. Then an iterator is created and used to move through
the linked list. The tenth line is remembered by copy-constructing a
second iterator from the first; later this line is printed and the
iterator — created dynamically — is destroyed. Here, dynamic
object creation is used to control the lifetime of the object.

This is very similar to earlier test examples for the **stack** class, but
now the contained objects are properly destroyed when the **tstack**
is destroyed.

string & integer

To facilitate the examples in the rest of this chapters, a more powerful string class is necessary, along with an integer object that guarantees its initialization

a string on the stack

This a more complete string class that has been used before in this book. In addition, this class uses templates to add a special feature: You can decide, when you instantiate the **SString**, whether it lives on the stack or the heap.

```
//: SSTRING.H -- Stack-based string
#ifndef SSTRING_H_
#define SSTRING_H_
#include <string.h>
#include <iostream.h>

template<int bsz = 0>
class SString {
  char buf[bsz + 1];
  char* s;
public:
  SString(const char* S = "") : s(buf) {
    if(!bsz) { // Make on heap
      s = new char[strlen(S) + 1];
      strcpy(s, S);
    } else { // Make on stack
      buf[bsz] = 0; // Ensure 0 termination
      strncpy(s, S, bsz);
    }
  }
  SString(const SString& rv) : s(buf) {
    if(!bsz) { // Make on heap
      s = new char[strlen(rv.s) + 1];
```

```
      strcpy(s, rv.s);
    } else { // Make on stack
      buf[bsz] = 0;
      strncpy(s, rv.s, bsz);
    }
}
SString& operator=(const SString& rv) {
  // Check for self-assignment:
  if(&rv == this) return *this;
  if(!bsz) { // Manage heap:
    delete s;
    s = new char[strlen(rv.s) + 1];
  }
  // Constructor guarantees length < bsz:
  strcpy(s, rv.s);
  return *this;
}
~SString() {
  if(!bsz) delete []s;
}
int operator==(const SString& rv) const {
  return !stricmp(s, rv.s);
}
int operator!=(const SString& rv) const {
  return stricmp(s, rv.s);
}
int operator>(const SString& rv) const {
  return stricmp(s, rv.s) > 0;
}
int operator<(const SString& rv) const {
  return stricmp(s, rv.s) < 0;
}
char* str() const { return s; }
friend ostream&
  operator<<(ostream& os,
             const SString<bsz>& S) {
    return os << S.s;
```

```
    }
};

typedef SString<> Hstring; // Heap string
#endif // SSTRING_H_
```

By using the **typedef Hstring**, you get an ordinary heap-based string. (A **typedef** was used here instead of inheritance because inheritance requires the new creation of the constructors and **operator=**.) But if you're concerned about the efficiency of creating and destroying a lot of strings, you can take a chance and assume the largest word size possible for the solution of your problem. When you give the template a size argument, it automatically creates the object totally on the stack rather than on the heap, which means the overhead of one **new** and one **delete** per object is eliminated. You can see that **operator=** is also speeded up.

The comparison operators for the string use a function called **stricmp( )**, which is *not* Standard C but which nonetheless is available with most compiler libraries. It performs a string compare while ignoring the case of the letters.

integer

The constructor for **class integer** zeroes the value, and it contains an automatic type conversion operator to an **int** so you can easily extract the value:

```
//: INTEGER.H -- Int wrapped in a class
#ifndef INTEGER_H_
#define INTEGER_H_
#include <iostream.h>

class integer {
  int i;
public:
  // Guaranteed zeroing:
```

```
  integer(int ii = 0) : i(ii) {}
  operator int() const { return i; }
  const integer& operator++() {
    i++;
    return *this;
  }
  const integer operator++(int) {
    integer returnval(i);
    i++;
    return returnval;
  }
  integer& operator+=(const integer& x) {
    i += x.i;
    return *this;
  }
  friend ostream&
  operator<<(ostream& os, const integer& x) {
      return os << x.i;
  }
};
#endif // INTEGER_H_
```

Although this class is quite minimal (it satisfies only the needs of this chapter), you can easily add as many operations as you need by following the examples in Chapter 10.

vectors

Although the **tstash** acts somewhat like a vector, it's convenient to have a class that looks exactly like a vector — that is, its only behavior is indexing. (Thus the only interface is through the **operator[]**.)

an "infinite" vector

This class is a vector that only holds pointers. It never needs sizing: You simply index to any location, and that location is magically there, without telling it ahead of time. The **operator[]** returns a pointer reference, so it can appear on the left-hand side of an **=**. (It can be an lvalue as well as an rvalue.) It only deals with pointers, so there's no limit on the type it can work with, and no assumptions are necessary about the behavior of the type.

Here's the header file:

```
//: VECTOR.H -- "Infinite" vector
#ifndef VECTOR_H_
#define VECTOR_H_
#include <stdlib.h>
#include "..\allege.h"

template<class T>
class vector {
  T** pos;
  int pos_sz;
  T** neg;
  int neg_sz;
  int owns;
  enum {
    chunk = 20, // Min allocation increase
    esz = sizeof(T*), // Element size
  };
  void expand(T**& array,int& size,int index);
public:
  vector(int Owns = 1);
  ~vector();
  T*& operator[](int index);
  int Owns() const { return owns; }
  void Owns(int newOwns) { owns = newOwns; }
};
```

```cpp
template<class T>
vector<T>::vector(int Owns)
  : pos(0), pos_sz(0),
    neg(0), neg_sz(0),
    owns(Owns) {}

template<class T>
vector<T>::~vector() {
  if(owns)
    for(int i = 0; i < pos_sz; i++)
      delete pos[i];
  free(pos);
  if(owns)
    for(int j = 0; j < neg_sz; j++)
      delete neg[j];
  free(neg);
}

template<class T>
T*& vector<T>::operator[](int index) {
  if(index < 0) {
    index *= -1;
    if(index >= neg_sz)
      expand(neg, neg_sz, index);
    return neg[index];
  }
  else { // Index >= 0
    if(index >= pos_sz)
      expand(pos, pos_sz, index);
    return pos[index];
  }
}

template<class T> void
vector<T>::expand(T**& array, int& size,
                  int index) {
  const newsize = index + chunk;
```

```
    const increment = newsize - size;
    void* v = realloc(array, newsize * esz);
    allegemem(v);
    array = (T**)v;
    memset(&array[size], 0, increment * esz);
    size = index + chunk;
  }
#endif // VECTOR_H_
```

The vector is divided into positive and negative sections for ease of implementation. You may, for some reason, want to change the underlying implementation so that a contiguous block of memory is always used.

The private **expand( )** function is used when the storage must be increased. It takes a reference **T**&** rather than a pointer because it must change the outside argument to point to a new physical location after the **realloc( )**. The old **size** and new **index** that caused the call to **expand( )** are also required so the new storage can be zeroed. (This is important because the destructor calls **delete** for all the pointers if the **vector** owns its objects.) The **size** is passed in as an **int&** because it must also be changed to reflect the new size.

In **operator[]**, if you ask for a location, either positive or negative, that is beyond the currently allocated storage, more storage is allocated. This is much more convenient than a built-in array because you simply make one and never worry about how big it needs to be:

```
//: VECTOR.CPP -- Test "infinite" vector
#include <fstream.h>
#include "..\allege.h"
#include "..\14\vector.h"
#include "..\14\sstring.h"
typedef SString<40> String;

main() {
```

```
ifstream source("vector.cpp");
allegefile(source);
const bsz = 255;
char buf[bsz];
vector<String> words;
int i = 0;
while(source.getline(buf, bsz)) {
  char* s = strtok(buf, " \t");
  while(s) {
    words[i++] = new String(s);
    s = strtok(0, " \t");
  }
  words[i++] = new String("\n");
}
for(int j = 0; words[j]; j++)
  cout << *words[j] << ' ';
}
```

This program uses the Standard C library function **strtok( )** that takes the starting address of a character buffer (the first argument) and looks for delimiters (the second argument). It replaces the delimiter with a zero and returns the address of the beginning of the token. If you call it subsequent times with a first argument of zero, it will continue extracting tokens from the rest of the string until it finds the end. In this case, the delimiters are spaces and tabs, so it extracts words. Each word is turned into a **String** and the pointer is placed into the **words** vector, which eventually contains the whole file, broken up into words.

a set

The constraint for a set is that it contains no duplicates. You can add elements to a set, and you can test to see if an element is a member of a set. The following **set** class uses a **vector** to hold its elements:

```
//: SET.H -- Each entry in a set is unique
```

```
#ifndef SET_H_
#define SET_H_
#include "..\14\vector.h"
#include <assert.h>

template<class Type>
class set {
  vector<Type> elem;
  int max;
  int lastindex; // Efficiency tool
  int within(const Type& e) {
    // Requires Type::operator== :
    for(lastindex = 0; lastindex < max;
        lastindex++)
      if(elem[lastindex]->operator==(e))
        return lastindex;
    return -1;
  }
  // Prevent assignment & copy-construction:
  void operator=(set&);
  set(set&);
public:
  set() : max(0), lastindex(0) {}
  void add(const Type&);
  int contains(const Type&);
  // Where is it in the set?:
  int index(const Type& e);
  Type& operator[] (int index) {
    // No check for shipping application:
    assert(index >= 0 && index < max);
    return *elem[index];
  }
  int length() const { return max; }
};

template<class Type> void
set<Type>::add(const Type& e) {
```

```
  if (!contains(e)) {
    elem[max] = new Type(e);//Copy-constructor
    max++;
  }
}

template<class Type> int
set<Type>::contains(const Type& e) {
  return within(e) != -1;
}

template<class Type> int
set<Type>::index(const Type& e) {
  // Prevent a new search if possible:
  if (elem[lastindex]->operator!=(e)) {
    int ind = within(e);
    assert(ind != -1); // Must know it's inside
  }
  return lastindex;
}
#endif // SET_H_
```

add( ) puts a new element in the set, checking to make sure it's not already there. **contains( )** tells you if your object is already in the set, and **index( )** tells you where in the set it is, so you can select it using **operator[]**. **length( )** tells you how many elements are in the set.

The implementation keeps track of the number of elements. As an efficiency aid, the last index element selected is also kept, so that if you do a **contains( )** followed directly by an **index( )**, you won't have to search through the entire set twice. This is facilitated by the **inline private** function **within( )**.

The following test uses the **set** class to create a *concordance*, which is a set of words that occur within a file:

```
//: SETTEST.CPP -- Test the "set" class
```

```
// Creates a concordance of text words
#include <fstream.h>
#include "..\14\set.h"
#include "..\14\sstring.h"
#include "..\allege.h"
const char* delimiters =
  " \t;()\"<>:{}[]+-=&*#.,/\\"
  "0123456789";

typedef SString<40> String;

main(int argc, char* argv[]) {
  allege(argc == 2, "need file argument");
  ifstream in(argv[1]);
  allegefile(in);
  ofstream out("settest.out");
  set<String> concordance;
  const sz = 255;
  char buf[sz];
  while(in.getline(buf, sz)) {
    // Capture individual words:
    char* s = strtok(buf, delimiters);
    while(s) {
      // Contains 1 entry per unique word:
      concordance.add(s); // Auto type conv.
      s = strtok(0, delimiters);
    }
  }
  for(int i = 0; i < concordance.length(); i++) {
    out << concordance[i] << endl;
  }
}
```

This program again uses **strtok( )**, but this time with a larger set of delimiters. In addition to stripping away most nonalpha characters, numbers are also removed.

Note that because **add( )** is expecting a string object but receives a **char***, automatic type conversion is performed using the **SString<40>** constructor that takes a single **char*** argument. This produces a temporary object whose address is passed to **add( )**. If **add( )** doesn't find this temporary in its list, it duplicates it. It's important that an object reference rather than a pointer be passed to **add( )** because the pointer wouldn't necessarily be placed in the container, so if you used **new** and handed the pointer in, you could end up losing the pointer.

an associative array

An ordinary array uses an integral value to index into a sequential set of elements of some type. An *associative array* uses any type as an index into the set of elements. Because, in the general case, you'd like to be able to use any type as the index and any other type for the elements, this is an ideal case for a template.

The associative array shown here uses both the **set** and **vector** classes to create two arrays of pointers: one for the input type, and one for the output type. If you use an index it hasn't seen before, it creates a new input object that's a copy of the index (the input type is assumed to have a copy-constructor and **operator=**) and a new output object using the default constructor. The **operator[]** simply returns a reference to the output object so you can perform an operation on it. You can also call two functions, **in_value( )** and **out_value( )** with an integer argument to produce all the input and output elements of the array:

```
//: ASSOC.H -- Associative array
#ifndef ASSOC_H_
#define ASSOC_H_
#include "..\14\set.h"
#include <assert.h>

template<class In, class Out>
class assoc_array {
  set<In> inVal;
```

```
    vector<Out> outVal;
    int max;
    // Prevent assignment & copy-construction:
    void operator=(assoc_array&);
    assoc_array(assoc_array&);
public:
    assoc_array() : max(0) {}
    Out& operator[](const In&);
    int length() const { return max; }
    In& in_value(int i) {
      // No check for shipping application:
      assert(i >= 0 && i < max);
      return inVal[i];
    }
    Out& out_value(int i) {
      assert(i >= 0 && i < max);
      return *outVal[i];
    }
};

template<class In, class Out> Out&
assoc_array<In,Out>::operator[](const In& in){
  if(!inVal.contains(in)) {
    inVal.add(in); // Copy-constructor
    outVal[max] = new Out; // Default constr.
    max++;
  }
  int x = inVal.index(in);
  return *outVal[inVal.index(in)];
}
#endif // ASSOC_H_
```

This is a fairly simple tool, but powerful in use. A classic example of an associative array is a program that counts the words in a file. One of the limitations of this associative array is that it doesn't work with built-in types as the output value. That's because built-in types don't have default constructors and are thus not initialized when they're created. To solve this problem for the word count program, the **integer** class is used along with the **SString** class to test the associative array:

```
//: ASSOC.CPP -- Test of associative array
#include "..\14\assoc.h"
#include "..\14\sstring.h"
#include "..\14\integer.h"
#include "..\allege.h"
#include <fstream.h>
#include <ctype.h>

main() {
  const char* delimiters =
    " \t;()\"<>:{}[]+-=&*#.,/\\";
  assoc_array<SString<80>, integer> strcount;
  ifstream source("assoc.cpp");
  allegefile(source);
  ofstream out("assoc.out");
  allegefile(out);
  const bsz = 255;
  char buf[bsz];
  while(source.getline(buf, bsz)) {
    char* s = strtok(buf, delimiters);
    while(s) {
      strcount[s]++; // Count word
      s = strtok(0, delimiters);
    }
  }
  for(int i = 0; i < strcount.length(); i++) {
    out << strcount.in_value(i) << " : "
        << strcount.out_value(i) << endl;
  }

  // The "shopping list" problem:
  assoc_array<SString<>, integer> shoplist;
  ifstream list("shoplist.txt");
```

```
    allegefile(list);
    ofstream olist("shoplist.out");
    allegefile(olist);
    while(list.getline(buf, bsz)) {
      int i = strlen(buf) - 1; // Last char
      while(isspace(buf[i]))
        i--; // Find nonzero char at end
      while(!isspace(buf[i]))
        i--; // Back up to space or tab
      int count = atoi(&buf[i+1]); // Use value
      while(isspace(buf[i]))
        i--; // Back up to non-whitespace
      buf[i+1] = 0; // Mark end of description
      i = 0;
      while(isspace(buf[i]))
        i++; // Find start of first word
      shoplist[&buf[i]] += count;
    }
    for(int j = 0; j < shoplist.length(); j++) {
      olist << shoplist.in_value(j) << " : "
            << shoplist.out_value(j) << endl;
    }
  }
```

The key line in the program is

```
strcount[s]++; // count word
```

Because **s** is a **char*** and the argument to **operator[]** is expected to be an **SString<80>**, the compiler creates a temporary object to pass to **operator[]** using the constructor **SString<80>(char*)**. This temporary is created entirely on the stack, so it's fairly quick to make and destroy.

The **operator[]** returns an **integer&** to the corresponding object in the **assoc_array**, and you can do anything you want to that object. Here, it's simply incremented to indicate another word was found.

The latter half of **main( )** solves the classic "shopping list" problem. Each line in the shopping list file contains an item (a name possibly separated with spaces) and a quantity. The items may appear more than once on the list, and an associative array is used to sum them all up. In this code, extra work is performed to compensate for surrounding spaces, using the Standard C **isspace( )**macro. Then the summation is performed with the line:

```
shoplist[&buf[i]] += count;
```

As before, the **char*** inside the index causes a temporary **SString** object to be created because that's what the indexing operator is expecting to see, and a type conversion exists via the constructor. When tracing the program, you'll see the extra constructor and destructor call caused by the temporary.

templates & inheritance

There's nothing to prevent you from using a class template in any way you'd use an ordinary class. For example, you can easily inherit from a template, and you can create a new template that instantiates and inherits from an existing template. If the **tstash** class does everything you want, but you'd also like it to sort itself, you can easily reuse the code and add value to it:

```
//: SORTED.H -- Template inheritance
#ifndef SORTED_H_
#define SORTED_H_
#include <stdlib.h>
#include <string.h>
#include <time.h>
#include "..\14\tstash.h"
#include "..\14\set.h"
template<class T>
class sorted : public tstash<T> {
  void bubblesort();
public:
```

```
    int add(T* element) {
      tstash<T>::add(element);
      bubblesort();
      return 0; // Sort moves the element
    }
};
template<class T>
void sorted<T>::bubblesort() {
  for(int i = count(); i > 0; i--)
    for(int j = 1; j < i; j++)
      if(*storage[j-1] > *storage[j]) {
        // Swap the two elements:
        T* t = storage[j-1];
        storage[j-1] = storage[j];
        storage[j] = t;
      }
}

// Quick & dirty sorted set:
template<class T>
class sortedSet : public set<T> {
  sorted<T> Sorted;
public:
  void add(T& e) {
    if(contains(e)) return;
    set<T>::add(e);
    Sorted.add(new T(e));
  }
  T& operator[] (int index) {
    assert(index >= 0 && index < length());
    assert(Sorted[index]);
    return *Sorted[index];
  }
  int length() {
    return Sorted.count();
  }
};
```

```
// Unique random number generator:
template<int upper_bound>
class urand {
  int map[upper_bound];
  int recycle;
public:
  urand(int Recycle = 0);
  int operator()();
};

template<int upper_bound>
urand<upper_bound>::urand(int Recycle = 0)
  : recycle(Recycle) {
  memset(map, 0, upper_bound * sizeof(int));
  // Seed the random number generator:
  time_t t;
  srand((unsigned)time(&t));
}

template<int upper_bound>
int urand<upper_bound>::operator()() {
  if(!memchr(map, 0, upper_bound)) {
    if(recycle)
      memset(map, 0,
             sizeof(map) * sizeof(int));
    else
      return -1; // No more spaces left
  }
  int newval;
  while(map[newval = rand() % upper_bound])
    ; // Until unique value is found
  map[newval]++; // Set flag
  return newval;
}
#endif // SORTED_H_
```

This example also contains a random number generator class that always produces a unique number and overloads **operator( )** to produce a familiar function-call syntax. The uniqueness of **urand** is produced by keeping a map of all the numbers possible in the random space (the upper bound is set with the template argument) and marking each one off as it's used. The optional second constructor argument allows you to reuse the numbers once they're all used up. Notice that this implementation is optimized for speed by allocating the entire map, regardless of how many numbers you're going to need. If you want to optimize for size, you can change the underlying implementation so it allocates storage for the map dynamically and puts the random numbers themselves in the map rather than flags. Notice that this change in implementation will not affect any client code.

The **sorted** template imposes a restriction on all classes it is instantiated for: They must contain a **>** operator. In **SString** this is added explicitly, but in **integer** the automatic type conversion **operator int( )** provides a path to the built-in **>** operator. When a template provides more functionality for you, the trade-off is usually that it puts more requirements on your class. Sometimes you'll have to inherit the contained class to add the required functionality. Notice the value of using an overloaded operator here — the **integer** class can rely on its underlying implementation to provide the functionality.

In this example you can see the usefulness of making the underlying **storage** in **tstash protected** rather than **private**. It *is* an important thing for the **sorted** class to know, a true dependency: If you were to change the underlying implementation of **tstash** to be something other than an array, like a linked list, the "swapping" of elements would be completely different, so the dependent class **sorted** would need to be changed. However, a preferable alternative (if possible) to making the implementation of **tstash protected** is to provide enough **protected** interface functions so that access and swapping can take place in a derived class without directly manipulating the underlying implementation. That way you can still change the underlying implementation without propagating modifications.

Note the additional **class sortedSet**, which is an example of how you can quickly paste together desired functionality from existing classes. **sortedSet** takes the interface from the **set** class, but when it adds a new element to the set it also adds it to a **sorted** object, and the return values are all sorted. You might consider designing a smaller, more efficient version of this class, but if it does what you need there's no point. (The Standard C++ template library contains a set class that sorts itself.)

Here's a test for SORTED.H:

```
//: SORTED.CPP -- Testing template inheritance
#include "..\14\sorted.h"
#include "..\14\sstring.h"
#include "..\14\integer.h"
typedef SString<40> String;

char* words[] = {
  "is", "running", "big", "dog", "a",
};
const wordsz = sizeof words / sizeof *words;

main() {
  sorted<String> ss;
  for(int i = 0; i < wordsz; i++)
    ss.add(new String(words[i]));
  for(int j = 0; j < ss.count(); j++)
    cout << ss[j]->str() << endl;
  sorted<integer> is;
  urand<47> rand1;
  for(int k = 0; k < 15; k++)
    is.add(new integer(rand1()));
  for(int l = 0; l < is.count(); l++)
    cout << *is[l] << endl;
}
```

Thinking in C++ Bruce Eckel

This tests both the **SString** and **integer** classes by created a **sorted** array for each.

design & efficiency

In **sorted**, every time you call **add( )** the element is inserted and the array is resorted. Here, the horribly inefficient and greatly deprecated (but easy to understand and code) bubble sort is used. This is perfectly appropriate, because it's part of the **private** implementation. During program development, your priorities are to

1. Get the class interfaces correct.

2. Create an accurate implementation as rapidly as possible so you can.

3. Prove your design.

Very often, you will discover problems with the class interface only when you assemble your initial "rough draft" of the working system. You may also discover the need for "helper" classes like containers and iterators during system assembly and during your first-pass implementation. Sometimes it's very difficult to discover these kinds of issues during analysis — your goal in analysis should be to get a big-picture design that can be rapidly implemented and tested. Only after the design has been proven should you spend the time to flesh it out completely and worry about performance issues. If the design fails, or if performance is not a problem, the bubble sort is good enough, and you haven't wasted any time. (Of course, the ideal solution is to use someone else's sorted container; the Standard C++ template library is the first place to look.)

preventing template bloat

Each time you instantiate a template, the code in the template is generated anew (except for **inline** functions). If some of the functionality of a template does not depend on type, it can be put in a common base class to prevent needless reproduction of that code. For example, in Chapter 12 in INHSTAK.CPP (page 518) inheritance was used to specify the types that a **stack** could accept and produce. Here's the templatized version of that code:

```
//: NOBLOAT.H -- Templatized INHSTAK.CPP
#ifndef NOBLOAT_H_
#define NOBLOAT_H_
#include "..\11\stack11.h"

template<class T>
class nbstack : public stack {
public:
  void push(T* str) {
    stack::push(str);
  }
  T* peek() const {
    return (T*)stack::peek();
  }
  T* pop() {
    return (T*)stack::pop();
  }
  ~nbstack();
};

// Defaults to heap objects & ownership:
template<class T>
nbstack<T>::~nbstack() {
  T* top = pop();
  while(top) {
    delete top;
    top = pop();
  }
}
#endif // NOBLOAT_H_
```

As before, the inline functions generate no code and are thus "free." The functionality is provided by creating the base-class code

---

only once. However, the ownership problem has been solved here by adding a destructor (which *is* type-dependent, and thus must be created by the template). Here, it defaults to ownership. Notice that when the base-class destructor is called, the stack will be empty, so no duplicate releases will occur.

polymorphism & containers

It's common to see polymorphism, dynamic object creation and containers, used together in a true object-oriented program. Containers and dynamic object creation solve the problem of not knowing how many or what type of objects you'll need, and because the container is configured to hold pointers to base-class objects, an upcast occurs every time you put a derived-class pointer into the container (with the associated code organization and extensibility benefits). The following example is a little simulation of trash recycling. All the trash is put into a single bin, then it's sorted out into separate bins. There's a function that goes through any trash bin and figures out what the resource value is. Notice this is not the most elegant way to implement this simulation; the example will be revisited in Chapter 17 when Run-Time Type Identification (RTTI) is explained.

```
//: RECYCLE.CPP -- Containers & polymorphism
#include <fstream.h>
#include <stdlib.h>
#include <time.h>
#include "..\14\tstack.h"
ofstream out("recycle.out");

enum type { Aluminum, Paper, Glass };

class trash {
```

```
  float Weight;
public:
  trash(float Wt) : Weight(Wt) {}
  virtual type trashType() const = 0;
  virtual const char* name() const = 0;
  virtual float value() const = 0;
  float weight() const { return Weight; }
  virtual ~trash() {}
};

class aluminum : public trash {
  static float val;
public:
  aluminum(float Wt) : trash(Wt) {}
  type trashType() const { return Aluminum; }
  virtual const char* name() const {
    return "aluminum";
  }
  float value() const { return val; }
  static void value(int newval) {
    val = newval;
  }
};

float aluminum::val = 1.67;

class paper : public trash {
  static float val;
public:
  paper(float Wt) : trash(Wt) {}
  type trashType() const { return Paper; }
  virtual const char* name() const {
    return "paper";
  }
  float value() const { return val; }
  static void value(int newval) {
    val = newval;
```

```
    }
};

float paper::val = 0.10;

class glass : public trash {
  static float val;
public:
  glass(float Wt) : trash(Wt) {}
  type trashType() const { return Glass; }
  virtual const char* name() const {
    return "glass";
  }
  float value() const { return val; }
  static void value(int newval) {
    val = newval;
  }
};

float glass::val = 0.23;

// Sums up the value of the trash in a bin:
void SumValue(const tstack<trash>& bin,ostream& os){
  tstackIterator<trash> tally(bin);
  float val = 0;
  while(tally) {
    val += tally->weight() * tally->value();
    os << "weight of " << tally->name()
       << " = " << tally->weight() << endl;
    tally++;
  }
  os << "Total value = " << val << endl;
}

main() {
  // Seed the random number generator
  time_t t;
```

```cpp
  srand((unsigned)time(&t));

  tstack<trash> bin; // Default to ownership
  // Fill up the trash bin:
  for(int i = 0; i < 30; i++)
    switch(rand() % 3) {
      case 0 :
        bin.push(new aluminum(rand() % 100));
        break;
      case 1 :
        bin.push(new paper(rand() % 100));
        break;
      case 2 :
        bin.push(new glass(rand() % 100));
        break;
    }
  // Bins to sort into:
  tstack<trash> glassbin(0); // No ownership
  tstack<trash> paperbin(0);
  tstack<trash> ALbin(0);
  tstackIterator<trash> sorter(bin);
  // Sort the trash:
  // (RTTI offers a nicer solution)
  while(sorter) {
    // Smart pointer call:
    switch(sorter->trashType()) {
      case Aluminum:
        ALbin.push(sorter.current());
        break;
      case Paper:
        paperbin.push(sorter.current());
        break;
      case Glass:
        glassbin.push(sorter.current());
        break;
    }
    sorter++;
```

```
        }
    SumValue(ALbin, out);
    SumValue(paperbin, out);
    SumValue(glassbin, out);
    SumValue(bin, out);
}
```

This uses the classic structure of virtual functions in the base class that are redefined in the derived class. The container **tstack** is instantiated for **trash**, so it holds **trash** pointers, which are pointers to the base class. However, it will also hold pointers to objects of classes derived from **trash**, as you can see in the call to **push( )**. When these pointers are added, they lose their specific identities and become simply **trash** pointers (they are *upcast*). However, because of polymorphism the proper behavior still occurs when the virtual function is called through the **tally** and **sorter** iterators. (Notice the use of the iterator's smart pointer, which causes the virtual function call.)

The **trash** class also includes a **virtual** destructor, something you should automatically add to any class with **virtual** functions. When the **bin** container goes out of scope, the container's destructor calls all the **virtual** destructors for the objects it contains, and thus properly cleans everything up.

Because container class templates are rarely subject to the inheritance and upcasting you see with "ordinary" classes, you'll almost never see **virtual** functions in these types of classes. Their reuse is implemented with templates, not with inheritance.

container types

There's a generally accepted set of container classes that correspond roughly to the tools you might have learned about in a "data structures" class. (Of course containers are much more than data structures because they're nothing without their associated functionality.) A container packages the functionality together with the data structure, so it seems a much more natural way to express these concepts.

Although a container may require a particular behavior (for example, you can only add and fetch stack elements from one end), you have much more freedom if you want it by using an iterator. Most of the types listed here can easily support an associated iterator.

All containers allow you to put things in and get things out. They are often differentiated by their function, but some containers seem to be only different types of holders. These are distinguished by their access speed: Some are easier to access linearly, but it's expensive to insert an element in the middle of the sequence; others have cheap insertions but expensive linear access. If you have a choice of this kind, it's best to start with the most flexible approach. If, after the program is working, you discover you haven't used the flexibility but need to optimize, change it out for a more efficient approach.

A subset of the following containers is in the C++ Standard Template Library (STL) which is discussed further in Appendix A:

Bag: Collection of (possibly duplicate) items. No particular order is assumed. Bag is not in the STL because you get this functionality with a vector or list.

Set: A bag that doesn't allow any duplicates. In the STL, this is described as a kind of *associative container* — something that provides retrieval of data based on keys. In a set, the data retrieved is the key itself. An STL *multiset* allows duplicates of the same key value within distinct objects.

Vector: Indexable sequence of items; generally your default choice because it has consistent access time.

Queue: Sequence in which items are added from one end and removed from the opposite end. This is a subset of a deque, and sometimes isn't implemented because you might as well use a deque.

Deque: (Pronounced "deck"): Double-ended queue. Sequence in which items are added and removed from either end. Used instead of a list when most insertions and deletions take place at the beginning or end of a sequence. A deque supports constant-time inserts and deletes at the beginning or end of the sequence, but inserts and deletes in the middle of the sequence require linear time.

Stack: Sequence in which items are added and removed from the same end. Although used as an example in this book, a stack is also just a subset of the functionality of a deque.

Ring: Sequence in which items are added and removed from the top of a circular structure — conceptually, a queue with the front and the back connected. It's usually created to support low-level activities very efficiently and with constant execution time. An example is an interrupt service routine for communication where you need to insert characters and later remove them, but can never run out of storage or worry about the time required to allocate it. Rings can overrun themselves without careful programming. The STL does not contain rings.

List: A rooted sequence of items that allows constant-time insertion and erasure at any point in the sequence. Fast random access is not provided; you use a list when there are frequent insertions and deletions from the middle of the sequence. Lists are generally implemented as *singly linked* and *doubly linked* lists. A singly linked list allows you to pass through it one way, and a doubly linked list allows you to move forward or backward from any point. The primary value of a singly linked list is that it has slightly lower overhead: Each node contains only a single pointer to the next node. (A doubly linked list also has a pointer to the previous node.) Insertions and deletions require slightly less work in a singly linked list than in a doubly linked list.

Dictionary: Mapping of key/value pairs; called a *map* in the STL. (It's another form of associative container.) These key/value pairs are sometimes called *associations*; a dictionary stores and retrieves these associations. You give it a key, and it produces the value associated with that key. The STL also provides a *multimap*, which allows multiple copies of the same key value — this is the equivalent of a *hash table*.

Tree: Collection of nodes and arcs (connections between nodes) with a single root. A tree cannot contain cycles (you can't have a path that takes you around and around) or cross-references. Trees are not provided by the STL; the functionality you need for a tree is generally provided by other STL types.

Binary tree: An ordinary tree has no restriction on the number of arcs that may grow from each node. In a binary tree, only two arcs may come out of a node, often thought of as simply "left" and "right." A binary tree is one of the fastest ways to retrieve information because the nodes are inserted according to their value, and you don't have to look through very many nodes to find what you want (as opposed to searching through a linear list). A "balanced" binary tree is reshuffled on each insertion to keep any part of the tree from growing too far down from the norm, thus causing an extra-long search in that part of the tree. However, the overhead of balancing the tree on each insertion can be high.

Graph: Collection of nodes and arcs without a root. A graph may contain cycles and cross-references. This is generally thought of in a more theoretical sense and is not often implemented. It's not part of the STL.

don't reinvent

Your goal should be to first find these common components in the STL that comes with your compiler or can be easily acquired, or buy them from third-party vendors. Creating them from scratch should be done only as an exercise or last resort.

function templates

A class template describes an infinite set of classes; the most common place you'll see templates is with classes. However, C++ also supports the concept of an infinite set of functions, which is sometimes useful. The syntax is virtually identical, except that you create a function instead of a class.

The clue that you should create a function template is, as you might suspect, if you find you're creating a number of functions that look identical except that they are dealing with different types. The classic example of a function template is a sorting function.[5] However, a function template is useful in all sorts of places, as demonstrated in the first example that follows. The second example shows a function template used with containers and iterators.

a memory allocation system

There are a few things you can do to make the raw memory allocation routines **malloc( )**, **calloc( )**, and **realloc( )** safer. The following function template produces one function **getmem( )** that either allocates a new piece of memory or resizes an existing piece (like **realloc( )**). In addition, it zeroes *only the new memory*, and it checks to see that the memory is successfully allocated. Also, you tell it only the number of elements of the type you want, not the number of bytes, so the possibility of a programmer error is reduced. Here's the header file:

```
//: GETMEM.H -- Function template for memory
#ifndef GETMEM_H_
#define GETMEM_H_
#include <stdlib.h>
```

---

[5] See *C++ Inside & Out* (Osborne/McGraw-Hill, 1993) by the author, Chapter 10.

```
#include <string.h>
#include "..\allege.h"

template<class T>
void getmem(T*& oldmem, int elems) {
  typedef int cntr; // Type of element counter
  const int csz = sizeof(cntr); // And size
  const int Tsz = sizeof(T);
  if(elems == 0) {
    free(&(((cntr*)oldmem)[-1]));
    return;
  }
  T* p = oldmem;
  cntr oldcount = 0;
  if(p) { // Previously allocated memory
    ((cntr*)p)--; // Back up by one cntr
    oldcount = *(cntr*)p; // Previous # elems
  }
  T* m = (T*)realloc(p, elems * Tsz + csz);
  allegemem(m);
  *((cntr*)m) = elems; // Keep track of count
  const cntr increment = elems - oldcount;
  if(increment > 0) {
    // Starting address of data:
    long startadr = (long)&(m[oldcount]);
    startadr += csz;
    // Zero the additional new memory:
    memset((void*)startadr, 0, increment * Tsz);
  }
  // Return the address beyond the count:
  oldmem = (T*)&(((cntr*)m)[1]);
}

template<class T>
inline void freemem(T * m) { getmem(m, 0); }

#endif // GETMEM_H_
```

To be able to zero only the new memory, a counter indicating the number of elements allocated is attached to the beginning of each block of memory. The **typedef cntr** is the type of this counter; it allows you to change from **int** to **long** if you need to handle larger chunks. (Other issues come up when using **long**, however — these are seen in compiler warnings.)

A pointer reference is used for the argument **oldmem** because the outside variable (a pointer) must be changed to point to the new block of memory. **oldmem** must point to zero (to allocate new memory) or to an existing block of memory *that was created with* **getmem( )**. This function assumes you're using it properly, but for debugging you could add an additional tag next to the counter containing an identifier, and check that identifier in **getmem( )** to help discover incorrect calls.

If the number of elements requested is zero, the storage is freed. There's an additional function template **freemem( )** that aliases this behavior.

You'll notice that **getmem( )** is very low-level — there are lots of casts and byte manipulations. For example, the **oldmem** pointer doesn't point to the true beginning of the memory block, but just *past* the beginning to allow for the counter. So to **free( )** the memory block, **getmem( )** must back up the pointer by the amount of space occupied by **cntr**. Because **oldmem** is a **T***, it must first be cast to a **cntr***, then indexed backward one place. Finally the address of that location is produced for **free( )** in the expression

```
free(&(((cntr*)oldmem)[-1]));
```

Similarly, if this is previously allocated memory, **getmem( )** must back up by one **cntr** size to get the true starting address of the memory and extract the previous number of elements. The true starting address is required inside **realloc( )**. If the storage size is being increased, the difference between the new number of elements and the old number is used to calculate the starting address and the amount of memory to zero in **memset( )**. Finally, the address beyond the count is produced to assign to **oldmem** in the statement:

```
oldmem = (T*)&(((cntr*)m)[1]);
```

Again, because **oldmem** is a reference to a pointer, this has the effect of changing the outside argument passed to **getmem( )**.

Here's a program to test **getmem( )**. It allocates storage and fills it up with values, then increases that amount of storage.

```
//: GETMEM.CPP -- Test memory function template
#include "..\14\getmem.h"
#include <iostream.h>

main() {
  int* p = 0;
  getmem(p, 10);
  for(int i = 0; i < 10; i++) {
    cout << p[i] << ' ';
    p[i] = i;
  }
  cout << '\n';
  getmem(p, 20);
  for(int j = 0; j < 20; j++) {
    cout << p[j] << ' ';
    p[j] = j;
  }
  cout << '\n';
  getmem(p, 25);
  for(int k = 0; k < 25; k++)
    cout << p[k] << ' ';
  freemem(p);
  cout << '\n';

  float* f = 0;
  getmem(f, 3);
  for(int u = 0; u < 3; u++) {
```

```
    cout << f[u] << ' ';
    f[u] = u + 3.14159;
  }
  cout << '\n';
  getmem(f, 6);
  for(int v = 0; v < 6; v++)
    cout << f[v] << ' ';
  freemem(f);
}
```

After each **getmem( )**, the values in memory are printed out to show that the new ones have been zeroed.

Notice that a different version of **getmem( )** is instantiated for the **int** and **float** pointers. You might think that because all the manipulations are so low-level, you could get away with a single nontemplate function and pass a **void*&** as **oldmem**. This doesn't work because then the compiler must do a conversion from your type to a **void***. To take the reference, it makes a temporary. This produces an error because you're modifying the temporary pointer, not the pointer you want to change. So the function template is necessary to produce the exact type for the argument.

applying a function to a tstack

Suppose you want to take a **tstack** and apply a function to all the objects it contains. A **tstack** can contain any type of object, so you need a function that works with any type of **tstack** and any type of object it contains:

```
//: APPLIST.CPP -- Apply a function to a tstack
#include "..\14\tstack.h"
#include <iostream.h>

// 0 arguments, any type of return value:
template<class T, class R>
void applist(tstack<T>& tl, R(T::*f)()) {
  tstackIterator<T> it(tl);
```

```
    while(it) {
      (it.current()->*f)();
      it++;
    }
  }

  // 1 argument, any type of return value:
  template<class T, class R, class A>
  void applist(tstack<T>& tl, R(T::*f)(A), A a) {
    tstackIterator<T> it(tl);
    while(it) {
      (it.current()->*f)(a);
      it++;
    }
  }

  // 2 arguments, any type of return value:
  template<class T, class R, class A1, class A2>
  void applist(tstack<T>& tl, R(T::*f)(A1, A2),
      A1 a1, A2 a2) {
    tstackIterator<T> it(tl);
    while(it) {
      (it.current()->*f)(a1, a2);
      it++;
    }
  }

  // Etc., to handle maximum probable arguments

  class gromit { // The techno-dog
    int arf;
  public:
    gromit(int Arf = 1) : arf(Arf + 1) {}
    void speak(int) {
      for(int i = 0; i < arf; i++)
        cout << "arf! ";
      cout << endl;
```

```
    }
    char eat(float) {
      cout << "chomp!" << endl;
      return 'z';
    }
    int sleep(char, double) {
      cout << "zzz..." << endl;
      return 0;
    }
    void sit(void) {}
};

main() {
  tstack<gromit> dogs;
  for(int i = 0; i < 5; i++)
    dogs.push(new gromit(i));
  applist(dogs, &gromit::speak, 1);
  applist(dogs, &gromit::eat, 2.0f);
  applist(dogs, &gromit::sleep, 'z', 3.0);
  applist(dogs, &gromit::sit);
}
```

The **applist( )** function template takes a reference to the container class and a pointer-to-member for a function contained in the class. It uses an iterator to move through the **stack** and apply the function to every object. If you've (understandably) forgotten the pointer-to-member syntax, you can refresh your memory at the end of Chapter 9.

You can see there is more than one version of **applist( )**, so it's possible to overload function templates. Although they all take any type of return value (which is ignored, but the type information is required to match the pointer-to-member), each version takes a different number of arguments, and because it's a template, those arguments can be of any type. (You can see different sets of functions in class **gromit**.)[6] The only limitation here is that there's no "super template" to create templates for you; thus you must decide how many arguments will ever be required.

Although the definition of **applist( )** is fairly complex and not something you'd ever expect a novice to understand, its use is remarkably clean and simple, and a novice could easily use it knowing only *what* it is intended to accomplish, not *how*. This is the type of division you should strive for in all of your program components: The tough details are all isolated on the designer's side of the wall, and users are concerned only with accomplishing their goals, and don't see, know about, or depend on details of the underlying implementation

Of course, this type of functionality is strongly tied to the **tstack** class, so you'd normally find these function templates in the header file along with **tstack**.

member function templates

It's also possible to make **applist( )** a *member function template* of the class, that is, a separate template definition from the class's template, and yet a member of the class. Thus, you can end up with the cleaner syntax:

```
dogs.applist(&gromit::sit);
```

This is analogous to the act (in Chapter 1) of bringing ordinary functions inside a class.[7]

---

[6] A reference to the British animated short *The Wrong Trousers* by Nick Park.

[7] Check your compiler version information to see if it supports member function templates.

controlling instantiation

At times it is useful to explicitly instantiate a template; that is, to tell the compiler to lay down the code for a specific version of that template even though you're not creating an object at that point. To do this, you reuse the **template** keyword as follows:

```
template class bobbin<thread>;
template void sort<char>(char*[]);
```

Here's a version of the SORTED.CPP example (page 622) that explicitly instantiates a template before using it:

```
//: GENERATE.CPP -- Explicit instantiation
#include "..\14\sorted.h"
#include "..\14\integer.h"
// Explicit instantiation:
template class sorted<integer>;

main() {
  sorted<integer> is;
  urand<47> rand1;
  for(int k = 0; k < 15; k++)
    is.add(new integer(rand1()));
  for(int l = 0; l < is.count(); l++)
    cout << *is[l] << endl;
}
```

In this example, the explicit instantiation doesn't really accomplish anything; the program would work the same without it. Explicit instantiation is only for special cases where extra control is needed.

template specialization

The **sorted** vector only works with objects of user-defined types. It won't instantiate properly to sort an array of **char***, for example. To create a special version you write the instantiation yourself as if the compiler had gone through and substituted your type(s) for the

---

template argument(s). But you put your own code in the function bodies of the specialization. Here's an example that shows a **char*** for the **sorted** vector:

```
//: SPECIAL.CPP -- Template specialization
// A special sort for char*
#include "..\14\sorted.h"
#include <iostream.h>
class sorted<char> :  public tstash<char> {
  void bubblesort();
public:
  int add(char* element) {
    tstash<char>::add(element);
    bubblesort();
    return 0; // Sort moves the element
  }
};

void sorted<char>::bubblesort() {
  for(int i = count(); i > 0; i--)
    for(int j = 1; j < i; j++)
      if(strcmp(storage[j], storage[j-1]) < 0) {
        // Swap the two elements:
        char* t = storage[j-1];
        storage[j-1] = storage[j];
        storage[j] = t;
      }
}

char* words[] = {
  "is", "running", "big", "dog", "a",
};
const wsz = sizeof words/sizeof *words;

main() {
  sorted<char>`sc;
  for(int k = 0; k < wsz; k++)
```

```
        sc.add(words[k]);
    for(int l = 0; l < sc.count(); l++)
        cout << sc[l] << endl;
}
```

In the **bubblesort( )** you can see that **strcmp( )** is used instead
of **>**.

summary

Container classes are an essential part of object-oriented
programming; they are another way to simplify and hide the details
of a program and to speed the process of program development. In
addition, they provide a great deal of safety and flexibility by
replacing the primitive arrays and relatively crude data structure
techniques found in C.

Because the client programmer needs containers, it's essential that
they be easy to use. This is where the **template** comes in. With
templates the syntax for source-code reuse (as opposed to object-
code reuse provided by inheritance and composition) becomes
trivial enough for the novice user. In fact, reusing code with
templates is notably easier than inheritance and composition.

Although you've learned about creating container and iterator
classes in this book, in practice it's much more expedient to learn
the containers and iterators that come with your compiler or, failing
that, to buy a library from a third-party vendor.[8] The standard C++
library includes a very complete but nonexhaustive set of
containers and iterators.

---

[8] See, for example, Rogue Wave, which has a well-designed set of
C++ tools for all platforms.

The issues involved with container-class design have been touched upon in this chapter, but you may have gathered that they can go much further. A complicated container-class library may cover all sorts of additional issues, including persistence (introduced in Chapter 15) and garbage collection (introduced in Chapter 11), as well as additional ways to handle the ownership problem.

exercises

1. Modify the result of Exercise 1 from Chapter 13 to use a **tstack** and **tstackIterator** instead of an array of **shape** pointers. Add destructors to the class hierarchy so you can see that the **shape** objects are destroyed when the **tstack** goes out of scope.

2. Modify the SSHAPE2.CPP example from Chapter 13 to use **tstack** instead of an array.

3. Modify RECYCLE.CPP to use a **tstash** instead of a **tstack**.

4. Change SETTEST.CPP to use a **sortedSet** instead of a **set**.

5. Duplicate the functionality of APPLIST.CPP for the **tstash** class.

6. Copy TSTACK.H to a new header file and add the function templates in APPLIST.CPP as *member* function templates of **tstack**. You can do this exercise only if your compiler supports member function templates.

7. (Advanced) Modify the **tstack** class to further increase the granularity of ownership. Add a flag to each link indicating whether that link owns the object it points to, and support this information in the **add( )** function and destructor. Add member functions to read and change the ownership for each link, and decide what the **owns** flag means in this new context.

8. (Advanced) Modify the **tstack** class so each entry contains reference-counting information (*not* the objects they contain), and add member functions to support the reference counting behavior.

9. (Advanced) Change the underlying implementation of **urand** in SORTED.CPP so it is space-efficient (as described in the paragraph following SORTED.CPP) rather than time-efficient.

10. (Advanced) Change the **typedef cntr** from an **int** to a **long** in GETMEM.H and modify the code to eliminate the resulting warning messages about the loss of precision. This is a pointer arithmetic problem.

11. (Advanced) Devise a test to compare the execution speed of an **SString** created on the stack versus one created on the heap.

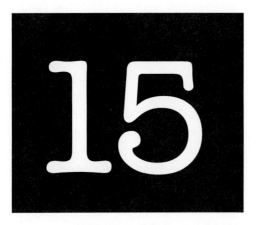

multiple inheritance

The basic concept of multiple inheritance (MI) sounds simple enough.

You create a new type by inheriting from more than one base class. The syntax is exactly what you'd expect, and as long as the inheritance diagrams are simple, MI is simple as well.

However, MI can introduce a number of ambiguities and strange situations, which are covered in this chapter. But first, it helps to get a perspective on the subject.

perspective

Before C++, the most successful object-oriented language was Smalltalk. Smalltalk was created from the ground up as an OO language. It is often referred to as *pure,* whereas C++, because it was built on top of C, is called *hybrid.* One of the design decisions made with Smalltalk was that all classes would be derived in a single hierarchy, rooted in a single base class (called **Object** — this is the model for the *object-based hierarchy*). You cannot create a new class in Smalltalk without inheriting it from an existing class, which is why it takes a certain amount of time to become productive in Smalltalk — you must learn the class library before you can start making new classes. So the Smalltalk class hierarchy is always a single monolithic tree.

Classes in Smalltalk usually have a number of things in common, and always have *some* things in common (the characteristics and behaviors of **Object**), so you almost never run into a situation where you need to inherit from more than one base class. However, with C++ you can create as many hierarchy trees as you want. Therefore, for logical completeness the language must be able to combine more than one class at a time — thus the need for multiple inheritance.

However, this was not a crystal-clear case of a feature that no one could live without, and there was (and still is) a lot of disagreement about whether MI is really essential in C++. MI was added in AT&T **cfront** release 2.0 and was the first significant change to the language. Since then, a number of other features have been added (notably templates) that change the way we think about programming and place MI in a much less important role. You can think of MI as a "minor" language feature that shouldn't be involved in your daily design decisions.

One of the most pressing issues that drove MI involved containers. Suppose you want to create a container that everyone can easily use. One approach is to use **void*** as the type inside the container, as with **pstash** and **stack**. The Smalltalk approach, however, is to make a container that holds **Object**s. (Remember that **Object** is the base type of the entire Smalltalk hierarchy.) Because everything in Smalltalk is ultimately derived from **Object**, any container that holds **Object**s can hold anything, so this approach works nicely.

Now consider the situation in C++. Suppose vendor **A** creates an object-based hierarchy that includes a useful set of containers including one you want to use called **holder**. Now you come across vendor **B**'s class hierarchy that contains some other class that is important to you, a **BitImage** class, for example, which holds graphic images. The only way to make a **holder** of **BitImage**s is to inherit a new class from both **Object**, so it can be held in the **holder**, and **BitImage**:

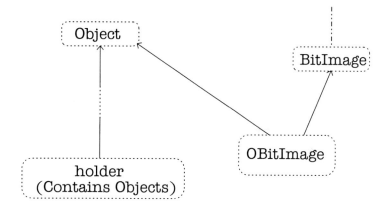

This was seen as an important reason for MI, and a number of class libraries were built on this model. However, as you saw in Chapter 14, the addition of templates has changed the way containers are created, so this situation isn't a driving issue for MI.

The other reason you may need MI is logical, related to design. Unlike the above situation, where you don't have control of the base classes, in this one you do, and you intentionally use MI to make the design more flexible or useful. (At least, you may believe this to be the case.) An example of this is in the original iostream library design:

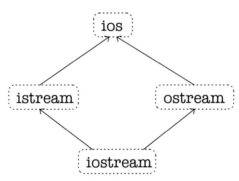

Both **istream** and **ostream** are useful classes by themselves, but they can also be inherited into a class that combines both their characteristics and behaviors.

Regardless of what motivates you to use MI, a number of problems arise in the process, and you need to understand them to use it.

duplicate subobjects

When you inherit from a base class, you get a copy of all the data members of that base class in your derived class. This copy is referred to as a *subobject*. If you multiply inherit from class **d1** and class **d2** into class **mi**, class **mi** contains one subobject of **d1** and one of **d2**. So your **mi** object looks like this:

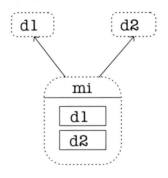

Now consider what happens if **d1** and **d2** both inherit from the same base class, called **base**:

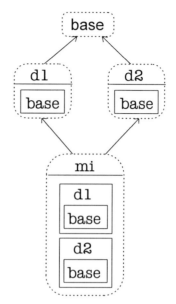

In the above diagram, both **d1** and **d2** contain a subobject of **base**, so **mi** contains *two* subobjects of **base**. Because of the path produced in the diagram, this is sometimes called a "diamond" in the inheritance hierarchy. Without diamonds, multiple inheritance is quite straightforward, but as soon as a diamond appears, trouble starts because you have duplicate subobjects in your new class. This takes up extra space, which may or may not be a problem depending on your design. But it also introduces an ambiguity.

ambiguous upcasting

What happens, in the above diagram, if you want to cast a pointer to an **mi** to a pointer to a **base**? There are two subobjects of type **base**, so which address does the cast produce? Here's the diagram in code:

```
//: MULTIPL1.CPP -- MI & ambiguity
#include <iostream.h>
```

```
#include "..\14\tstash.h"

class base {
public:
  virtual char* vf() const = 0;
};

class d1 : public base {
public:
  char* vf() const { return "d1"; }
};

class d2 : public base {
public:
  char* vf() const { return "d2"; }
};

// Causes error: ambiguous override of vf():
//! class mi : public d1, public d2 {};

main() {
  tstash<base> b;
  b.add(new d1);
  b.add(new d2);
  // Cannot upcast: which subobject?:
//!  b.add(new mi);
  for(int i = 0; i < b.count(); i++)
    cout << b[i]->vf() << endl;
}
```

Two problems occur here. First, you cannot even create the class **mi** because doing so would cause a clash between the two definitions of **vf( )** in **d1** and **d2**.

Second, in the array definition for **b[]** this code attempts to create a **new mi** and upcast the address to a **base***. The compiler won't accept this because it has no way of knowing whether you want to use **d1**'s subobject **base** or **d2**'s subobject **base** for the resulting address.

virtual base classes

To solve the first problem, you must explicitly disambiguate the function **vf( )** by writing a redefinition in the class **mi**.

The solution to the second problem is a language extension: The meaning of the **virtual** keyword is overloaded. If you inherit a base class as **virtual**, only one subobject of that class will ever appear as a base class. Virtual base classes are implemented by the compiler with pointer magic in a way suggesting the implementation of ordinary virtual functions.

Because only one subobject of a virtual base class will ever appear during multiple inheritance, there is no ambiguity during upcasting. Here's an example:

```
//: MULTIPL2.CPP -- Virtual Base Classes
#include <iostream.h>
#include "..\14\tstash.h"

class base {
public:
  virtual char* vf() const = 0;
};

class d1 : virtual public base {
public:
  char* vf() const { return "d1"; }
};

class d2 : virtual public base {
public:
  char* vf() const { return "d2"; }
};
```

```
// MUST explicitly disambiguate vf():
class mi : public d1, public d2 {
public:
   char* vf() const { return d1::vf();}
};

main() {
   tstash<base> b;
   b.add(new d1);
   b.add(new d2);
   b.add(new mi); // OK
   for(int i = 0; i < b.count(); i++)
      cout << b[i]->vf() << endl;
}
```

The compiler now accepts the upcast, but notice that you must still explicitly disambiguate the function **vf( )** in **mi**; otherwise the compiler wouldn't know which version to use.

the "most derived" class and virtual base initialization

The use of virtual base classes isn't quite as simple as that. The above example uses the compiler-synthesized default constructor. If the virtual base has a constructor, things become a bit strange. To understand this, you need a new term: *most-derived* class.

The most-derived class is the one you're currently in, and is particularly important when you're thinking about constructors. In the previous example, **base** is the most-derived class inside the **base** constructor. Inside the **d1** constructor, **d1** is the most-derived class, and inside the **mi** constructor, **mi** is the most-derived class.

When you are using a virtual base class, the most-derived constructor is responsible for initializing that virtual base class. That means any class, no matter how far away it is from the virtual base, is responsible for initializing it. Here's an example:

```
//: MULTIPL3.CPP -- Virtual base initialization
// Virtual base classes must always be
// Intialized by the "most-derived" class
#include <iostream.h>
#include "..\14\tstash.h"

class base {
public:
  base(int) {}
  virtual char* vf() const = 0;
};

class d1 : virtual public base {
public:
  d1() : base(1) {}
  char* vf() const { return "d1"; }
};

class d2 : virtual public base {
public:
  d2() : base(2) {}
  char* vf() const { return "d2"; }
};

class mi : public d1, public d2 {
public:
  mi() : base(3) {}
  char* vf() const {
    return d1::vf(); // MUST disambiguate
  }
};

class x : public mi {
public:
```

```
  // You must ALWAYS init the virtual base:
  x() : base(4) {}
};

main() {
  tstash<base> b;
  b.add(new d1);
  b.add(new d2);
  b.add(new mi); // OK
  b.add(new x);
  for(int i = 0; i < b.count(); i++)
    cout << b[i]->vf() << endl;
}
```

As you would expect, both **d1** and **d2** must initialize **base** in their constructor. But so must **mi** and **x**, even though they are more than one layer away! That's because each one in turn becomes the most-derived class. The compiler can't know whether to use **d1**'s initialization of **base** or to use **d2**'s version. Thus you are always forced to do it in the most-derived class. Note that only the single selected virtual base constructor is called.

"tying off" virtual bases with a default constructor

Forcing the most-derived class to initialize a virtual base that may be buried deep in the class hierarchy can seem like a tedious and confusing task to put upon the client programmer of your class. It's better to make this invisible, which is done by creating a default constructor for the virtual base class, like this:

```
//: MULTIPL4.CPP -- "Tying off" virtual bases
// so you don't have to worry about them
// in derived classes
#include <iostream.h>
#include "..\14\tstash.h"
```

```
class base {
public:
 // Default constructor removes responsibility:
  base(int = 0) {}
  virtual char* vf() const = 0;
};

class d1 : virtual public base {
public:
  d1() : base(1) {}
  char* vf() const { return "d1"; }
};

class d2 : virtual public base {
public:
  d2() : base(2) {}
  char* vf() const { return "d2"; }
};

class mi : public d1, public d2 {
public:
  mi() {} // Calls default constructor for base
  char* vf() const {
    return d1::vf(); // MUST disambiguate
  }
};

class x : public mi {
public:
  x() {} // Calls default constructor for base
};

main() {
  tstash<base> b;
  b.add(new d1);
  b.add(new d2);
  b.add(new mi); // OK
```

```
  b.add(new x);
  for(int i = 0; i < b.count(); i++)
    cout << b[i]->vf() << endl;
}
```

If you can always arrange for a virtual base class to have a default
constructor, you'll make things much easier for anyone who
inherits from that class.

overhead

The term "pointer magic" has been used to describe the way virtual
inheritance is implemented. You can see the physical overhead of
virtual inheritance with the following program:

```
//: OVERHEAD.CPP -- Virtual base class overhead
#include <fstream.h>
ofstream out("overhead.out");

class base {
public:
  virtual void f() const {};
};

class nonvirtual_inheritance
  : public base {};

class virtual_inheritance
  : virtual public base {};

class virtual_inheritance2
  : virtual public base {};

class mi
  : public virtual_inheritance,
    public virtual_inheritance2 {};
```

```
#define WRITE(arg) \
out << #arg << " = " << arg << endl;

main() {
  base b;
  WRITE(sizeof(b));
  nonvirtual_inheritance nonv_inheritance;
  WRITE(sizeof(nonv_inheritance));
  virtual_inheritance v_inheritance;
  WRITE(sizeof(v_inheritance));
  mi MI;
  WRITE(sizeof(MI));
}
```

Each of these classes contains a single byte, and the "core size" is that byte. Because all these classes contain virtual functions, you expect the object size to be bigger than the core size by a pointer (at least — your compiler may also pad extra bytes into an object for alignment). The results are a bit surprising. (These are from one particular compiler; yours may do it differently.)

```
sizeof(b) = 2
sizeof(nonv_inheritance) = 2
sizeof(v_inheritance) = 6
sizeof(MI) = 12
```

Both **b** and **nonv_inheritance** contain the extra pointer, as expected. But when virtual inheritance is added, it would appear that the VPTR and *two extra pointers* are added! By the time the multiple inheritance is performed, the object appears to contain five extra pointers. (However, one of these is probably a second VPTR for the second multiply inherited subobject.)

The curious can certainly probe into your particular implementation and look at the assembly language for member selection to

---

determine exactly what these extra bytes are for, and the cost of member selection with multiple inheritance[1]. The rest of you have probably seen enough to guess that quite a bit more goes on with virtual multiple inheritance, so it should be used sparingly (or avoided) when efficiency is an issue.

upcasting

When you embed subobjects of a class inside a new class, whether you do it by creating member objects or through inheritance, each subobject is placed within the new object by the compiler. Of course, each subobject has its own **this** pointer, and as long as you're dealing with member objects, everything is quite straightforward. But as soon as multiple inheritance is introduced, a funny thing occurs: An object can have more than one **this** pointer because the object represents more than one type during upcasting. The following example demonstrates this point:

```
//: MITHIS.CPP -- MI and the "this" pointer
#include <fstream.h>
ofstream out("mithis.out");

class base1 {
  char c[0x10];
public:
  void printthis1() {
    out << "base1 this = " << this << endl;
  }
};

class base2 {
  char c[0x10];
```

---

[1] See also Jan Gray, *"C++ Under the Hood"*, a chapter in *Black Belt C++* (edited by Bruce Eckel, M&T Press, 1995).

```
public:
  void printthis2() {
    out << "base2 this = " << this << endl;
  }
};

class member1 {
  char c[0x10];
public:
  void printthism1() {
    out << "member1 this = " << this << endl;
  }
};

class member2 {
  char c[0x10];
public:
  void printthism2() {
    out << "member2 this = " << this << endl;
  }
};

class mi : public base1, public base2 {
  member1 m1;
  member2 m2;
public:
  void printthis() {
    out << "mi this = " << this << endl;
    printthis1();
    printthis2();
    m1.printthism1();
    m2.printthism2();
  }
};

main() {
  mi MI;
```

```
out << "sizeof(mi) = "
    << hex << sizeof(mi) << " hex" << endl;
MI.printthis();
// A second demonstration:
base1* b1 = &MI; // Upcast
base2* b2 = &MI; // Upcast
out << "base 1 pointer = " << b1 << endl;
out << "base 2 pointer = " << b2 << endl;
}
```

The arrays of bytes inside each class are created with hexadecimal sizes, so the output addresses (which are printed in hex) are easy to read. Each class has a function that prints its **this** pointer, and these classes are assembled with both multiple inheritance and composition into the class **mi,** which prints its own address and the addresses of all the other subobjects. This function is called in **main( )**. You can see clearly that you get two different **this** pointers for the same object. The address of the **mi** object is taken and upcast to the two different types. Here's the output:[2]

```
sizeof(mi) = 40 hex
mi this = 0x223e
base1 this = 0x223e
base2 this = 0x224e
member1 this = 0x225e
member2 this = 0x226e
base 1 pointer = 0x223e
base 2 pointer = 0x224e
```

Although object layouts vary from compiler to compiler and are not specified in Standard C++, this one is fairly typical. The starting address of the object corresponds to the address of the first class in

---

[2] For easy readability the code was generated for a small-model Intel processor.

the base-class list. Then the second inherited class is placed, followed by the member objects in order of declaration.

When the upcast to the **base1** and **base2** pointers occur, you can see that, even though they're ostensibly pointing to the same object, they must actually have different **this** pointers, so the proper starting address can be passed to the member functions of each subobject. The only way things can work correctly is if this implicit upcasting takes place when you call a member function for a multiply inherited subobject.

persistence

Normally this isn't a problem, because you want to call member functions that are concerned with that subobject of the multiply inherited object. However, if your member function needs to know the true starting address of the object, multiple inheritance causes problems. Ironically, this happens in one of the situations where multiple inheritance seems to be useful: *persistence*.

The lifetime of a local object is the scope in which it is defined. The lifetime of a global object is the lifetime of the program. A *persistent object* lives between invocations of a program: You can normally think of it as existing on disk instead of in memory. One definition of an object-oriented database is "a collection of persistent objects."

To implement persistence, you must move a persistent object from disk into memory in order to call functions for it, and later store it to disk before the program expires. Four issues arise when storing an object on disk:

1. The object must be converted from its representation in memory to a series of bytes on disk.

2. Because the values of any pointers in memory won't have meaning the next time the program is invoked, these pointers must be converted to something meaningful.

3. What the pointers *point to* must also be stored and retrieved.

4. When restoring an object from disk, the virtual pointers in the object must be respected.

Because the object must be converted back and forth between a layout in memory and a serial representation on disk, the process is called *serialization* (to write an object to disk) and *deserialization* (to restore an object from disk). Although it would be very convenient, these processes require too much overhead to support directly in the language. Class libraries will often build in support for serialization and deserialization by adding special member functions and placing requirements on new classes. (Usually some sort of **serialize( )** function must be written for each new class.) Also, persistence is generally not automatic; you must usually explicitly write and read the objects.

MI-based persistence

Consider sidestepping the pointer issues for now and creating a class that installs persistence into simple objects using multiple inheritance. By inheriting the **persistence** class along with your new class, you automatically create classes that can be read from and written to disk. Although this sounds great, the use of multiple inheritance introduces a pitfall, as seen in the following example.

```
//: PERSIST1.CPP -- Simple persistence with MI
#include <fstream.h>

class persistent {
  int objSize; // Size of stored object
public:
  persistent(int sz) : objSize(sz) {}
  void write(ostream& out) const {
    out.write((char*)this, objSize);
  }
  void read(istream& in) {
    in.read((char*)this, objSize);
  }
};
```

```
class data {
  float f[3];
public:
  data(float f0 = 0.0, float f1 = 0.0,
    float f2 = 0.0) {
    f[0] = f0;
    f[1] = f1;
    f[2] = f2;
  }
  void print(const char* msg = "") const {
    if(*msg) cout << msg << "   ";
    for(int i = 0; i < 3; i++)
      cout << "f[" << i << "] = "
          << f[i] << endl;
  }
};

class wdata1 : public persistent, public data {
public:
  wdata1(float f0 = 0.0, float f1 = 0.0,
    float f2 = 0.0) : data(f0, f1, f2),
    persistent(sizeof(wdata1)) {}
};

class wdata2 : public data, public persistent {
public:
  wdata2(float f0 = 0.0, float f1 = 0.0,
    float f2 = 0.0) : data(f0, f1, f2),
    persistent(sizeof(wdata2)) {}
};

main() {
  {
    ofstream f1("f1.dat"), f2("f2.dat");
    wdata1 d1(1.1, 2.2, 3.3);
    wdata2 d2(4.4, 5.5, 6.6);
    d1.print("d1 before storage");
```

```
    d2.print("d2 before storage");
    d1.write(f1);
    d2.write(f2);
  } // Closes files
  ifstream f1("f1.dat"), f2("f2.dat");
  wdata1 d1;
  wdata2 d2;
  d1.read(f1);
  d2.read(f2);
  d1.print("d1 after storage");
  d2.print("d2 after storage");
}
```

In this very simple version, the **persistent::read( )** and **persistent::write( )** functions take the **this** pointer and call **iostream read( )** and **write( )** functions. (Note that any type of **iostream** can be used). A more sophisticated **persistent** class would call a **virtual write( )** function for each subobject.

With the language features covered so far in the book, the number of bytes in the object cannot be known by the persistent class so it is inserted as a constructor argument. (In Chapter 17, *run-time type identification* shows how you can find the exact type of an object given only a base pointer; once you have the exact type you can find out the correct size with the **sizeof** operator.)

The **data** class contains no pointers or VPTR, so there is no danger in simply writing it to disk and reading it back again. And it works fine in class **wdata1** when, in **main( )**, it's written to file F1.DAT and later read back again. However, when **persistent** is put second in the inheritance list in class **wdata1**, the **this** pointer for **persistent** is offset to the end of the object, so it reads and writes past the end of the object. This not only produces garbage when reading the object from the file, it's dangerous because it walks over any storage that occurs after the object.

This problem occurs in multiple inheritance any time a class must produce the **this** pointer for the actual object from a subobject's

this pointer. Of course, if you know your compiler always lays out objects in order of declaration in the inheritance list, you can ensure that you always put the critical class at the beginning of the list (assuming there's only one critical class). However, such a class may exist in the inheritance hierarchy of another class and you may unwittingly put it in the wrong place during multiple inheritance. Fortunately, using run-time type identification (the subject of Chapter 17) will produce the proper pointer to the actual object, even if multiple inheritance is used.

improved persistence

A more practical approach to persistence, and one you will see employed more often, is to create virtual functions in the base class for reading and writing and then require the creator of any new class that must be streamed to redefine these functions. The argument to the function is the stream object to write to or read from.[3] Then the creator of the class, who knows best how the new parts should be read or written, is responsible for making the correct function calls. This doesn't have the "magical" quality of the previous example, and it requires more coding and knowledge on the part of the user, but it works and doesn't break when pointers are present.

```
//: PERSIST2.CPP -- Improved MI persistence
#include <fstream.h>
#include <string.h>

class persistent {
public:
  virtual void write(ostream& out) const = 0;
  virtual void read(istream& in) = 0;
};
```

---

[3] Sometimes there's only a single function for streaming, and the argument contains information about whether you're reading or writing.

```
class data {
protected:
  float f[3];
public:
  data(float f0 = 0.0, float f1 = 0.0,
    float f2 = 0.0) {
    f[0] = f0;
    f[1] = f1;
    f[2] = f2;
  }
  void print(const char* msg = "") const {
    if(*msg) cout << msg << endl;
    for(int i = 0; i < 3; i++)
      cout << "f[" << i << "] = "
           << f[i] << endl;
  }
};

class wdata1 : public persistent, public data {
public:
  wdata1(float f0 = 0.0, float f1 = 0.0,
    float f2 = 0.0) : data(f0, f1, f2) {}
  void write(ostream& out) const {
    out << f[0] << " " << f[1] << " " << f[2];
  }
  void read(istream& in) {
    in >> f[0] >> f[1] >> f[2];
  }
};

class wdata2 : public data, public persistent {
public:
  wdata2(float f0 = 0.0, float f1 = 0.0,
    float f2 = 0.0) : data(f0, f1, f2) {}
  void write(ostream& out) const {
    out << f[0] << " " << f[1] << " " << f[2];
```

```
    }
  void read(istream& in) {
    in >> f[0] >> f[1] >> f[2];
  }
};

class conglomerate : public data,
public persistent {
  char* name; // Contains a pointer
  wdata1 d1;
  wdata2 d2;
public:
  conglomerate(const char* nm = "",
    float f0 = 0.0, float f1 = 0.0,
    float f2 = 0.0, float f3 = 0.0,
    float f4 = 0.0, float f5 = 0.0,
    float f6 = 0.0, float f7 = 0.0,
    float f8= 0.0) : data(f0, f1, f2),
    d1(f3, f4, f5), d2(f6, f7, f8) {
    name = new char[strlen(nm) + 1];
    strcpy(name, nm);
  }
  void write(ostream& out) const {
    int i = strlen(name) + 1;
    out << i << " "; // Store size of string
    out << name << endl;
    d1.write(out);
    d2.write(out);
    out << f[0] << " " << f[1] << " " << f[2];
  }
  // Must read in reverse order as write:
  void read(istream& in) {
    delete []name; // Remove old storage
    int i;
    in >> i >> ws; // Get int, strip whitespace
    name = new char[i];
    in.getline(name, i);
```

```
      d1.read(in);
      d2.read(in);
      in >> f[0] >> f[1] >> f[2];
    }
  void print() const {
    data::print(name);
    d1.print();
    d2.print();
    }
};

main() {
  {
    ofstream data("data.dat");
    conglomerate C("This is conglomerate C",
        1.1, 2.2, 3.3, 4.4, 5.5,
        6.6, 7.7, 8.8, 9.9);
    cout << "C before storage" << endl;
    C.print();
    C.write(data);
  } // Closes file
  ifstream data("data.dat");
  conglomerate C;
  C.read(data);
  cout << "after storage: " << endl;
  C.print();
}
```

The pure virtual functions in **persistent** must be redefined in the derived classes to perform the proper reading and writing. If you already knew that **data** would be persistent, you could inherit directly from **persistent** and redefine the functions there, thus eliminating the need for multiple inheritance. This example is based on the idea that you don't own the code for **data**, that it was created elsewhere and may be part of another class hierarchy so you don't have control over its inheritance. However, for this scheme to work correctly, you must have access to the underlying implementation so it can be stored; thus the use of **protected**.

The classes **wdata1** and **wdata2** use familiar iostream inserters and extractors to store and retrieve the **protected** data in **data** to and from the iostream object. In **write( )**, you can see that spaces are added after each floating point number is written; these are necessary to allow parsing of the data on input.

The class **conglomerate** not only inherits from **data**, it also has member objects of type **wdata1** and **wdata2**, as well as a pointer to a character string. In addition, all the classes that inherit from **persistent** also contain a VPTR, so this example shows the kind of problem you'll actually encounter when using persistence.

When you create **write( )** and **read( )** function pairs, the **read( )** must exactly mirror what happens during the **write( )**, so **read( )** pulls the bits off the disk the same way they were placed there by **write( )**. Here, the first problem that's tackled is the **char***, which points to a string of any length. The size of the string is calculated and stored on disk as an **int** (followed by a space to enable parsing) to allow the **read( )** function to allocate the correct amount of storage.

When you have subobjects that have **read( )** and **write( )** member functions, all you need to do is call those functions in the new **read( )** and **write( )** functions. This is followed by direct storage of the members in the base class.

People have gone to great lengths to automate persistence, for example, by creating modified preprocessors to support a "persistent" keyword to be applied when defining a class. One can imagine a more elegant approach than the one shown here for implementing persistence, but it has the advantage that it works under all implementations of C++, doesn't require special language extensions, and is relatively bulletproof.

avoiding MI

The need for multiple inheritance in PERSIST2.CPP is contrived, based on the concept that you don't have control of some of the code in the project. Upon examination of the example, you can see that MI can be easily avoided by using member objects of type **data** and putting the virtual **read( )** and **write( )** members inside **data** or **wdata1** and **wdata2** rather than in a separate class. There are many situations like this one where multiple inheritance may be avoided; the language feature is included for unusual, special-case situations that would otherwise be difficult or impossible to handle. But when the question of whether to use multiple inheritance comes up, you should ask two questions:

1. Do I need to show the public interfaces of both these classes, or could one class be embedded with some of its interface produced with member functions in the new class?

2. Do I need to upcast to both of the base classes? (This applies when you have more than two base classes, of course.)

If you can't answer "no" to both questions, you can avoid using MI and should probably do so.

One situation to watch for is when one class only needs to be upcast as a function argument. In that case, the class can be embedded and an automatic type conversion operator provided in your new class to produce a reference to the embedded object. Any time you use an object of your new class as an argument to a function that expects the embedded object, the type conversion operator is used. However, type conversion can't be used for normal member selection; that requires inheritance.

repairing an interface

One of the best arguments for multiple inheritance involves code that's out of your control. Suppose you've acquired a library that consists of a header file and compiled member functions, but no source code for member functions. This library is a class hierarchy with virtual functions, and it contains some global functions that take pointers to the base class of the library; that is, it uses the library objects polymorphically. Now suppose you build an application around this library, and write your own code that uses the base class polymorphically.

Later in the development of the project or sometime during its maintenance, you discover that the base-class interface provided by the vendor is incomplete: A function may be nonvirtual and you need it to be virtual, or a virtual function is completely missing in the interface, but essential to the solution of your problem. If you had the source code, you could go back and put it in. But you don't, and you have a lot of existing code that depends on the original interface. Here, multiple inheritance is the perfect solution.

For example, here's the header file for a library you acquire:

```
//: VENDOR.H -- Vendor-suppplied class header
// You only get this & the compiled VENDOR.OBJ
#ifndef VENDOR_H_
#define VENDOR_H_

class vendor {
public:
  virtual void v() const;
  void f() const;
  ~vendor();
};

class vendor1 : public vendor {
public:
```

```
    void v() const;
    void f() const;
    ~vendor1();
};

void A(const vendor&);
void B(const vendor&);
// Etc.
#endif // VENDOR_H_
```

Assume the library is much bigger, with more derived classes and a
larger interface. Notice that it also includes the functions **A( )** and
B( ), which take a base pointer and treat it polymorphically. Here's
the implementation file for the library:

```
//: VENDOR.CPP -- Implementation of VENDOR.H
// This is compiled and unavailable to you
#include <fstream.h>
#include "..\15\vendor.h"

extern ofstream out; // For trace info

void vendor::v() const {
  out << "vendor::v()\n";
}

void vendor::f() const {
  out << "vendor::f()\n";
}

vendor::~vendor() {
  out << "~vendor()\n";
}

void vendor1::v() const {
  out << "vendor1::v()\n";
}
```

```
void vendor1::f() const {
  out << "vendor1::f()\n";
}

vendor1::~vendor1() {
  out << "~vendor1()\n";
}

void A(const vendor& V) {
  // ...
  V.v();
  V.f();
  //...
}

void B(const vendor& V) {
  // ...
  V.v();
  V.f();
  //...
}
```

In your project, this source code is unavailable to you. Instead, you get a compiled file as VENDOR.OBJ or VENDOR.LIB (or the equivalent for your system).

The problem occurs in the use of this library. First, the destructor isn't virtual. This is actually a design error on the part of the library creator. In addition, **f( )** was not made virtual; assume the library creator decided it wouldn't need to be. And you discover that the interface to the base class is missing a function essential to the solution of your problem. Also suppose you've already written a fair amount of code using the existing interface (not to mention the functions **A( )** and **B( ),** which are out of your control), and you don't want to change it.

To repair the problem, create your own class interface and multiply inherit a new set of derived classes from your interface and from the existing classes:

```
//: PASTE.CPP -- Fixing a mess with MI
#include <fstream.h>
#include "..\15\vendor.h"

ofstream out("paste.out");

class mybase { // Repair vendor interface
public:
  virtual void v() const = 0;
  virtual void f() const = 0;
  // New interface function:
  virtual void g() const = 0;
  virtual ~mybase() { out << "~mybase()\n"; }
};

class paste1 : public mybase, public vendor1 {
public:
  void v() const {
    out << "paste1::v()\n";
    vendor1::v();
  }
  void f() const {
    out << "paste1::f()\n";
    vendor1::f();
  }
  void g() const {
    out << "paste1::g()\n";
  }
  ~paste1() { out << "~paste1()\n"; }
};

main() {
  paste1& p1p = *new paste1;
```

```
    mybase& mp = p1p; // Upcast
    out << "calling f()\n";
    mp.f();   // Right behavior
    out << "calling g()\n";
    mp.g(); // New behavior
    out << "calling A(p1p)\n";
    A(p1p); // Same old behavior
    out << "calling B(p1p)\n";
    B(p1p);   // Same old behavior
    out << "delete mp\n";
    // Deleting a reference to a heap object:
    delete &mp; // Right behavior
}
```

In **mybase** (which does *not* use MI), both **f( )** and the destructor
are now virtual, and a new virtual function **g( )** has been added to
the interface. Now each of the derived classes in the original library
must be recreated, mixing in the new interface with MI. The
functions **paste1::v( )** and **paste1::f( )**need to call only the original
base-class versions of their functions. But now, if you upcast to
mybase as in **main( )**,

```
mybase* mp = p1p; // upcast
```

any function calls made through **mp** will be polymorphic, including
delete. Also, the new interface function **g( )** can be called through
mp. Here's the output of the program:

```
calling f()
paste1::f()
vendor1::f()
calling g()
paste1::g()
calling A(p1p)
paste1::v()
vendor1::v()
vendor::f()
calling B(p1p)
```

```
paste1::v()
vendor1::v()
vendor::f()
delete mp
~paste1()
~vendor1()
~vendor()
~mybase()
```

The original library functions **A( )** and **B( )** still work the same (assuming the new **v( )** calls its base-class version). The destructor is now virtual and exhibits the correct behavior.

Although this is a messy example, it does occur in practice and it's a good demonstration of where multiple inheritance is clearly necessary: You must be able to upcast to both base classes.

summary

The reason MI exists in C++ and not in other OOP languages is that C++ is a hybrid language and couldn't enforce a single monolithic class hierarchy the way Smalltalk does. Instead, C++ allows many inheritance trees to be formed, so sometimes you may need to combine the interfaces from two or more trees into a new class.

If no "diamonds" appear in your class hierarchy, MI is fairly simple, although identical function signatures in base classes must be resolved. If a diamond appears, then you must deal with the problems of duplicate subobjects by introducing virtual base classes. This not only adds confusion, but the underlying representation becomes more complex and less efficient.

Multiple inheritance has been called the "goto of the 90's".[4] This seems appropriate because, like a goto, MI is best avoided in normal programming, but can occasionally be very useful. It's a "minor" but more advanced feature of C++, designed to solve problems that arise in special situations. If you find yourself using it often, you may want to take a look at your reasoning. A good Occam's Razor is to ask, "Must I upcast to all of the base classes?" If not, your life will be easier if you embed instances of all the classes you *don't* need to upcast to.

exercises

1. This exercise will take you step-by-step through the traps of MI. Create a base class **X** with a single constructor that takes an **int** argument and a member function **f( )** that takes no arguments and returns **void**. Now inherit **X** into **Y** and **Z**, creating constructors for each of them that take a single **int** argument. Now multiply inherit **Y** and **Z** into **A**. Create an object of class **A**, and call **f( )** for that object. Fix the problem with explicit disambiguation.

   Create a pointer to an **X** called **px**, and assign to it the address of the object of type **A** you created before. Fix the problem using a virtual base class. Now fix **X** so you no longer have to call the constructor for **X** inside **A**.

   Remove the explicit disambiguation for **f( )**, and see if you can call **f( )** through **px**. Trace it to see which function gets called. Fix the problem so the correct function will be called in a class hierarchy.

---

[4] A phrase coined by Zack Urlocker.

exception handling

Improved error recovery is one of the most powerful ways you can increase the robustness of your code.

Unfortunately, it's almost accepted practice to ignore error conditions, as if we're in a state of denial about errors. Some of the reason is no doubt the tediousness and code bloat of checking for many errors. For example, **printf( )** returns the number of arguments that were successfully printed, but virtually no one checks this value. The proliferation of code alone would be disgusting, not to mention the difficulty it would add in reading the code.

The problem with C's approach to error handling could be thought of as one of coupling — the user of a function must tie the error-handling code so closely to that function that it becomes too ungainly and awkward to use.

One of the major features in C++ is *exception handling*, which is a better way of thinking about and handling errors. With exception handling,

1. Error-handling code is not nearly so tedious to write, and it doesn't become mixed up with your "normal" code. You write the code you *want* to happen; later in a separate section you write the code to cope with the problems. If you make multiple calls to a function, you handle the errors from that function once, in one place.

2. Errors cannot be ignored. If a function needs to send an error message to the caller of that function, it "throws" an object representing that error out of the function. If the caller doesn't "catch" the error and handle it, it goes to the next enclosing scope, and so on until *someone* catches the error.

This chapter examines C's approach to error handling (such as it is), why it did not work very well for C, and why it won't work at all for C++. Then you'll learn about **try**, **throw**, and **catch**, the C++ keywords that support exception handling.

error handling in C

Until Chapter 7, this book used the Standard C library **assert( )** macro as a shorthand for error handling. After Chapter 7, **assert( )** was used as it was intended: for debugging during development with code that could be disabled with **#define NDEBUG** for the shipping product. For run-time error checking, **assert( )** was replaced by the **allege( )** functions and macros developed in Chapter 7. These were convenient to say, "There's a problem here you'll probably want to handle with some more sophisticated code, but you don't need to be distracted by it in this example." The **allege( )** functions may be enough for small programs, but for complicated products you'll need to write more sophisticated error-handling code.

Thinking in C++ Bruce Eckel

Error handling is quite straightforward in situations where you check some condition and you know exactly what to do because you have all the necessary information in that context. Of course, you just handle the error at that point. These are ordinary errors and not the subject of this chapter.

The problem occurs when you *don't* have enough information in that context, and you need to pass the error information into a larger context where that information does exist. There are three typical approaches in C to handle this situation.

1. Return error information from the function or, if the return value cannot be used this way, set a global error condition flag. (Standard C provides **errno** and **perror( )** to support this.) As mentioned before, the programmer may simply ignore the error information because tedious and obfuscating error checking must occur with each function call. In addition, returning from a function that hits an exceptional condition may not make sense.

2. Use the little-known Standard C library signal-handling system, implemented with the **signal( )** function (to determine what happens when the event occurs) and **raise( )** (to generate an event). Again, this has high coupling because it requires the user of any library that generates signals to understand and install the appropriate signal-handling mechanism; also in large projects the signal numbers from different libraries may clash with each other.

3. Use the nonlocal goto functions in the Standard C library: **setjmp( )** and **longjmp( )**. With **setjmp( )** you save a known good state in the program, and if you get into trouble, **longjmp( )** will restore that state. Again, there is high coupling between the place where the state is stored and the place where the error occurs.

When considering error-handling schemes with C++, there's an additional very critical problem: The C techniques of signals and setjmp/longjmp do not call destructors, so objects aren't properly cleaned up. This makes it virtually impossible to effectively recover from an exceptional condition because you'll always leave objects behind that haven't been cleaned up and that can no longer be accessed. The following example demonstrates this with setjmp/longjmp:

```
//: NONLOCAL.CPP -- setjmp & longjmp
#include <iostream.h>
#include <setjmp.h>

class rainbow {
public:
  rainbow() { cout << "rainbow()" << endl; }
  ~rainbow() { cout << "~rainbow()" << endl; }
};

jmp_buf kansas;

void OZ() {
  rainbow RB;
  for(int i = 0; i < 3; i++)
    cout << "there's no place like home\n";
  longjmp(kansas, 47);
}

main() {
  if(setjmp(kansas) == 0) {
    cout << "tornado, witch, munchkins...\n";
    OZ();
  } else {
    cout << "Auntie Em! "
         << "I had the strangest dream..."
         << endl;
  }
}
```

setjmp( ) is an odd function because if you call it directly, it stores all the relevant information about the current processor state in the **jmp_buf** and returns zero. In that case it has the behavior of an ordinary function. However, if you call **longjmp( )** using the same **jmp_buf**, it's as if you're returning from **setjmp( )** again — you pop right out the back end of the **setjmp( )**. This time, the value returned is the second argument to **longjmp( )**, so you can detect that you're actually coming back from a **longjmp( )**. You can imagine that with many different **jmp_bufs**, you could pop around to many different places in the program. The difference between a local **goto** (with a label) and this nonlocal goto is that you can go *anywhere* with setjmp/longjmp (with some restrictions not discussed here).

The problem with C++ is that **longjmp( )** doesn't respect objects; in particular it doesn't call destructors when it jumps out of a scope.[1] Destructor calls are essential, so this approach won't work with C++.

throwing an exception

If you encounter an exceptional situation in your code — that is, one where you don't have enough information in the current context to decide what to do — you can send information about the error into a larger context by creating an object containing that information and "throwing" it out of your current context. This is called *throwing an exception*. Here's what it looks like:

```
throw myerror("something bad happened");
```

myerror is an ordinary class, which takes a **char*** as its argument. You can use any type when you throw (including built-in types), but often you'll use special types created just for throwing exceptions.

---

[1] You may be surprised when you run the example — some C++ compilers have extended **longjmp( )** to clean up objects on the stack. This is nonportable behavior.

The keyword **throw** causes a number of relatively magical things to happen. First it creates an object that isn't there under normal program execution, and of course the constructor is called for that object. Then the object is, in effect, "returned" from the function, even though that object type isn't normally what the function is designed to return. A simplistic way to think about exception handling is as an alternate return mechanism, although you get into trouble if you take the analogy too far — you can also exit from ordinary scopes by throwing an exception. But a value is returned, and the function or scope exits.

Any similarity to function returns ends there because *where* you return to is someplace completely different than for a normal function call. (You end up in an appropriate exception handler that may be miles away from where the exception was thrown.) In addition, only objects that were successfully created at the time of the exception are destroyed (unlike a normal function return that assumes all the objects in the scope must be destroyed). Of course, the exception object itself is also properly cleaned up at the appropriate point.

In addition, you can throw as many different types of objects as you want. Typically, you'll throw a different type for each different type of error. The idea is to store the information in the object and the *type* of object, so someone in the bigger context can figure out what to do with your exception.

catching an exception

If a function throws an exception, it must assume that exception is caught and dealt with. As mentioned before, one of the advantages of C++ exception handling is that it allows you to concentrate on the problem you're actually trying to solve in one place, and then deal with the errors from that code in another place.

the try block

If you're inside a function and you throw an exception (or a called function throws an exception), that function will exit in the process of throwing. If you don't want a **throw** to leave a function, you can set up a special block within the function where you try to solve your actual programming problem (and potentially generate exceptions). This is called the *try block* because you try your various function calls there. The try block is an ordinary scope, preceded by the keyword **try**:

```
try {
  // code that may generate exceptions
}
```

If you were carefully checking for errors without using exception handling, you'd have to surround every function call with setup and test code, even if you call the same function several times. With exception handling, you put everything in a try block without error checking. This means your code is a lot easier to write and easier to read because the goal of the code is not confused with the error checking.

exception handlers

Of course, the thrown exception must end up someplace. This is the *exception handler*, and there's one for every exception type you want to catch. Exception handlers immediately follow the try block and are denoted by the keyword **catch**:

```
try {
// code that may generate exceptions
} catch(type1 id1) {
  // handle exceptions of type1
} catch(type2 id2) {
  // handle exceptions of type2
}
// etc...
```

Each catch clause (exception handler) is like a little function that takes a single argument of one particular type. The identifier (**id1**, **id2**, and so on) may be used inside the handler, just like a function argument, although sometimes there is no identifier because it's not needed in the handler — the exception type gives you enough information to deal with it.

The handlers must appear directly after the try block. If an exception is thrown, the exception-handling mechanism goes hunting for the first handler with an argument that matches the type of the exception. Then it enters that catch clause, and the exception is considered handled. (The search for handlers stops once the catch clause is finished.) Only the matching catch clause executes; it's not like a **switch** statement where you need a **break** after each **case** to prevent the remaining ones from executing.

Notice that, within the try block, a number of different function calls might generate the same exception, but you only need one handler.

termination vs. resumption

There are two basic models in exception-handling theory. In *termination* (which is what C++ supports) you assume the error is so critical there's no way to get back to where the exception occurred. Whoever threw the exception decided there was no way to salvage the situation, and they don't *want* to come back.

The alternative is called *resumption*. It means the exception handler is expected to do something to rectify the situation, and then the faulting function is retried, presuming success the second time. If you want resumption, you still hope to continue execution after the exception is handled, so your exception is more like a function call — which is how you should set up situations in C++ where you want resumption-like behavior (that is, don't throw an exception; call a function that fixes the problem). Alternatively, place your **try** block inside a **while** loop that keeps reentering the **try** block until the result is satisfactory.

Historically, programmers using operating systems that supported resumptive exception handling eventually ended up using termination-like code and skipping resumption. So although resumption sounds attractive at first, it seems it isn't quite so useful in practice. One reason may be the distance that can occur between the exception and its handler; it's one thing to terminate to a handler that's far away, but to jump to that handler and then back again may be too conceptually difficult for large systems where the exception can be generated from many points.

the exception specification

You're not required to inform the person using your function what exceptions you might throw. However, this is considered very uncivilized because it means he cannot be sure what code to write to catch all potential exceptions. Of course, if he has your source code, he can hunt through and look for **throw** statements, but very often a library doesn't come with sources. C++ provides a syntax to allow you to politely tell the user what exceptions this function throws, so the user may handle them. This is the *exception specification* and it's part of the function declaration, appearing after the argument list.

The exception specification reuses the keyword **throw**, followed by a parenthesized list of all the potential exception types. So your function declaration may look like

```
void f() throw(toobig, toosmall, divzero);
```

With exceptions, the traditional function declaration

```
void f();
```

means that any type of exception may be thrown from the function. If you say

```
void f() throw();
```

it means that no exceptions are thrown from a function.

For good coding policy, good documentation, and ease-of-use for the function caller, you should always use an exception specification when you write a function that throws exceptions.

unexpected( )

If your exception specification claims you're going to throw a certain set of exceptions and then you throw something that isn't in that set, what's the penalty? The special function **unexpected( )** is called when you throw something other than what appears in the exception specification.

set_unexpected( )

unexpected( ) is implemented with a pointer to a function, so you can change its behavior. You do so with a function called **set_unexpected( )** which, like **set_new_handler( )**, takes the address of a function with no arguments and **void** return value. Also, it returns the previous value of the **unexpected( )** pointer so you can save it and restore it later. To use **set_unexpected( )**, you must include the header file EXCEPT.H. Here's an example that shows a simple use of all the features discussed so far in the chapter:

```
//: EXCEPT.CPP -- Basic exceptions
// Exception specifications & unexpected()
#include <except.h>
#include <iostream.h>
#include <stdlib.h>
#include <string.h>

class up {};
class fit {};
void g();

void f(int i) throw (up, fit) {
  switch(i) {
    case 1: throw up();
    case 2: throw fit();
```

```
    }
    g();
}

// void g() {} // version 1
void g() { throw 47; } // Version 2
// (can throw built-in types)

void my_unexpected() {
  cout << "unexpected exception thrown";
  exit(1);
}

main() {
  set_unexpected(my_unexpected);
  // (ignores return value)
  for(int i = 1; i <=3; i++)
    try {
      f(i);
    } catch(up) {
      cout << "up caught" << endl;
    } catch(fit) {
      cout << "fit caught" << endl;
    }
}
```

The classes **up** and **fit** are created solely to throw as exceptions. Often exception classes will be this small, but sometimes they contain additional information so that the handlers can query them.

f( ) is a function that promises in its exception specification to throw only exceptions of type **up** and **fit**, and from looking at the function definition this seems plausible. Version one of **g( )**, called by **f( )**, doesn't throw any exceptions so this is true. But then someone changes **g( )** so it throws exceptions and the new **g( )** is linked in with **f( )**. Now **f( )** begins to throw a new exception,

---

unbeknown to the creator of **f( )**. Thus the exception specification is violated.

The **my_unexpected( )** function has no arguments or return value, following the proper form for a custom **unexpected( )** function. It simply prints a message so you can see it has been called, then exits the program. Your new **unexpected( )** function must not return (that is, you can write the code that way but it's an error). However, it can throw another exception (you can even rethrow the same exception), or call **exit( )** or **abort( )**. If **unexpected( )** throws an exception, the search for the handler starts at the function call that threw the unexpected exception. (This behavior is unique to **unexpected( )**.)

Although the **new_handler( )** function pointer can be null and the system will do something sensible, the **unexpected( )** function pointer should never be null. The default value is **terminate( )** (mentioned later), but whenever you use exceptions and specifications you should write your own **unexpected( )** to log the error and either rethrow it, throw something new, or terminate the program.

In **main( )**, the **try** block is within a **for** loop so all the possibilities are exercised. Note that this is a way to achieve something like resumption — nest the **try** block inside a **for**, **while**, **do**, or **if** and cause any exceptions to attempt to repair the problem; then attempt the **try** block again.

Only the **up** and **fit** exceptions are caught because those are the only ones the programmer of **f( )** said would be thrown. Version two of **g( )** causes **my_unexpected( )** to be called because **f( )** then throws an **int**. (You can throw any type, including a built-in type.)

In the call to **set_unexpected( )**, the return value is ignored, but it can also be saved in a pointer to function and restored later.

better exception specifications?

You may feel the existing exception specification rules aren't very safe, and that

```
void f();
```

should mean that no exceptions are thrown from this function. If the programmer wants to throw any type of exception, you may think she *should* have to say

```
void f() throw(...); // not in C++
```

This would surely be an improvement because function declarations would be more explicit. Unfortunately you can't always know by looking at the code in a function whether an exception will be thrown — it could happen because of a memory allocation, for example. Worse, existing functions written before exception handling was introduced may find themselves inadvertently throwing exceptions because of the functions they call (which may be linked into new, exception-throwing versions). Thus, the ambiguity, so

```
void f();
```

means "Maybe I'll throw an exception, maybe I won't." This ambiguity is necessary to avoid hindering code evolution.

catching any exception

As mentioned, if your function has no exception specification, *any* type of exception can be thrown. One solution to this problem is to create a handler that *catches* any type of exception. You do this using the ellipses in the argument list (á la C):

```
catch(...) {
  cout << "an exception was thrown" << endl;
}
```

This will catch any exception, so you'll want to put it at the *end* of your list of handlers to avoid pre-empting any that follow it.

The ellipses give you no possibility to have an argument or to know anything about the type of the exception. It's a catch-all.

rethrowing an exception

Sometimes you'll want to rethrow the exception that you just caught, particularly when you use the ellipses to catch any exception because there's no information available about the exception. This is accomplished by saying **throw** with no argument:

```
catch(...) {
  cout << "an exception was thrown" << endl;
  throw;
}
```

Any further **catch** clauses for the same **try** block are still ignored — the **throw** causes the exception to go to the exception handlers in the next-higher context. In addition, everything about the exception object is preserved, so the handler at the higher context that catches the specific exception type is able to extract all the information from that object.

uncaught exceptions

If none of the exception handlers following a particular **try** block matches an exception, that exception moves to the next-higher context, that is, the function or **try** block surrounding the **try** block that failed to catch the exception. (The location of this higher-context **try** block is not always obvious at first glance.) This process continues until, at some level, a handler matches the exception. At that point, the exception is considered "caught," and no further searching occurs.

If no handler at any level catches the exception, it is "uncaught" or "unhandled." An uncaught exception also occurs if a new exception is thrown before an existing exception reaches its handler — the most common reason for this is that the constructor for the exception object itself causes a new exception.

terminate( )

If an exception is uncaught, the special function **terminate( )** is automatically called. Like **unexpected( )**, terminate is actually a pointer to a function. Its default value is the Standard C library function **abort( )**, which immediately exits the program with no calls to the normal termination functions (which means that destructors for global and static objects might not be called).

No cleanups occur for an uncaught exception; that is, no destructors are called. If you don't wrap your code (including, if necessary, all the code in **main( )**) in a try block followed by handlers and ending with a default handler (**catch(...)**) to catch all exceptions, then you will take your lumps. An uncaught exception should be thought of as a programming error.

set_terminate( )

You can install your own **terminate( )** function using the standard **set_terminate( )** function, which returns a pointer to the **terminate( )** function you are replacing, so you can restore it later if you want. Your custom **terminate( )** must take no arguments and have a **void** return value. In addition, any **terminate( )** handler you install must not return or throw an exception, but instead must call some sort of program-termination function. If **terminate( )** is called, it means the problem is unrecoverable.

Like **unexpected( )**, the **terminate( )** function pointer should never be null.

Here's an example showing the use of **set_terminate( )**. Here, the return value is saved and restored so the **terminate( )** function can be used to help isolate the section of code where the uncaught exception is occurring:

```
//: TRMNATOR.CPP -- Use of set_terminate()
// Also shows uncaught exceptions
```

```
#include <except.h>
#include <iostream.h>
#include <stdlib.h>

void terminator() {
  cout << "I'll be back!" << endl;
  abort();
}

void (*old_terminate)()
  = set_terminate(terminator);

class botch {
public:
  class fruit {};
  void f() {
    cout << "botch::f()" << endl;
    throw fruit();
  }
  ~botch() { throw 'c'; }
};

main() {
  try{
    botch b;
    b.f();
  } catch(...) {
    cout << "inside catch(...)" << endl;
  }
}
```

The definition of **old_terminate** looks a bit confusing at first: It not
only creates a pointer to a function, but it initializes that pointer to
the return value of **set_terminate( )**. Even though you may be
familiar with seeing a semicolon right after a pointer-to-function
definition, it's just another kind of variable and may be initialized
when it is defined.

The class **botch** not only throws an exception inside **f( )**, but also in its destructor. This is one of the situations that causes a call to **terminate( )**, as you can see in **main( )**. Even though the exception handler says **catch(...)**, which would seem to catch everything and leave no cause for **terminate( )** to be called, **terminate( )** is called anyway, because in the process of cleaning up the objects on the stack to handle one exception, the **botch** destructor is called, and that generates a second exception, forcing a call to **terminate( )**. Thus, a destructor that throws an exception or causes one to be thrown is a design error.

cleaning up

Part of the magic of exception handling is that you can pop from normal program flow into the appropriate exception handler. This wouldn't be very useful, however, if things weren't cleaned up properly as the exception was thrown. C++ exception handling guarantees that as you leave a scope, all objects in that scope *whose constructors have been completed* will have destructors called.

Here's an example that demonstrates that constructors that aren't completed don't have the associated destructors called. It also shows what happens when an exception is thrown in the middle of the creation of an array of objects, and an **unexpected( )** function that rethrows the unexpected exception:

```
//: CLEANUP.CPP -- Exceptions clean up objects
#include <fstream.h>
#include <except.h>
#include <string.h>

ofstream out("cleanup.out");
```

```
class noisy {
  static int i;
  int objnum;
  enum { sz = 40 };
  char name[sz];
public:
  noisy(const char* nm="array elem") throw(int){
    objnum = i++;
    memset(name, 0, sz);
    strncpy(name, nm, sz - 1);
    out << "constructing noisy " << objnum
      << " name [" << name << "]" << endl;
    if(objnum == 5) throw int(5);
    // Not in exception specification:
    if(*nm == 'z') throw char('z');
  }
  ~noisy() {
    out << "destructing noisy " << objnum
      << " name [" << name << "]" << endl;
  }
  void* operator new[](size_t sz) {
    out << "noisy::new[]" << endl;
    return ::new char[sz];
  }
  void operator delete[](void* p) {
    out << "noisy::delete[]" << endl;
    ::delete []p;
  }
};

int noisy::i = 0;

void unexpected_rethrow() {
  out << "inside unexpected_rethrow()" << endl;
  throw; // Rethrow same exception
}
```

```
main() {
  set_unexpected(unexpected_rethrow);
  try {
    noisy n1("before array");
    // Throws exception:
    noisy* array = new noisy[7];
    noisy n2("after array");
  } catch(int i) {
    out << "caught " << i << endl;
  }
  out << "testing unexpected:" << endl;
  try {
    noisy n3("before unexpected");
    noisy n4("z");
    noisy n5("after unexpected");
  } catch(char c) {
    out << "caught " << c << endl;
  }
}
```

The class **noisy** keeps track of objects so you can trace program progress. It keeps a count of the number of objects created with a **static** data member **i**, and the number of the particular object with **objnum**, and a character buffer called **name** to hold an identifier. This buffer is first set to zeroes. Then the constructor argument is copied in. (Note that a default argument string is used to indicate array elements, so this constructor also acts as a default constructor.) Because the Standard C library function **strncpy( )** stops copying after a null terminator *or* the number of characters specified by its third argument, the number of characters copied in is one minus the size of the buffer, so the last character is always zero, and a print statement will never run off the end of the buffer.

There are two cases where a **throw** can occur in the constructor. The first case happens if this is the fifth object created (not a real exception condition, but demonstrates an exception thrown during array construction). The type thrown is **int**, which is the type promised in the exception specification. The second case, also contrived, happens if the first character of the argument string is **'z'**, in which case a **char** is thrown. Because **char** is not listed in the exception specification, this will cause a call to **unexpected( )**.

The array versions of **new** and **delete** are overloaded for the class, so you can see when they're called.

The function **unexpected_rethrow( )** prints a message and rethrows the same exception. It is installed as the **unexpected( )** function in the first line of **main( )**. Then some objects of type **noisy** are created in a **try** block, but the array causes an exception to be thrown, so the object **n2** is never created. You can see the results in the output of the program:

```
constructing noisy 0 name [before array]
noisy::new[]
constructing noisy 1 name [array elem]
constructing noisy 2 name [array elem]
constructing noisy 3 name [array elem]
constructing noisy 4 name [array elem]
constructing noisy 5 name [array elem]
destructing noisy 4 name [array elem]
destructing noisy 3 name [array elem]
destructing noisy 2 name [array elem]
destructing noisy 1 name [array elem]
noisy::delete[]
destructing noisy 0 name [before array]
caught 5
testing unexpected:
constructing noisy 6 name [before unexpected]
constructing noisy 7 name [z]
inside unexpected_rethrow()
destructing noisy 6 name [before unexpected]
caught z
```

Four array elements are successfully created, but in the middle of the constructor for the fifth one, an exception is thrown. Because the fifth constructor never completes, only the destructors for objects 1–4 are called.

The storage for the array is allocated separately with a single call to the global **new**. Notice that even though **delete** is never explicitly called anywhere in the program, the exception-handling system knows it must call **delete** to properly release the storage. This behavior happens only with "normal" versions of **operator new**. If you use the placement syntax described in Chapter 11, the exception-handling mechanism will not call **delete** for that object because then it might release memory that was not allocated on the heap.

Finally, object **n1** is destroyed, but not object **n2** because it was never created.

In the section testing **unexpected_rethrow( )**, the **n3** object is created, and the constructor of **n4** is begun. But before it can complete, an exception is thrown. This exception is of type **char**, which violates the exception specification, so the **unexpected( )** function is called (which is **unexpected_rethrow( )**, in this case). This rethrows the same exception, which is expected this time, because **unexpected_rethrow( )** can throw any type of exception. The search begins right after the constructor for **n4**, and the **char** exception handler catches it (after destroying **n3**, the only successfully created object). Thus, the effect of **unexpected_rethrow( )** is to take any unexpected exception and make it expected; used this way it provides a filter to allow you to track the appearance of unexpected exceptions and pass them through.

constructors

When writing code with exceptions, it's particularly important that you always be asking, "If an exception occurs, will this be properly

---

cleaned up?" Most of the time you're fairly safe, but in constructors there's a problem: If an exception is thrown before a constructor is completed, the associated destructor will not be called for that object. This means you must be especially diligent while writing your constructor.

The general difficulty is allocating resources in constructors. If an exception occurs in the constructor, the destructor doesn't get a chance to deallocate the resource. This problem occurs most often with "naked" pointers. For example,

```cpp
//: NUDEP.CPP -- Naked pointers
#include <fstream.h>
#include <stdlib.h>
ofstream out("nudep.out");

class bonk {
public:
  bonk() { out << "bonk()" << endl; }
  ~bonk() { out << "~bonk()" << endl; }
};

class og {
public:
  void* operator new(size_t sz) {
    out << "allocating an og" << endl;
    throw int(47);
    return 0;
  }
  void operator delete(void* p) {
    out << "deallocating an og" << endl;
    ::delete p;
  }
};

class useResources {
  bonk* bp;
```

```
    og* op;
public:
  useResources(int count = 1) {
    out << "useResources()" << endl;
    bp = new bonk[count];
    op = new og;
  }
  ~useResources() {
    out << "~useResources()" << endl;
    delete []bp; // Array delete
    delete op;
  }
};

main() {
  try {
    useResources ur(3);
  } catch(int) {
    out << "inside handler" << endl;
  }
};
```

The output is the following:

```
useResources()
bonk()
bonk()
bonk()
allocating an og
inside handler
```

The **useResources** constructor is entered, and the **bonk**
constructor is successfully completed for the array objects.
However, inside **og::operator new**, an exception is thrown (as an
example of an out-of-memory error). Suddenly, you end up inside
the handler, *without* the **useResources** destructor being called.
This is correct because the **useResources** constructor was unable

to finish, but it means the **bonk** object that was successfully created on the heap is never destroyed.

making everything an object

To prevent this, guard against these "raw" resource allocations by placing the allocations inside their own objects with their own constructors and destructors. This way, each allocation becomes atomic, as an object, and if it fails, the other resource allocation objects are properly cleaned up. Templates are an excellent way to modify the above example:

```
//: WRAPPED.CPP -- Safe, atomic pointers
#include <fstream.h>
#include <stdlib.h>
ofstream out("wrapped.out");

// Simplified. Yours may have other arguments.
template<class T, int sz = 1> class pwrap {
  T* ptr;
public:
  class rangeError {}; // Exception class
  pwrap() {
    ptr = new T[sz];
    out << "pwrap constructor" << endl;
  }
  ~pwrap() {
    delete []ptr;
    out << "pwrap destructor" << endl;
  }
  T& operator[](int i) throw(rangeError) {
    if(i >= 0 && i < sz) return ptr[i];
    throw rangeError();
  }
};

class bonk {
```

```
public:
  bonk() { out << "bonk()" << endl; }
  ~bonk() { out << "~bonk()" << endl; }
  void g() {}
};

class og {
public:
  void* operator new[](size_t sz) {
    out << "allocating an og" << endl;
    throw int(47);
    return 0;
  }
  void operator delete[](void* p) {
    out << "deallocating an og" << endl;
    ::delete p;
  }
};

class useResources {
  pwrap<bonk, 3> Bonk;
  pwrap<og> Og;
public:
  useResources() : Bonk(), Og() {
    out << "useResources()" << endl;
  }
  ~useResources() {
    out << "~useResources()" << endl;
  }
  void f() { Bonk[1].g(); }
};

main() {
  try {
    useResources ur;
  } catch(int) {
    out << "inside handler" << endl;
```

```
  } catch(...) {
    out << "inside catch(...)" << endl;
  }
}
```

The difference is the use of the template to wrap the pointers and make them into objects. The constructors for these objects are called *before* the body of the **useResources** constructor, and any of these constructors that complete before an exception is thrown will have their associated destructors called.

The **pwrap** template shows a more typical use of exceptions than you've seen so far: A nested class called **rangeError** is created to use in **operator[]** if its argument is out of range. Because **operator[]** returns a reference it cannot return zero. (There are no null references.) This is a true exceptional condition — you don't know what to do in the current context, and you can't return an improbable value. In this example, **rangeError** is very simple and assumes all the necessary information is in the class name, but you may also want to add a member that contains the value of the index, if that is useful.

Now the output is

```
bonk()
bonk()
bonk()
pwrap constructor
allocating an og
~bonk()
~bonk()
~bonk()
pwrap destructor
inside handler
```

Again, the storage allocation for **og** throws an exception, but this time the array of **bonk** objects is properly cleaned up, so there is no memory leak.

Thinking in C++   Bruce Eckel

exception matching

When an exception is thrown, the exception-handling system looks through the "nearest" handlers in the order they are written. When it finds a match, the exception is considered handled, and no further searching occurs.

Matching an exception doesn't require a perfect match between the exception and its handler. An object or reference to a derived-class object will match a handler for the base class. (However, if the handler is for an object rather than a reference, the exception object is "sliced" as it is passed to the handler; this does no damage but loses all the derived-type information.) If a pointer is thrown, standard pointer conversions are used to match the exception. However, no automatic type conversions are used to convert one exception type to another in the process of matching. For example,

```
//: AUTOEXCP.CPP -- No matching conversions
#include <iostream.h>
class except1 {};
class except2 {
public:
  except2(except1&) {}
};

void f() { throw except1(); }

main() {
  try { f();
  } catch (except2) {
    cout << "inside catch(except2)" << endl;
  } catch (except1) {
    cout << "inside catch(except1)" << endl;
  }
}
```

Even though you might think the first handler could be used by converting an **except1** object into an **except2** using the constructor conversion, the system will not perform such a conversion during exception handling, and you'll end up at the **except1** handler.

The following example shows how a base-class handler can catch a derived-class exception:

```
//: BASEXCPT.CPP -- Exception hierarchies
#include <iostream.h>

class X {
public:
  class trouble {};
  class small : public trouble {};
  class big : public trouble {};
  void f() { throw big(); }
};

main() {
  X x;
  try {
    x.f();
  } catch(X::trouble) {
    cout << "caught trouble" << endl;
  // Hidden by previous handler:
  } catch(X::small) {
    cout << "caught small trouble" << endl;
  } catch(X::big) {
    cout << "caught big trouble" << endl;

  }
}
```

Here, the exception-handling mechanism will always match a **trouble** object, *or anything derived from* **trouble**, to the first handler. That means the second and third handlers are never called because the first one captures them all. It makes more sense to catch the derived types first and put the base type at the end to catch anything less specific (or a derived class introduced later in the development cycle).

In addition, if **small** and **big** represent larger objects than the base class **trouble** (which is often true because you regularly add data members to derived classes), then those objects are sliced to fit into the first handler. Of course, in this example it isn't important because there are no additional members in the derived classes and there are no argument identifiers in the handlers anyway. You'll usually want to use reference arguments rather than objects in your handlers to avoid slicing off information.

standard exceptions

The set of exceptions used with the Standard C++ library are also available for your own use. Generally it's easier and faster to start with a standard exception class than to try to define your own. If the standard class doesn't do what you need, you can derive from it.

The following tables describe the standard exceptions:

exception	The base class for all the exceptions thrown by the C++ standard library. You can ask **what( )** and get a result that can be displayed as a character representation.
logic_error	Derived from **exception**. Reports program logic errors, which could presumably be detected before the program executes.
runtime_error	Derived from **exception**. Reports run-time errors, which can presumably be detected only when the program executes.

The iostream exception class **ios::failure** is also derived from **exception**, but it has no further subclasses.

The classes in both of the following tables can be used as they are, or they can act as base classes to derive your own more specific types of exceptions.

Exception classes derived from **logic_error**	
domain_error	Reports violations of a precondition.
invalid_argument	Indicates an invalid argument to the function it's thrown from.
length_error	Indicates an attempt to produce an object whose length is greater than or equal to NPOS (the largest representable value of type **size_t**).
out_of_range	Reports an out-of-range argument.
bad_cast	Thrown for executing an invalid **dynamic_cast** expression in run-time type identification (see Chapter 17).
bad_typeid	Reports a null pointer **p** in an expression **typeid(*p)**. (Again, a run-time type identification feature in Chapter 17).

Exception classes derived from **runtime_error**	
range_error	Reports violation of a postcondition.
overflow_error	Reports an arithmetic overflow.
bad_alloc	Reports a failure to allocate storage.

programming with exceptions

For most programmers, especially C programmers, exceptions are not available in their existing language and take a bit of adjustment. Here are some guidelines for programming with exceptions.

when to avoid exceptions

Exceptions aren't the answer to all problems. In fact, if you simply go looking for something to pound with your new hammer, you'll cause trouble. The following sections point out situations where exceptions are *not* warranted.

not for asynchronous events

The Standard C **signal( )** system, and any similar system, handles asynchronous events: events that happen outside the scope of the program, and thus events the program cannot anticipate. C++ exceptions cannot be used to handle asynchronous events because the exception and its handler are on the same call stack. That is, exceptions rely on scoping, whereas asynchronous events must be handled by completely separate code that is not part of the normal program flow (typically, interrupt service routines or event loops).

This is not to say that asynchronous events cannot be *associated* with exceptions. But the interrupt handler should do its job as quickly as possible and then return. Later, at some well-defined point in the program, an exception might be thrown *based on* the interrupt.

not for ordinary error conditions

If you have enough information to handle an error, it's not an exception. You should take care of it in the current context rather than throwing an exception to a larger context.

Also, C++ exceptions are not thrown for machine-level events like divide-by-zero. It's assumed these are dealt with by some other mechanism, like the operating system or hardware. That way, C++ exceptions can be reasonably efficient, and their use is isolated to program-level exceptional conditions.

not for flow-of-control

An exception looks somewhat like an alternate return mechanism and somewhat like a **switch** statement, so you can be tempted to use them for other than their original intent. This is a bad idea, partly because the exception-handling system is significantly less efficient than normal program execution; exceptions are a rare event, so the normal program shouldn't pay for them. Also, exceptions from anything other than error conditions are quite confusing to the user of your class or function.

you're not forced to use exceptions

Some programs are quite simple, many utilities, for example. You may only need to take input and perform some processing. In these programs you might attempt to allocate memory and fail, or try to open a file and fail, and so on. It is acceptable in these programs to use **assert( )** or to print a message and **abort( )** the program, allowing the system to clean up the mess, rather than to work very hard to catch all exceptions and recover all the resources yourself. Basically, if you don't need to use exceptions, you don't have to.

new exceptions, old code

Another situation that arises is the modification of an existing program that doesn't use exceptions. You may introduce a library that *does* use exceptions and wonder if you need to modify all your code throughout the program. Assuming you have an acceptable error-handling scheme already in place, the most sensible thing to do here is surround the largest block that uses the new library (this may be all the code in **main( )**) with a **try** block, followed by a **catch(...)** and basic error message. You can refine this to whatever degree necessary by adding more specific handlers, but, in any case, the code you're forced to add can be minimal.

Thinking in C++ *Bruce Eckel*

You can also isolate your exception-generating code in a try block and write handlers to convert the exceptions into your existing error-handling scheme.

It's truly important to think about exceptions when you're creating a library for someone else to use, and you can't know how they need to respond to critical error conditions.

typical uses of exceptions

Do use exceptions to

1. Fix the problem and call the function (which caused the exception) again.

2. Patch things up and continue without retrying the function.

3. Calculate some alternative result instead of what the function was supposed to produce.

4. Do whatever you can in the current context and rethrow the *same* exception to a higher context.

5. Do whatever you can in the current context and throw a *different* exception to a higher context.

6. Terminate the program.

7. Wrap functions (especially C library functions) that use ordinary error schemes so they produce exceptions instead.

8. Simplify. If your exception scheme makes things more complicated, then it is painful and annoying to use.

9. Make your library and program safer. This is a short-term investment (for debugging) and a long-term investment (for application robustness).

always use exception specifications

The exception specification is like a function prototype: It tells the user to write exception-handling code and what exceptions to handle. It tells the compiler the exceptions that may come out of this function.

Of course, you can't always anticipate by looking at the code what exceptions will arise from a particular function. Sometimes the functions it calls produce an unexpected exception, and sometimes an old function that didn't throw an exception is replaced with a new one that does, and you'll get a call to **unexpected( )**. Anytime you use exception specifications or call functions that do, you should create your own **unexpected( )** function that logs a message and rethrows the same exception.

start with standard exceptions

Check out the Standard C++ library exceptions before creating your own. If a standard exception does what you need, chances are it's a lot easier for your user to understand and handle.

If the exception type you want isn't part of the standard library, try to derive one from an existing standard **exception**. It's nice for your users if they can always write their code to expect the **what( )** function defined in the **exception( )** class interface.

nest your own exceptions

If you create exceptions for your particular class, it's a very good idea to nest the exception classes inside your class to provide a clear message to the reader that this exception is used only for your class. In addition, it prevents the pollution of the namespace.

You can nest your exceptions even if you're deriving them from C++ standard exceptions.

use exception hierarchies

Exception hierarchies provide a valuable way to classify the different types of critical errors that may be encountered with your class or library. This gives helpful information to users, assists them in organizing their code, and gives them the option of ignoring all the specific types of exceptions and just catching the base-class type. Also, any exceptions added later by inheriting from the same

Thinking in C++   Bruce Eckel

base class will not force all existing code to be rewritten — the base-class handler will catch the new exception.

Of course, the Standard C++ exceptions are a good example of an exception hierarchy, and one that you can use to build upon.

multiple inheritance

You'll remember from Chapter 14 that the only *essential* place for MI is if you need to upcast a pointer to your object into two different base classes — that is, if you need polymorphic behavior with both of those base classes. It turns out that exception hierarchies are a useful place for multiple inheritance because a base-class handler from any of the roots of the multiply inherited exception class can handle the exception.

catch by reference, not by value

If you throw an object of a derived class and it is caught *by value* in a handler for an object of the base class, that object is "sliced" — that is, the derived-class elements are cut off and you'll end up with the base-class object being passed. Chances are this is not what you want because the object will behave like a base-class object and not the derived class object it really is (or rather, was — before it was sliced). Here's an example:

```
//: CATCHREF.CPP -- Why catch by reference?
#include <iostream.h>

class base {
public:
  virtual void what() {
    cout << "base" << endl;
  }
};

class derived : public base {
public:
  void what() {
    cout << "derived" << endl;
```

```
    }
};

void f() { throw derived(); }

main() {
  try {
    f();
  } catch(base b) {
    b.what();
  }
  try {
    f();
  } catch(base& b) {
    b.what();
  }
}
```

The output is

```
base
derived
```

because, when the object is caught by value, it is *turned into* a **base** object (by the copy-constructor) and must behave that way in all situations, whereas when it's caught by reference, only the address is passed and the object isn't truncated, so it behaves like what it really is, a **derived** in this case.

Although you can also throw and catch pointers, by doing so you introduce more coupling — the thrower and the catcher must agree on how the exception object is allocated and cleaned up. This is a problem because the exception itself may have occurred from heap exhaustion. If you throw exception objects, the exception-handling system takes care of all storage.

throw exceptions in constructors

Because a constructor has no return value, you've previously had two choices to report an error during construction:

1. Set a nonlocal flag and hope the user checks it.

2. Return an incompletely created object and hope the user checks it.

This is a serious problem because C programmers have come to rely on an implied guarantee that object creation is always successful, which is not unreasonable in C where types are so primitive. But continuing execution after construction fails in a C++ program is a guaranteed disaster, so constructors are one of the most important places to throw exceptions — now you have a safe, effective way to handle constructor errors. However, you must also pay attention to pointers inside objects and the way cleanup occurs when an exception is thrown inside a constructor.

don't cause exceptions in destructors

Because destructors are called in the process of throwing other exceptions, you'll never want to throw an exception in a destructor or cause another exception to be thrown by some action you perform in the destructor. If this happens, it means that a new exception may be thrown *before* the catch-clause for an existing exception is reached, which will cause a call to **terminate( )**.

This means that if you call any functions inside a destructor that may throw exceptions, those calls should be within a **try** block in the destructor, and the destructor must handle all exceptions itself. None must escape from the destructor.

avoid naked pointers

See WRAPPED.CPP (page 704). A naked pointer usually means vulnerability in the constructor if resources are allocated for that pointer. A pointer doesn't have a destructor, so those resources won't be released if an exception is thrown in the constructor.

overhead

Of course it costs something for this new feature; when an exception is thrown there's considerable run-time overhead. This is the reason you never want to use exceptions as part of your normal flow-of-control, no matter how tempting and clever it may seem. Exceptions should occur only rarely, so the overhead is piled on the exception and not on the normally executing code. One of the important design goals for exception handling was that it could be implemented with no impact on execution speed when it *wasn't* used; that is, as long as you don't throw an exception, your code runs as fast as it would without exception handling. Whether or not this is actually true depends on the particular compiler implementation you're using.

Exception handling also causes extra information to be put on the stack by the compiler, to aid in stack unwinding.

Exception objects are properly passed around like any other objects, except that they can be passed into and out of what can be thought of as a special "exception scope" (which may just be the global scope). That's how they go from one place to another. When the exception handler is finished, the exception objects are properly destroyed.

summary

Error recovery is a fundamental concern for every program you write, and it's especially important in C++, where one of the goals is to create program components for others to use. To create a robust system, each component must be robust.

The goals for exception handling in C++ are to simplify the creation of large, reliable programs using less code than currently possible, with more confidence that your application doesn't have an unhandled error. This is accomplished with little or no performance penalty, and with low impact on existing code.

Basic exceptions are not terribly difficult to learn, and you should begin using them in your programs as soon as you can. Exceptions are one of those features that provide immediate and significant benefits to your project.

exercises

1. Create a class with member functions that throw exceptions. Within this class, make a nested class to use as an exception object. It takes a single **char*** as its argument; this represents a description string. Create a member function that throws this exception. (State this in the function's exception specification.) Write a try block that calls this function and a catch clause that handles the exception by printing out its description string.

2. Rewrite the **stash** class from Chapter 11 so it throws out-of-range exceptions for **operator[]**.

3. Write a generic **main( )** that takes all exceptions and reports them as errors.

4. Create a class with its own **operator new**. This operator should allocate 10 objects, and on the 11th "run out of memory" and throw an exception. Also add a static member function that reclaims this memory. Now create a **main( )** with a **try** block and a **catch** clause that calls the memory-restoration routine. Put these inside a **while** loop, to demonstrate recovering from an exception and continuing execution.

5. Create a destructor that throws an exception, and write code to prove to yourself that this is a bad idea by showing that if a new exception is thrown before the handler for the existing one is reached, **terminate( )** is called.

6. Prove to yourself that all exception objects (the ones that are thrown) are properly destroyed.

7. Prove to yourself that if you create an exception object on the heap and throw the pointer to that object, it will *not* be cleaned up.

8. (Advanced). Track the creation and passing of an exception using a class with a constructor and copy-constructor that announce themselves and provide as much information as possible about how the object is being created (and in the case of the copy-constructor, what object it's being created from). Set up an interesting situation, throw an object of your new type, and analyze the result.

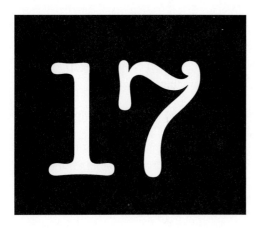

run-time type identification

Run-time type identification (RTTI) lets you find the exact type of an object when you have only a pointer or reference to the base type.

This can be thought of as a "secondary" feature in C++, a pragmatism to help out when you get into messy situations. Normally, you'll want to intentionally ignore the exact type of an object and let the virtual function mechanism implement the correct behavior for that type. But occasionally it's useful to know the exact type of an object for which you only have a base pointer. Often this information allows you to perform a special-case operation more efficiently or prevent a base-class interface from becoming ungainly. It happens enough that most class libraries

contain virtual functions to produce run-time type information.
When exception handling was added to C++, it required the exact
type information about objects. It became an easy next step to build
access to that information into the language.

This chapter explains what RTTI is for and how to use it. In addition,
it explains the why and how of the new C++ cast syntax, which
has the same appearance as RTTI.

the "shape" example

This is an example of a class hierarchy that uses polymorphism.
The generic type is the base class **shape**, and the specific derived
types are **circle**, **square**, and **triangle**:

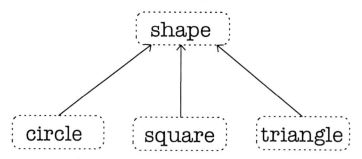

This is a typical class-hierarchy diagram, with the base class at the
top and the derived classes growing downward. The normal goal in
object-oriented programming is for the bulk of your code to
manipulate pointers to the base type (**shape**, in this case) so if you
decide to extend the program by adding a new class (**rhomboid**,
derived from **shape**, for example), the bulk of the code is not
affected. In this example, the virtual function in the **shape** interface
is **draw( )**, so the intent is for the client programmer to call **draw( )**
through a generic **shape** pointer. **draw( )** is redefined in all the
derived classes, and because it is a virtual function, the proper
behavior will occur even though it is called through a generic
shape pointer.

Thus, you generally create a specific object (**circle**, **square**, or **triangle**), take its address and cast it to a **shape*** (forgetting the specific type of the object), and use that anonymous pointer in the rest of the program. Historically, diagrams are drawn as seen above, so the act of casting from a more derived type to a base type is called *upcasting*.

what is RTTI?

But what if you have a special programming problem that's easiest to solve if you know the exact type of a generic pointer? For example, suppose you want to allow your users to highlight all the shapes of any particular type by turning them purple. This way, they can find all the triangles on the screen by highlighting them. Your natural first approach may be to try a virtual function like **TurnColorIfYouAreA( )**, which allows enumerated arguments of some type **color** and of **shape::circle**, **shape::square**, or **shape::triangle**.

To solve this sort of problem, most class library designers put virtual functions in the base class to return type information about the specific object at run-time. You may have seen library member functions with names like **isA( )** and **typeOf( )**. These are vendor-defined RTTI functions. Using these functions, as you go through the list you can say, "If you're a triangle, turn purple."

When exception handling was added to C++, the implementation required that some run-time type information be put into the virtual function tables. This meant that with a small language extension the programmer could also get the run-time type information about an object. All library vendors were adding their own RTTI anyway, so it was included in the language.

RTTI, like exceptions, depends on type information residing in the virtual function table. If you try to use RTTI on a class that has no virtual functions, you'll get unexpected results.

Two syntaxes for RTTI

There are two different ways to use RTTI. The first acts like **sizeof( )** because it looks like a function, but it's actually implemented by the compiler. **typeid( )** takes an argument that's an object, a reference, or a pointer and returns a reference to a global **const** object of type **typeinfo**. These can be compared to each other with the **operator==** and **operator!=**, and you can also ask for the **name( )** of the type, which returns a string representation of the type name. Note that if you hand **typeid( )** a **shape***, it will say that the type is **shape***, so if you want to know the exact type it is pointing to, you must dereference the pointer. For example, if **s** is a **shape***,

```
cout << typeid(*s).name() << endl;
```

will print out the type of the object **s** points to.

You can also ask a **typeinfo** object if it precedes another **typeinfo** object in the implementation-defined "collation sequence," using **before(typeinfo&)**, which returns true or false. When you say,

```
if(typeid(me).before(typeid(you))) // ...
```

you're asking if **me** occurs before **you** in the collation sequence.

The second syntax for RTTI is called a "type-safe downcast." The reason for the term "downcast" is (again) the historical arrangement of the class hierarchy diagram. If casting a **circle*** to a **shape*** is an upcast, then casting a **shape*** to a **circle*** is a downcast. However, you know a **circle*** is also a **shape***, and the compiler freely allows an upcast assignment, but you *don't* know that a **shape*** is necessarily a **circle***, so the compiler doesn't allow you to perform a downcast assignment without using an explicit cast. You can of course force your way through using ordinary C-style casts or a C++ **static_cast** (described at the end of this chapter), which says, "I hope this is actually a **circle***, and I'm going to pretend it is." Without some explicit knowledge that it *is* in fact a circle, this is a totally dangerous thing to do. A common approach in vendor-defined RTTI is to create some function that attempts to assign (for this example) a **shape*** to a **circle***, checking the type in the process. If this function returns the address, it was successful; if it returns null, you didn't have a **circle***.

The C++ RTTI typesafe-downcast follows this "attempt-to-cast" function form, but it uses (very logically) the template syntax to produce the special function **dynamic_cast**. So the example becomes

```
shape* sp = new circle;
circle* cp = dynamic_cast<circle*>(sp);
if(cp) cout << "cast successful";
```

The template argument for **dynamic_cast** is the type you want the function to produce, and this is the return value for the function. The function argument is what you are trying to cast from.

Normally you might be hunting for one type (triangles to turn purple, for instance), but the following example fragment can be used if you want to count the number of various shapes.

```
circle* cp = dynamic_cast<circle*>(sh);
square* sp = dynamic_cast<square*>(sh);
triangle* tp = dynamic_cast<triangle*>(sh);
```

Of course this is contrived — you'd probably put a **static** data member in each type and increment it in the constructor. You would do something like that *if* you had control of the source code for the class and could change it. Here's an example that counts shapes using both the **static** member approach and **dynamic_cast**:

```
//: RTSHAPES.CPP -- Counting shapes
#include <iostream.h>
#include <time.h>
#include <typeinfo.h>
#include "..\14\tstash.h"

class shape {
```

```
protected:
  static int count;
public:
  shape() { count++; }
  virtual ~shape() = 0 { count--; }
  virtual void draw() const = 0;
  static int quantity() { return count; }
};

int shape::count = 0;

class rectangle : public shape {
  void operator=(rectangle&); // Disallow
protected:
  static int count;
public:
  rectangle() { count++; }
  rectangle(const rectangle&) { count++;}
  ~rectangle() { count--; }
  void draw() const {
    cout << "rectangle::draw()" << endl;
  }
  static int quantity() { return count; }
};

int rectangle::count = 0;

class ellipse : public shape {
  void operator=(ellipse&); // Disallow
protected:
  static int count;
public:
  ellipse() { count++; }
  ellipse(const ellipse&) { count++; }
  ~ellipse() { count--; }
  void draw() const {
    cout << "ellipse::draw()" << endl;
```

```
  }
  static int quantity() { return count; }
};

int ellipse::count = 0;

class circle : public ellipse {
  void operator=(circle&); // Disallow
protected:
  static int count;
public:
  circle() { count++; }
  circle(const circle&) { count++; }
  ~circle() { count--; }
  void draw() const {
    cout << "circle::draw()" << endl;
  }
  static int quantity() { return count; }
};

int circle::count = 0;

main() {
  tstash<shape> shapes;
  time_t t;
  // Seed random number generator:
  srand((unsigned)time(&t));
  const mod = 12;
  for(int i = 0; i < rand() % mod; i++)
    shapes.add(new rectangle);
  for(int j = 0; j < rand() % mod; j++)
    shapes.add(new ellipse);
  for(int k = 0; k < rand() % mod; k++)
    shapes.add(new circle);
  int Ncircles = 0;
  int Nellipses = 0;
  int Nrects = 0;
```

```
int Nshapes = 0;
for(int u = 0; u < shapes.count(); u++) {
  shapes[u]->draw();
  if(dynamic_cast<circle*>(shapes[u]))
    Ncircles++;
  if(dynamic_cast<ellipse*>(shapes[u]))
    Nellipses++;
  if(dynamic_cast<rectangle*>(shapes[u]))
    Nrects++;
  if(dynamic_cast<shape*>(shapes[u]))
    Nshapes++;
}
cout << endl << endl
     << "circles = " << Ncircles << endl
     << "ellipses = " << Nellipses << endl
     << "rectangles = " << Nrects << endl
     << "shapes = " << Nshapes << endl
     << endl
     << "circle::quantity() = "
     << circle::quantity() << endl
     << "ellipse::quantity() = "
     << ellipse::quantity() << endl
     << "rectangle::quantity() = "
     << rectangle::quantity() << endl
     << "shape::quantity() = "
     << shape::quantity() << endl;
}
```

Both types work for this example, but the **static** member approach can be used only if you own the code and have installed the **static** members and functions (or if a vendor provides them for you). In addition, the syntax for RTTI may then be different from one class to another.

syntax specifics

This section looks at the details of how the two forms of RTTI work, and how they differ.

typeid( ) with built-in types

For consistency, the **typeid( )** operator works with built-in types. So the following expressions are true:

```
typeid(47) == typeid(int)
typeid(0) == typeid(int)
int i;
typeid(i) == typeid(int)
typeid(&i) == typeid(int*)
```

producing the proper type name

typeid( ) must work properly in all situations. For example, the following class contains a nested class:

```
//: RNEST.CPP -- Nesting and RTTI
#include <iostream.h>
#include <typeinfo.h>

class one {
  class nested {};
  nested* n;
public:
  one() { n = new nested; }
  ~one() { delete n; }
  nested* N() { return n; }
};

main() {
  one O;
  cout << typeid(*O.N()).name() << endl;
```

```
}
```

The **typeinfo::name( )** member function will still produce the proper class name; the result is **one::nested**.

nonpolymorphic types

Although **typeid( )** works with nonpolymorphic types (those that don't have a virtual function in the base class), the information you get this way is dubious. For the following class hierarchy,

```
class X {
  int i;
public:
  // ...
};
class Y : public X {
  int j;
public:
  // ...
};
```

If you create an object of the derived type and upcast it,

```
X* xp = new Y;
```

The **typeid( )** operator will produce results, but not the ones you might expect. Because there's no polymorphism, the static type information is used:

```
typeid(*xp) == typeid(X)
typeid(*xp) != typeid(Y)
```

RTTI is intended for use only with polymorphic classes.

casting to intermediate levels

dynamic_cast can detect both exact types and, in an inheritance hierarchy with multiple levels, intermediate types. For example,

---

Thinking in C++   *Bruce Eckel*

```
class d1 {
public:
  virtual void foo() {}
};
class d2 {
public:
  virtual void bar() {}
};
class mi : public d1, public d2 { };
class mi2 : public mi {};

d2* D2 = new mi2;
mi2* MI2 = dynamic_cast<mi2*>(D2);
mi* MI = dynamic_cast<mi*>(D2);
```

This has the extra complication of multiple inheritance. If you create an **mi2** and upcast it to the root (in this case, one of the two possible roots is chosen), then the **dynamic_cast** back to either of the derived levels **mi** or **mi2** is successful.

You can even cast from one root to the other:

```
d1* D1 = dynamic_cast<d1*>(D2);
```

This is successful because **D2** is actually pointing to an **mi2** object, which contains a subobject of type **d1**.

Casting to intermediate levels brings up an interesting difference between **dynamic_cast** and **typeid( )**. **typeid( )** always produces a reference to a **typeinfo** object that describes the *exact* type of the object. Thus it doesn't give you intermediate-level information. In the following expression (which is true), **typeid( )** doesn't see **D2** as a pointer to the derived type, like **dynamic_cast** does:

```
typeid(D2) != typeid(mi2*)
```

The type of **D2** is simply the exact type of the pointer:

```
typeid(D2) == typeid(d2*)
```

---

void pointers

Run-time type identification doesn't work with **void** pointers:

```
//: VOIDRTTI.CPP -- RTTI & void pointers
#include <iostream.h>
#include <typeinfo.h>

class stimpy {
public:
  virtual void happy() {}
  virtual void joy() {}
};

main() {
  void* v = new stimpy;
  // Error:
//!  stimpy* s = dynamic_cast<stimpy*>(v);
  // Error:
//!  cout << typeid(*v).name() << endl;
}
```

A **void*** truly means "no type information at all."

using RTTI with templates

Templates generate many different class names, and sometimes you'd like to print out information about what class you're in. RTTI provides a convenient way to do this. The following example revisits the code in Chapter 12 to print out the order of constructor and destructor calls without using a preprocessor macro:

```
//: INHORDER.CPP -- Order of constructor calls
#include <iostream.h>
#include <typeinfo.h>

template<int id> class announce {
public:
```

```
  announce() {
    cout << typeid(*this).name()
         << " constructor " << endl;
  }
  ~announce() {
    cout << typeid(*this).name()
         << " destructor " << endl;
  }
};

class X : public announce<0> {
  announce<1> m1;
  announce<2> m2;
public:
  X() { cout << "X::X()" << endl; }
  ~X() { cout << "X::~X()" << endl; }
};

main() { X x; }
```

The TYPEINFO.H header must be included to call any member functions for the **typeinfo** object returned by **typeid( )**. The template uses a constant **int** to differentiate one class from another, but class arguments will work as well. Inside both the constructor and destructor, RTTI information is used to produce the name of the class to print. The class **X** uses both inheritance and composition to create a class that has an interesting order of constructor and destructor calls.

This technique is often useful in situations when you're trying to understand how the language works.

references

RTTI must adjust somewhat to work with references. The contrast between pointers and references occurs because a reference is

---

always dereferenced for you by the compiler, whereas a pointer's type *or* the type it points to may be examined. Here's an example:

```
class B {
public:
  virtual float f() { return 1.0;}
};
class D : public B { /* ... */ };
B* p = new D;
B& r = *p;
```

Whereas the type of pointer that **typeid( )** sees is the base type and not the derived type, the type it sees for the reference is the derived type:

```
typeid(p)  == typeid(B*)
typeid(p)  != typeid(D*)
typeid(r)  == typeid(D)
```

Conversely, what the pointer points to is the derived type and not the base type, and taking the address of the reference produces the base type and not the derived type:

```
typeid(*p)  == typeid(D)
typeid(*p)  != typeid(B)
typeid(&r)  == typeid(B*)
typeid(&r)  != typeid(D*)
```

Expressions may also be used with the **typeid( )** operator because they have a type as well:

```
typeid(r.f())  == typeid(float)
```

exceptions

When you perform a **dynamic_cast** to a reference, the result must be assigned to a reference. But what happens if the cast fails? There are no null references, so this is the perfect place to throw an exception; the Standard C++ exception type is **bad_cast**, but in the following example the ellipses are used to catch any exception:

```
class X {};

mi MI;
d1 & D1 = MI; // upcast to reference
try {
  X& xr = dynamic_cast<X&>(D1);
} catch(...) {
  cout << "dynamic_cast<X&>(D1) failed"
       << endl;
}
```

The failure, of course, is because **D1** doesn't actually point to an **X** object. If an exception was not thrown here, then **xr** would be unbound, and the guarantee that all objects or references are constructed storage would be broken.

An exception is also thrown if you try to dereference a null pointer in the process of calling **typeid( )**. The Standard C++ exception is called **bad_typeid**:

```
B* bp = 0;
try {
  typeid(*bp); // throws exception
} catch(bad_typeid) {
  cout << "Bad typeid() expression" << endl;
}
```

Here (unlike the reference example above) you can avoid the exception by checking for a nonzero pointer value before attempting the operation; this is the preferred practice.

multiple inheritance

Of course, the RTTI mechanisms must work properly with all the complexities of multiple inheritance, including **virtual** base classes:

```
//: MIRTTI.CPP -- MI & RTTI
```

```
#include <iostream.h>
#include <typeinfo.h>

class BB {
public:
 virtual void f() {}
};
class B1 : virtual public BB {};
class B2 : virtual public BB {};
class MI : public B1, public B2 {};

main() {
  BB* bbp = new MI; // Upcast
  // Proper name detection:
  cout << typeid(*bbp).name() << endl;
  // Dynamic_cast works properly:
  MI* mip = dynamic_cast<MI*>(bbp);
  // Can't force old-style cast:
  //! MI* mip2 = (MI*)bbp; // Compile error
}
```

typeid( ) properly detects the name of the actual object, even through the **virtual** base class pointer. The **dynamic_cast** also works correctly. But the compiler won't even allow you to try to force a cast the old way:

```
MI* mip = (MI*)bbp; // compile-time error
```

It knows this is never the right thing to do, so it requires that you use a **dynamic_cast**.

sensible uses for RTTI

Because it allows you to discover type information from an anonymous polymorphic pointer, RTTI is ripe for misuse by the novice because RTTI may make sense before virtual functions do.

For many people coming from a procedural background, it's very difficult not to organize their programs into sets of **switch** statements. They could accomplish this with RTTI and thus lose the very important value of polymorphism in code development and maintenance. The intent of C++ is that you use virtual functions throughout your code, and you only use RTTI when you must.

However, using virtual functions as they are intended requires that you have control of the base-class definition because at some point in the extension of your program you may discover the base class doesn't include the virtual function you need. If the base class comes from a library or is otherwise controlled by someone else, a solution to the problem is RTTI: You can inherit a new type and add your extra member function. Elsewhere in the code you can detect your particular type and call that member function. This doesn't destroy the polymorphism and extensibility of the program, because adding a new type will not require you to hunt for switch statements. However, when you add new code in your main body that requires your new feature, you'll have to detect your particular type.

Putting a feature in a base class might mean that, for the benefit of one particular class, all the other classes derived from that base require some meaningless stub of a virtual function. This makes the interface less clear and annoys those who must redefine pure virtual functions when they derive from that base class. For example, suppose that in the WIND5.CPP program in Chapter 13 (page 553) you wanted to clear the spit valves of all the instruments in your orchestra that had them. One option is to put a **virtual ClearSpitValve( )** function in the base class **instrument**, but this is confusing because it implies that **percussion** and **electronic** instruments also have spit valves. RTTI provides a much more reasonable solution in this case because you can place the function in the specific class (**wind** in this case) where it's appropriate.

Finally, RTTI will sometimes solve efficiency problems. If your code uses polymorphism in a nice way, but it turns out that one of your objects reacts to this general-purpose code in a horribly inefficient way, you can pick that type out using RTTI and write case-specific code to improve the efficiency.

revisiting the trash recycler

Here's the trash recycling simulation from Chapter 14, rewritten to use RTTI instead of building the information into the class hierarchy:

```
//: RECYCLE2.CPP -- Chapter 14 example w/ RTTI
#include <fstream.h>
#include <stdlib.h>
#include <time.h>
#include <typeinfo.h>
#include "..\14\tstack.h"
ofstream out("recycle2.out");

class trash {
  float Weight;
public:
  trash(float Wt) : Weight(Wt) {}
  virtual float value() const = 0;
  float weight() const { return Weight; }
  virtual ~trash() {}
};

class aluminum : public trash {
  static float val;
public:
  aluminum(float Wt) : trash(Wt) {}
  float value() const { return val; }
  static void value(int newval) {
    val = newval;
  }
};

float aluminum::val = 1.67;
```

```
class paper : public trash {
  static float val;
public:
  paper(float Wt) : trash(Wt) {}
  float value() const { return val; }
  static void value(int newval) {
    val = newval;
  }
};

float paper::val = 0.10;

class glass : public trash {
  static float val;
public:
  glass(float Wt) : trash(Wt) {}
  float value() const { return val; }
  static void value(int newval) {
    val = newval;
  }
};

float glass::val = 0.23;

// Sums up the value of the trash in a bin:
template<class T> void
SumValue(const tstack<T>& bin, ostream& os) {
  tstackIterator<T> tally(bin);
  float val = 0;
  while(tally) {
    val += tally->weight() * tally->value();
    os << "weight of "
        << typeid(*tally.current()).name()
        << " = " << tally->weight() << endl;
    tally++;
  }
```

```
  os << "Total value = " << val << endl;
}

main() {
  // Seed the random number generator
  time_t t;
  srand((unsigned)time(&t));

  tstack<trash> bin; // Default to ownership
  // Fill up the trash bin:
  for(int i = 0; i < 30; i++)
    switch(rand() % 3) {
      case 0 :
        bin.push(new aluminum(rand() % 100));
        break;
      case 1 :
        bin.push(new paper(rand() % 100));
        break;
      case 2 :
        bin.push(new glass(rand() % 100));
        break;
    }
  // Note difference w/ chapter 14: Bins hold
  // exact type of object, not base type:
  tstack<glass> glassbin(0); // No ownership
  tstack<paper> paperbin(0);
  tstack<aluminum> ALbin(0);
  tstackIterator<trash> sorter(bin);
  // Sort the trash:
  while(sorter) {
    aluminum* ap =
      dynamic_cast<aluminum*>(sorter.current());
    paper* pp =
      dynamic_cast<paper*>(sorter.current());
    glass* gp =
      dynamic_cast<glass*>(sorter.current());
    if(ap) ALbin.push(ap);
```

```
        if(pp) paperbin.push(pp);
        if(gp) glassbin.push(gp);
        sorter++;
    }
    SumValue(ALbin, out);
    SumValue(paperbin, out);
    SumValue(glassbin, out);
    SumValue(bin, out);
}
```

The nature of this problem is that the trash is thrown unclassified into a single bin, so the specific type information is lost. But later, the specific type information must be recovered to properly sort the trash, and so RTTI is used. In Chapter 14, an RTTI system was inserted into the class hierarchy, but as you can see here, it's more convenient to use C++'s built-in RTTI.

mechanism & overhead of RTTI

Typically, RTTI is implemented by placing an additional pointer in the VTABLE. This pointer points to the **typeinfo** structure for that particular type. (Only one instance of the **typeinfo** structure is created for each new class.) So the effect of a **typeid( )** expression is quite simple: The VPTR is used to fetch the **typeinfo** pointer, and a reference to the resulting **typeinfo** structure is produced. Also, this is a deterministic process — you always know how long it's going to take.

For a **dynamic_cast<destination*>(source_pointer)**, most cases are quite straightforward: **source_pointer**'s RTTI information is retrieved, and RTTI information for the type **destination*** is fetched. Then a library routine determines whether **source_pointer**'s type is of type **destination*** or a base class of **destination***. The pointer it returns may be slightly adjusted because of multiple inheritance if the base type isn't the first base of the derived class. The situation is (of course) more complicated with multiple inheritance where a base type may appear more than once in an inheritance hierarchy and where virtual base classes are used.

Because the library routine used for **dynamic_cast** must check through a list of base classes, the overhead for **dynamic_cast** is higher than **typeid( )** (but of course you get different information, which may be essential to your solution), and it's nondeterministic because it may take more time to discover a base class than a derived class. In addition, **dynamic_cast** allows you to compare any type to any other type; you aren't restricted to comparing types within the same hierarchy. This adds extra overhead to the library routine used by **dynamic_cast**.

creating your own RTTI

If your compiler doesn't yet support RTTI, you can build it into your class libraries quite easily. This makes sense because RTTI was added to the language after observing that virtually all class libraries had some form of it anyway (and it was relatively "free" after exception handling was added because exceptions require exact knowledge of type information).

Essentially, RTTI requires only a virtual function to identify the exact type of the class, and a function to take a pointer to the base type and cast it down to the more derived type; this function must produce a pointer to the more derived type. (You may also wish to handle references.) There are a number of approaches to implement your own RTTI, but all require a unique identifier for each class and a virtual function to produce type information. The following uses a **static** member function called **dynacast( )** that calls a type information function **dynamic_type( )**. Both functions must be defined for each new derivation:

```
//: SELFRTTI.CPP -- Your own RTTI system
#include "..\14\tstack.h"
#include <iostream.h>
class security {
protected:
  enum { baseID = 1000 };
public:
  virtual int dynamic_type(int ID) {
    if(ID == baseID) return 1;
    return 0;
  }
};

class stock : public security {
protected:
  enum { typeID = baseID + 1 };
public:
  int dynamic_type(int ID) {
    if(ID == typeID) return 1;
    return security::dynamic_type(ID);
  }
  static stock* dynacast(security* s) {
    if(s->dynamic_type(typeID))
      return (stock*)s;
    return 0;
  }
};

class bond : public security {
protected:
  enum { typeID = baseID + 2 };
public:
  int dynamic_type(int ID) {
    if(ID == typeID) return 1;
    return security::dynamic_type(ID);
  }
  static bond* dynacast(security* s) {
```

```
    if(s->dynamic_type(typeID))
      return (bond*)s;
    return 0;
  }
};

class commodity : public security {
protected:
  enum { typeID = baseID + 3};
public:
  int dynamic_type(int ID) {
    if(ID == typeID) return 1;
    return security::dynamic_type(ID);
  }
  static commodity* dynacast(security* s) {
    if(s->dynamic_type(typeID))
      return (commodity*)s;
    return 0;
  }
  void special() {
    cout << "special commodity function\n";
  }
};

class metal : public commodity {
protected:
  enum { typeID = baseID + 4};
public:
  int dynamic_type(int ID) {
    if(ID == typeID) return 1;
    return commodity::dynamic_type(ID);
  }
  static metal* dynacast(security* s) {
    if(s->dynamic_type(typeID))
      return (metal*)s;
    return 0;
  }
```

```
};

main() {
  tstack<security> portfolio;
  portfolio.push(new metal);
  portfolio.push(new commodity);
  portfolio.push(new bond);
  portfolio.push(new stock);
  tstackIterator<security> it(portfolio);
  while(it) {
    commodity* cm =
      commodity::dynacast(it.current());
    if(cm) cm->special();
    else cout << "not a commodity" << endl;
    it++;
  }
  cout << "cast from intermediate pointer:\n";
  security* sp = new metal;
  commodity* cp = commodity::dynacast(sp);
  if(cp) cout << "it's a commodity\n";
  metal* mp = metal::dynacast(sp);
  if(mp) cout << "it's a metal too!\n";
}
```

Each subclass must create its own **typeID**, redefine the **virtual dynamic_type( )** function to return that **typeID**, and define a **static** member called **dynacast( )**, which takes the base pointer (or a pointer at any level in a deeper hierarchy — in that case, the pointer is simply upcast).

In the classes derived from **security**, you can see that each defines its own **typeID** enumeration by adding to **baseID**. It's essential that **baseID** be directly accessible in the derived class because the **enum** must be evaluated at compile-time, so the usual approach of reading private data with an **inline** function would fail. This is a good example of the need for the **protected** mechanism.

The **enum baseID** establishes a base identifier for all types derived from **security**. That way, if an identifier clash ever occurs, you can change all the identifiers by changing the base value. (However, because this scheme doesn't compare different inheritance trees, an identifier clash is unlikely). In all the classes, the class identifier number is **protected**, so it's directly available to derived classes but not to the end user.

This example illustrates what built-in RTTI must cope with. Not only must you be able to determine the exact type, you must also be able to find out whether your exact type is *derived from* the type you're looking for. For example, **metal** is derived from **commodity**, which has a function called **special( )**, so if you have a **metal** object you can call **special( )** for it. If **dynamic_type( )** told you only the exact type of the object, you could ask it if a **metal** were a **commodity**, and it would say "no," which is untrue. Therefore, the system must be set up so it will properly cast to intermediate types in a hierarchy as well as exact types.

The **dynacast( )** function determines the type information by calling the **virtual dynamic_type( )** function for the **security** pointer it's passed. This function takes an argument of the **typeID** for the class you're trying to cast to. It's a virtual function, so the function body is the one for the exact type of the object. Each **dynamic_type( )** function first checks to see if the identifier it was passed is an exact match for its own type. If that isn't true, it must check to see if it matches a base type; this is accomplished by making a call to the base class **dynamic_type( )**. Just like a recursive function call, each **dynamic_type( )** checks against its own identifier. If it doesn't find a match, it returns the result of calling the base class **dynamic_type( )**. When the root of the hierarchy is reached, zero is returned to indicate no match was found.

If **dynamic_type( )** returns one (for "true") the object pointed to is either the exact type you're asking about or derived from that type, and **dynacast( )** takes the **security** pointer and casts it to the desired type. If the return value is false, **dynacast( )** returns zero to indicate the cast was unsuccessful. In this way it works just like the C++ **dynamic_cast** operator.

The C++ **dynamic_cast** operator does one more thing the above scheme can't do: It compares types from one inheritance hierarchy to another, completely separate inheritance hierarchy. This adds generality to the system for those unusual cases where you want to compare across hierarchies, but it also adds some complexity and overhead.

You can easily imagine how to create a DYNAMIC_CAST macro that uses the above scheme and allows an easier transition to the built-in **dynamic_cast** operator.

new cast syntax

Whenever you use a cast, you're breaking the type system.[1] You're telling the compiler that even though you know an object is a certain type, you're going to pretend it is a different type. This is an inherently dangerous activity, and a clear source of errors.

Unfortunately, each cast is different: the name of the pretender type surrounded by parentheses. So if you are given a piece of code that isn't working correctly and you know you want to examine all casts to see if they're the source of the errors, how can you guarantee that you find all the casts? In a C program, you can't. For one thing, the C compiler doesn't always require a cast (it's possible to assign dissimilar types *through* a void pointer without being forced to use a cast), and the casts all look different, so you can't know if you've searched for every one.

To solve this problem, C++ provides a consistent casting syntax using four reserved words: **dynamic_cast** (the subject of the first

---

[1] See Josée Lajoie, "The new cast notation and the bool data type," C++ Report, September, 1994 pp. 46-51.

part of this chapter), **const_cast**, **static_cast,** and **reinterpret_cast**. This window of opportunity opened up when the need for **dynamic_cast** arose — the meaning of the existing cast syntax was already far too overloaded to support any additional functionality.

By using these casts instead of the **(newtype)** syntax, you can easily search for all the casts in any program. To support existing code, most compilers have various levels of error/warning generation that can be turned on and off. But if you turn on full errors for the new cast syntax, you can be guaranteed that you'll find all the places in your project where casts occur, which will make bug-hunting much easier.

The following table describes the different forms of casting:

static_cast	For "well-behaved" and "reasonably well-behaved" casts, including things you might now do without a cast (e.g., an upcast or automatic type conversion).
const_cast	To cast away **const** and/or **volatile**.
dynamic_cast	For type-safe downcasting (described earlier in the chapter).
reinterpret_cast	To cast to a completely different meaning. The key is that you'll need to cast back to the original type to use it safely. The type you cast to is typically used only for bit twiddling or some other mysterious purpose. This is the most dangerous of all the casts.

The three new casts will be described more completely in the following sections.

static_cast

A **static_cast** is used for all conversions that are well-defined. These include "safe" conversions that the compiler would allow you to do without a cast and less-safe conversions that are nonetheless well-defined. The types of conversions covered by **static_cast** include typical castless conversions, narrowing (information-losing) conversions, forcing a conversion from a **void***, implicit type conversions, and static navigation of class hierarchies:

```
//: STATCAST.CPP -- Examples of static_cast

class base { /* ... */ };
class derived : public base {
public:
  // ...
  // Automatic type conversion:
  operator int() { return 1; }
};

void func(int) {}

class other {};

main() {
  int i = 0x7fff; // Max pos value = 32767
  long l;
  float f;
  //(1) typical castless conversions:
  l = i;
  f = i;
  // Also works:
  l = static_cast<long>(i);
  f = static_cast<float>(i);

  //(2) narrowing conversions:
  i = l; // May lose digits
  i = f; // May lose info
```

```
// Says "I know," eliminates warnings:
i = static_cast<int>(l);
i = static_cast<int>(f);
char c = static_cast<char>(i);

//(3) forcing a conversion from void* :
void* vp = &i;
// Old way produces a dangerous conversion:
float* fp = (float*)vp;
// The new way is equally dangerous:
fp = static_cast<float*>(vp);

//(4) implicit type conversions, normally
// Performed by the compiler:
derived d;
base* bp = &d; // Upcast: normal and OK
bp = static_cast<base*>(&d); // More explicit
int x = d; // Automatic type conversion
x = static_cast<int>(d); // More explicit
func(d); // Automatic type conversion
func(static_cast<int>(d)); // More explicit

//(5) Static Navigation of class hierarchies:
derived* dp = static_cast<derived*>(bp);
// ONLY an efficiency hack. dynamic_cast is
// Always safer. However:
// Other* op = static_cast<other*>(bp);
// Conveniently gives an error message, while
other* op2 = (other*)bp;
// Does not.
}
```

In Section (1), you see the kinds of conversions you're used to doing in C, with or without a cast. Promoting from an **int** to a **long** or **float** is not a problem because the latter can always hold every value that an **int** can contain. Although it's unnecessary, you can use **static_cast** to highlight these promotions.

Converting back the other way is shown in (2). Here, you can lose data because an **int** is not as "wide" as a **long** or a **float** — it won't hold numbers of the same size. Thus these are called "narrowing conversions." The compiler will still perform these, but will often give you a warning. You can eliminate this warning and indicate that you really did mean it using a cast.

Assigning from a **void*** is not allowed without a cast in C++ (unlike C), as seen in (3). This is dangerous and requires that a programmer know what he's doing. The **static_cast**, at least, is easier to locate than the old standard cast when you're hunting for bugs.

Section (4) shows the kinds of implicit type conversions that are normally performed automatically by the compiler. These are automatic and require no casting, but again **static_cast** highlights the action in case you want to make it clear what's happening or hunt for it later.

If a class hierarchy has no **virtual** functions or if you have other information that allows you to safely downcast, it's slightly faster to do the downcast statically than with **dynamic_cast**, as shown in (5). In addition, **static_cast** won't allow you to cast out of the hierarchy, as the traditional cast will, so it's safer. However, statically navigating class hierarchies is always risky and you should use **dynamic_cast** unless you have a special situation.

const_cast

If you want to convert from a **const** to a non**const** or from a **volatile** to a non**volatile**, you use **const_cast**. This is the *only* conversion allowed with **const_cast**; if any other conversion is involved it must be done separately or you'll get a compile-time error.

```
//: CONSTCST.CPP -- Const casts

main() {
  const int i = 0;
  int* j = (int*)&i; // Deprecated form
```

```
    j  = const_cast<int*>(&i); // Preferred
    // Can't do simultaneous additional casting:
//! long* l = const_cast<long*>(&i); // Error
    volatile int k = 0;
    int* u = const_cast<int*>(&k);
}

class X {
    int i;
// mutable int i; // a better approach
public:
    void f() const {
        // Casting away const-ness:
        (const_cast<X*>(this))->i = 1;
    }
};
```

If you take the address of a **const** object, you produce a pointer to a **const**, and this cannot be assigned to a non**const** pointer without a cast. The old-style cast will accomplish this, but the **const_cast** is the appropriate one to use. The same holds true for **volatile**.

If you want to change a class member inside a **const** member function, the traditional approach is to cast away constness by saying **(X*)this**. You can still cast away constness using the better **const_cast**, but a superior approach is to make that particular data member **mutable**, so it's clear in the class definition, and not hidden away in the member function definitions, that the member may change in a **const** member function.

reinterpret_cast

This is the least safe of the casting mechanisms, and the one most likely to point to bugs. At the very least, your compiler should contain switches to allow you to force the use of **const_cast** and **reinterpret_cast**, which will locate the most unsafe of the casts.

A **reinterpret_cast** pretends that an object is just a bit pattern that can be treated (for some dark purpose) as if it were an entirely different type of object. This is the low-level bit twiddling that C is notorious for. You'll virtually always need to **reinterpret_cast** back to the original type before doing anything else with it.

```
//: REINTERP.CPP -- Reinterpret_cast
// Example depends on VPTR location,
// Which may differ between compilers.
#include <string.h>
#include <fstream.h>
ofstream out("reinterp.out");

class X {
  enum { sz = 5 };
  int a[sz];
public:
  X() { memset(a, 0, sz * sizeof(int)); }
  virtual void f() {}
  // Size of all the data members:
  int membsize() { return sizeof(a); }
  friend ostream&
    operator<<(ostream& os, const X& x) {
      for(int i = 0; i < sz; i++)
        os << x.a[i] << ' ';
      return os;
    }
};

main() {
  X x;
  out << x << endl; // Initialized to zeroes
  int* xp = reinterpret_cast<int*>(&x);
  xp[1] = 47;
  out << x << endl; // Oops!

  X x2;
```

```
const vptr_size = sizeof(X) - x2.membsize();
long l = reinterpret_cast<long>(&x2);
// *IF* the VPTR is first in the object:
l += vptr_size; // Move past VPTR
xp = reinterpret_cast<int*>(l);
xp[1] = 47;
out << x2 << endl;
}
```

The **class X** contains some data and a **virtual** member function. In **main( )**, an **X** object is printed out to show that it gets initialized to zero, and then its address is cast to an **int*** using a **reinterpret_cast**. Pretending it's an **int***, the object is indexed into as if it were an array and (in theory) element one is set to 47. But here's the output:[2]

```
0 0 0 0 0
47 0 0 0 0
```

Clearly, it's not safe to assume that the data in the object begins at the starting address of the object. In fact, this compiler puts the VPTR at the beginning of the object, so if **xp[0]** had been selected instead of **xp[1]**, it would have trashed the VPTR.

To fix the problem, the size of the VPTR is calculated by subtracting the size of the data members from the size of the object. Then the address of the object is cast (again, with **reinterpret_cast**) to a **long**, and the starting address of the actual data is established, *assuming* the VPTR is placed at the beginning of the object. The resulting number is cast back to an **int*** and the indexing now produces the desired result:

```
0 47 0 0 0
```

---

[2] For this particular compiler. Yours will probably be different.

Of course, this is inadvisable and nonportable programming. That's the kind of thing that a **reinterpret_cast** indicates, but it's available when you decide you have to use it.

summary

RTTI is a convenient extra feature, a bit of icing on the cake. Although normally you upcast a pointer to a base class and then use the generic interface of that base class (via virtual functions), occasionally you get into a corner where things can be more effective if you know the exact type of the object pointed to by the base pointer, and that's what RTTI provides. Because some form of virtual-function-based RTTI has appeared in almost all class libraries, this is a useful feature because it means

1. You don't have to build it into your own libraries.

2. You don't have to worry whether it will be built into someone else's library.

3. You don't have the extra programming overhead of maintaining an RTTI scheme during inheritance.

4. The syntax is consistent, so you don't have to figure out a new one for each library.

While RTTI is a convenience, like most features in C++ it can be misused by either a naive or determined programmer. The most common misuse may come from the programmer who doesn't understand virtual functions and uses RTTI to do type-check coding instead. The philosophy of C++ seems to be to provide you with powerful tools and guard for type violations and integrity, but if you want to deliberately misuse or get around a language feature, there's nothing to stop you. Sometimes a slight burn is the fastest way to gain experience.

The new cast syntax will be a big help during debugging because casting opens a hole into your type system and allows errors to slip in. The new cast syntax will allow you to more easily locate these error entryways.

exercises

1. Use RTTI to assist in program debugging by printing out the exact name of a template using **typeid( )**. Instantiate the template for various types and see what the results are.

2. Implement the function **TurnColorIfYouAreA( )** described earlier in this chapter using RTTI.

3. Modify the **instrument** hierarchy from Chapter 13 by first copying WIND5.CPP to a new location. Now add a **virtual ClearSpitValve( )** function to the **wind** class, and redefine it for all the classes inherited from **wind**. Instantiate a **tstash** to hold **instrument** pointers and fill it up with various types instrument objects created using **new**. Now use RTTI to move through the container looking for objects in class **wind**, or derived from **wind**. Call the **ClearSpitValve( )** function for these objects. Notice that it would unpleasantly confuse the **instrument** base class if it contained a **ClearSpitValve( )** function.

Thinking in C++ *Bruce Eckel*

et cetera

At this writing, the C++ standard is unfinished. Although virtually all features that will end up in the language have been added to the standard, some haven't appeared in all compilers. This appendix briefly mentions some of the other features you should look for in your compiler (or in future releases of your compiler).

bool, true, & false

Virtually everyone uses Booleans, and everyone defines them differently.[1] Some use enumerations, others use **typedef**s. A **typedef** is a particular problem because you can't overload on it (a **typedef** to an **int** is still an **int**) or instantiate a unique template with it.

A class could have been created for **bool** in the standard library, but this doesn't work very well either, because you can only have one automatic type conversion operator from a class without causing overload resolution problems.

The best approach for such a useful type is to build it into the language. A **bool** type can have two states expressed by the built-in constants **true** (which converts to an integral one) and **false** (which converts to an integral zero). All three names are keywords. In addition, some language elements have been adapted:

Element	Usage with bool
&& || !	Take **bool** arguments and return **bool**.
< > <= **>= == !=**	Produce **bool** results
if, for, **while, do**	Conditional expressions convert to **bool** values
? :	First operand converts to **bool** value

Because there's a lot of existing code that uses an **int** to represent a flag, the compiler will implicitly convert from an **int** to a **bool**.

---

[1] See Josée Lajoie, "The new cast notation and the bool data type," C++ Report, September 1994.

Ideally, the compiler will give you a warning as a suggestion to correct the situation.

An idiom that falls under "poor programming style" is the use of **++** to set a flag to true. This is still allowed, but deprecated, which means that at some time in the future it will be made illegal. The problem is the same as incrementing an **enum**: You're making an implicit type conversion from **bool** to **int**, incrementing the value (perhaps beyond the range of the normal **bool** values of zero and one), and then implicitly converting it back again.

Pointers will also be automatically converted to **bool** when necessary.

new include format

As C++ has evolved, different compiler vendors chose different extensions for file names. In addition, various operating systems have different restrictions on file names, in particular on name length. To smooth over these rough edges, the standard adopts a new format that allows file names longer than the notorious eight characters and eliminates the extension. For example, including IOSTREAM.H becomes

```
#include <iostream>
```

The translator can implement the includes in a way to suit the needs of that particular compiler and operating system, if necessary truncating the name and adding an extension. Of course, you can also copy the headers given you by your compiler vendor to ones without extensions if you want to use this style before a vendor has provided support for it.

All of the libraries that have been inherited from Standard C still use the **.h** extension when you're including them. This provides a nice distinction to the reader indicating when you're using C versus C++ libraries.

the Standard C++ Libraries

Standard C++ not only incorporates all the Standard C libraries, with small additions and changes to support type safety, it also adds libraries of its own. These libraries are far more powerful than those in Standard C; the leverage you get from them is analogous to the leverage you get from changing from C to C++. The best reference to the full libraries is the Standard itself,[2] which you should be able to find in electronic form by hunting around on the Internet or on BBSs.

The iostream library was introduced in this book (see Chapter 5). Other useful libraries in Standard C++ include the following:

Language Support. Elements inherent to the language itself, like implementation limits in **<climits>** and **<cfloat>**; dynamic memory declarations in **<new>** like **bad_alloc** (the exception thrown when you're out of memory) and **set_new_handler**; the **<typeinfo>** header for RTTI and the **<exception>** header that declares the **terminate( )** and **unexpected( )** functions.

Diagnostics Library. Components C++ programs can use to detect and report errors. The **<stdexcept>** header declares the standard exception classes and **<cassert>** declares the same thing as C's ASSERT.H.

General Utilities Library. These components are used by other parts of the Standard C++ library, but you can also use them in your own programs. Included are templatized versions of operators **!=, >, <=**, and **>=** (to prevent redundant definitions), a **pair** template class with a **tuple**-making template function, a set of *function objects* for support of the STL (described in the next section of this appendix), and storage allocation functions for use with the STL so you can easily modify the storage allocation mechanism.

---

[2] Available at this writing in draft form only.

Strings Library. The string class may be the most thorough string manipulation tool you've ever seen. Chances are, anything you've done to character strings with lines of code in C can be done with a member function call in the string class, including **append( )**, **assign( )**, **insert( )**, **remove( )**, **replace( )**, **resize( )**, **copy( )**, **find( )**, **rfind( )**, **find_first_of( )**, **find_last_of( )**, **find_first_not_of( )**, **find_last_not_of( )**, **substr( )**, and **compare( )**. The operators **=**, **+=**, and **[]** are also overloaded to perform the intuitive operations. In addition, there's a "wide" **wstring** class designed to support international character sets. Both **string** and **wstring** (declared in **<string>**, not to be confused with C's STRING.H) are created from a common template class called **basic_string**. Note that the string classes are seamlessly integrated with iostreams, virtually eliminating the need for you to ever use **strstream** (or worry about the associated memory-management gotchas described in Chapter 5).

Localization Library. This allows you to localize strings in your program to adapt to usage in different countries, including money, numbers, date, time, and so on.

Containers Library. This includes the Standard Template Library (described in the next section of this appendix) and also the **bits** and **bit_string** classes in **<bits>** and **<bitstring>**, respectively. Both **bits** and **bit_string** are more complete implementations of the bitvector concept introduced in Chapter 4 (see page 188). The **bits** template creates a fixed-sized array of bits that can be manipulated with all the bitwise operators, as well as member functions like **set( )**, **reset( )**, **count( )**, **length( )**, **test( )**, **any( )**, and **none( )**. There are also conversion operators **to_ushort( )**, **to_ulong( )**, and **to_string( )**.

The **bit_string** class is, by contrast, a dynamically sized array of bits, with similar operations to **bits**, but also with additional operations that make it act somewhat like a **string**. There's a fundamental difference in bit weighting: With **bits**, the right-most bit (bit zero) is the least significant bit, but with **bit_string**, the right-most bit is the *most* significant bit. There are no conversions between **bits** and

bit_string. You'll use **bits** for a space-efficient set of on-off flags and **bit_string** for manipulating arrays of binary values (like pixels).

Iterators Library. Includes iterators that are tools for the STL (described in the next section of this appendix), streams, and stream buffers.

Algorithms Library. These are the template functions that perform operations on the STL containers using iterators. The algorithms include: **adjacent_find, prev_permutation, binary_search, push_heap, copy, random_shuffle, copy_backward, remove, count, remove_copy, count_if, remove_copy_if, equal, remove_if, equal_range, replace, fill, replace_copy, fill_n, replace_copy_if, find, replace_if, find_if, reverse, for_each, reverse_copy, generate, rotate, generate_n, rotate_copy, includes, search, inplace_merge, set_difference, lexicographical_compare, set_intersection, lower_bound, set_symmetric_difference, make_heap, set_union, max, sort, max_element, sort_heap, merge, stable_partition, min, stable_sort, min_element, swap, mismatch, swap_ranges, next_permutation, transform, nth_element, unique, partial_sort, unique_copy, partial_sort_copy, upper_bound,** and **partition**.

Numerics Library. The goal of this library is to allow the compiler implementor to take advantage of the architecture of the underlying machine when used for numerical operations. This way, creators of higher level numerical libraries can write to the numerics library and produce efficient algorithms without having to customize to every possible machine. The numerics library also includes the complex number class (which appeared in the first version of C++ as an example, and has become an expected part of the library) in **float, double,** and **long double** forms.

the Standard Template Library (STL)

The templates provided in Chapter 14 demonstrate the power and flexibility of C++ templates, but they are not intended to be

---

complete general-purpose tools, although they may certainly help solve some of your problems. The C++ STL[3] is a powerful library intended to satisfy the vast bulk of your needs for containers and algorithms, but in a completely portable fashion. This means that not only are your programs easier to port to other platforms, but that your knowledge itself does not depend on the libraries provided by a particular compiler vendor. Thus, it will benefit you greatly to look first to the STL for containers and algorithms, *before* looking at vendor-specific solutions.

A fundamental principle of software design is that *all problems can be simplified by introducing an extra level of indirection*. This simplicity is achieved in the STL using iterators to perform operations on a data structure while knowing as little as possible about that structure, thus producing data structure independence. With the STL, this means that any operation that can be performed on a built-in type can also be performed on a user-defined type and vice versa. If you learn the library, it will work on everything.

The drawback to this independence is that you'll have to take a little time at first getting used to the way things are done in the STL. However, the STL uses a consistent pattern, so once you fit your mind around it, it doesn't change from one STL tool to another.

Consider an example using the STL **set** class. A simple **set** can be created that works with **int**s:

```
//: INTSET.CPP -- Simple use of STL set
#include <set.h>

void main() {
  set<int, less<int> > intset;
  for(int i = 0; i < 25; i++)
    for(int j = 0; j < 10; j++)
```

---

[3] Contributed to the C++ Standard by Alexander Stepanov and Meng Lee at Hewlett-Packard.

```
      // Try to insert multiple copies:
      intset.insert(j);
  // Print to output:
  copy(intset.begin(), intset.end(),
      ostream_iterator<int>(cout, "\n"));
}
```

The first argument to **set** is the type to be contained in the set, and the second creates a less-than operation to be used for inserting elements into the set (in the **insert( )** function). The set will allow only one of each key to be inserted into itself.

The **copy( )** function shows the use of iterators. The **set** member functions **begin( )** and **end( )** produce iterators as their return values. These are used by **copy( )** as beginning and ending points for its operation, which is simply to move between the boundaries established by the iterators and copy the elements to the third argument, which is also an iterator but a special type created for iostreams. This places **int** objects on **cout** and separates them with a newline.

Because of its genericity, **copy( )** is certainly not restricted to printing on a stream. It can be used in virtually any situation: it needs only three iterators to talk to. All of the algorithms follow the form of **copy( )** and simply manipulate iterators (that's the extra indirection).

Now consider taking the form of INTSET.CPP and reshaping it to solve the concordance problem shown in SETTEST.CPP in Chapter 14 (page 612). The solution becomes remarkably simple.

```
//: CONCORD.CPP -- Concordance with STL
#include <set.h>
#include <fstream.h>
#include "..\allege.h"
#include "..\14\sstring.h"
const char* delimiters =
  " \t;()\"<>:{}[]+-=&*#.,/\\"
```

```
    "0123456789";

main(int argc, char* argv[]) {
  allege(argc == 2, "usage: concord filename");
  ifstream in(argv[1]);
  allegefile(in);
  set<Hstring, less<Hstring> > concordance;
  const sz = 1024;
  char buf[sz];
  while(in.getline(buf,sz)) {
    // Capture individual words:
    char* s = strtok(buf, delimiters);
    while(s) {
      concordance.insert(s); // Auto type conv.
      s = strtok(0, delimiters);
    }
  }
  // output results:
  copy(concordance.begin(), concordance.end(),
       ostream_iterator<Hstring>(cout, "\n"));
}
```

The only substantive difference here is that **Hstring** is used instead of **int**. The words inserted are pulled from a file and tokenized with **strtok( )**, but everything else is the same as in INTSET.CPP. Conveniently, the concordance is automatically sorted.

Other classes in the STL include the following:

Container	Use
vector	Random-access iteration and constant-time insert/erase operations at the end. Insert/erase in the middle takes linear time. There's also a specialization for **bool**.

Container	Use
list	Bi-directional iteration and constant-time insert/erase operations anywhere in the sequence.
deque	Random-access iteration and constant-time insert/erase at the beginning or the end. Insert/erase in the middle takes linear time.
stack	You choose with the template argument whether to build it using a **vector, list**, or **deque**.
queue	Templatized to be built using a **list** or **deque**.
priority_queue	For random-access iteration. Provides **top( )**, **push( )**, and **pop( )** operations. Templatized to be created from **vector** or **deque**.
multiset	A set that allows duplicate keys.
map	An associative container with unique keys.
multimap	An associative container that allows duplicate keys, like a hash table.

This section has only given a hint of the power of the STL. You won't regret the time you spend learning it.

the asm keyword

This is an escape mechanism that allows you to write assembly code for your hardware within a C++ program. Often you're able to reference C++ variables within the assembly code, which means you can easily communicate with your C++ code and limit the assembly code to that necessary for efficiency tuning or to utilize special processor instructions. The exact syntax of the assembly language is compiler-dependent and can be discovered in your compiler's documentation.

explicit operators

These are keywords for bitwise and logical operators. Non-U.S. programmers without keyboard characters like **&**, **|**, **^**, and so on, were forced to use C's horrible *trigraphs*, which were not only annoying to type, but obscure when reading. This is repaired in C++ by the addition of new keywords:

Keyword	Meaning
and	&& (logical AND)
or	|| (logical OR)
not	! (logical NOT)
not_eq	!= (logical not-equivalent)
bitand	& (bitwise AND)
and_eq	&= (bitwise AND-assignment)
bitor	| (bitwise OR)
or_eq	|= (bitwise OR-assignment)
xor	^ (bitwise exclusive-OR)
xor_eq	^= (bitwise exclusive-OR-assignment)
compl	~ (ones complement)

programming
guidelines

This appendix[1] is a collection of suggestions for C++ programming. They've been collected over the course of my teaching and programming experience and

also from the insights of friends including Dan Saks (coauthor with Tom Plum of *C++ Programming Guidelines*, Plum Hall, 1991), Scott Meyers (author of *Effective C++*, Addison-Wesley, 1992), and Rob

---

[1] This appendix was suggested by Andrew Binstock, editor of Unix Review, as an article for that magazine.

Murray (author of *C++ Strategies & Tactics*, Addison-Wesley, 1993). Many of these tips are summarized from the pages of this book.

1. Don't automatically rewrite all your existing C code in C++ unless you need to significantly change its functionality (that is, don't fix it if it isn't broken). *Recompiling* in C++ is a very valuable activity because it may reveal hidden bugs. However, taking C code that works fine and rewriting it in C++ may not be the most valuable use of your time, unless the C++ version will provide a lot of opportunities for reuse as a class.

2. Separate the class creator from the class user (*client programmer*). The class user is the "customer" and doesn't need or want to know what's going on behind the scenes of the class. The class creator must be the expert in class design and write the class so it can be used by the most novice programmer possible, yet still work robustly in the application. Library use will be easy only if it's transparent.

3. When you create a class, make your names as clear as possible. Your goal should be to make the user's interface conceptually simple. To this end, use function overloading and default arguments to create a clear, easy-to-use interface.

4. Data hiding allows you (the class creator) to change as much as possible in the future without damaging client code in which the class is used. In this light, keep everything as **private** as possible, and make only the class interface **public**, always using functions rather than data. Make data **public** only when forced. If class users don't need to access a function, make it **private**. If a part of your class must be exposed to inheritors as **protected**, provide a function interface rather than expose the actual data. In this way, implementation changes will have minimal impact on derived classes.

5. Don't fall into analysis paralysis. Some things you don't learn until you start coding and get some kind of system working. C++ has

built-in firewalls; let them work for you. Your mistakes in a class or set of classes won't destroy the integrity of the whole system.

6. Your analysis and design must produce, at minimum, the classes in your system, their public interfaces, and their relationships to other classes, especially base classes. If your method produces more than that, ask yourself if all the elements have value over the lifetime of the program. If they do not, maintaining them will cost you. Members of development teams tend not to maintain anything that does not contribute to their productivity; this is a fact of life that many design methods don't account for.

7. Remember the fundamental rule of software engineering: *All problems can be simplified by introducing an extra level of conceptual indirection.*[2] This one idea is the basis of abstraction, the primary feature of object-oriented programming.

8. Make classes as atomic as possible; that is, give each class a single, clear purpose. If your classes or your system design grows too complicated, break complex classes into simpler ones.

9. From a design standpoint, look for and separate things that change from things that stay the same. That is, search for the elements in a system that you might want to change without forcing a redesign, then encapsulate those elements in classes.

10. Watch out for *variance*. Two semantically different objects may have identical actions, or responsibilities, and there is a natural temptation to try to make one a subclass of the other just to benefit from inheritance. This is called variance, but there's no real justification to force a superclass/subclass relationship where it doesn't exist. A better solution is to create a general superclass that contains both as subclasses — it requires a bit more space, but you still benefit from inheritance and will probably make an important discovery about the natural language solution.

---

[2] Explained to me by Andrew Koenig.

---

11. Watch out for *limitation* during inheritance. The clearest designs add new capabilities to inherited ones. A suspicious design removes old capabilities during inheritance without adding new ones. But rules are made to be broken, and if you are working from an old class library, it may be more efficient to restrict an existing class in its subclass than it would be to restructure the hierarchy so your new class fits in where it should, above the old class.

12. Don't extend fundamental functionality by subclassing. If an interface element is essential to a class it should be in the base class, not added during derivation. If you're adding member functions by inheriting, perhaps you should rethink the design.

13. Start with a minimal interface to a class, as small and simple as you need. As the class is used, you'll discover ways you must expand the interface. However, once a class is in use you cannot shrink the interface without disturbing client code. If you need to add more functions, that's fine; it won't disturb code, other than forcing recompiles. But even if new member functions replace the functionality of old ones, leave the existing interface alone (you can combine the functionality in the underlying implementation if you want). If you need to expand the interface of an existing function by adding more arguments, leave the existing arguments in their current order, and put default values on all the new arguments; this way you won't disturb any existing calls to that function.

14. Read your classes aloud to make sure they're logical, referring to base classes as "is-a" and member objects as "has-a.."

15. When deciding between inheritance and composition, ask if you need to upcast to the base type. If not, prefer composition (member objects) to inheritance. This can eliminate the perceived need for multiple inheritance. If you inherit, users will think they are supposed to upcast.

16. Sometimes you need to inherit in order to access **protected** members of the base class. This can lead to a perceived need for multiple inheritance. If you don't need to upcast, first derive a new

class to perform the protected access. Then make that new class a member object inside any class that needs to use it, rather than inheriting.

17. Typically, a base class will only be an interface to classes derived from it. When you create a base class, default to making the member functions pure virtual. The destructor can also be pure virtual (to force inheritors to explicitly redefine it), but remember to give the destructor a function body, because all destructors in a hierarchy are always called.

18. When you put a **virtual** function in a class, make all functions in that class **virtual**, and put in a **virtual** destructor. Start removing the **virtual** keyword when you're tuning for efficiency. This approach prevents surprises in the behavior of the interface.

19. Use data members for variation in value and **virtual** functions for variation in behavior. That is, if you find a class with state variables and member functions that switch behavior on those variables, you should probably redesign it to express the differences in behavior within subclasses and **virtual** functions.

20. If you must do something nonportable, make an abstraction for that service and localize it within a class. This extra level of indirection prevents the nonportability from being distributed throughout your program.

21. Avoid multiple inheritance. It's for getting you out of bad situations, especially repairing class interfaces where you don't have control of the broken class (see Chapter 15). You should be an experienced programmer before designing multiple inheritance into your system.

22. Don't use private inheritance. Although it's in the language and seems to have occasional functionality, it introduces significant ambiguities when combined with run-time type identification. Create a private member object instead of using private inheritance.

---

23. Operator overloading is only "syntactic sugar": a different way to make a function call. If overloading an operator doesn't make the class interface clearer and easier to use, don't do it. Create only one automatic type conversion operator for a class. In general, follow the guidelines and format given in Chapter 10 when overloading operators.

24. First make a program work, then optimize it. In particular, don't worry about writing **inline** functions, making some functions non**virtual**, or tweaking code to be efficient when you are first constructing the system. Your primary goal should be to prove the design, unless the design requires a certain efficiency.

25. Don't let the compiler create the constructors, destructors, or the **operator=** for you. Those are training wheels. Class designers should always say exactly what the class should do and keep the class entirely under control. If you don't want a copy-constructor or **operator=**, declare them private. Remember that if you create any constructor, it prevents the default constructor from being synthesized.

26. If your class contains pointers, you must create the copy-constructor, **operator=**, and destructor for the class to work properly.

27. To minimize recompiles during development of a large project, use the handle class/Cheshire cat technique demonstrated in Chapter 2, and remove it only if run-time efficiency is a problem.

28. Avoid the preprocessor. Always use **const** for value substitution and **inline**s for macros.

29. Keep scopes as small as possible so the visibility and lifetime of your objects are as small as possible. This reduces the chance of using an object in the wrong context and hiding a difficult-to-find bug. For example, suppose you have a container and a piece of code that iterates through it. If you copy that code to use with a new container, you may accidentally end up using the size of the old

container as the upper bound of the new one. If, however, the old container is out of scope, the error will be caught at compile time.

30. Avoid global variables. Always strive to put data inside classes. Global functions are more likely to occur naturally than global variables, although you may later discover that a global function may fit better as a **static** member of a class.

31. If you need to declare a class or function from a library, always do so by including a header file. For example, if you want to create a function to write to an **ostream**, never declare **ostream** yourself using an incomplete type specification like this,

```
class ostream;
```

This approach leaves your code vulnerable to changes in representation. (For example, **ostream** could actually be a **typedef**.) Instead, always use the header file:

```
#include <iostream.h>
```

When creating your own classes, if a library is big, provide your users an abbreviated form of the header file with incomplete type specifications (that is, class name declarations) for cases where they only need to use pointers. (It can speed compilations.)

32. When choosing the return type of an overloaded operator, think about chaining expressions together. When defining **operator=**, remember x=x. Return a copy or reference to the lvalue (**return *this**) so it can be used in a chained expression (**A = B = C**).

33. When writing a function, pass arguments by **const** reference as your first choice. As long as you don't need to modify the object being passed in, this practice is best because it has the simplicity of pass-by-value syntax but doesn't require expensive constructions and destructions to create a local object, which occurs when passing by value. Normally you don't want to be worrying too much about efficiency issues when designing and building your system, but this habit is a sure win.

34. Be aware of temporaries. When tuning for performance, watch out for temporary creation, especially with operator overloading. If your

constructors and destructors are complicated, the cost of creating and destroying temporaries can be high. When returning a value from a function, always try to build the object "in place" with a constructor call in the return statement:

```
return foo(i, j);
```

rather than

```
foo x(i, j);
return x;
```

The former return statement eliminates a copy-constructor call and destructor call.

35. When creating constructors, consider exceptions. In the best case, the constructor won't do anything that throws an exception. In the next-best scenario, the class will be composed and inherited from robust classes only, so they will automatically clean themselves up if an exception is thrown. If you must have naked pointers, you are responsible for catching your own exceptions and then deallocating any resources pointed to before you throw an exception in your constructor. If a constructor must fail, the appropriate action is to throw an exception.

36. Do only what is minimally necessary in your constructors. Not only does this produce a lower overhead for constructor calls (many of which may not be under your control) but your constructors are then less likely to throw exceptions or cause problems.

37. The responsibility of the destructor is to release resources allocated during the lifetime of the object, not just during construction.

38. Use exception hierarchies, preferably derived from the Standard C++ exception hierarchy and nested as public classes within the class that throws the exceptions. The person catching the exceptions can then catch the specific types of exceptions, followed by the base type. If you add new derived exceptions, client code will still catch the exception through the base type.

39. Throw exceptions by value and catch exceptions by reference. Let the exception-handling mechanism handle memory management.

If you throw pointers to exceptions created on the heap, the catcher must know to destroy the exception, which is bad coupling. If you catch exceptions by value, you cause extra constructions and destructions; worse, the derived portions of your exception objects may be sliced during upcasting by value.

40. Don't write your own class templates unless you must. Look first in the Standard Template Library, then to vendors who create special-purpose tools. Become proficient with their use and you'll greatly increase your productivity.

41. When creating templates, watch for code that does not depend on type and put that code in a nontemplate base class to prevent needless code bloat. Using inheritance or composition, you can create templates in which the bulk of the code they contain is type-dependent and therefore essential.

42. Don't use the STDIO.H functions such as **printf( )**. Learn to use iostreams instead; they are type-safe and type-extensible, and significantly more powerful. Your investment will be rewarded regularly (see Chapter 5). In general, always use C++ libraries in preference to C libraries.

43. Avoid C's built-in types. They are supported in C++ for backward compatibility, but they are much less robust than C++ classes, so your bug-hunting time will increase.

44. Whenever you use built-in types as globals or automatics, don't define them until you can also initialize them. Define variables one per line along with their initialization. When defining pointers, put the '*' next to the type name. You can safely do this if you define one variable per line. This style tends to be less confusing for the reader.

45. Guarantee that initialization occurs in all aspects of your code. Perform all member initialization in the constructor initializer list, even built-in types (using pseudo-constructor calls). Use any bookkeeping technique you can to guarantee no uninitialized objects are running around in your system. Using the constructor

initializer list is often more efficient when initializing subobjects; otherwise the default constructor is called, and you end up calling other member functions — probably **operator=** — on top of that in order to get the initialization you want.

46. Don't use the form **foo a = b;** to define an object. This one feature is a major source of confusion because it calls a constructor instead of the **operator=**. For clarity, always be specific and use the form **foo a(b);** instead. The results are identical, but other programmers won't be confused.

47. Use the new casts in C++. A cast overrides the normal typing system and is a potential error spot. By dividing C's one-cast-does-all into classes of well-marked casts, anyone debugging and maintaining the code can easily find all the places where logical errors are most likely to happen.

48. For a program to be robust, each component must be robust. Use all the tools provided by C++: implementation hiding, exceptions, const-correctness, type checking, and so on in each class you create. That way you can safely move to the next level of abstraction when building your system.

49. Build in **const**-correctness. This allows the compiler to point out bugs that would otherwise be subtle and difficult to find. This practice takes a little discipline and must be used consistently throughout your classes, but it pays off.

50. Use compiler error checking to your advantage. Perform all compiles with full warnings, and fix your code to remove all warnings. Write code that utilizes the compiler errors and warnings rather than that which causes run-time errors (for example, don't use variadic argument lists, which disable all type checking). Use **assert( )** for debugging, but use exceptions to work with run-time errors.

51. Prefer compile-time errors to run-time errors. Try to handle an error as close to the point of its occurrence as possible. Prefer dealing with the error at that point to throwing an exception. Catch any

exceptions in the nearest handler that has enough information to deal with them. Do what you can with the exception at the current level; if that doesn't solve the problem, rethrow the exception.

52. If you're using exception specifications, install your own **unexpected( )** function using **set_unexpected( )**. Your **unexpected( )** should log the error and rethrow the current exception. That way, if an existing function gets redefined and starts throwing exceptions, it won't abort the program.

53. Create a user-defined **terminate( )** (indicating a programmer error) to log the error that caused the exception, then release system resources, and exit the program.

54. If a destructor calls any functions, those functions may throw exceptions. A destructor cannot throw an exception (this can result in a call to **terminate( )**, which indicates a programming error), so any destructor that calls functions must catch and manage its own exceptions.

55. Don't create your own "mangled" private data member names, unless you have a lot of pre-existing global values; otherwise, let classes and namespaces do that for you.

56. If you're going to use a loop variable after the end of a **for** loop, define the variable *before* the **for** control expression. This way, you won't have any surprises when implementations change to limit the lifetime of variables defined within **for** control-expressions to the controlled expression.

57. Watch for overloading. A function should not conditionally execute code based on the value of an argument, default or not. In this case, you should create two or more overloaded functions instead.

58. Hide your pointers inside container classes. Bring them out only when you are going to immediately perform operations on them. Pointers have always been a major source of bugs. When you use **new**, try to drop the resulting pointer into a container. Prefer that a container "own" its pointers so it's responsible for cleanup. If you

must have a free-standing pointer, always initialize it, preferably to an object address, but to zero if necessary. Set it to zero when you delete it to prevent accidental multiple deletions.

59. Don't overload global **new** and **delete**; always do it on a class-by-class basis. Overloading the global versions affects the entire client programmer project, something only the creators of a project should control. When overloading **new** and **delete** for classes, don't assume you know the size of the object; someone may be inheriting from you. Use the provided argument. If you do anything special, consider the effect it could have on inheritors.

60. Don't repeat yourself. If a piece of code is recurring in many functions in derived classes, put that code into a single function in the base class and call it from the derived class functions. Not only do you save code space, you provide for easy propagation of changes. This is possible even for pure virtual functions (see Chapter 13). You can use an inline function for efficiency. Sometimes the discovery of this common code will add valuable functionality to your interface.

61. Prevent object slicing. It virtually never makes sense to upcast an object by value. To prevent this, put pure virtual functions in your base class.

62. Sometimes simple aggregation does the job. A "passenger comfort system" on an airline consists of disconnected elements: seat, air conditioning, video, etc., and yet you need to create many of these in a plane. Do you make private members and build a whole new interface? No — in this case, the components themselves are also part of the public interface, so you should create public member objects. Those objects have their own private implementations, which are still safe.

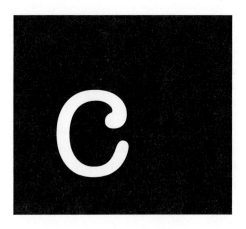

simulating virtual constructors

During a constructor call, the virtual mechanism does not operate (early binding occurs). Sometimes this is awkward.

In addition, you may want to organize your code so you don't have to select an exact type of constructor when creating an object. That is, you'd like to say, "I don't know precisely what type of object you are, but here's the information: Create yourself." This appendix demonstrates two approaches to "virtual construction." The first is a full-blown technique that works on both the stack and the heap, but is also fairly complex to implement. The second is much simpler to implement and maintain, but restricts you to creating objects on the heap.

all-purpose virtual constructors

Consider the oft-cited "shapes" example. It seems logical that inside the constructor for a **shape** object, you would want to set everything up and then **draw( )** the shape. **draw( )** should be a virtual function, a message to the **shape** that it should draw itself appropriately, depending on whether it is a circle, square, line, and so on. However, this doesn't work inside the constructor, for the reasons given in Chapter 13: Virtual functions resolve to the "local" function bodies when called in constructors.

If you want to be able to call a virtual function inside the constructor and have it do the right thing, you must use a technique to *simulate* a virtual constructor. This is a conundrum. Remember the idea of a virtual function is that you send a message to an object and let the object figure out the right thing to do. But a constructor builds an object. So a virtual constructor would be like saying, "I don't know exactly what type of object you are, but build yourself anyway." In an ordinary constructor, the compiler must know which VTABLE address to bind to the VPTR, and if it existed, a virtual constructor couldn't do this because it doesn't know all the type information at compile-time. It makes sense that a constructor can't be virtual because it is the one function that absolutely must know everything about the type of the object.

And yet there are times when you want something approximating the behavior of a virtual constructor.

In the **shape** example, it would be nice to hand the **shape** constructor some specific information in the argument list and let the constructor create a specific type of shape (a **circle**, **square**, or **triangle**) with no further intervention. Ordinarily, you'd have to make an explicit call to the **circle**, **square**, or **triangle** constructor yourself.

Thinking in C++   *Bruce Eckel*

Coplien[1] calls his solution to this problem "envelope and letter classes." The "envelope" class is the base class, a shell that contains a pointer to an object of the base class. The constructor for the "envelope" determines (at run-time, when the constructor is called, not at compile-time, when the type checking is normally done) what specific type to make, then creates an object of that specific type (on the heap) and assigns the object to its pointer. All the function calls are then handled by the base class through its pointer.

Here's a simplified version of the shape example:

```
//: SSHAPE.CPP -- "Virtual constructors"
// Used in a simple "shape" framework
#include <iostream.h>
#include "..\14\tstash.h"

class shape {
  shape* S;
  // Prevent copy-construction & operator=
  shape(shape&);
  shape operator=(shape&);
protected:
  shape() { S = 0; };
public:
  enum type { Circle, Square, Triangle };
  shape(type);  // "Virtual" constructor
  virtual void draw() { S->draw(); }
  virtual ~shape() {
    cout << "~shape\n";
    delete S;
  }
};
```

---

[1] James O. Coplien, *Advanced C++ Programming Styles and Idioms*, Addison-Wesley, 1992.

```
class circle : public shape {
  // Prevent copy-construction & operator=
  circle(circle&);
  circle operator=(circle&);
public:
  circle() {}
  void draw() { cout << "circle::draw\n"; }
  ~circle() { cout << "~circle\n"; }
};

class square : public shape {
  // Prevent copy-construction & operator=
  square(square&);
  square operator=(square&);
public:
  square() {}
  void draw() { cout << "square::draw\n"; }
  ~square() { cout << "~square\n"; }
};

class triangle : public shape {
  // Prevent copy-construction & operator=
  triangle(triangle&);
  triangle operator=(triangle&);
public:
  triangle() {}
  void draw() { cout << "triangle::draw\n"; }
  ~triangle() { cout << "~triangle\n"; }
};

shape::shape(type t) {
  switch(t) {
    case Circle: S = new circle; break;
    case Square: S = new square; break;
    case Triangle: S = new triangle; break;
  }
```

```
    draw();  // Virtual call in the constructor
}

main() {
  tstash<shape> shapes; // Default to ownership
  cout << "virtual constructor calls:" << endl;
  shapes.add(new shape(shape::Circle));
  shapes.add(new shape(shape::Square));
  shapes.add(new shape(shape::Triangle));
  cout << "virtual function calls:" << endl;
  for(int i = 0; i < shapes.count(); i++)
    shapes[i]->draw();
  shape c(shape::Circle); // Can create on stack
}
```

The base class **shape** contains a pointer to an object of type **shape** as its only data member. When you build a "virtual constructor" scheme, you must exercise special care to ensure this pointer is always initialized to a live object.

The **type** enumeration inside **class shape** and the requirement that the constructor for **shape** be defined after all the derived classes are two of the restrictions of this method. Each time you derive a new subtype from **shape**, you must go back and add the name for that type to the **type** enumeration. Then you must modify the **shape** constructor to handle the new case. The disadvantage is you now have a dependency between the **shape** class and all classes derived from it. However, the advantage is that the dependency that normally occurs in the body of the program (and possibly in more than one place, which makes it less maintainable) is isolated inside the class. In addition, this produces an effect like the "cheshire cat" technique in Chapter 2; in this case all the specific shape class definitions can be hidden inside the implementation files. That way, the base-class interface is truly the only thing the user sees.

In this example, the information you must hand the constructor about what type to create is very explicit: It's an enumeration of the type. However, your scheme may use other information — for example, in a parser the output of the scanner may be handed to the "virtual constructor," which then uses that text string to determine what exact token to create.

The "virtual constructor" **shape(type)** can only be *declared* inside the class; it cannot be *defined* until after all the base classes have been declared. However, the default constructor can be defined inside **class shape**, but it should be made **protected** so temporary **shape** objects cannot be created. This default constructor is only called by the constructors of derived-class objects. You are forced to explicitly create a default constructor because the compiler will create one for you automatically only if there are *no* constructors defined. Because you must define **shape(type)**, you must also define **shape( )**.

The default constructor in this scheme has at least one very important chore — it must set the value of the **S** pointer to zero. This sounds strange at first, but remember that the default constructor will be called as part of the construction of the *actual object* — in Coplien's terms, the "letter," not the "envelope." However, the "letter" is derived from the "envelope," so it also inherits the data member **S**. In the "envelope," **S** is important because it points to the actual object, but in the "letter," **S** is simply excess baggage. Even excess baggage should be initialized, however, and if **S** is not set to zero by the default constructor called for the "letter," bad things happen (as you'll see later).

The "virtual constructor" takes as its argument information that completely determines the type of the object. Notice, though, that this type information isn't read and acted upon until run-time, whereas normally the compiler must know the exact type at compile-time (one other reason this system effectively imitates virtual constructors).

Inside the virtual constructor there's a **switch** statement that uses the argument to construct the actual object, which is then assigned to the pointer inside the "envelope." After that, the construction of the "letter" is completed, so any virtual calls will be properly directed.

As an example, consider the call to **draw( )** inside the virtual constructor. If you trace this call (either by hand or with a debugger), you can see that it starts in the **draw( )** function in the base class, **shape**. This function calls **draw( )** for the "envelope" **S** pointer to its "letter." All types derived from **shape** share the same interface, so this virtual call is properly executed, even though it seems to be in the constructor. (Actually, the constructor for the "letter" has already completed.) As long as all virtual calls in the base class simply make calls to identical virtual function through the pointer to the "letter," the system operates properly.

To understand how it works, consider the code in **main( )**. To create the array **s[ ]**, "virtual constructor" calls are made to **shape**. Ordinarily in a situation like this, you would call the constructor for the actual type, and the VPTR for that type would be installed in the object. Here, however, the VPTR used in each case is the one for **shape**, not the one for the specific **circle**, **square**, or **triangle**.

In the **for** loop where the **draw( )** function is called for each **shape**, the virtual function call resolves, through the VPTR, to the corresponding type. However, this is **shape** in each case. In fact, you might wonder why **draw( )** was made **virtual** at all. The reason shows up in the next step: The base-class version of **draw( )** makes a call, through the "letter" pointer **S**, to the **virtual** function **draw( )** for the "letter." This time the call resolves to the actual type of the object, not just the base class **shape**. Thus the run-time cost of using "virtual constructors" is one more virtual call every time you make a virtual function call.

a remaining conundrum

In the "virtual constructor" scheme presented here, calls made to virtual functions inside destructors will be resolved in the normal way, at compile-time. You might think that you can get around this restriction by cleverly calling the base-class version of the virtual

---

function inside the destructor. Unfortunately, this results in disaster. The base-class version of the function is indeed called. However, its **this** pointer is the one for the "letter" and not the "envelope." So when the base-class version of the function makes its call — remember, the base-class versions of virtual functions always assume they are dealing with the "envelope" — it will go to the **S** pointer to make the call. For the "letter," **S** is zero, set by the **protected** default constructor. Of course, you could prevent this by adding even more code to each virtual function in the base class to check that **S** is not zero. Or, you can follow two rules when using this "virtual constructor" scheme:

1. Never explicitly call root class virtual functions from derived-class functions.

2. Always redefine virtual functions defined in the root class.

   The second rule results from the same problem as rule one. If you call a virtual function inside a "letter," the function gets the "letter" **this** pointer. If the virtual call resolves to the base-class version, which will happen if the function was never redefined, then a call will be made through the "letter" **this** pointer to the "letter" **S**, which is again zero.

   You can see that there are costs, restrictions, and dangers to using this method, which is why you don't want to have it as part of the programming environment all the time. It's one of those features that's very useful for solving certain types of problems, but it isn't something you want to cope with all the time. Fortunately, C++ allows you to put it in when you need it, but the standard way is the safest and, in the end, easiest.

destructor operation

The activities of destruction in this scheme are also tricky. To understand, let's verbally walk through what happens when you call **delete** for a pointer to a **shape** object — specifically, a **square** — created on the heap. (This is more complicated than an object created on the stack.) This will be a **delete** through the polymorphic interface, as in the statement **delete s[i]** in **main( )**.

The type of the pointer **s[i]** is of the base class **shape**, so the compiler makes the call through **shape**. Normally, you might say that it's a virtual call, so **square**'s destructor will be called. But with this "virtual constructor" scheme, the compiler is creating actual **shape** objects, even though the constructor initializes the "letter" pointer to a specific type of shape. The virtual mechanism *is* used, but the VPTR inside the **shape** object is **shape**'s VPTR, not **square**'s. This resolves to **shape**'s destructor, which calls **delete** for the "letter" pointer **S**, which actually points to a **square** object. This is again a virtual call, but this time it resolves to **square**'s destructor.

With a destructor, however, all destructors in the hierarchy must be called. **Square**'s destructor is called first, followed by any intermediate destructors, in order, until finally the base-class destructor is called. This base-class destructor has code that says **delete S**. When this destructor was called originally, it was for the "envelope" **S**, but now it's for the "letter" **S**, which is there because the "letter" was inherited from the "envelope," and not because it contains anything. So *this* call to **delete** should do nothing.

The solution to the problem is to make the "letter" **S** pointer zero. Then when the "letter" base-class destructor is called, you get **delete 0**, which by definition does nothing. Because the default constructor is protected, it will be called *only* during the construction of a "letter," so that's the only situation where **S** is set to zero.

a simpler alternative

This "virtual constructor" scheme is unnecessarily complicated for most needs. If you can restrict yourself to objects created on the heap, things can be made a lot simpler. All you really want is some function (which I'll call an *object-maker function*) into which you can throw a bunch of information and it will produce the right object. This function doesn't have to be a constructor if it's OK to produce a pointer to the base type rather than an object itself. Here's the envelope-and-letter example redesigned using an object-maker function:

```
//: SSHAPE2.CPP -- Alternative to SSHAPE.CPP
#include <iostream.h>
#include "..\14\tstash.h"

class shape {
  shape(shape&); // Prevent copy-construction
protected:
  shape() {} // Prevent stack objects
  // But allow access to derived constructors
public:
  enum type { Circle, Square, Triangle };
  virtual void draw() = 0;
  virtual ~shape() { cout << "~shape\n"; }
  static shape* make(type);
};

class circle : public shape {
  circle(circle&); // No copy-construction
  circle operator=(circle&); // No operator=
protected:
  circle() {};
public:
  void draw() { cout << "circle::draw\n"; }
  ~circle() { cout << "~circle\n"; }
  friend shape* shape::make(type t);
};

class square : public shape {
  square(square&); // No copy-construction
  square operator=(square&); // No operator=
protected:
  square() {};
```

```cpp
public:
  void draw() { cout << "square::draw\n"; }
  ~square() { cout << "~square\n"; }
  friend shape* shape::make(type t);
};

class triangle : public shape {
  triangle(triangle&); // No copy-construction
  triangle operator=(triangle&); // Prevent
protected:
  triangle() {};
public:
  void draw() { cout << "triangle::draw\n"; }
  ~triangle() { cout << "~triangle\n"; }
  friend shape* shape::make(type t);
};

shape* shape::make(type t) {
  shape* S;
  switch(t) {
    case Circle: S = new circle; break;
    case Square: S = new square; break;
    case Triangle: S = new triangle; break;
  }
  S->draw(); // Virtual function call
  return S;
}

main() {
  tstash<shape> shapes; // Default to ownership
  shapes.add(shape::make(shape::Circle));
  shapes.add(shape::make(shape::Square));
  shapes.add(shape::make(shape::Triangle));
  cout << "virtual function calls:\n";
  for(int i = 0; i < shapes.count(); i++)
    shapes[i]->draw();
  //Circle c; // error: can't create on stack
```

```
}
```

You can see that everything's a lot simpler, and you don't have to worry about strange cases with an internal pointer. The only restrictions are that the **enum** in the base class must be changed every time you derive a new class (true also with the envelope-and-letter approach) and that objects must be created on the heap. This latter restriction is enforced by making all the constructors **protected**, so the user can't create an object of the class, but the derived-class constructors can still access the base-class constructors during object creation. This is an excellent example of where the **protected** keyword is essential.

where to find it...

internal, 273, 276, 312, 338
  no, 338
  type-safe, 179
linked list, 118, 141, 164
linker, 100
  collision, 117
Lisp, 47
list, 631
  constructor initializer, 289
  constructor initializer list, 503
  linked, 118, 141, 164
  standard template library, 765
Lister, Timothy, 62
local
  classes, 352
  static object, 335
localtime( ), 265
logic_error
  Standard C++ library exception type, 710
logical
  explicit bitwise and logical operators, 767
  operators, 420
longjmp( ), 154, 683
loop, for, 158
Love, Tom, 62
lvalue, 282
macro
  argument, 308
  preprocessor, 305
  preprocessor macros for parameterized
    types, instead of templates, 582
magic numbers, 272
main( )
  executing code after exiting, 337
  executing code before entering, 337
maintaining class library source, 252
make, 101
malloc( ), 96, 229, 462, 464, 466, 633
  and free( ), interaction with new and delete,
    472
  and time, 466
mangling, name, 103, 111, 177, 361
manipulator, 209
  creating, 246
  iostreams formatting, 242
map, 632
  standard template library, 765
McKee, Robert, 63

member
  calling a member function, 113
  const member function, 288
  const member functions, 294
  defining storage for static data member, 348
  friend function, 129
  initializing const data members, 290
  member function selection, 108
  member function template, 640
  member object initialization, 503
  member selection operator, 111
  overloaded member operator, 399
  pointers to members, 390
  static data member, 443
  static data member inside a class, 348
  static member function, 302, 382
  static member functions, 353
  versus nonmember operators, 428
memberwise
  assignment, 445
  initialization, 388
  memberwise const, 297
memcpy( ), 95
memory
  a memory allocation system, 633
  allocation, 481
  dynamic allocation, 461
  dynamic memory allocation, 95
  exhausting heap, 486
  management, reference counting, 436
  memory manager overhead, 466
  read-only (ROM), 299
  simple storage allocation system, 484
memset( ), 291
message, sending, 113, 540
Meyers, Scott, 769
MI
  multiple inheritance, 647
minimum size of a struct, 115
mistakes, and design, 146
modeling problems, 112
modes, iostream open, 217
modulus operator, 266
monolithic, 648
Mortensen, Owen, 393
multimap, 632
  standard template library, 765
multiple inheritance, 528, 647
  ambiguity, 651